Reference Modeling for Business Systems Analysis

Peter Fettke
Institute for Information Systems (IWi) at the German Research
Center for Artificial Intelligence (DFKI), Saarbrücken, Germany

Peter Loos
Institute for Information Systems (IWi) at the German Research
Center for Artificial Intelligence (DFKI), Saarbrücken, Germany

T0321695

IDEA GROUP PUBLISHING
Hershey • London • Melbourne • Singapore

Acquisition Editor:	Michelle Potter
Senior Managing Editor:	Jennifer Neidig
Managing Editor:	Sara Reed
Development Editor:	Kristin Roth
Copy Editor:	Mike Goldberg
Typesetter:	Marko Primorac
Cover Design:	Lisa Tosheff
Printed at:	Integrated Book Technology

Published in the United States of America by
> Idea Group Publishing (an imprint of Idea Group Inc.)
> 701 E. Chocolate Avenue
> Hershey PA 17033
> Tel: 717-533-8845
> Fax: 717-533-8661
> E-mail: cust@idea-group.com
> Web site: http://www.idea-group.com

and in the United Kingdom by
> Idea Group Publishing (an imprint of Idea Group Inc.)
> 3 Henrietta Street
> Covent Garden
> London WC2E 8LU
> Tel: 44 20 7240 0856
> Fax: 44 20 7379 3313
> Web site: http://www.eurospan.co.uk

Library of Congress Cataloging-in-Publication Data

Reference modeling for business systems analysis / Peter Fettke and
   Peter Loos, editors.
      p. cm.
   Summary: "This book provides insights into state-of-the-art modeling languages and methods used for reference modeling. A reference model provides a blueprint for information systems development and analysis. Well-established reference models for industrial, retail and other industries are described"--Provided by publisher.
   Includes bibliographical references and index.
   ISBN 1-59904-054-9 -- ISBN 1-59904-055-7 (softcover) -- ISBN
   1-59904-056-5 (ebook)
   1. Information technology. 2. System analysis. 3. System design.
   4. Database management.   I. Fettke, Peter, 1973-   . II. Loos, Peter,
   1960-   .
   T58.5R435 2007
   658.4'038011--dc22
                                           2006027715

British Cataloguing in Publication Data
A Cataloguing in Publication record for this book is available from the British Library.

All work contributed to this book is new, previously-unpublished material. The views expressed in this book are those of the authors, but not necessarily of the publisher.

Reference Modeling for Business Systems Analysis

Table of Contents

Chapter I
> Peter Fettke, Institute for Information Systems (IWi) at the German Research
>   Center for Artificial Intelligence (DFKI), Saarbrücken, Germany
> Peter Loos, Institute for Information Systems (IWi) at the German Research
>   Center for Artificial Intelligence (DFKI), Saarbrücken, Germany

Section I: Reference Modeling Languages

Chapter II
> Jan Recker, Queensland University of Technology, Australia
> Michael Rosemann, Queensland University of Technology, Australia
> Wil M. P. van der Aalst, Queensland University of Technology, Australia,
>   & Eindhoven University of Technology, The Netherlands
> Monique Jansen-Vullers,; Eindhoven University of Technology, The Netherlands
> Alexander Dreiling, SAP Research CEC Brisbane, SAP Australia Pty Ltd,
>   Australia

Foreword

Introduction

Based on nearly 10 years of data modeling experience, in 1995 I published *Data Model Patterns: Conventions of Thought in the United States* (cf. Hay, 1995). It was simply a compendium of standard data models I had built for standard business situations that I encountered. Two years later, Silverston et al. (1997) published *The Data Model Resource Book: A Library of Logical Data and Data Warehouse Designs*, which contained their versions of similar models. Fowler (1997) added an object-oriented flavor to the set of common data modeling patterns with *Analysis Patterns: Reusable Object Models*.

In all cases, we were writing from practical experience, describing models that we found ourselves recreating over and over again for various (mostly American) clients. None of us was working from an academic background in computer science, and none of us saw any particular reason to do academic research on the subject. Both the need for these models and the shape of the models themselves were relatively self-evident to all of us.

And we have been successful both at selling books and at marketing ourselves as conceptual data modeling consultants.

Mr. Silverston's and my modeling approach was derived from work done in the UK, and we both have traveled some, but our orientation, at least, was clearly toward the American and UK environments.

Imagine my surprise, then, to come across the articles in this volume, which presented an extensive bibliography of academic works primarily from Germany and Austria on the subject of data model patterns—here called "reference models."

The chapters here go beyond what Mr. Silverston, Mr. Fowler and I have done in three ways:

First, several of the chapters address process models as well as data models. In my experience, it is more difficult to identify generic processes beyond the first few levels of a function decomposition diagram, and I for one found data models more interesting as a way to understand the subtle nuances of what makes a company what it is. Still, addressing process and/or function models is clearly a worthwhile effort.

Second, several of the chapters address the problem of managing pattern configurations. As I describe more informally in my book, it is often the case that there isn't a single "right" answer for a generic model. It is often the case, however, that there are reasonable alternatives to select from when using the patterns to build a specific enterprise's model. The management of these alternate patterns is a task that has not been well addressed in the past.

Finally, and perhaps most important, several chapters specifically address the question of how to evaluate the quality of reference models. This, of course, is a continuation of the more general question of how to evaluate the quality of models in general. The industry thus far has not been as articulate as it could be in addressing either question.

What is a "Reference Model"

The term "reference model" as it is used here is problematic. Different articles describe very different things under this title.

Reference Data or All Data?

In the United States, the meaning of the term "reference model" is different from the one used in this volume. There it refers to any data model that portrays only reference data—the entity classes that describe an organization's configuration. These include primarily the "___ type" entity classes, such as EVENT TYPE, ORDER TYPE, ACTIVITY TYPE and so forth, and not any transaction data elements. While both our patterns and some of the reference models described here make extensive use of these entity classes, they also include, in a generic sense, the transactional data types as well, such as ORDER, EMPLOYMENT, ACTIVITY and so forth.

That is, our *patterns* represent a generic version of all sides of an enterprise data model, not just the *reference* data.

Data or Process?

It is clear that different practitioners address different dimensions of the business. The two primary dimensions are data and activities. Mr. Silverston and I have addressed data in our patterns for the simple reason that it is harder to find universal processes that are common to all businesses. Or at least harder to find any in sufficient detail to be interesting.

In this volume, both data and process models are addressed, to varying degrees. In at least one case, the models focus on aggregate functions more than detailed processes, but in others, process models are included. In some cases, only process models and no data models are discussed.

Ovidiu Noran's article on "Reference Models in Enterprise Architecture" asserts that "The reuse of EA [enterprise architecture] knowledge [involves] identifying commonalities in enterprise models (EMs) and grouping them accordingly. Their common features can then be abstracted into a *partial* enterprise model (PEM) or *reference* enterprise model." In his discussion, he does not specify whether such models are of data or process. Indeed, later in the article he asserts that "Reference models represent reusable templates for human roles (organisational), processes (common functionality) or technology (resources, e.g., IT)." This, in turn, supports an "enterprise engineering tool," which in turn is used to build an "enterprise model," but is not shown to be a template for that model *per se*.

Dr. Noran's overall point, however, is about a "generalized enterprise reference architecture, that is, an architecture that can model activities involved in the implementation of a project spanning over a part or the entire life of an entity." That is, rather than addressing specific pattens in data or process structure, he is concerned with creating a template that describes the system development effort overall. His model is in fact a meta model addressing the nature and artefacts of the development process itself.

Detail or Overall Functions?

This raises a separate question about the definition of "reference model."

In these articles, there is considerable variety in the level of detail involved. In the article presenting a reference model for industrial enterprises, only a high-level function breakdown is presented, with emphasis on describing the overall functions involved. Along with that is representation of bills of material, routing and equipment as data categories, but without any data model details. By contrast, the article describing retail reference models contained both basic process and data models.

Description or Prescription

An ongoing controversy in the United States, that was alluded to only obliquely here, is whether a data model is *descriptive* or *prescriptive*. Is it simply a description of the nature of an enterprise, or is it a blueprint for building new systems. In the United States, at least, the term "data model" is used in several different contexts to mean different things. Some view data modeling as being equivalent to database design. While it is important for the model to reflect the business world that systems will address, the model itself is the design of database artifacts. (IBM Rational's product, for example, a few years ago added a "data modeling" facility, which is nothing other than a tool for modeling relational database design.) As such, the model is *prescriptive*.

I and others, meanwhile, contend that a data model (well, a "conceptual" data model, anyway) should focus entirely on the business at hand as a first step in the development process. It should be done completely without regard for the technologies that might be used to implement its findings. In this sense, a data model is *descriptive*.[1]

Graeme Simsion has written a lot on this subject. See, for example, his article in *The Data Administration Newsletter,* "You're Making It Up: Data Modeling Analysis or Design" (Simsion, 2006).

The answer in the data modeling world at large is, of course, both. In the data world, a conceptual model describes the underlying structure of a business in terms of the data it uses. A logical (some call it the physical) data model then describes either table and column or object class structures for a system design. Similarly, in the process world, an "essential data flow diagram" describes business processes without regard for the technologies that might be invoked to carry them out (McMenamin & Palmer, 1984). A "to be" process model, then, describes the automated or manual mechanisms that will be implemented to carry out the processes.

The reader's view of the models being addressed affect his or her view of the way to approach reference models. Reference models can be created for all of these views. A *conceptual reference model* is concerned with generic concepts that will be made particular in describing actual enterprises. A general concept might be "facility, which in the petroleum industry means any collection of physical equipment configured to carry out a function. Specific company (conceptual) models might then describe the configuration of their facilities in more detail. In the logical model, there might be a "facility" table in a piece of commercial software, with the ability to tailor it as necessary for each customer installation.

Logical reference (data) models, on the other hand, are more specific database designs, but they have been created with the idea that as designs they will be reused.

Most of the articles in this volume beg this question by not addressing the actual modeling in great detail, but at least one ("configuration management for reference models") did go so far as to assert that what the authors considered a "conceptual model" is "…the result of a construct done by a modeler, who examines the elements of a system for a specific purpose such as redesign of an organization or the development of an information system at a given point of time with a specific language."

Managing the Modeling Process and the Models

Several of the chapters discuss the process of developing models. Ostensibly, they are about developing reference models, but the steps they describe apply to the creation of any model: interviews, draft models, review of the models and so forth. In fact, in my experience, it is rare to set out to develop reference models in isolation. Both Mr. Silverston and I had over ten years experience developing enterprise models for clients before we wrote our books describing the models we inferred from our experiences. Fowler's (1997) *Analysis Patterns* similarly came from his actual modeling experiences.

As Gamma et al. (1995) describe the origin of their *Design Patterns* book, "Design patterns capture solutions that have developed and evolved over time. Hence they aren't the designs people tend to generate initially. They reflect untold redesign and recoding as developers have struggled for greater reuse and flexibility in their software" (p. xi).

One measure of quality that came up more than once in these articles was the extent to which a reference model is used by those who develop more specific enterprise models.

This is similar to the general data model quality criterion that a model is only "good" if it is used as the basis for the design of systems. In this case, though, the question is whether a *reference model* has been used as the basis to create other models. This is less compelling, since, if a *reference* model is derived from a specific model, by definition it already is sufficient for that situation. If it is then generalized enough to cover a second situation, by definition it now is suitable for at least two situations. If it is then generalized for a third situation, it is pretty likely that the generalization should now cover not only those three, but indeed most situations.

The heart of this process, however, is that for developing the specialized models in the first place—the processes described by the authors here apply.

The issue of configuration management is more difficult. Between the most general and the most concrete specific model there are families of models that deal with variations in business situations. These could vary in the level of generality, the granularity of sub-types or language. Underlying patterns still apply, but in applying them to specific situations, it is necessary to make decisions between alternatives.

Several articles described this problem, although it is not clear to me that any of them provided a clear solution. Technology for managing models is still relatively primitive, which means that at best, the skill of the modeler in selecting from his or her intellectual toolkit will be key to success for some years to come.

Technology

This raises another issue: Technology. This is problematic in three areas:

The first problem is that, as an industry, we still haven't agreed on modeling notations. In the field of entity/relationship modeling, there is the original Chen (1997) notation, information engineering (developed by Finkelstein (1989) and James Martin), SSADM (cf. Eva 1994, promoted by the Oracle Corporation, and Barker (1990)) and UML (Rumbaugh et al. (1998)). In addition, the technique originally developed in the Netherlands called NIAM (cf. Nijssen, 1976)) and promoted in the United States as Object Role Modeling (cf. Halpin, 2001)) takes a different approach. Each of these has its promoters, and, indeed, each is particularly well suited for different purposes. That UML is becoming popular in the object-oriented community does not mean that it will be accepted readily by those already proficient with Information Engineering. As one who is particularly prejudiced in favor of a particular technique, I think I can speak for all equally prejudiced practitioners when I say that I am not going to give it up willingly.

Note that this is also an issue in the area of function and process modeling. The data flow diagrams of the 1970s have been largely replaced by business process diagrams, IDEF0 diagrams and use cases. Each of these has its promoters as well.

This will undoubtedly be a problem for some years.

The second problem, which is related to the first, is one of the tools available for creating models. Of those on the market, very few are able to accommodate more than one notation. A few can convert a conceptual entity/relationship model into a design UML model, but even this is not a smooth process. The notation that prevails may be determined by the modeling technology that prevails.

The third area is the technology used to convert data models into database or object designs. In this regard, the technology is relatively mature, although changes in development practices are making it difficult for tool vendors to keep up. As business rules become more important, the tools that allow specification of rules and generation of systems from those specifications will become progressively more important. But they don't necessarily link to the CASE tools.

Market for Reference Models

In reading these essays, the question prominent in my mind is: Is the IT industry ready for all of this? It is clear that many years of research are behind what is written here, with extensive thought having gone into the best ways to both create and deploy reference models.

My personal experience, however, makes me wonder about the willingness of industry to make use of this research.

First, there is the question of industry's willingness to adopt modeling techniques at all. In my experience, there are many companies that think this is a good idea in principle, but are not prepared to invest even in the amount of time and resources that would be required to carryout a simple modeling exercise. They want to see something tangible in the way of program code as quickly as possible.

The current movement toward "agile" development techniques is in response to what some people consider too much effort spent on modeling at the expense of actually producing systems. Techniques such as "extreme programming" advocate simply developing a small piece of code, passing it to the user for evaluation and then modifying and adding to it as necessary. Drawing models is seen as a waste of time. This is a movement that is meeting resistance, but it is growing.

Many companies (and their information technology departments) are not sophisticated when it comes to modeling, so considerable salesmanship is required just to be allowed to do it in the first place.

In this context, reference models are valuable because a consultant who has them in his head can make the case that a tailored enterprise model can be completed in a matter of a few months instead of the year or more that people expect. But this presupposes the models already exist. The elaborate processes of developing them, as described in the essays contained here, would already have already taken place.

As mentioned, much of what is written here applies to data modeling in general, not just to the development of reference models. It is important to interview subject matter experts, gain consensus for the model and provide a means for maintaining it. These are not issues just for reference models.

One thing missing from the essays here is discussion of the skill of the modeler. Surveys have shown that given the same problem, ten data modelers will come up with ten different models (Hobermann, 2006; Shanks et al., 1993). This makes the question of data model quality problematic. I contend, however, that, given a particular level of abstraction, the modelers will come up with the same model. At any particular level of abstraction, the contents of a model are ultimately constrained by the reality of the things being modeled.

Where the data modeler's skill comes into play is in determining an appropriate level of abstraction. The more abstract the model, the more general it is and the more adaptable it is to variations in the business's situation, but the farther it is from the concrete language of the business. The more concrete it is, the more familiar and understandable it is to the people who will be using it, but the more vulnerable it is to changes in the business.

In 1999, I attempted to package the models in *Data Model Patterns: Conventions of Thought* into a product that would allow a customer to simply read the models into a CASE tool, and then modify them to meet its particular requirements. It included documentation that the customer could also tailor. The product was not a commercial success. No one was confident enough of their own abilities to make use of such a tool.

On the other hand, in the years since then, my consulting business has thrived as people invite me to produce company-specific enterprise data models—which I can do quickly because I have the patterns in my head.

This leads to a question about the need for the extensive project management and configuration management techniques described here for reference models. A good reference model is a view of the enterprise that is most effective when it resides in the mind of a data modeler. It is the skill of the data modeler that determines the usefulness—the success—of that model. The project management skills are required for the *rest* of the project.

Conclusion

Clearly the disciplines described by the academic articles in this volume are long overdue their implementation in real companies. As mentioned, however, much of what is prescribed here represents simple good practice in the development of any kind of model.

The development of data model (and process model) *reference patterns,* however, must fundamentally remain an inductive process, based on extensive experience with real, specific models.

David C. Hay
Essential Strategies, Inc., USA

References

Barker, R. (1990). *CASE*Method: Entity relationship modelling.* Wokingham, UK: Addison-Wesley.

Chen, P. (1977). *The entity-relationship approach to logical data base design.* Wellesly, MA: QED Information Sciences.

Eva, M. (1994). *SSADM version 4: A user's guide* (2nd ed.). London: McGraw-Hill.

Finkelstein, C. (1989). *An introduction to information engineering: From strategic planning to information systems.* Sydney: Addison-Wesley.

Fowler, M. (n.d.). *Analysis patterns: Reusable object models.* Reading, MA: Addison-Wesley.

Gamma, E., Helm, R., Johnson, R., & Vlissides, J. (1995). *Design patterns: Elements of reusable object-oriented software.* Reading, MA: Addison-Wesley.

Halpin, T. (2001). *Information modeling and relational databases.* San Francisco: Morgan Kaufmann.

Hay, D. (1995). *Data model patterns: Conventions of thought.* New York: Dorset House.

Hoberman, S. (2006). *Design challenge.* Retrieved from http://www.stevehoberman.com/designchallenge.htm.

McMenamin, S., & Palmer, J. (1984). *Essential systems analysis.* Englewood Cliffs, NJ: Yourdon Press.

Nijssen, G. M. (1976). A gross architecture for the next generation database management systems. In G. M. Nijssen (Ed.), *Proceedings of the 1976 IFIP Working Conference on Modeling in Data Base Management Systems,* Freudenstadt, Germany (pp. 1-24). Amsterdam: North-Holland Publishing.

Rumbaugh, J., Jacobson, I., & Booch, G. (1998). *The unified modeling language reference manual.* Reading, MA: Addison-Wesley.

Shanks, G.G., Simsion, G.C., & Rembach, M. (1993).The role of experience in conceptual schema design. In *Proceedings of the 4ᵗʰ Australian Conference on Information Systems,* Brisbane Australia.

Silverston, L., Inmon, B., & Graziano K. (1997). The data model resource book: A library of logical data and data warehouse designs.

Simsion, G. (2006). You're making it up: Data modeling analysis or design. *The data administration newsletter.* http://www.tdan.com/i031ht02.htm

Endnote

[1] This is why, by the way, I vigourously objected to the concept of "object-oriented Analysis." To me, analysis of requirements is just that, and should be done without regard for whether the findings are implemented with object-oriented technology, COBOL programs, or something else.

Dave Hay, a veteran of the information industry since the days of punched cards, paper tape and teletype machines, has been producing data models to support strategic information planning and requirements analysis since the mid-1980s. He has worked in a variety of industries including, among others, power generation, clinical pharmaceutical research, upstream and downstream oil production and processing, forestry, banking, foster care and broadcast. He is the founder and president of Essential Strategies, Inc., a consulting firm dedicated to helping clients define corporate information architecture, identify requirements and plan strategies for the implementation of new systems, including data warehouses. More recently, the company has become deeply immersed in the problems of defining, specifying and implementing metadata repositories. Hay's background in philosophy and data modeling leave him perfectly situated to participate in the new/old field of semantics. His work with clients is usually concerned with defining an organization's semantics. A pioneer in the use of standard data models for standard business situations, he is the author of the book, *Data Model Patterns: Conventions of Thought.* He has brought his considerable experience in requirements analysis into play in writing *Requirements Analysis: From Business Views to Architecture.* His latest book, *Data Model Patterns: A Metadata Map,* describes a comprehensive schema encompassing all aspects of metadata. He is a member of DAMA International, the International Oracle User's Group, the Oracle Development Tools User Group, as well as local chapters of both. He has spoken numerous times at events sponsored by these groups and others. Hay's bachelor's degree in philosophy is from Claremont McKenna College, and he has an MBA in quantitative analysis from New York University.

Preface

Within the information systems field, conceptual modeling is a promising instrument to develop information systems. However, the modeling process is often resource-consuming and faulty. As a way to overcome these failures and to improve and accelerate the development of enterprise-specific models, the concept of reference modeling has been introduced.

Research on reference modeling has become quite popular in the 1990s. Interest in reference modeling, both in industry and in academia, has grown rapidly over the past decade, and continues to grow. The output of the various research streams is documented in the literature. However, non-experts cannot easily access most of this work because it is spread around in different conference proceedings, scholar journals, project reports, and so forth. The objective of this book is to consolidate the already-available knowledge in this area and to point to open problems. The book will provide insights and support for:

- Professionals and researchers working in the field of conceptual modeling in general and reference modeling in particular
- Practitioners and managers concerned with business systems analysis

We want to stimulate further research and provide one building block for an international community on reference modeling with the help of this book.

At the beginning of 2005, we published a call for chapters and invited several experts in the reference modeling field to provide us with proposal chapters for this book. The response to our book was indeed overwhelming. We received 27 full chapters, which forced us to spend a considerable amount of time on the selection process. All chapters received have been reviewed by at least two experts in the field of conceptual modeling or reference modeling respectively. Finally, we selected 16 chapters for inclusion in our book.

Chapter I by Fettke and Loos motivates research on reference modeling and introduces the chapters of this book on using reference models for business systems analysis. Their discussion is based on a framework for research on reference modeling that consists of four

Figure 1. Reference modeling framework used in the book

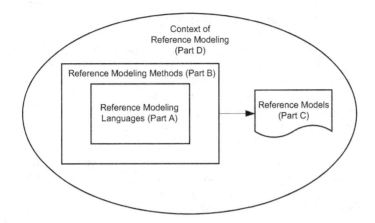

elements: reference modeling languages, reference modeling methods, reference models and reference modeling context (cf. Figure 1). Each element of the framework is discussed with respect to prior research, the contributions of chapters in this book and future research opportunities.

Section I of the book consists of Chapters II and III. In **Chapter II**, Recker, Rosemann, van der Aalst, Jansen-Vullers and Dreiling reflect on the area of configurable reference modeling languages. Their chapter discusses typical requirements for and the development of a reference modeling language. The proposed approach is discussed against the background of ERP systems and exemplified by so-called configurable event-driven process chains (C-EPCs), an extension of a well-known process modeling language in the area of business process management. The usefulness of their approach is demonstrated by applications in the area of SAP enterprise system configuration, process mining and integration of configurable data and process models.

Chapter III by vom Brocke provides an excellent summary of well-known design principles for reference models. In his chapter, he proposes a framework for reuse relations between conceptual models. The framework presented does not only stress the need for configuration concepts to reuse conceptual models, but also elaborates other design principles such as instantiation, aggregation, specialization and analogy. As a special feature, a precise meta model defines each design principle. Furthermore, vom Brocke discusses the trade-off between the costs of designing reference models *for* reuse and the costs of designing reference models *with* reuse. Some guidelines for applying the design principles complete this chapter.

Section II of the book consists of Chapters IV to VII. In **Chapter IV**, Ahlemann and Gastl introduce a process model for the construction of reference models. The proposal describes how to base the model construction process on empirical data. To achieve this objective, typical empirical data gathering methods such as interviews, systems analysis, and so forth, are used. The construction process of reference models consists of four phases: (1) planning the reference model project, (2) model construction, (3) practical testing and (4) documentation. Each phase is described in detail. Furthermore, the authors present many concrete examples illustrating how the proposed process model can be applied in reality.

In **Chapter V,** Duarte, Fernandes, and Machado investigate methods for business modeling in process-oriented organizations from a software development perspective. The authors propose a generic framework for process-oriented software houses. The framework can be understood as a particular reference model and describes important software development processes such as management, support and add-value processes. The instantiation of this framework is demonstrated with the well-known rational unified process (RUP). Additionally, it is explained how the framework can be used with other kinds of processes. The chapter concludes with the results from a case study investigating a real software development project.

It can be assumed that the effectiveness and efficiency of the application of a reference model is strongly determined by the quality of the model. To evaluate the quality of reference models, Frank develops a multi-perspective framework in **Chapter VI**. This framework consists of four perspectives: (1) costs and benefits of reference model use are assessed from an economic perspective; (2) the deployment perspective describes criteria for the ability and willingness of users to deal with a reference model; (3) from an engineering perspective, a reference model is viewed as a design artifact that has to fulfill particular requirements; and (4) finally, reference models can be assessed from an epistemological point of view. Additionally, the chapter explains a generic process model for performing a reference model evaluation.

Noran demonstrates in **Chapter VII** how reference models can be used in the area of enterprise architecture. The complete description of the methodology used is beyond the scope of this chapter. Instead, the author exemplifies the usefulness of his approach with a particular example. This example shows how to assess and organize reference models into a structured repository using a generalized architectural framework. Further, the chapter provides guidance for the selection of an appropriate reference model. The chapter concludes with reflections on improving the quality of reference models and some interesting aspects used to structure and select reference models.

Section III of the book consists of Chapters VIII to XIII. In **Chapter VIII**, Scheer, Jost and Güngöz summarize the results of 20 years of research on developing and applying a reference model for industrial enterprises. The so-called Y-CIM reference model is established and recognized as the standard reference model in the industrial sector and is also being deployed more by other industries. This chapter focuses on the development of CIM and how the Y-CIM reference model can implement it. Some particular features of the Y-CIM reference model are discussed. Additionally, the applicability of the model in the service industry is investigated.

In **Chapter IX**, Becker and Schütte give an overview of a reference model for retail enterprises, the so-called "retail-H model." This reference model provides a structural framework for information systems for the retail sector. The reference model and its graphical representation aim at enhancing the orientation within the numerous conceptual models applied in the retail sector. These conceptual models are pivotal for the management of information systems and business processes. Furthermore, the authors describe some exemplary reference data models in the retail sector.

In **Chapter X**, Mäuser describes the SKO data model, a reference model for the Sparkassenorganisation (the organization of German Saving Banks). The SKO data model was initially developed approximately 15 years ago and is derived from the Financial Services Data Model, which had been provided by IBM. Currently, the model is probably the most extensive reference data model in the banking area with more than 17,000 well-defined modeling objects. Until now, this reference model has been utilized in about 30 projects. The model is organized around five abstraction layers that provide different levels of modeling granularity. A dedicated software tool guarantees the efficient use of the SKO data model.

Faced with changing market conditions and higher pressure on cost and productivity, enterprises have started to concentrate on their core competencies. This results in a paradigm shift in the domain of strategic sourcing from a supplier centric to a supply network scope. In order to support the paradigm shift, Albani, Müssigmann and Zaha have developed a reference model for the domain of strategic supply network development in **Chapter XI**. This reference model extends the traditional frame of reference in strategic sourcing to a supply network perspective. Additionally, the authors describe the development of a prototype that is based on the proposed reference model.

While the Y-CIM and retail-H reference models, as well as the SKO data model, primarily address traditional business areas, numerous reference models have been proposed in the meantime to facilitate the development of electronic business systems and applications. Mišić and Zhao conduct a comparative analysis of existing electronic reference models in **Chapter XII**. Such an analysis is the first step in selecting the right foundation for the system that is being developed. This chapter presents some results of a comparative analysis of four well-known reference models for electronic businesses. Their analysis is primarily conducted from the viewpoint of a reference model's suitability to support the development of flexible and interoperable electronic business applications.

In **Chapter XIII**, Van Belle presents the results of the evaluation of 10 reference models that are well-known in theory and practice. His analysis is based on an evaluation framework that encompasses syntactic, semantic and pragmatic aspects. Most evaluation criteria used allow a quantitative evaluation of reference models. However, not all criteria proposed can be measured using clear or unambiguous metrics. To overcome these limitations, the author suggests some novel, exploratory approaches. The chapter does not only evaluate selected reference models but also provides some insights into the methodological problems of reference model evaluation.

Section IV of the book consists of Chapters XIV to XVII. In **Chapter XIV**, Thomas explores the idea of reference model management. His work is motivated by the fact that today's reference modeling processes are not well supported by software tools. Of course, there are tools that support a particular reference modeling activity. However, there is no integrated approach to computer-supported management of reference models. Such an approach is developed by the author. The proposed system is described with the help of particular data structures and system architectures. Additionally, experiences from a prototypical implementation of a reference model management system are reported.

In **Chapter XV**, Braun, Esswein, Gehlert and Weller investigate the topic of configuration management for reference models. They argue that the modification of reference models should be systematically supported by a model configuration management system, which has to address versioning and referencing. Versioning is needed to trace changes made to reference models over time. The concept of referencing describes the relationship between a generic reference model and a particular enterprise model. The chapter discusses several requirements of configuration management and shows how these requirements can be supported by an adequate system.

In **Chapter XVI**, Mendling, Neumann, and Nüttgens discuss interchange formats for reference modeling. Interchange formats build on isomorphic mapping between a domain-specific meta model and the scheme of the interchange format. First, the authors explain general aspects of interchange formats, including their pragmatic, economic and conceptual efforts and present general design guidelines for interchange formats. After that, they illustrate interchange formats for EPCs and UML, two frequently used modeling languages for reference modeling. Additionally, the authors illustrate the benefits of interchange formats for three important areas of reference modeling: model interchange, separation of process modeling and execution as well as model transformation.

Finally, in **Chapter XVII**, Höhnel, Krahl, and Schreiber report on several lessons learned in reference modeling. The authors gained their experience from more than 40 reference modeling projects in different industries. The lessons learned described by the authors can be grouped into five critical success factors: open communication, open construction principles and quality criteria, tool support, business justification and "use what you bought." Each success factor is derived from their practical experience and is extensively discussed. Furthermore, the authors especially demonstrate which factors are of particular importance for successful reference modeling during which phases.

We hope that you will enjoy this book as much as we have enjoyed the effort involved in preparing it. May this book and the work reported in it offer guidance for your work and stimulation for your own research.

Peter Fettke & Peter Loos

Acknowledgments

The fact that this book is able to provide a comprehensive, detailed and current overview about reference modeling in the context of business systems analysis is due to the excellent contributions we received by academics and practitioners who are globally perceived as the thought leaders in this area.

We would like to thank our reviewers for spending the time and energy preparing critical, but constructive reviews (in alphabetical order):

Jörg Becker, Westfälische Wilhelms-Universität Münster, Germany

Oliver Braun, Saarland University, Germany

Jan vom Brocke, European Research Center for Information Systems, University of Münster, Germany

Wilhelm Dangelmaier, University of Paderborn, Germany

Jörg Desel, Catholic University of Eichstätt-Ingolstadt, Germany

Jörg Evermann, Victoria University Wellington, New Zealand

Ulrich Frank, University of Duisburg-Essen, Germany

David C. Hay, Essential Strategies, Inc., USA

Ekkart Kindler, University of Paderborn, Germany

Stefan Kirn, University of Hohenheim, Germany

Helmut Krcmar, Technische Universität München, Germany

Susanne Leist, University of Regensburg, Germany

Vojislav B. Mišić, University of Manitoba, Canada

Daniel Moody, University of Iceland, Iceland

Markus Nüttgens, University of Hamburg, Germany

Andreas Opdahl, University of Bergen, Norway

Jeffrey Parsons, Memorial University of Newfoundland, Canada

Geert Poels, Ghent University, Belgium

Peter Rittgen, University College of Borås, Sweden

Michael Rosemann, Queensland University of Technology, Australia

Reinhard Schütte, Dohle Handelsgruppe GmbH & Co. KG, Germany

Klaus Turowski, University of Augsburg, Germany

Jean-Paul Van Belle, University of Cape Town, South Africa

Wil van der Aalst, Queensland University of Technology, Australia, & Eindhoven University of Technology, The Netherlands

Robert Winter, University of St. Gallen, Switzerland

Boris Wyssusek, Queensland University of Technology, Australia

Special thanks goes to David Hay, who provided an interesting foreword for our book. Furthermore, Idea Group Inc., especially our development editor, Kristin Roth, who gave us excellent support while preparing this book. Last, but not least, we would like to thank all authors, including those whose work could not be included in this book, for their interest in, and support for, our project.

Peter Fettke & Peter Loos

Chapter I

Perspectives on Reference Modeling

Peter Fettke, Institute for Information Systems (IWi) at the German Research
Center for Artificial Intelligence (DFKI), Saarbrücken, Germany

Peter Loos, Institute for Information Systems (IWi) at the German Research
Center for Artificial Intelligence (DFKI), Saarbrücken, Germany

Abstract

Conceptual models play an increasingly important role in all phases of the information systems life cycle. For instance, they are used for business engineering, information systems development and customizing of enterprise resource planning (ERP) systems. Despite conceptual modeling being a vital instrument for developing information systems, the modeling process often is resource consuming and faulty. As a way to overcome these failures and to improve the development of enterprise-specific models, the concept of reference modeling has been introduced. A reference model is a conceptual framework and may be used as a blueprint for information systems development. In this chapter, we seek to motivate research on reference modeling and introduce the chapters of this book on using reference models for business systems analysis. Our discussion is based on a framework for research on reference modeling that consists of four elements: reference modeling languages, reference modeling methods, reference models and reference modeling context. Each element of the framework is discussed with respect to prior research, the contributions of chapters in this book and future research opportunities.

Motivation

Within the information systems discipline, conceptual modeling aims at building some kind of formal representation of a modeling domain (Frank, 1999; Mylopoulos, 1998; Scheer & Hars, 1992; Wand & Weber, 2002). Conceptual models, which are often graphically represented, are used to grasp both static and dynamic aspects of a particular discourse world. They play an increasingly important role in activities such as business engineering (Scheer, 1998a, 1998b), information systems development (Winter, 1994) and customizing of enterprise resource planning (ERP) systems (Rosemann, 2003b). Despite conceptual modeling being a vital instrument for developing information systems, the modeling process is often resource-consuming and faulty. As a way to overcome these failures and to improve and accelerate the development of enterprise-specific models, the concept of reference modeling has been introduced (Mertins & Bernus, 1998; Mišic & Zhao, 2000; Scheer & Nüttgens, 2000; Schütte, 1998).

A reference model is a model representing a class of domains (Fettke & Loos, 2003a, pp. 35-36). It is a conceptual framework that can be used as a blueprint for information system development. In order to be able to use reference models, they must be adapted to the requirements of a specific enterprise. Reference models are also called universal models, generic models or model patterns. Concrete examples of reference models are (e.g., SAP's reference model, Keller & Teufel, 1998), Hay's (1996) data model patterns or Scheer's (1994) reference model for production planning and control systems.

Although the ideas of reference modeling can be traced back to at least the 1930s (Thomas, 2005, p. 18), research on reference modeling has become quite popular in Germany in the 1990s. For instance, in February 2006, the conference "Referenzmodellierung" (this term is the German word for "reference modeling") was held for the ninth time. More than 50 papers have been published in the proceedings of this conference. However, today's reference modeling research is mainly conducted in Germany, as can be seen by two library searches: More than two hundred books on reference modeling are catalogued by "Die Deutsche Bibliothek" (German National Library, see Figure 1; the search was conducted on February 2, 2006, using the search string "referenzmodell*"). In comparison, in the catalogue of the Library of Congress, only 11 titles can be found on the topic (the search was conducted on February 2, 2006, using the search string "reference model*").

One reason for the tremendous interest in reference modeling in Germany may be that worldwide leading German information technology enterprises made extensive use of reference models. For example, SAP, the world's leading ERP developer, decided in the early 1990s to describe their software packages with reference models. The reference models developed were used by SAP as a marketing instrument to penetrate the American market for client/server ERP systems (Ricciuti & Semich, 1993). The IDS Scheer AG, a software and consulting company that developed the ARIS Toolset, is another leading enterprise. The ARIS Toolset is a worldwide leading business process modeling tool, which is very often used for reference modeling. Additionally, IDS Scheer AG developed several reference models for different industries, which are used by consultants in projects (Reiter, 1999).

These two examples demonstrate that reference modeling is relevant for all businesses worldwide. Since reference modeling has such a potential for effective and efficient business

Figure 1. Number of publications on reference modeling catalogued by "Die Deutsche Bibliothek" and the Library of Congress

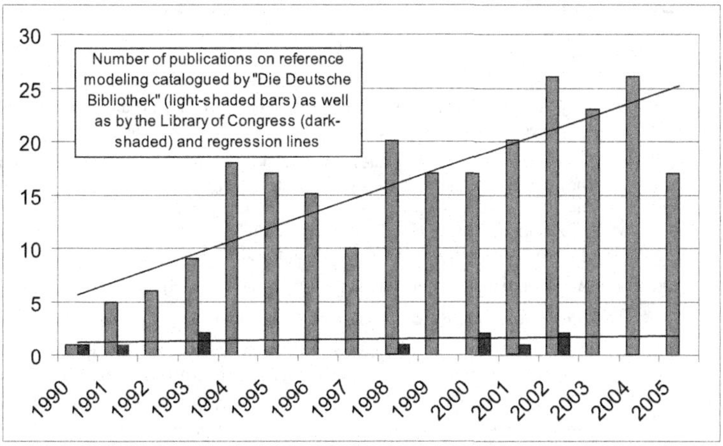

systems analysis, we want to stimulate further research and build an international community on reference modeling with the help of this book. In particular, the objective of this introductory chapter is twofold: first, we seek to motivate research on reference modeling and, second, we introduce the chapters of this book.

The remainder of this chapter is structured as follows: We first discuss the term "reference model." Next, we describe some application areas and benefits of reference modeling. We then introduce a framework for research on reference modeling that consists of four elements: reference modeling languages, reference modeling methods, reference models and the reference modeling context. Each element of the framework is discussed with respect to prior research, the contributions of the chapters in this book and future research opportunities. Finally, we present some concluding remarks.

Theoretical Background

Explicating the Term "Reference Model"

Despite the popularity of the term "reference model," both in academia and practice, the term is used to designate different objects. Amongst others, it is used to designate theoretical statements (Schmid & Lindemann, 1998), standardized technical architectures (ISO, 1994) or documentations of enterprise systems (Curran & Keller, 1999). Hence, considerable confusion remains as to the meaning of the term "reference model."

Several definitions of the term "reference model" are depicted in Table 1. It is almost undisputed that a reference model is a conceptual model and that not all conceptual models are reference models. However, different distinguishing features are discussed in the literature:

Table 1. Definitions of the term "reference model"

Author(s)	Definition
Bernus (1999)	Reference models "capture characteristics common to many enterprises within or across one or more industrial sectors." (p. 7)
	"Reference components provide normalized descriptions of key concepts of a given domain. They can be used as the starting point for developing a new application similar to applications developed before in the domain, thus extending reuse to the early development (1998)
Castano, Antonellis de, Fugini, & Pernici (1998)	"Reference components provide normalized descriptions of key concepts of a given domain. They can be used as the starting point for developing a new application similar to applications developed before in the domain, thus extending reuse to the early development phases. Reference components can also be used as a validation tool, to check the quality of existing schemas and promote their standardization." (p. 309)
Fettke & Loos (2003a)	"A reference model represents a class of domains." (p. 35)
Frank (1999)	"A generic reference model represents a class of domains." (p. 695)
Mertins & Bernus (1998)	"An information system reference model is... a typical, or paradigmatic model, which describes the information system or a well identified part of it." (p. 615)
Mišic & Zhao (2000)	A "reference model is a conceptual framework for describing system architecture, thus providing a high-level specification for a class of systems." (p. 484)
Rosemann (2003a)	"Reference models are generic conceptual models that formalise recommended practices for a certain domain." (p. 595)
Schütte (1998)	"A reference information model is the result of a construction created by a modeler who declares for IT and business people universal elements and relationships of a system as a recommendation with the help of a language in one point of time so that a point of reference is created." [translation by the authors] (p. 69)
vom Brocke (2003)	"A reference model ... is an information model that people develop or use for supporting the construction of application models, though the relationship between the reference and application model can be characterized by the fact that object or content of the reference model is reused by the construction of the object or content of the application model." [translation by the authors] (p. 34)
"What is a process reference model?" (1998)	A process reference model "integrates best practices into a cross-functional framework." (p. 52)

- **Best practices:** A reference model provides best practices for conducting business.

- **Universal applicability:** A reference model does not represent a particular enterprise, but a class of domains. Hence, a reference model is valid for a class of domains.

- **Reusability:** Reference models can be understood as blueprints for information systems development. Thus a reference model is a conceptual framework that could be reused in a multitude of information system projects.

Using these characteristics to define the term "reference model" leads to a further problem. Although these characteristics have an appealing intuitive meaning, until now the definition of all characteristics has not been accomplished satisfactorily. Consequently, some authors reject one ore more of these characterizations as being constitutional for the term "reference model," for instance Thomas (2005) and vom Brocke (2003, pp. 31-34).

Within computer science, the meaning of the term "design pattern" is similar to the meaning of the term "reference model." Design patterns are "proven solutions to recurring design problems" (Coplien, 2000, p. 1604). This idea is pursued with reference models, too. However, design patterns are normally finely granulated, reusable artifacts that are mostly used for designing an information system. The main idea of business patterns or analysis patterns is quite similar to the concept of reference modeling. For a deeper discussion on this differentiation, see Fettke, Zwicker, and Loos (2006).

In this book, we do not prescribe a particular definition of the term "reference model." Instead, the different authors have developed their own meaning.

Application Areas and Benefits of Reference Modeling

Reference modeling provides both theoretical and practical benefits. From a theoretical perspective, a reference model provides a general description of an enterprise. Hence, a reference model is an important artifact that is designed during the research process. The construction and evolution of a reference model can be understood as a design science (Hevner, March, Park, & Ram, 2004) research process.

From a practical perspective, reference modeling can be used in different application scenarios (Fettke & Loos, 2004b, pp. 21-23):

- **Deriving a particular enterprise model:** A reference model representing a class of domain can be reused and adapted to the needs of a particular enterprise.

- **Validating enterprise-specific models:** A reference model can be used as a benchmark for analyzing enterprise-specific models. With the help of the reference model it is possible to identify gaps in enterprise-specific models.

- **Developing off-the-shelf-applications:** Reference models represent classes of domains. Hence, they provide a generic framework for the development of off-the-shelf-applications.

- **Selecting ERP packages:** Reference models can be used to describe the features of different ERP packages. Based on such a description, it is possible to compare and select an appropriate ERP package for an enterprise.

The use of reference modeling has different economic effects on the modeling process (Becker & Knackstedt, 2003):

- **Decrease in costs:** Reference models can be reused, so the development costs of the reference model can be saved.

- **Decrease in modeling time:** Additionally, the development time of an enterprise model can be reduced with the help of a reference model.

- **Increase in model quality:** Normally, reference models are proven solutions and provide a better model quality.

- **Decrease in modeling risk:** The risk of failures during reference model usage can be reduced because reference models are already validated.

To conclude, reference modeling can be used to improve the enterprise's market position. However, reference models can also have some negative effects. For instance, the selection of an appropriate reference model is a pivotal activity during reference modeling. Furthermore, a modeler normally needs to have greater experience with modeling when using reference models, as adapting them requires particular skills.

Framework for Research on Reference Modeling

There is a great deal of terminological confusion in modeling literature. For example, the term "model" is often used for different purposes. Adopting the well-established framework of Wand and Weber (2002) for conceptual modeling, we conceptualize the field of research on reference modeling using four perspectives (cf. Figure 2, Fettke & Loos, 2004c):

- **Reference modeling languages:** A reference modeling language provides a set of constructs and rules that show how to combine the constructs to model real-world domains. For instance, event-driven process chains (EPC; Scheer, 1998a, 1998b), the entity-relationship model (ERM, (Chen, 1976)) or the unified modeling language (UML); (Fettke, 2005; Rumbaugh, Jacobson, & Booch, 1998) are languages used for reference modeling.

- **Reference modeling methods:** A modeling method provides procedures by which a language can be used (e.g., the unified software development process, USDP; Jacobson, Booch & Rumbaugh, 1998). Reference modeling methods can be distinguished with regards to supporting the developing or application process of a reference model.

- **Reference models:** A reference model is a model representing a class of domains, (e.g., Scheer's, 1994, reference model for production planning and control systems). It is a conceptual framework or blueprint for system development.

- **Context:** Each modeling process is embedded in a specific context setting that comprises technical, economic, social and other factors. For instance, tools used for reference modeling (Becker, Algermissen, Delfmann, & Niehaves, 2004) or markup languages for reference models (Mendling & Nüttgens, 2004) constitute particular technical factors.

Reference Modeling Languages

Overview of Some Existing Research

To represent a reference model, a modeling language is needed. Until now, no standardized (reference) modeling language is established in theory or practice. Nevertheless, there is a tendency to standardize the concepts used to represent a modeling domain. Typical model-

Figure 2. Reference modeling framework (Based on Wand & Weber, 2002)

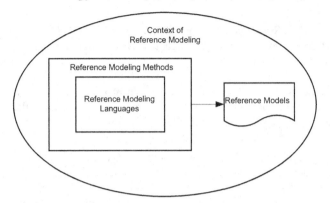

ing languages used are, amongst others, ERM, the UML or EPC (Fettke, Loos, & Zwicker, 2006).

Three aspects of modeling language are of particular importance for reference modeling:

- **Multi-perspective modeling:** The representation of modeling domains from different perspectives is a vital modeling concept (Finkelstein, Gabbay, Hunter, Kramer, & Nuseibeh, 1994; Pohl, 1994). A particular perspective on a model can be designed from different construction criteria. Basically, perspectives can be constructed based on analytical criteria or subjective needs. For instance, if objective criteria are used to represent a model perspective, then data, function or process views are used to describe information systems (Scheer, 1998a, 1998b). If subjective needs are taken into consideration, model perspectives are conceptualized based on perception, presuppositions and preferences of a model user (Frank, 2002).

- **Management of variants:** The management of conceptual model variants fosters the systematic utilization of alternative configurations of information systems. The industrial management of variants of product components is a useful instrument for controlling the complexity of production processes and can also be used to specify different model variants (Schütte, 1998, pp. 207-211). While model perspectives offer different views on a particular modeling object, model variants represent different modeling objects that are similar or comparable regarding a particular aspect. Typical approaches to manage model variants are described by Schlagheck (2000, pp. 74-76) and Schwegmann (1999, pp. 140-165).

- **Reuse and adaptation:** Reusing conceptual models is a central concept of reference modeling. In the simplest case, a reference model is duplicated manually without any technical assistance, which does not restrict its adaptation in any way. However, problematic redundancies and inconsistencies between the original and duplicated model can arise. To support the reuse and adaptation of models, various, more powerful concepts have been proposed (Becker, Delfmann, Dreiling, Knackstedt, & Kuropka, 2004; Dreiling, Rosemann, van der Aalst, Sadiq, & Khan, 2005).

Chapters in This Book

In Chapter II, Recker, Rosemann, van der Aalst, Jansen-Vullers and Dreiling reflect on the area of configurable reference modeling languages. Their chapter discusses typical requirements for, and the development of, a reference modeling language. The proposed approach is discussed against the background of ERP systems and exemplified by so-called configurable event-driven process chains (C-EPCs), an extension of a well-known process modeling language in the area of business process management. The usefulness of their approach is demonstrated by applications in the area of SAP enterprise system configuration, process mining and integration of configurable data and process models.

Chapter III by vom Brocke provides an excellent summary of well-known design principles for reference models. In his chapter, he proposes a framework for reuse relations between conceptual models. The framework presented does not only stress the need for configuration concepts to reuse conceptual models, but other design principles such as instantiation, aggregation, specialization and analogy are elaborated as well. As a special feature, a precise meta model defines each design principle. Furthermore, vom Brocke discusses the trade-off between the costs of designing reference models *for* reuse and the costs of designing reference models *with* reuse. Some guidelines for applying the design principles complete this chapter.

Some Future Research Opportunities

We propose that further research on languages for reference modeling can be undertaken in at least the following areas:

- **Formalization:** Often, reference models are represented using languages without formal semantics and only limited syntax definition. In the future, it will be necessary to define syntax and semantics of a reference model language more precisely.

- **Standardization:** Formalization goes along with the standardization of a reference modeling language. If a standardized reference modeling language is used, reusing or integrating different reference models becomes easier.

- **Empirical research:** Until now, the effectiveness or efficiency of reference modeling languages has almost only been based on intuitive argumentations. There are not many well-founded empirical research approaches to assess the quality of reference modeling languages. Hence, it is necessary to conduct more empirical research on the quality of reference modeling languages.

Reference Modeling Methods

Overview of Some Existing Research

Several authors describe and propose various procedure models for reference modeling (Lang, 1997; Schlagheck, 2000; Schütte, 1998; Schwegmann, 1999). From a conceptual point of view, reference modeling consists of two processes (cf. Figure 3; Fettke, Zwicker, et al., 2006). The objective of the construction process is to design and build a particular reference model. The reuse of the reference model for the development of a particular enterprise model is the objective of the application process. Both processes are always temporally separated. Normally, different organizations and personal staff are allocated for these processes. The separation is a requirement for reusing reference models in different contexts, yet it requires careful coordination of both processes.

Typical activities during the construction process of reference models are problem definition, development, evaluation and maintenance of a reference model. To apply a reference model, four main activities have to be executed: selection, adaptation, utilization and integration.

Furthermore, various methods are proposed for particular activities during the construction and application of reference models. For instance, Rosemann (2003c) describes how to utilize reference models for the ERP life cycle; Algermissen, Delfmann, and Niehaves (2005) report about reference modeling in public administration and Esswein, Zumpe, and Sunke (2004) discuss how to assess the quality of reference models in electronic commerce.

Chapters in This Book

In Chapter IV, Ahlemann and Gastl introduce a process model for the construction of reference models. The proposal describes how to base the model construction process on empirical data. To achieve this objective, typical empirical data gathering methods such as interviews, systems analysis, etc. are used. The construction process of reference models consists of four phases: (1) planning the reference model project, (2) model construction,

Figure 3. Reference modeling processes

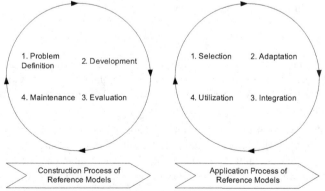

(3) practical testing, and (4) documentation. Each phase is described in detail. Furthermore, the authors present many concrete examples illustrating how the proposed process model can be applied in reality.

In Chapter V, Duarte, Fernandes and Machado investigate methods for business modeling in process-oriented organizations from a software development perspective. The authors propose a generic framework for process-oriented software houses. The framework can be understood as a particular reference model and describes important software development processes such as management, support and add-value processes. The instantiation of this framework is demonstrated with the well-known rational unified process (RUP). Additionally, it is explained how the framework can be used with other kinds of processes. The chapter concludes with the results from a case study investigating a real software development project.

It can be assumed that the effectiveness and efficiency of the application of a reference model is strongly determined by the quality of the model. To evaluate the quality of reference models, Frank develops a multi-perspective framework in Chapter VI. This framework consists of four perspectives: (1) costs and benefits of reference model use are assessed from an economic perspective; (2) deployment perspective describes criteria for the ability and willingness of users to deal with a reference model; (3) from an engineering perspective, a reference model is viewed as a design artifact that has to fulfill particular requirements; and (4) finally, reference models can be assessed from an epistemological point of view. Additionally, the chapter explains a generic process model for performing a reference model evaluation.

Noran demonstrates in Chapter VII how reference models can be used in the area of enterprise architecture. The complete description of the methodology used is beyond the scope of this chapter. Instead, the author exemplifies the usefulness of his approach with a particular example. This example shows how to assess and organize reference models into a structured repository using a generalized architecture framework. Further, the chapter provides guidance for the selection of an appropriate reference model. The chapter concludes with reflections on improving the quality of reference models and some interesting aspects used to structure and select reference models.

Future Research Opportunities

We propose that further research on reference modeling methods can be undertaken in at least the following areas:

- **Consolidation:** So far, numerous approaches to reference modeling exist in theory and practice. Hence, there is a need to "chop down the reference method jungle" (an analogy to Hofstede & Weide, 1993) and to standardize different methodological contributions.

- **Particular contributions:** Nevertheless, there is a lack of particular contributions. For instance, despite the fact that several approaches to evaluate reference models are known, there are only few results available on the evaluation of reference models. Furthermore, there are almost no guidelines on how to select an appropriate reference model. Additionally, it is necessary to develop application methods for particular domains (e.g., knowledge management, business process management and supply chain management).

- **Empirical research:** The relevance and usefulness of known reference model methods is almost only demonstrated on intuitive grounds. Hence, more empirical research is needed to make precise propositions on the usefulness of reference modeling methods.

Reference Models

Overview of Some Existing Research

Within theory and practice, numerous more or less elaborated reference models are proposed. Detailed analyses and comparisons of known reference models are provided by Fettke and Loos (2003a), Fettke et al. (2006), Fettke et al. (2006), Mišic and Zhao (2000), Van Belle (2003), and others. When surveying existing reference models, several aspects are conspicuous:

- **Domain:** Early developed reference models only address industrial enterprises. Since then, reference models have been developed for several other domains (e.g., financial service providers, Gesamtverband der Deutschen Versicherungswirtschaft e. V., 2000; publishing houses, Tzouvaras, 2003; and supply chain management, Stephens, 2001).
- **Size:** The size of existent reference models fluctuates significantly. While some models contain several hundred process and data entities, other models are rather small. For instance, compare the models developed by Scheer (1994b) and Frank (2001).
- **Reuse and customization:** Dedicated concepts for reusing reference models are seldom used in known reference models. Hence, reference models are often reused by manual copying. However, build- and runtime-operators are used by some reference modelers (e.g., Schlagheck, 2000).
- **Evaluation:** The evaluation of a reference model is not an obligatory activity. Some results of an ontological approach are reported by Fettke and Loos (2003c, 2004a, 2005). However, neither acceptable evaluation criteria nor methods are established yet (Fettke & Loos, 2003b). If a particular reference model is evaluated, often quite simple research designs are used (e.g., case studies or experience reports).

Chapters in This Book

In Chapter VIII, Scheer, Jost, and Güngöz summarize the results of 20 years of research on developing and applying a reference model for industrial enterprises. The so-called Y-

CIM reference model is established and recognized as the standard reference model in the industrial sector and is also being deployed more and more by other industries. This Chapter focuses on the development of CIM and how the Y-CIM reference model can implement it. Some particular features of the Y-CIM reference model are discussed. Additionally, the applicability of the model in the service industry is investigated.

In Chapter IX, Becker and Schütte give an overview of a reference model for retail enterprises, the so-called "retail-H model." This reference model provides a structural framework for information systems for the retail sector. The reference model and its graphical representation aim at enhancing the orientation within the numerous conceptual models applied in the retail sector. These conceptual models are pivotal for the management of information systems and business processes. Furthermore, the authors describe some exemplary reference data models in the retail sector.

In Chapter X, Mäuser describes the SKO data model, a reference model for the Sparkassenorganisation (the organization of German Saving Banks). The SKO data model was initially developed approximately 15 years ago and is derived from the financial services data model, which had been provided by IBM. Currently, the model is probably the most extensive reference data model in the banking area, with more than 17,000 well-defined modeling objects. Until now, this reference model has been utilized in about 30 projects. The model is organized around five abstraction layers that provide different levels of modeling granularity. A dedicated software tool guarantees the efficient use of the SKO data model.

Faced with changing market conditions and higher pressure on cost and productivity, enterprises have started to concentrate on their core competencies. This results in a paradigm shift in the domain of strategic sourcing from a supplier-centric to a supply network scope. In order to support the paradigm shift, Albani, Müssigmann, and Zaha have developed a reference model for the domain of strategic supply network development in Chapter XI. This reference model extends the traditional frame of reference in strategic sourcing to a supply network perspective. Additionally, the authors describe the development of a prototype that is based on the proposed reference model.

While the Y-CIM and retail-H reference models as well as the SKO data model primarily address traditional business areas, numerous reference models have been proposed in the meantime to facilitate the development of electronic business systems and applications. Mišic and Zhao conduct a comparative analysis of existing electronic reference models in Chapter XII. Such an analysis is the first step in selecting the right foundation for the system that is being developed. This chapter presents some results of a comparative analysis of four well-known reference models for electronic businesses. Their analysis is primarily conducted from the viewpoint of a reference model's suitability to support the development of flexible and interoperable electronic business applications.

In Chapter XIII, Van Belle presents the results of the evaluation of 10 reference models that are well-known in theory and practice. His analysis is based on an evaluation framework which encompasses syntactic, semantic and pragmatic aspects. Most evaluation criteria used allow a quantitative evaluation of reference models. However, not all criteria proposed can be measured using clear or unambiguous metrics. To overcome these limitations, the author suggests some novel, exploratory approaches. The chapter does not only evaluate selected reference models but also provides some insights into the methodological problems of reference model evaluation.

Some Future Research Opportunities

We propose that future research on reference models can be done in at least the following areas:

- **Consolidation:** The known set of reference models has to be consolidated. Existing reference models consist of largely redundant parts. These redundancies have to be identified. After eliminating these redundancies, it will be necessary to invent adequate abstraction and reuse concepts for reference models. Otherwise, it will be impossible to reuse the consolidated reference models efficiently.

- **Evaluation:** As already mentioned before, little research has been done on the systematic evaluation of reference models. In the meantime, there are several frameworks for the evaluation of reference models. However, it is necessary to apply these frameworks to assess each known reference model.

- **Empirical research:** Furthermore, it is necessary to conduct more empirical research on the application of a particular reference model. Such approaches should study how a particular reference model is used in practice.

Reference Modeling Context

Overview of Existing Research

Reference modeling processes are embedded in a particular context that encompasses technical, economic, social, psychological and other factors. Two aspects are stressed in the literature:

- **Modeling tools:** Modeling tools are software systems supporting the construction and application of reference models (Scheer, 1994a). Although there is still no all-purpose reference modeling tool, several important concepts are already proposed in the literature. For instance, meta case tools are already available and their continuously improving modeling flexibility has large benefits for reference modeling (Becker, Delfmann, Knackstedt, & Kuropka, 2002; Fettke, Loos, & Pastor, 2004). Distributed modeling tools and virtual engineering communities for reference modeling support the collaborative development of (reference) models (Fettke, Zwicker, et al., 2006; Ram & Ramesh, 1998; vom Brocke, 2003). Furthermore, discussions are under way to enhance the graphical representation of reference models with virtual reality technology (Leinenbach, 2000).

- **Meta-theoretical assumptions:** Each scientific investigation is based on a particular set of unquestioned theories, assumed assumptions, pursued objectives, used research methods and a particular Weltanschauung. Until now, no research paradigm is well-established in Information Systems (Iivari, Hirschheim, & Klein, 1998; Mingers, 2001).

Nevertheless, several paradigmatic questions are already discussed in the context of (reference) modeling (Becker, Niehaves, & Knackstedt, 2004; Hirschheim, Klein, & Lyytinen, 1995; Niehaves, Ribbert, Dreiling, & Holten, 2004).

Chapters in this Book

In Chapter XIV, Thomas explores the idea of reference model management. His work is motivated by the fact that today's reference modeling processes are not well supported by software tools. Of course, there are tools that support a particular reference modeling activity. However, there is no integrated approach to computer-supported management of reference models. Such an approach is developed by the author. The proposed system is described with the help of particular data structures and system architectures. Additionally, experiences from a prototypical implementation of a reference model management system are reported.

In Chapter XV, Braun, Esswein, Gehlert, and Weller investigate the topic of configuration management for reference models. They argue that the modification of reference models should be systematically supported by a model configuration management system which has to address versioning and referencing. Versioning is needed to trace changes made to reference models over time. The concept of referencing describes the relationship between a generic reference model and a particular enterprise model. The chapter discusses several requirements of configuration management and shows how these requirements can be supported by an adequate system.

In Chapter XVI, Mendling, Neumann, and Nüttgens discuss interchange formats for reference modeling. Interchange formats build on isomorphic mapping between a domain-specific meta model and the scheme of the interchange format. First, the authors explain general aspects of interchange formats, including their pragmatic, economic and conceptual efforts and present general design guidelines for interchange formats. After that, they illustrate interchange formats for EPCs and UML, two frequently used modeling languages for reference modeling. Additionally, the authors illustrate the benefits of interchange formats for three important areas of reference modeling: model interchange, separation of process modeling and execution as well as model transformation.

Finally, in Chapter XVII, Höhnel, Krahl, and Schreiber report about several lessons learned in reference modeling. The authors gained their experience from more than 40 reference modeling projects in different industries. The lessons learned described by the authors can be grouped into five critical success factors: open communication, open construction principles and quality criteria, tool support, business justification and "use what you bought." Each success factor is derived from their practical experience and is extensively discussed. Furthermore, the authors especially demonstrate which factors are of particular importance for successful reference modeling during which phases.

Some Future Research Opportunities

Future research that might be undertaken in this context encompasses the following aspects:

- **Influence of modeling paradigms:** Today, the influence of different research paradigms on research results is undisputable. However, it is unclear how different research paradigms influence reference modeling practice and research.

- **Improved understanding of reference modeling processes:** Most research on reference modeling conceptualizes reference modeling as an analytic process that can be supported by methods and is grounded on rationality. However, these assumptions may be violated in practice. In other words, it is necessary to explore real reference modeling processes.

- **Improved tool support:** The practice of reference modeling can benefit greatly from new tools that particularly support reuse concepts of reference modeling.

Final Remarks

With the help of reference models, business systems analysis will become more effective and efficient. In this chapter, we discussed the state-of-the-art of reference modeling and future trends. Furthermore, we introduced the chapters of this book. This chapter demonstrates that reference modeling has an interesting history and, hopefully, will have a promising future.

Numerous case studies demonstrate that practical experience with reference modeling is very promising. Nevertheless, it is necessary to develop sound methods and techniques to assess and evaluate the existent languages, methods, models and tools for reference modeling. The results obtained by investigating real reference model processes can be of tremendous value for developing future reference modeling concepts because this feedback provides important insights into reality. In other words, the design science research approach often deployed in reference modeling has to be complemented with an empirical research perspective (Fettke et al., 2005).

Acknowledgments

In parts, this chapter presents results from the research project "Reference modeling with reference model catalogs" funded by the Deutsche Forschungsgemeinschaft (DFG, German Research Foundation). The authors would like to thank Jörg Zwicker for translating some draft manuscript passages into English. Additional thanks go to Christian Seel, Boris Wyssusek, and Jörg Zwicker for commenting on earlier versions of this text.

References

Algermissen, L., Delfmann, P., & Niehaves, B. (2005, May 26-28). *Experiences in process-oriented reorganisation through reference modelling in public administrations: The case study Regio@KomM.* Paper presented at the European Conference on Information Systems (ECIS), Regensburg.

Becker, J., Algermissen, L., Delfmann, P., & Niehaves, B. (2004). A web based platform for the design of administrational reference process models. In K. G. Jeffery (Ed.), *Web information systems—WISE 2004: 5th International Conference on Web Information Systems Engineering* (LNCS 3306, pp. 159-168). Berlin: Springer.

Becker, J., Delfmann, P., Dreiling, A., Knackstedt, R., & Kuropka, D. (2004). *Configurative process modeling: Outlining an approach to increased business process model usability.* Paper presented at the Information Resources Management Association International Conference (IRMA), New Orleans, LA.

Becker, J., Delfmann, P., Knackstedt, R., & Kuropka, D. (2002). Configurative reference modeling. In J. Becker & R. Knackstedt (Eds.), *Wissensmanagement mit Referenzmodellen. Konzepte für die Anwendungssystem- und Organisationsgestaltung* (pp. 25-144). Berlin: Springer. [in German]

Becker, J., & Knackstedt, R. (2003). Construction and application of reference models for data warehousing. In W. Uhr, W. Esswein, & E. Schoop (Eds.), *Wirtschaftsinformatik 2003/Band II - Medien - Märkte - Mobilität* (pp. 415-433). Heidelberg: Physica. [in German]

Becker, J., Niehaves, B., & Knackstedt, R. (2004). Epistemological foundations of reference modeling: A consensus-based approach. In J. Becker & B. Niehaves (Eds.), *Referenzmodellierung - Grundlagen, Techniken und domänenbezogene Anwendungen.* Berlin: Springer. [in German]

Bernus, P. (1999). *GERAM: Generalised Enterprise Reference Architecture and Methodology, Version 1.6.3.* o. O.

Castano, S., Antonellis de, V., Fugini, M. G., & Pernici, B. (1998). Conceptual schema analysis: Techniques and applications. *ACM Transactions on Database Systems, 23*(3), 286-333.

Chen, P. P.-S. (1976). The entity-relationship model: Toward a unified view of data. *ACM Transactions on Database Systems, 1*(1), 9-36.

Coplien, J. O. (2000). Software design patterns. In A. Ralston, E. D. Reilly, & D. Hemmendinger (Eds.), *Encyclopedia of computer science* (4th ed., pp. 1604-1606). New York: Nature Publishing Group, Grovs Dictionaries.

Curran, T. A., & Keller, G. (1999). *SAP R/3 business blueprint: Business engineering mit den R/3-Referenzprozessen.* Bonn: Addison-Wesley.

Dreiling, A., Rosemann, M., van der Aalst, W. M. P., Sadiq, W., & Khan, S. (2005). Model-driven process configuration of enterprise systems. In O. K. Ferstl, E. J. Sinz, S. Eckert, & T. Isselhorst (Eds.), *Wirtschaftsinformatik 2005: eEconomy, eGovernment, eSociety* (pp. 687-706). Heidelberg: Physica.

Esswein, W., Zumpe, S., & Sunke, N. (2004, October 25-27). *Identifying the quality of e-commerce reference models*. Paper presented at the Towards a New Services Landscape-ICEC, Sixth International Conference on Electronic Commerce, Delft, Niederlande.

Fettke, P. (2005). Unified modeling language. In M. Khosrow-Pour (Ed.), *Encyclopedia of information science and technology, Volume I-V* (pp. 2921-2928). Hershey, PA: Idea Group Reference.

Fettke, P., & Loos, P. (2003a). Classification of reference models: A methodology and its application. *Information Systems and E-Business Management, 1*(1), 35-53.

Fettke, P., & Loos, P. (2003b, October 13). Multiperspective evaluation of reference models—towards a framework. In M. A. Jeusfeld & Ó. Pastor (Eds.), *Conceptual modeling for novel application domains: ER 2003 Workshops ECOMO, IWCMQ, AOIS, and XSDM*, Chicago (pp. 80-91). Berlin: Springer.

Fettke, P., & Loos, P. (2003c, August 4-6). *Ontological evaluation of reference models using the Bunge-Wand-Weber Model*. Paper presented at the Americas Conference on Information Systems (AMCIS), Tampa, FL.

Fettke, P., & Loos, P. (2004a). Ontological evaluation of Scheer's reference model for production planning and control systems: Outline. In B. Rumpe & W. Hesse (Eds.), *Modellierung 2004 - Proceedings zur Tagung, 23-26.03.2004*, Marburg, Germany (pp. 317-318). Bonn: Köllen.

Fettke, P., & Loos, P. (2004b). Reference models for retail enterprises. *HMD: Praxis der Wirtschaftsinformatik, 235*, 15-25. [in German]

Fettke, P., & Loos, P. (2004c). Reference modeling research. *Wirtschaftsinformatik, 46*(5), 331-340. [in German]

Fettke, P., & Loos, P. (2005). Ontological analysis of reference models. In P. Green & M. Rosemann (Eds.), *Business systems analysis with ontologies* (pp. 56-81). Hershey, PA: Idea Group Inc.

Fettke, P., Loos, P., Frank, U., Moody, D. L., Parsons, J., Rosemann, M., et al. (2005). Empirical research strategies in conceptual modeling: Silver bullet or academic toys? A written discussion with an editorial by Hans Ulrich Buhl and Bernd Heinrich. *Wirtschaftsinformatik, 47*(2), 152-159.

Fettke, P., Loos, P., & Pastor, K. (2004). GenGraph: A multi-grammar and multi-perspective business modeling tool: Overview on conceptualization and implementation. In M. Rebstock (Ed.), *Modellierung betrieblicher Informationssysteme - MobIS 2004 - Proceedings der Tagung MobIS 2004 im Rahmen der Multi-Konferenz Wirtsschaftsinformatik (MKWI 2004) vom 9. bis 11. März 2004, 10.03.2004 in* Essen, Germany (pp. 79-90). Bonn: Köllen.

Fettke, P., Loos, P., & Zwicker, J. (2006). Business process reference models: Survey and classification. In C. Bussler & A. Haller (Eds.), *Business process management workshops: BPM 2005 international workshops, BPI, BPD, ENEI, BPRM, WSCOBPM, BPS,* Nancy, France, September 5, 2005. *Revised Selected Papers* (pp. 469-483). Berlin: Springer.

Fettke, P., Zwicker, J., & Loos, P. (2006). Using UML for reference modeling (forthcoming). In P. Rittgen (Ed.), *Enterprise modeling and computing with UML*. Hershey, PA: Idea Group Inc.

Finkelstein, A., Gabbay, D., Hunter, A., Kramer, J., & Nuseibeh, B. (1994). Inconsistency handling in multiperspective specifications. *IEEE Transactions on Software Engineering, 20*, 569-578.

Frank, U. (1999, August 13-15). *Conceptual modelling as the core of the information systems discipline: Perspectives and epistemological challenges.* Paper presented at the Fifth Americas Conference on Information Systems (AMCIS 1999), Milwaukee, Wisconsin.

Frank, U. (2001). A conceptual foundation for versatile e-commerce platforms. *Journal of Electronic Commerce Research, 2*(2), 48-57.

Frank, U. (2002). *Multi-perspective enterprise modeling (MEMO): Conceptual framework and modeling languages.* Paper presented at the Proceedings of the 35th Hawaii International Conference on Systems Science (CD-ROM).

Gesamtverband der Deutschen Versicherungswirtschaft e. V. (Ed.). (2000). *The application architecture of the German insurance industry.* Retrieved March 30, 2002 from, http://www.gdv-online.de/vaa/ [in German]

Hay, D. C. (1996). *Data model patterns: Conventions of thought.* New York: Dorset House.

Hevner, A. R., March, S. T., Park, J., & Ram, S. (2004). Design science in information systems research. *MIS Quarterly, 28*(1), 75-105.

Hirschheim, R., Klein, H. K., & Lyytinen, K. (1995). *Information systems development and data modeling: Conceptual and philosophical foundations.* Cambridge: Press Syndicate for the University of Cambridge.

Hofstede, A. H. M., & Weide, T. P. v. d. (1993). Formalisation of techniques: Chopping down the methodology jungle. *Information & Software Technology, 34*(1), 57-65.

Iivari, J., Hirschheim, R., & Klein, H. K. (1998). A paradigmatic analysis contrasting information systems development approaches and methodologies. *Information Systems Research, 9*(2), 164-193.

ISO. (1994). *Information technology: Open systems interconnections—basic reference model: The basic model, ISO/IEC 7498-1:1994(E), second edition corrected and reprinted 1996-06-15,* Genève, Switzerland.

Jacobson, I., Booch, G., & Rumbaugh, J. (1998). *The unified software development process.* Reading, MA: Addison-Wesley.

Keller, G., & Teufel, T. (1998). *SAP R/3 process oriented implementation: Iterative process prototyping.* Harlow: Addison-Wesley.

Lang, K. (1997). *Business process management with reference model components.* Wiesbaden: DUV. [in German]

Leinenbach, S. (2000). *Interactive business process modeling.* Wiesbaden: DUV. [in German]

Mendling, J., & Nüttgens, M. (2004). XML-based reference modelling: Foundations of an EPC markup language. In P. Delfmann (Ed.), *Referenzmodellierung - grundlagen, techniken und domänenbezogene Anwendung* (pp. 51-72). Berlin: Springer.

Mertins, K., & Bernus, P. (1998). Reference models. In P. Bernus, K. Mertins, & G. Schmidt (Eds.), *Handbook on architectures of information systems* (pp. 615-617). Berlin: Springer.

Mingers, J. (2001). Combining IS research methods: Towards a pluralist methodology. *Information Systems Research, 12*(3), 240-259.

Mišic, V. B., & Zhao, J. L. (2000, October 9-12). Evaluating the quality of reference models. In A. H. F. Laender, S. W. Liddle, & V. C. Storey (Eds.), *Conceptual modeling: ER 2000, 19th International Conference on Conceptual Modeling,* Salt Lake City, UT (pp. 484-498). Berlin: Springer.

Mylopoulos, J. (1998). Information modeling in the time of the revolution. *Information Systems, 23*(3/4), 127-155.

Niehaves, B., Ribbert, M., Dreiling, A., & Holten, R. (2004). *Conceptual modeling: An epistemological foundation.* Paper presented at the Americas Conference on Information Systems 2004, New York City.

Pohl, K. (1994). The three dimensions of requirements engineering: A framework and its applications. *Information Systems, 19*(3), 243-258.

Ram, S., & Ramesh, V. (1998). Collaborative conceptual schema design: A process model and prototype system. *ACM Transactions on Information Systems, 16*(4), 347-371.

Reiter, C. (1999). Toolbasierte Referenzmodellierung - State-of-the-Art und Entwicklungstrends. In J. Becker, M. Rosemann, & R. Schütte (Eds.), *Referenzmodellierung—State-of-the-art und entwicklungsperspektiven* (pp. 45-68). Heidelberg: Physica.

Ricciuti, M., & Semich, W. J. (1993). SAP's client/server battle plan. *Datamation, 39*(6), 26-31.

Rosemann, M. (2003a). Application reference models and building blocks for management and control (ERP Systems). In P. Bernus, L. Nemes, & G. Schmidt (Eds.), *Handbook of enterprise architecture* (pp. 595-615). Berlin: Springer.

Rosemann, M. (2003b). *Configuration of enterprise systems reference models.* o. O.

Rosemann, M. (2003c). Using reference models within the enterprise resource planning lifecycle. *Australian Accounting Review, 10*(3), 19-30.

Rumbaugh, J., Jacobson, I., & Booch, G. (1998). *The unified modeling language reference manual.* Reading, MA: Addison-Wesley.

Scheer, A.-W. (1994a). ARIS toolset: A software product is born. *Information Systems, 19*(8), 607-624.

Scheer, A.-W. (1994b). *Business process engineering: Reference models for industrial enterprises* (2nd ed.). Berlin: Springer.

Scheer, A.-W. (1998a). *ARIS: Business process frameworks* (2nd ed.). Berlin: Springer.

Scheer, A.-W. (1998b). *ARIS: Business process modeling* (2nd ed.). Berlin: Springer.

Scheer, A.-W., & Hars, A. (1992). Extending data modeling to cover the whole enterprise. *Communications of the ACM, 35*(9), 166-172.

Scheer, A.-W., & Nüttgens, M. (2000). ARIS architecture and reference models for business process management. In W. v. d. Aalst, J. Desel, & A. Oberweis (Eds.), *Busi-*

ness process management: Models, techniques, and empirical studies (pp. 376-389). Berlin: Springer.

Schlagheck, B. (2000). *Object-oriented reference models for controlling processes and projects*. Wiesbaden: DUV. [in German]

Schmid, B. F., & Lindemann, M. A. (1998). *Elements of a reference model for electronic markets*. Paper presented at the Proceedings of the 31st Hawaii International Conference on Systems Science (HICSS98).

Schütte, R. (1998). *Guidelines for reference modeling*. Wiesbaden: Gabler. [in German]

Schwegmann, A. (1999). *Object-oriented reference modeling*. Wiesbaden: DUV. [in German]

Stephens, S. (2001). Supply chain operations reference model version 5.0: A new tool to improve supply chain efficiency and achieve best practices. *Information Systems Frontiers, 3*(4), 471-476.

Thomas, O. (2005). Understanding the term reference model in information systems research: History, literature analysis and explanation. In *Workshop on Business Process Reference Models (BPRM), in Verbindung mit der International Conference on Business Process Management (BPM 2005)* (pp. 16-29) Nancy, Frankreich.

Tzouvaras, A. (2003). *Reference modeling for publishing houses*. Göttingen: Cuvillier. [in German]

Van Belle, J.-P. W. G. D. (2003). *A framework for the analysis and evaluation of enterprise models*. Unpublished Thesis Submitted for the Degree of Doctor of Philosophy, University of Cape Town, Cape Town, South Africa.

vom Brocke, J. (2003). *Reference modelling, towards collaborative arrangements of design processes*. Berlin: Logos. [in German]

Wand, Y., & Weber, R. (2002). Research commentary: Information systems and conceptual modeling—a research agenda. *Information Systems Research, 13*(4), 363-377.

What is a process reference model? (1998). *Automatic I. D. News, 14*(10), 52.

Winter, R. (1994). Formalised conceptual models as a foundation of information systems development. In P. Loucopoulos (Ed.), *Entity-relationship approach—ER'94, business modelling and re-engineering, 13th International Conference on the Entity-Relationship Approach,* Manchester, UK (pp. 437-455). Berlin: Springer.

Section I

Reference Modeling Languages

Chapter II

Configurable Reference Modeling Languages

Jan Recker, Queensland University of Technology, Australia

Michael Rosemann, Queensland University of Technology, Australia

Wil M. P. van der Aalst, Quensland University of Technology, Australia, &
Eindhoven University of Technology, The Netherlands

Monique Jansen-Vullers, Eindhoven University of Technology, The Netherlands

Alexander Dreiling, SAP Research CEC Brisbane,
SAP Australia Pty Ltd, Australia

Abstract

This chapter discusses reference modeling languages for business systems analysis and design. In particular, it reports on reference models in the context of the design-for/by-reuse paradigm, explains how traditional modeling techniques fail to provide adequate conceptual expressiveness to allow for easy model reuse by configuration or adaptation and elaborates on the need for reference modeling languages to be configurable. We discuss requirements for and the development of reference modeling languages that reflect the need for configurability. Exemplarily, we report on the development, definition and configuration of configurable event-driven process chains. We further outline how configurable reference modeling languages and the corresponding design principles can be used in future scenarios such as process mining and data modeling.

Introduction

Business systems have evolved as computer-based information systems that present them-selves as comprehensive commercial packages for the support of business requirements. Being IT-supported software solutions, they presumptively support and enhance organiza-tions in all their business operations. First attempts towards such corporate-wide integrated information systems were developed in the 1960s (Beer, 1966). The huge success of this idea has led to the proliferation of comprehensive business information systems such as enterprise resource planning (ERP) systems or enterprise systems (ES), the current generation of which is known under the label of process-aware information systems (Dumas, van der Aalst, & ter Hofstede, 2005). This label has emerged from an act of "silent revolution" that has embraced the IS discipline over the last decades and which has started to shift the focus of attention from a data perspective towards a process perspective. As a result, an increasing number of business processes are now conducted under the governance of process-aware information systems, with the intention of bridging not only business and IT but also people and software through process-based technology.

The successful implementation of process-aware business systems is, however, dependent on a seamless alignment between the system capabilities and the organizational require-ments of the enterprise. The process of aligning organizational requirements and system functionality (Rosemann, Vessey, & Weber, 2004) is known as configuration and rests on the assumption of similarity between enterprises, in the sense that generic business system functionality, with some customization, is assumed to be applicable to all enterprises in a given industry sector. Following the idea of process-orientation, business system vendors often offer their solutions in the form of pre-defined generic business processes for a set of industry sectors. Oracle, for example, offers system-supported business process solutions that cover 19 industrial sectors (Oracle, 2006) while SAP offers business process solutions for 24 industrial sectors (SAP, 2006). These industry-specific process "templates" are in-troduced to organizations to offer a final implementation of the business system in the form of a configured, enterprise-specific set of business processes that are enabled, enacted and supported by the system.

Yet, the act of aligning generic industry-specific with enterprise-specific business processes that reflect organizational requirements has been shown to imply extensive configuration efforts and may lead to significant implementation costs that exceed the price of software licenses by factors of five to ten (Davenport, 2000). Some instances even indicate that a misalignment may result in severe business failure if conducted badly. Consider the example of FoxMeyer, once a \$5 billion wholesale drug distributor, which filed for bankruptcy in 1996 after Andersen Consulting concluded that the insufficiently aligned SAP installation crippled the firm's distribution (Stein, 1998). Other examples include Mobil Europe and Dow Chemical (Davenport, 1998).

Business systems vendors are aware of these problems and try to increase the manageability of the configuration process of their software solutions. One respective measure is to deliver the products along with extensive documentation and specific implementation and configura-tion support tools. Conceptual models play a central role within such documentation. They describe functionality and structure of the business systems on a semi-formal level and have become popular under the notion of reference models. Though such reference models for business systems exist in the form of function, data, system organization, object and process models, the latter is by far the most popular model type (Rosemann, 2000) and often forms a constituent part of the documentation of software packages.

While the existence of such reference models as part of the system documentation in general is valuable in software implementation projects (Kesari, Chang, & Seddon, 2003), traditional reference models offer little or no support for configuration (Daneva, 2000) This is mainly due to a lack of conceptual support in the form of a configurable modeling language underlying the reference models (Rosemann & van der Aalst, in press).

Nevertheless, the business system configuration process can significantly benefit from the usage of reference models, for instance, in terms of consistency, completeness, adaptability and communicability. Since most business information systems are quite extensively depicted in their reference models, it motivates the idea of utilizing these reference models for the configuration task. However, the language that is used to formulate reference models for the task of system configuration needs to be configurable to support this delicate task. A configurable reference process model should, for instance, provide rules defining how a generic reference process model can be adapted to suit a specific organizational context.

This chapter provides an introduction to configurable reference modeling languages and their role in the configuration process of business information systems. It covers discussions of current shortcomings of reference modeling languages, the need for configurable reference models and the different stages towards the development and application of configurable reference modeling languages, particularly in the context of business information systems. While we will, during the course of this chapter, address multiple perspectives using the examples of process and data models, our foremost focus lies on the process perspective. We will explicate our argumentations using the example of a configurable reference process modeling language called configurable EPCs (Rosemann & van der Aalst, in press).

Forthcoming from this introduction we will first discuss traditional reference modeling languages. Then, we will present and discuss design principles for the design of configurable reference modeling languages and then apply the principles in the development of EPCs. Next, we will briefly outline future scenarios for configurable reference modeling languages and their design principles. We close this chapter by discussing some conclusions from our work.

Reference Modeling Languages

Reference models are generic conceptual models that formalize recommended practices for a certain domain (Fettke & Loos, 2003; Misic & Zhao, 2000). Often labeled with the term "best practice," reference models claim to capture reusable state-of-the-art practices (Silverston, 2001a, 2001b). The depicted domains can be very different and range from selected functional areas, such as financial accounting or customer relationship management, to the scope of an entire industry sector (e.g., higher education).

The main objective of reference models is to streamline the design of enterprise-individual (particular) models by providing a generic solution (Rosemann, 2000). The application of reference models is motivated by the "design-for/by-reuse" paradigm, postulating that they should accelerate the modeling process by providing a repository of potentially relevant business processes and structures, ideally in an easy "plug & play" modus. Thus, reference modeling is closely related to the reuse of information models (Wisse, 2000) by providing a generic model solution that can be adapted to a specific model reflecting individual requirements.

Reference models are often used for describing the structure and functionality of business systems. In these cases, a reference model can be interpreted as a structured, semi-formal description of a particular application. Such application reference models correspond to an existing off-the-shelf solution that supports the functionality and structure described in the model (Rosemann, 2002). They can, for example, be used for a better understanding and evaluation of the appropriateness of the software.

One of the most comprehensive models is the SAP reference model (Curran, Keller, & Ladd, 1997). In version 4.6, its data model includes more than 4,000 entity types and the reference process models cover more than 1,000 system processes and inter-organizational business scenarios. Most of the other market leading business systems vendors have alternative or similar approaches toward such reference models.

Foundational conceptual work for the SAP reference model had been conducted by SAP AG and the IDS Scheer AG in a collaborative research project in the years 1990-1992 (Keller, Nüttgens, & Scheer, 1992). The outcome of this project was the process modeling language event-driven process chains (EPCs) (Keller et al., 1992; Scheer, 2000), which has been used for the design of the reference process models in SAP. EPCs have become one of the most popular reference modeling languages overall and have, for instance, been used for the design of many SAP-independent reference models (e.g., Siebel CRM, ITIL, eTOM and PMBOK).

EPCs basically denote directed graphs, which visualize the control flow and consist of events, functions and connectors. Each EPC starts and ends with at least one event. An event triggers a function, which leads to a new event. Three types of connectors (logical AND ∧, logical exclusive OR XOR and logical OR ∨) can be used to specify the logical links that exist between sequences of events and functions in process chains. They model control flow splits and joins. An AND-split activates all outgoing branches in concurrency while an AND-join waits for all incoming branches to synchronize before propagating control to the following EPC element. An OR-split activates one, two or up to all outgoing branches based on certain conditions while an OR-join synchronizes all incoming branches that are active and then propagates control to the following EPC element. An XOR-split activates one of multiple outgoing branches based on certain conditions while an OR-join propagates control to the following EPC element when the first active incoming branch arrives.

Figure 1 gives an example for an EPC as it potentially can be found as part of a reference model. This model shows an extract of a procurement process. The EPC contains eight events, six functions and three connectors. The events can be seen as pre- and/or post-conditions of functions. For example, the function Verify Invoice can be executed if event Invoice posted is received and the completion of this function will trigger the event Payment to be effected. There are two functions triggering event Invoice arrived. The XOR-connector in the lower half of the diagram shows that there is no need to synchronize these two functions (e.g., the completion of Store Goods directly triggers event Invoice posted). The XOR-connector in the upper half of the diagram splits the control flow in accordance to the condition whether the purchase performed relates to goods (left branch) or services (right branch). The remaining connector denotes an AND-join, meaning that both input events need to be triggered in order to enable function Create Purchase Order.

Figure 1. An example for a potential reference model in EPC notation

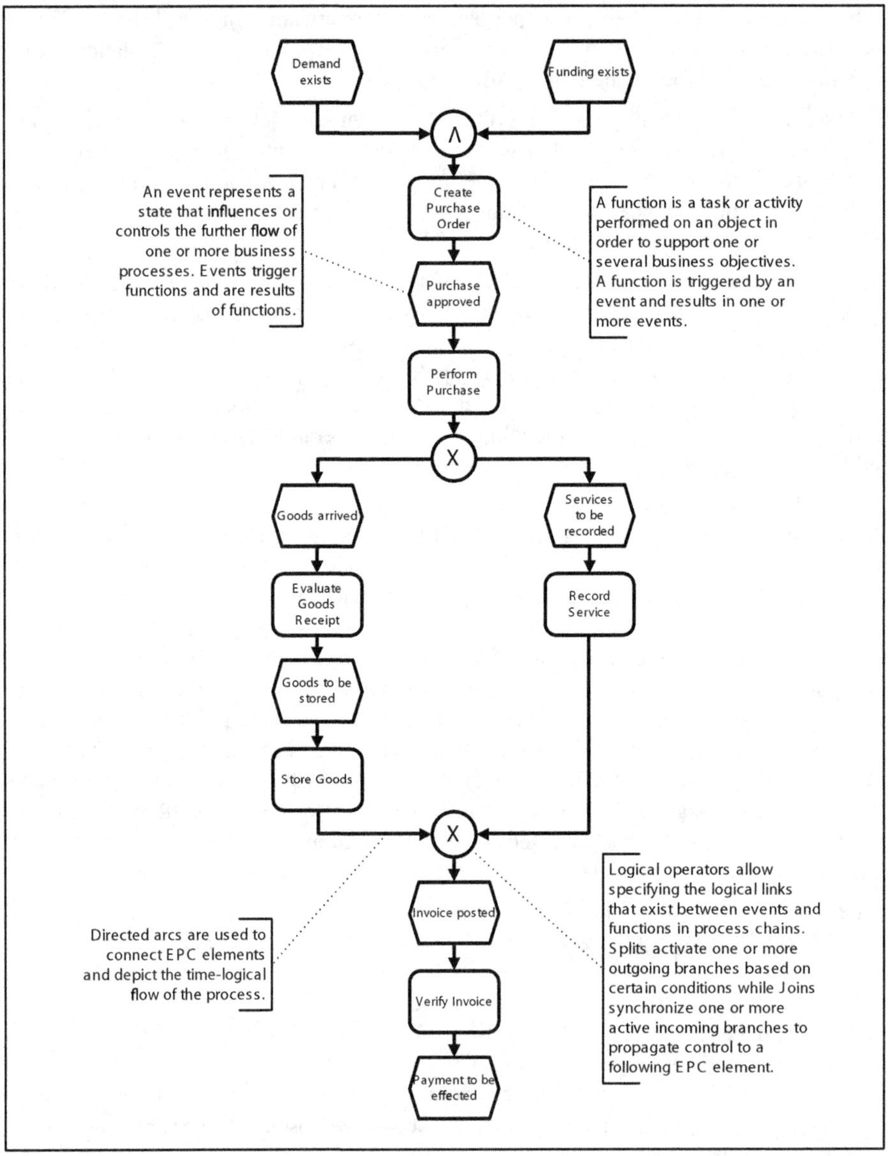

As can be observed from Figure 1, regular EPCs do not contain any configuration information. Therefore, valuable information is lacking. For example, it is not shown that Record Service (i.e., the scenario in which procured services need to be audited during execution, is only of interest for a subset of all procurement scenarios, namely those where services are being procured instead of goods). There are cases imaginable where enterprises only enact a procurement process for goods but not services. In these cases the accordant part of the reference model is not applicable to the organization and should be eliminated from the enterprise-specific process model. This implies that the XOR connector may be a choice made for the whole process rather than for an individual process instance. Consider a second example. The EPC shown in Figure 1 neither shows that Store Goods is only relevant if Evaluate Goods Receipt is conducted. If organizations opt never to procure goods but only services, there is no need to implement functionality for goods storage. Also, the model neither gives any insights into the necessity or criticality of potential configurations nor into possible inter-dependencies between configuration decisions. Thus, the model expressive power is limited and cannot guide the configuration of a corresponding business system. Hence, a reference model designed using a traditional reference modeling language is only of limited use for the configuration process due to a lack of support on a conceptual level.

Design of Configurable Reference Modeling Languages

Design Principles for a Configurable Reference Modeling Language

Following the elaborations in the preceding section and the idea of reference modeling (i.e., the streamlined development of individual models through "design-for/by-reuse") we postulate that reference modeling languages ought to be configurable. We can reason our argumentation by introducing a simple reference model lifecycle that depicts the different stages of a reference model, ranging from model design to execution (see Figure 2).

The lifecycle is initiated by ES vendors who depict the functionality of their software packages in reference models (design time). Such a reference model typically does not include merely one proposed alternative for conducting business in a certain domain but a range of often mutually exclusive alternatives. It denotes an "upper-bound" of business system models that may possibly be implemented in a particular enterprise. An organization might merely favor one of the depicted alternatives and thus only to a subset of system functionality to be implemented. Accordingly they only refer to a subset of the reference model. Figure 2 demonstrates this problem in a simple example. The upper-bound reference model depicts two mutually exclusive alternatives of conducting business, either the sequence A-B-C or A-B-D. A particular enterprise has to select one of these two substitutive alternatives of conducting business under the governance of the respective business system. The XOR split in this case represents a decision point that is of relevance during configuration time. Note that a model in this phase cannot necessarily be executed. It rather captures different alternatives for a

Figure 2. Reference model lifecycle

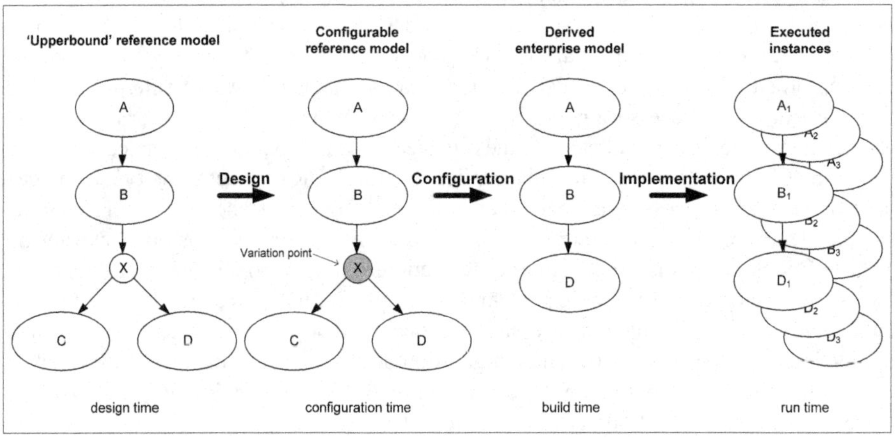

domain and thus needs to be configured before it can serve as the actual build time model, a template for implementing and executing process instances at run time.

These types of decisions cannot be reflected in traditional reference models due to a lack of conceptual support of the underlying reference modeling language. Existing reference modeling techniques do not support the highlighting and selection of different alternatives. The resulting lack of expressiveness denotes a major issue for model users, as (a) it does not become obvious what configuration alternatives exist during system implementation, and (b) the models do not provide any decision support towards the selection of different alternatives.

Contemplating the reference model lifecycle and the shortcomings of traditional reference modeling languages, we have identified the following design principles for a configurable reference modeling language:

a.   A configurable modeling language is characterized by its capability to support decisions for the transformation of reference models from configuration time to build time (i.e., the model user can individualize the model by selecting from alternative options before instances will be derived from it). Such configuration decisions on a type level have to be clearly differentiated from decisions on an instance level and can be highlighted as variation points in a model (Halmans & Pohl, 2003) that should capture a decision point together with the related possible choices.

b.   A configurable modeling language has to support configurations of business systems regarding processes, functions, control flow and data. In terms of processes, configuration should address the active parts of process models (i.e., functionality—functions, tasks, transitions and the like—and control flow). As events (or states), being more passive parts of processes cannot actively be influenced by an organization, these should not be covered by a configurable reference process modeling language.

c.   It should be possible to differentiate configuration decisions into mandatory and optional decisions. Mandatory decisions have to be made before the very first instance can be derived from this model. Optional decisions can initially be neglected. It should be possible to maintain defaults for optional configuration decisions. This allows the instantiation of the model even without explicitly making all possible decisions.

d.   Configuration should be differentiated into global and local decisions. Global decisions are based on the general context, including factors such as industry, country, size, and so forth. The relevant context factors have to be maintained for every variation point. As soon as information regarding the relevant context has been provided, a first (hidden or background) configuration of the reference model can take place, which would lead to "context-aware models." Local configurations require an explicit study of the relevant reference model as the related decisions may be based on local or individual factors such as available budget, risk profile, time, and so forth.

e.   Configuration decisions should be differentiated into critical and non-critical decisions. Critical decisions have significant impact on the use of the system and other business processes, can often not be re-done and should be made by the project team. Non-critical decisions are of minor importance, can be made by individual team members and change over time.

f.   Configuration decisions can have interrelationships. Such pre-requisites for a configuration decision should be clearly highlighted. This can include other decisions that have to be made before. Moreover, any impact of one decision on other decisions has to be depicted. This means a logical order between configuration decisions has to be considered. This includes interrelationships within one model, between two process models or even interrelationships between reference process and related data models (Rosemann & Shanks, 2001).

g.   Variation points should refer to further related information within the part of the business system it depicts. This may include the system online help and the system configuration module, such as the SAP implementation guide (IMG) (Bancroft, Seip, & Sprengel, 1997). Such information can provide valuable support for the decision maker.

h.   The entire configuration process should be guided by recommendations in the form of guidelines. Such information could come as benchmarking data from the outside of the system if a critical mass of system users is willing to provide such data. It may include information such as the processing time of a given process path, the number of times a decision has been made in the same industry or the required investments and implementation time for a certain configuration. Such recommendations may as well assist reference model users in assessing the compliance of their configuration to industry best practices.

i.   Reference models can be very comprehensive. Any extension of the underlying modeling languages has to carefully consider the impact on the perceived model complexity. It is advisable to extend existing reference modeling languages rather than developing new ones.

In the following we will apply these design principles in the development of a configurable reference modeling language. As process modeling is key to acquiring, communicating and validating business requirements (Daneva, 2004; Welti, 1999) we will focus the process perspective (i.e., the alignment of IT functionality to the actual business processes of an organization). The following section introduces Configurable EPCs as the representation language of a reference process modeling approach that considers the configurable nature of a business system and reflects the design principles for configurable modeling techniques.

Configurable Event-Driven Process Chains

This section introduces the notion of a Configurable EPC (C-EPC). We start our elaborations by referring back to the procurement example given before. Figure 1 shows a potential reference model for the process of procurement in the form of a classical EPC. Following this diagram, procurement starts with the creation of a purchase order (function Create Purchase Order) when a demand for services or goods exists (event Demand exists) and (logical AND-connector ∧) when sufficient funding for the procurement exists (event Funding exists). Once the created purchase order has been approved, the procurement can be conducted. The process succeeds with either reception and storage of the arrived goods, or recording of the enactment of the requested service. In either case, an invoice will arrive at some point in time demanding payment for the delivery of goods or services. Then, the invoice needs to be verified, which in turn triggers the effectuation of payment, which ends the process.

However, not all organizations implement procurement the same way. For example, not only goods may be purchased but also services, with the former being in a need for appropriate storage while the latter need to be audited during enactment. A particular organization may only want to implement procurement functionality of a business system for either services or goods. Furthermore, for illustration purposes, let us assume that a purchase may or may not be related to a purchase order. Similarly, the verification of invoices may or may not be essential for the effectuation of payment, for example in cases where long-term contracts to trusted vendors or sophisticated support exists (e.g., in the form of Evaluated Receipt Settlement functionality). None of these potential configuration decisions can be visualized using the traditional EPC reference modeling language. In particular, the model does not express possible configuration alternatives and scenarios with respect to the process it represents.

This section introduces configurable EPCs as an approach to depict variation points in a reference process model as well as further configuration information (Rosemann & van der Aalst, in press).

Adhering to design principle (b), we seek to make the active parts of processes configurable (i.e., functionality and control flow). Accordingly, in a C-EPC, functions and connectors can be configured. As an example, Figure 3 shows the procurement reference process model introduced in the preceding section depicted in C-EPC notation. We will use this example model throughout the remainder of this section to introduce the notion of C-EPCs.

Adhering to design principle (i), C-EPCs extend regular EPCs with the specification of variation points (configurable functions and connectors), configuration requirements and configuration guidelines.

Configurable functions may be included (ON), excluded (OFF) or conditionally skipped (OPT). To be more specific, a decision has to be made whether to perform such a function in every process instance during run time (ON), whether to exclude this function permanently (i.e., it will not be executed in any process instance (OFF) or whether to defer this decision to run time, i.e., for each process instance it has to be decided whether or not to execute the function (OPT)). Referring to the example given in Figure 3, it is possible, for instance, to configure the procurement process in a way that Create Purchase Order and Verify Invoice are not to be implemented; therefore, they are to be excluded from the enterprise-individual process model. Reflecting this decision in the configurable reference process model, the accordant configurable functions can be switched OFF.

Configurable connectors subsume possible build time connectors that are less or equally expressive. Hence, a configurable connector can only be mapped to a connector type that restricts its behavior. A configurable OR-connector may be mapped to a regular OR-, XOR- or AND-connector. Or, the OR-connector may be mapped to a single sequence of events and functions (indicated by SEQ_n for some process path starting with node n). That is, out of the incoming/outgoing branches of a configurable OR-connector, a single branch is chosen that is to be included in the individual model while the remaining branches are to be excluded from the model. A configurable AND-connector may only be mapped to a regular AND-connector with a decision being made as to how many of n available process paths are to be executed in synchronization. A configurable XOR-connector may be mapped to a regular XOR-connector, or the XOR-connector may be mapped to a single process sequence SEQ_n. Table 1 summarizes these mapping constraints.

Referring back to the example given in Figure 3, consider the decision that a particular enterprise does not want to implement procurement for both goods and services but instead only for goods. The assessment and recording of services would then be deemed unnecessary. In the reference process model, such a decision can be reflected by mapping the configurable XOR-connector to a single sequence $SEQ_{Goods\ arrived}$ specifying the process branch containing the handling of received goods.

In order to depict inter-dependencies between configurable EPC nodes, configuration requirements can be introduced to limit the configuration possibilities between inter-related configurable nodes. These constraints are best defined via logical expressions in the form of If-Then statements and denote predicates for a set of configurable nodes that must hold true for a valid configuration. Consider again the example given in Figure 3. If the goods receipt sub-process is deemed unnecessary, there is no need for the storage of goods, as services cannot be physically stored. A configuration constraint could be that if Evaluate Goods Receipt is switched OFF, so must be function Store Goods.

In order to provide input in terms of recommendations and proposed best practices, configuration guidelines may be depicted (also in the form of logical expressions) to guide the configuration process semantically. They, too, may be expressed in the form of If-Then statements. They denote logical predicates for a set of configurable nodes that may but not need hold true for a given configuration. Again, consider Figure 3. Verify invoice may be an unnecessary task if long-term procurement contracts with trusted vendors or advanced Evaluated Receipt Settlement functionality exists that automatically settles invoices based on goods issued. For these scenarios a configuration guideline suggests switching Verify Invoice OFF.

Figure 3. Potential configurable reference model for the procurement process, depicted in C-EPC notation

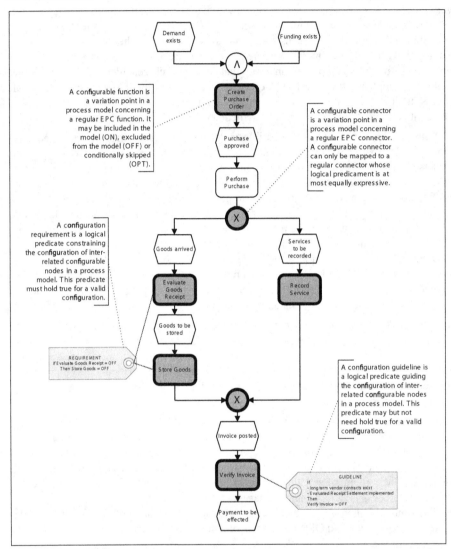

In summation, the notion of a C-EPC potentially facilitates a selection and modification of process flows and process activities within a reference process model. As can be seen from Figure 3, configurable nodes are denoted as usual EPC nodes shaped by thick circles, while both configuration requirements and guidelines are depicted as notes-like boxes attached to a number of configurable nodes.

Table 1. Constraints for the configuration of connectors

Configurable connector	Mapping to OR	Mapping to XOR	Mapping to AND	Mapping to SEQ_n
OR	✓	✓	✓	✓
XOR		✓		✓
AND			✓	

Configuration Using Configurable EPCs

According to the reference model lifecycle (see Figure 2), at configuration time a configurable reference process model can be configured in the sense that configuration alternatives within the model are selected in a way that a configuration scenario is created which is deemed desirable for the particular organization. Such a configuration maps all configurable nodes to concrete values (i.e., regular EPC nodes) while adhering to configuration requirements (and possibly also configuration guidelines). Figure 4 shows two possible regular EPCs resulting from a configuration of the C-EPC shown in Figure 3.

Consider the EPC depicted in the left part of Figure 4: In this case, the particular enterprise decided to relate purchase requests to purchase orders, hence, the function Create Purchase Order is included. Similarly, as the organization only purchases from long-known, trusted vendors, an extra invoice verification activity was deemed unnecessary. Hence, the accordant function Verify Invoice was excluded from the model. Furthermore, procurement in this case has to cater to either physical goods or services. Hence, the configurable XOR-connector has been mapped to a regular XOR-connector, allowing for the procurement of either services or goods at run time, for both of which accordant activities have been included as well. In the left part of Figure 4, Configuration (a) shows the process model resulting from the configuration {(Create Purchase Order,ON),(XOR,XOR),(Evaluate Goods Receipt,ON),(Store Goods,ON),(Record Service,ON),(XOR,XOR),(Verify Invoice,OFF)}.

Configuration (b) shows an EPC resulting from the configuration {(Create Purchase Order,OFF),(XOR,$SEQ_{\text{Services to be recorded}}$),(Goods Receipt,OFF),(Storage,OFF),(Service recording,ON),(XOR,$SEQ_{\text{Services to be recorded}}$),(Verify Invoice,ON)}. As both EPC models do not conflict against the configuration requirements depicted in Figure 3, both configurations are valid. Note here that a valid configuration is also suitable if it further satisfies all configuration guidelines.

Strictly speaking, deriving a correct build time EPC from a configured C-EPC involves three kinds of tasks: (a) derivation of a partial EPC model for each configured function, (b) derivation of a partial EPC model for each configured connector and (c) recalculation of the complete EPC process graph by excluding unnecessary paths. The calculation of the build time EPC should be governed by the minimality criterion: if elements have to be added by configuration, add as few elements as possible; if elements have to be removed by configuration, remove as many as possible, and optimize the graph so as to include no unnecessary paths (Mendling, Recker, Rosemann, & van der Aalst, 2006; Recker, Rosemann, van der Aalst, & Mendling, 2006).

Theoretically, there are four constellations in which a configured function may appear in a C-EPC (Dreiling, Chiang, Rosemann, & van der Aalst, 2005; Recker, Rosemann, van der Aalst, & Mendling, 2006): (a) between two events, (b) between a connector and an event, (c) between an event and a connector and (d) between two connectors. Figure 5 illustrates the derivation rules for these four cases (connectors labeled with any indicate that any connector type is allowed to make the rule applicable). In case (a) a configurable function mapped to OPT generates two additional XOR-connectors. This mapping is proposed in accordance to the minimality criterion as it introduces a minimal set of additional elements. In case (b) the configurable function mapped to OPT generates an additional function and two XOR-connectors. This additional function allows for the XOR-split decision, otherwise there would have been a split connector subsequent to a join connector, which is not lawful. Case (c) is similar to case (a)—instead of the succeeding event a successor split connector (any) is given. In Case (d) the configurable function mapped to OFF may not simply be excluded. As the any join may be the last connector in a chain of several connectors, the exclusion of the configurable function may not be possible in every case (if the connector chain is composed of join connectors only, events preceding the connector chain can be eliminated together with the function. If the connector chain also includes split connectors, there are further functions at the end of the chain that require the events in order to comply with the EPC alternation rule). The optional function follows a similar idea as applied in case (b). All of these derivation rules preserve the correctness of the model.

Configured connectors can mostly be derived in a straightforward manner. If a configurable connector is not configured to a sequence, only its label has to be adopted. If a connector is configured to a sequence SEQ_n, those succeeding paths that are not to be included in the build time model have to be eliminated. This means that all subsequent elements are to be excluded from the model until a join connector is reached. If there are no more paths to be eliminated, it must further be checked whether there are join connectors in the model that do not link to any incoming arc. Paths starting with these joins have to be eliminated, too, and the check must be repeated. This procedure is iterated until there are no more connectors without incoming arcs. Figure 6 illustrates this procedure by presenting the case of a split connector whose outgoing paths are eliminated. Following our argumentation, this connector and its successor path must be eliminated until a join connector is reached. Again, these derivation rules preserve the correctness of the model.

After deriving configured functions and configured connectors, the resulting EPC may still include unnecessary process graph structures. Functions that are switched OFF and connectors that are configured to SEQ_n may lead to empty paths or connectors with only one incoming and one outgoing arc (for instance the XOR connector in the resulting model shown in Figure 6). In order to comply with the minimality criterion, certain graph reduction rules have to be applied. Figure 7 gives five reduction rules that are sufficient to derive EPCs that comply with the minimality criterion. Rule (a) eliminates arcs a from an AND-split to an AND-join if there is a path from the split to the join that does not pass a. Rule (b) deletes a path of concurrency if that path only includes an event and no function. Rule (c) eliminates connectors that only have one incoming and one outgoing arc. Rule (d) deletes an arc between an OR split or an XOR split and a join connector if there is another arc between them.

Figure 4. Two possible configurations of the C-EPC shown in Figure 3

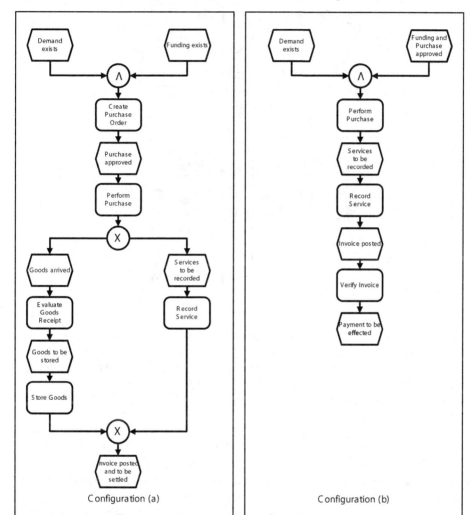

Configuration (a)

Configuration (b)

Rule (e) merges two events if they both are successors of an OR split or an XOR split and predecessor of the same join connector. These reduction rules preserve a minimal process graph structure that represents the control flow of the configured process flow variant.

The previous derivation rules can be summarized in the definition of a respective derivation algorithm. The algorithm includes the steps 1-4 for connector configuration, 5-6 for graph reduction, 7 for function configuration and 8-9 for graph reduction. We start with the configuration of connectors as sequence configurations might already reduce the model; in

Figure 5. Derivation rules for configured functions

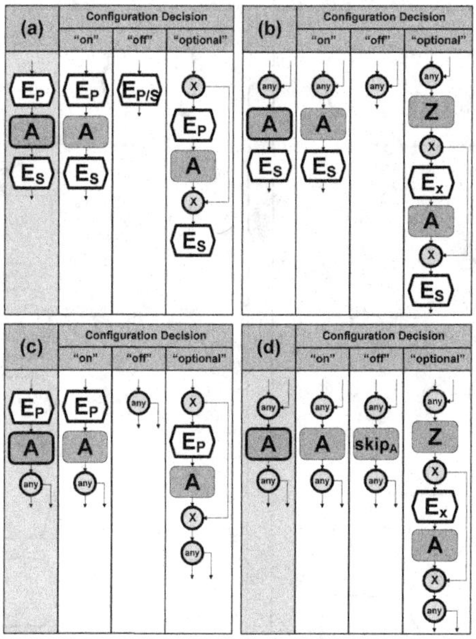

particular, it may lead to the exclusion of configurable functions. Furthermore, connector configuration may result in unnecessary connectors. The graph is reduced in steps 5-6, as the removal of unnecessary connectors before handling configurable functions allows applying the derivation rules (a) and (c) of Figure 7, which in turn result in a smaller graph than rules (b) and (d). Still, function configuration may also result in unnecessary connectors that have to be removed in steps 8-9.

1. Map configured connectors to regular connectors in adherence to the configuration value.
2. If the configuration value is SEQ_n eliminate paths (including all nodes) $i \neq n$, until a join connector or an end node is reached.
3. Check whether there is a connector c without any incoming arcs. If yes, go to 4. If no, go to 5.
4. Eliminate all paths starting with connector c until a join connector or an end node is reached. Go to 3.
5. Check whether one of the reduction rules shown in Figure 7 is applicable. If yes, go to 6. If no, go to 7.
6. Apply one reduction rule and go to 5.
7. Configure functions according to the rules shown in Figure 5.
8. Check whether one of the reduction rules shown in Figure 7 is applicable. If yes, go to 9. If no, end.
9. Apply one reduction rule and go to 7.

Figure 6. Example: Connector configured to SEQ_{E2}

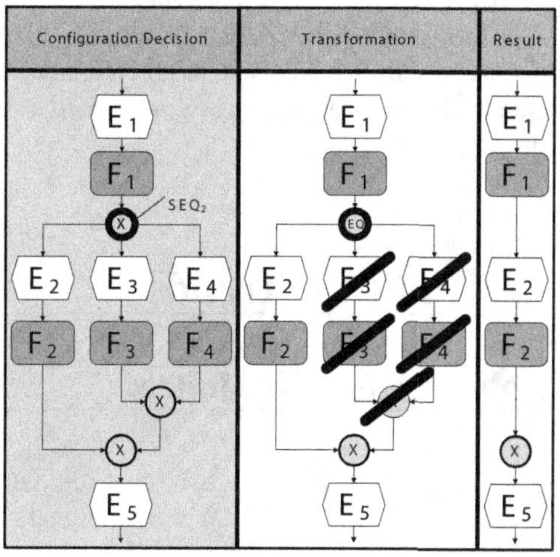

Steps 1 to 9 ensure that all configurable nodes in a C-EPC are either deleted from the model or mapped to regular EPC counterparts. At this stage, we can ensure that the resulting process graph neither contains semantically ambiguous process paths nor unnecessary ones. What we cannot ensure is a formal semantics of the resulting EPC (Kindler, 2005; van der Aalst, 1999). Yet, our extension (and the respective reduction) approach allows for the application of existing formalization approaches (e.g., Kindler, 2005; van der Aalst, 1999) as a semantic foundation for (derived) EPCs.

Figure 7. Reduction rules to derive minimal EPCs

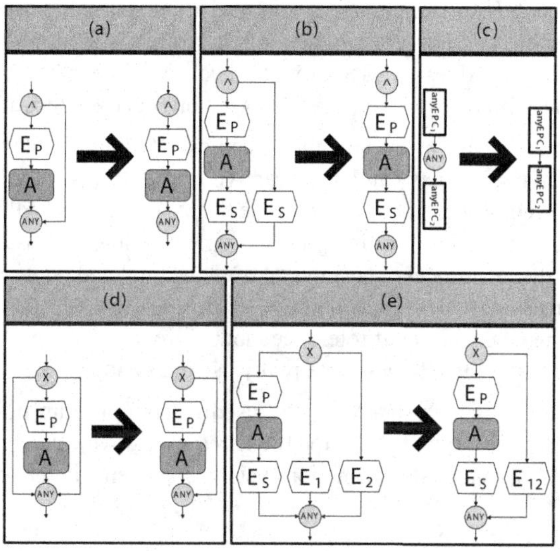

The algorithm as shown here rests on the specification of C-EPCs in XML (Mendling, Recker, Rosemann, & van der Aalst, 2005; Recker, Rosemann, van der Aalst, & Mendling, 2006) using the interchange format EPML (Mendling & Nüttgens, 2006) and can be implemented using the object-oriented scripting language XOTcl (Neumann & Zdun, 2000) (the prototype program and the EPML specifications can be downloaded from http://wi.wu-wien.ac.at/~mendling/EPML).

Future Trends

Mining Configurable Reference Models

Most of the work reported in this Chapter discusses the use of configurable process models as a way to actually configure an ES (i.e., the model is used to realize the system). However, configurable process models (e.g., C-EPCs) can also be used as a way to analyze the processes supported by the system and to "discover" the actual system configuration. As a starting point for such types of analysis, one can use audit trails (also known as event or transaction logs) and apply process mining techniques.

The goal of process mining is to extract information about processes from event logs (van der Aalst et al., 2003). Process mining techniques such as the alpha algorithm (van der Aalst, Weijters, & Maruster, 2004) typically assume that it is possible to sequentially record events such that (a) each event refers to an activity (i.e., a well-defined step in the process), and (b) each event refers to a case (i.e., a process instance). Moreover, there are other techniques explicitly using additional information such as (c) the performer also referred to as originator of the event (i.e., the person/resource executing or initiating the activity), (d) the timestamp of the event or (e) data elements recorded with the event (e.g., the size of an order). This information can be used to automatically construct process models. For example, the Multi-Phase Mining approach (van Dongen & van der Aalst, 2004) can be used to construct an EPC describing the behavior observed in the log. There are mature tools such as the ProM framework (van Dongen, Alves de Medeiros, Verbeek, Weijters, & van der Aalst, 2005) available to construct different types of models based on process executions.

There are several ways to use event logs in the context of configurable reference models (see Figure 8). Reference models can be descriptive or prescriptive (i.e., they are used to describe a process or control to respectively guide the system). The SAP reference models are expressed in terms of EPCs describing how people should/could use the SAP system. In reality, however, the real process may deviate from the modeled process (e.g., the implementation is not consistent with the specification, or people use a SAP solution in a way not modeled in any of the EPCs). Even if reference models are more of a prescriptive nature, it is still interesting to investigate how people really use the system.

Figure 8 shows that reference models can be used to configure an information system (prescriptive) or to merely model the desired process (descriptive). Independent of the way the reference model is used, most information systems log events in the form of audit trails or transaction logs. The information can be used for process discovery and conformance testing. Process discovery aims at the construction of models based on the logs without explicitly using some apriori reference model. This approach is used to construct models that can be used for comparison with existing reference models, or to generate input for the construction of new reference models. Conformance testing can be used to compare real processes with some a priori knowledge represented in the form of a reference model. It may be used to see if some descriptive reference model is actually followed in reality. Note that system users may deviate from the procedure prescribed in the reference models. Such information can be used for auditing or process improvement. Moreover, the configuration itself can be investigated (e.g., analyzing which configuration is used, what is the effect of using a specific configuration, etc.).

Process mining is far from trivial. Knowledge of the many ways in which a system may be used can assist process mining techniques, as illustrated by Jansen-Vullers, van der Aalst, and Rosemann (2006). Based on inspecting the event logs, it is relatively easy to discover the particular configuration being used. Moreover, event logs can be used to "diagnose" a configuration. For example, using process mining it is possible to automatically locate the bottlenecks and present them in the context of the configurable process model (e.g., a function in the C-EPC). This may assist the reconfiguration of the system. Furthermore, process mining techniques can be used to compare different configurations and their effects on the performance of the resulting process, which supports an "evidence-based" approach towards business process management.

Figure 8. Relation between reference models and process mining

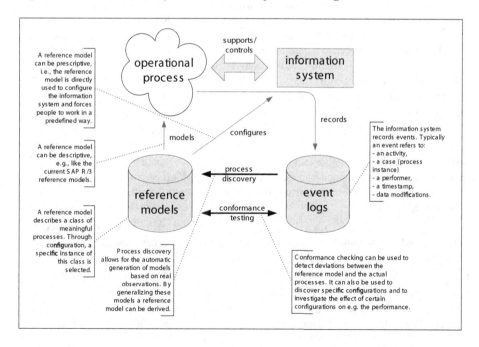

Configurable Data Modeling Languages

So far, we have covered the configurability of reference process models. Yet, given that reference models are often used in the context of business systems, there are more perspectives to consider. Business systems are not only popular, since they provide process-oriented support for typical functional areas such as Procurement or Materials Management, but also since they provide integrated data repositories across the whole enterprise. Accordingly, available reference models not only depict business processes but also the data structure of business systems. As an example, in version 4.6, the SAP reference data model covers more than 230 business objects clustering more than 4,000 entity types. A configuration approach needs to place emphasis on the configuration of reference data models as well. Consider an organizational perspective: Reference data models are of particular importance to the configuration of system organizational units as they precisely depict the given opportunities of a business system. A subset of the SAP reference data model (approximately 30-40 entity types) allows for a complete description of the interrelations between system organizational units such as company, factory or distribution channel, which facilitates configuration decisions as to the system organizational structure.

Similar to the process perspective, current reference data models are typically based on traditional modeling techniques such as the Entity-Relationship Modeling (ERM) notation (Chen, 1976). Entity types are used to group and depict distinct subjects of interest (e.g., customers, organizations, sales order items, etc.). These entities may possess various attributes for further specification. Relationships between such elements of interest are depicted using relationship types that specify the type of association between distinct entities. Cardinalities can further be used to specify the extent of dependency between associated entity types.

Classical data modeling techniques do not allow for the depiction of configuration information, such as variation points or configuration requirements (Rosemann & Shanks, 2001). In the following, we discuss some configuration decisions that can be made and how they could be depicted in reference data models. Extracts of the SAP reference data model are used as an example. The structure of this analysis follows the main constructs of Entity-Relationship-Models (i.e., entity and relationship types, Chen, 1976). Note that the variant used here is called SAP-Structured ERM; refer, for instance, to Seubert, Schäfer, Schorr, and Wagner (1994).

Transparent examples for model configurations related to optional entity types can be found in Enterprise Systems in the definition of system organizational structures. The Sales & Distribution solution in SAP, for example, requires a decision whether shipping points of an enterprise are to be subdivided into loading points. The IMG (Bancroft et al., 1997) marks this decision as optional. This variation point, however, cannot be reflected in the available reference data model (see Figure 9) as the data structure is statically fixed.

In a configurable reference data model, optional entity types such as Loading Point could be highlighted with a dotted line, thereby indicating that such organizational structure may (a) or may not be (b) implemented.

The configuration of optional relationship types includes two decisions. First, if the relationship type is required at all. If the relationship is required, a second decision is related to what cardinalities the relationship should have. Again, consider an organizational perspective: The IMG allows for the decision whether or not to assign a purchasing organization to a company code (i.e., whether procurement may be effectuated company-specific for all plants assigned to that company, Figure 10, configuration (a)), or whether procurement may be effectuated plant-specific for all the plants assigned to the purchasing organization (Figure 10, configuration (b)), irrespective of the super-ordinate company code. Again, the available reference data model cannot reflect this decision as the relationship between the entity types Company Code and Purchasing Organization is fixed.

A configurable reference data model could highlight this variation point by using a dotted line for the connection between these entity types.

There is a need to further explore configurability of reference data models. We only presented a brief outline of a proposed conceptual extension to existing reference data modeling techniques. Our short discussion revealed that, following the idea of configurable reference process modeling, the design principles that led to the development of C-EPCs may also be used to extend or refine other reference modeling techniques towards configurability (leading for example to C-ERMs). Exemplarily, we elaborated on the conceptual development of a configurable data modeling technique that allows for the modeling of optional entity types and optional relationship types. Clearly, this has to be considered a work-in-progress but nevertheless denotes an important and interesting research facet in the future of (configurable) reference modeling.

Figure 9. Configuration of reference data models: Entity types

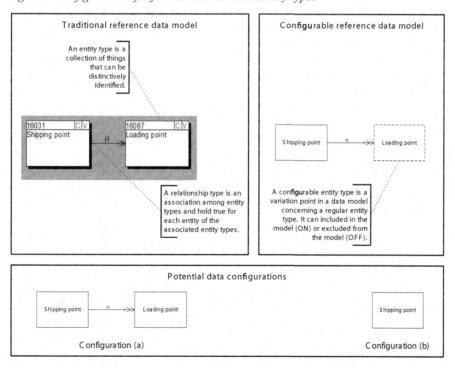

Conclusion

This chapter discussed and introduced extensions to conceptual modeling languages in order to facilitate the configuration of reference models. These modeling languages have been developed in light of a number of critical design principles which are of relevance following the paradigm of information model reuse. We used an extension of the event-driven process chain to demonstrate the design of a configurable reference process modeling language. Furthermore, we gave first insights into how configurable models can be derived via process mining from executed business system-supported processes. In principle, other modeling languages could be extended in similar ways. It has been discussed how the idea of configuring process models can be applied to other views, such as the data perspective. We briefly reported on the development of a configurable data modeling language as an example.

We expect research on configurable reference modeling to give a stimulating input to both academic and practical work around reference models in the future. The development of generic, configurable languages such as the C-EPC and the establishment of tool-neutral interchange formats such as EPML (Mendling & Nüttgens, 2006) or the XML metadata interchange (XMI) format (OMG, 2005) provide promising prototype examples that strive

Figure 10. Configuration of reference data models: Relationship types

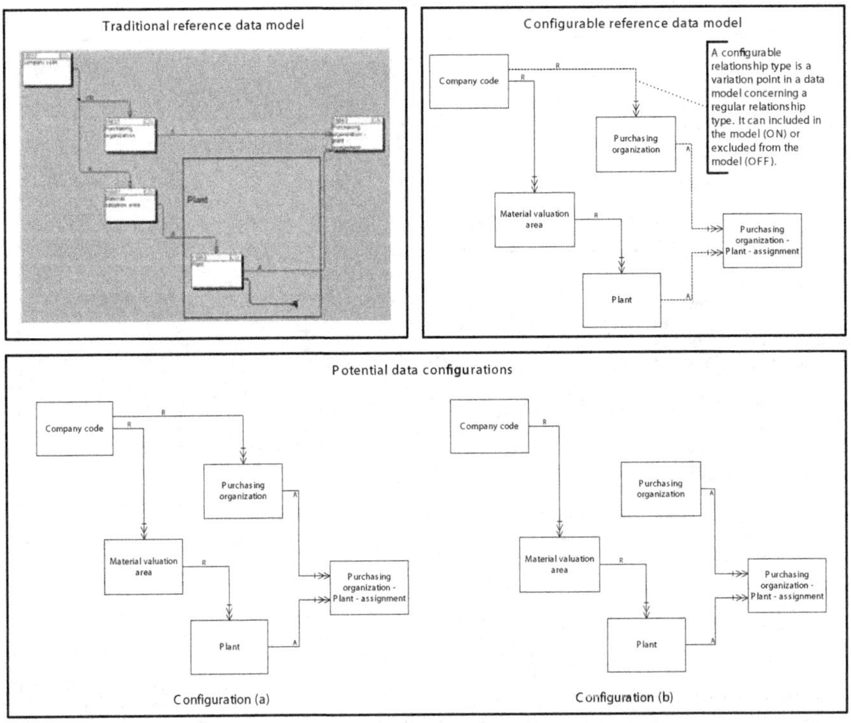

for practical adoption in the form of commercial solutions. Configurable reference models may be used to facilitate a model-driven implementation process of business systems (Recker, Mendling, van der Aalst, & Rosemann, 2006),or the usage of configurable reference models can lead to the cross-organizational consolidation of previous process configurations, thereby accumulating an evidence-based body of knowledge as to the configuration and enactment of business processes across multiple industry sectors, regions and cultures. These are just a few ideas, but they already indicate that reference modeling and model configurability continue to emerge as a vibrant and influential research discipline in the future.

References

Bancroft, N. H., Seip, H., & Sprengel, A. (1997). *Implementing Sap R/3: How to introduce a large system into a large organization* (2nd ed.). Englewood Cliffs, NJ: Prentice Hall.

Beer, S. (1966). *Decision and control: The meaning of operational research and management cybernetics.* London: John Wiley & Sons.

Chen, P. P.-S. (1976). The entity relationship model: Toward a unified view of data. *ACM Transactions on Database Systems, 1*(1), 9-36.

Curran, T., Keller, G., & Ladd, A. (1997). *SAP R/3 business blueprint: Understanding the business process reference model.* Upper Saddle River, NJ: Prentice Hall.

Daneva, M. (2000). Practical reuse measurement in ERP requirements engineering. In B. Wangler & L. Bergmann (Eds.), *Advanced information systems engineering: 12th International Conference* (Vol. 1789, pp. 309-324). Stockholm, Sweden: Springer.

Daneva, M. (2004). ERP requirements engineering practice: Lessons learned. *IEEE Software, 21*(2), 26-33.

Davenport, T. H. (1998). Putting the enterprise into the enterprise system. *Harvard Business Review, 76*(4), 121-131.

Davenport, T. H. (2000). *Mission critical: Realizing the promise of enterprise systems.* Boston: Harvard Business School Press.

Dreiling, A., Chiang, M., Rosemann, M., & van der Aalst, W. M. P. (2005). Towards an understanding of model-driven process configuration and its support at large. In N. C. Romano (Ed.), *2005 Americas Conference on Information Systems* (pp. 2084-2092). Omaha, NE: Association for Information Systems.

Dumas, M., van der Aalst, W. M. P., & ter Hofstede, A. H. M. (Eds.). (2005). *Process aware information systems: Bridging people and software through process technology.* Hoboken, NJ: John Wiley & Sons.

Fettke, P., & Loos, P. (2003). Classification of reference models: A methodology and its application. *Information Systems and E-Business Management, 1*(1), 35-53.

Halmans, G., & Pohl, K. (2003). Communicating the variability of a software-product family to customers. *Software and System Modeling, 2*(1), 15-36.

Jansen-Vullers, M. H., van der Aalst, W. M. P., & Rosemann, M. (2006). Mining configurable enterprise information systems. *Data & Knowledge Engineering, 56*(3), 195-244.

Keller, G., Nüttgens, M., & Scheer, A.-W. (1992). *Semantische Prozessmodellierung auf der Grundlage "Ereignisgesteuerter Prozessketten (EPK)"* (Working Paper No. 89). Saarbrücken, Germany: Institut für Wirtschaftsinformatik, Universität Saarbrücken. [in German]

Kesari, M., Chang, S., & Seddon, P. B. (2003). A content-analytic study of the advantages and disadvantages of process modelling. In J. Ang & S.-A. Knight (Eds.), *14th Australasian Conference on Information Systems* [CD-ROM]. Perth, Australia: School of Management Information Systems.

Kindler, E. (2005). On the semantics of EPCs: Resolving the vicious circle. *Data & Knowledge Engineering, 56*(1), 23-40.

Mendling, J., & Nüttgens, M. (2006). EPC markup language (EPML): An XML-based interchange format for event-driven process chains (EPC). *Information Systems and E-Business Management, 4*(3), 245-263.

Mendling, J., Recker, J., Rosemann, M., & van der Aalst, W. M. P. (2005). Towards the interchange of configurable EPCs: An XML-based approach for reference model configuration. In U. Frank & J. Desel (Eds.), *Enterprise modelling and information systems architectures 2005* (Vol. P-75, pp. 8-21). Klagenfurt, Germany: German Computer Society.

Mendling, J., Recker, J., Rosemann, M., & van der Aalst, W. M. P. (2006). Generating correct EPCs from configured CEPCs. In H. M. Haddad (Ed.), *2006 ACM Symposium on Applied Computing* (pp. 1505-1510). Dijon, France: ACM.

Misic, V. B., & Zhao, J. L. (2000). Evaluating the quality of reference models. In A. H. F. Laender, S. W. Liddle, & V. C. Storey (Eds.), *Conceptual modeling—ER 2000* (Vol. 1920, pp. 484-498). Salt Lake City, UT: Springer.

Neumann, G., & Zdun, U. (2000). XOTcl: An object-oriented scripting language. In *7th USENIX Tcl/Tk Conference* (pp. 163-174). Austin, TX.

OMG. (2005). *MOF 2.0/XMI mapping specification, v2.1.* Retrieved January 17, 2006, from http://www.omg.org/docs/formal/05-09-01.pdf

Oracle. (2006). *Oracle consulting business solutions.* Retrieved January 13, 2006, from http://www.oracle.com/consulting/solutions/index.html

Recker, J., Mendling, J., van der Aalst, W. M. P., & Rosemann, M. (2006). Model-driven enterprise systems configuration. In E. Dubois & K. Pohl (Eds.), *Advanced information systems engineering—CAiSE 2006* (Vol. 4001, pp. 369-383). Luxembourg, Grand-Duchy of Luxembourg: Springer.

Recker, J., Rosemann, M., van der Aalst, W. M. P., & Mendling, J. (2006). On the syntax of reference model configuration. Transforming the C-EPC into lawful EPC models. In C. Bussler & A. Haller (Eds.), *Business process management workshops* (Vol. 3812, pp. 497-511). Berlin, Germany: Springer.

Rosemann, M. (2000). Using reference models within the enterprise resource planning lifecycle. *Australian Accounting Review, 10*(3), 19-30.

Rosemann, M. (2002). Application reference models and building blocks for management and control (ERP Systems). In P. Bernus, L. Nemes, & G. Schmidt (Eds.), *Handbook of enterprise architecture* (pp. 595-616). Berlin, Germany: Springer.

Rosemann, M., & Shanks, G. (2001). Extension and configuration of reference models for enterprise resource planning systems. In G. Finnie, D. Cecez-Kecmanovic, & B. Lo (Eds.), *12ᵗʰ Australasian Conference on Information Systems* (pp. 537-546). Coffs Harbour, Australia: School of Multimedia and Information Technology.

Rosemann, M., & van der Aalst, W. M. P. (in press). A configurable reference modelling language. *Information Systems,* (forthcoming).

Rosemann, M., Vessey, I., & Weber, R. (2004). Alignment in enterprise systems implementations: The role of ontological distance. In *25ᵗʰ International Conference on Information Systems* (pp. 439-448). Washington, DC: Association for Information Systems.

SAP. (2006). *SAP business maps: Solution composer.* Retrieved January 13, 2006, from http://www.sap.com/solutions/businessmaps/composer/

Scheer, A.-W. (2000). *ARIS: Business process modeling* (3ʳᵈ ed.). Berlin, Germany: Springer.

Seubert, M., Schäfer, T., Schorr, M., & Wagner, J. (1994). Praxisorientierte datenmodellierung mit der SAP-SERM-Methode. *EMISA Forum, 4*(2), 71-79. [in German]

Silverston, L. (2001a). *The data model resource book, Volume 1: A library of universal data models for all enterprises.* New York: John Wiley & Sons.

Silverston, L. (2001b). *The data model resource book, Volume 2: A library of data models for specific industries* (2ⁿᵈ ed.). New York: John Wiley & Sons.

Stein, T. (1998, August 31). SAP sued over R/3. *Information Week,* p. 134.

van der Aalst, W. M. P. (1999). Formalization and verification of event-driven process chains. *Information and Software Technology, 41*(10), 639-650.

van der Aalst, W. M. P., van Dongen, B. F., Herbst, J., Maruster, L., Schimm, G., & Weijters, A. J. M. M. (2003). Workflow mining: A survey of issues and approaches. *Data & Knowledge Engineering, 47*(2), 237-267.

van der Aalst, W. M. P., Weijters, A. J. M. M., & Maruster, L. (2004). Workflow mining: Discovering process models from event logs. *IEEE Transactions on Knowledge and Data Engineering, 16*(9), 1128-1142.

van Dongen, B. F., Alves de Medeiros, A. K., Verbeek, M., Weijters, A. J. M. M., & van der Aalst, W. (2005). The ProM framework: A new era in process mining tool support. In G. Ciardo & P. Darondeau (Eds.), *Applications and theory of Petri Nets 2005* (Vol. 3536, pp. 444-454). Berlin, Germany: Springer.

van Dongen, B. F., & van der Aalst, W. M. P. (2004). Multi-phase process mining: Building instance graphs. In P. Atzeni, W. W. Chu, H. Lu, S. Zhou, & T. W. Ling (Eds.), *Conceptual modeling: ER 2004* (pp. 362-376). Shanghai, China: Springer.

Welti, N. (1999). *Successful SAP R/3 implementation: Practical management of ERP projects.* Reading, MA: Addison-Wesley.

Wisse, P. (2000). *Metapattern: Context and time in information models.* Boston: Addison-Wesley.

Chapter III

Design Principles for Reference Modeling:
Reusing Information Models by Means of Aggregation, Specialisation, Instantiation, and Analogy

Jan vom Brocke,
European Research Center for Information Systems,
University of Münster, Germany

Abstract

With the design of reference models, an increase in the efficiency of information systems engineering is intended. This is expected to be achieved by reusing information models. Current research focuses mainly on configuration as one principle for reusing artifacts. According to this principle, all variants of a model are incorporated in the reference model facilitating adaptations by choices. In practice, however, situations arise whereby various requirements to a model are unforeseen: Either results are inappropriate or costs of design are rising strongly. This chapter introduces additional design principles aiming at giving more flexibility to both the design and application of reference models.

Introduction

Modeling comprises a concentration on special aspects in design processes by means of abstraction. In particular, information (system) models are built in order to describe relevant aspects of information systems. Due to an increasing demand of these models addressing similar design problems to a certain extent, the development of reference (information) models is subject to research.[1] The essential idea is to provide information models as a kind of "reference" in order to increase both efficiency and effectiveness of modeling processes (Becker et al., 2004; Fettke & Loos, 2003; Scheer & Nüttgens, 2000).

Practical applications of reference models are widespread in the domain of ERP-systems (Becker & Schütte, 2004; Huschens & Rumpold-Preining, 2006; Kittlaus & Krahl, 2006; Scheer, 1994). In this domain, reference models set the basis for general business solutions that can be adapted to individual customer needs. In order to support this kind of customising process, reference models are built in a configurative way (Becker et al., 2004; Meinhardt & Popp, 2006; Recker et al., 2005); for a review on German literature (see vom Brocke, 2003, pp. 95-158). This work intends to encounter all relevant variants of prospective applications during build-time of the model in order to facilitate adaptability by means of choices (van der Aalst et al., 2005, p. 77). A vital factor for the economic efficiency of reference modeling is in how far a single variant of the model fits the customer's requirements. As this fit indicates the value of the model, it is also essential for the return on investment in building reference models from a supplier's perspective. Considering the variety of requirements to be faced in today's software engineering, the design principle of configuration illuminates specific limitations. In particular, it is increasingly hard to take into account the various requirements that may be relevant and to incorporate them in the reference model. Hence, supplementary design principles that may enlarge the "tool-kit" of reference modeling appear to be useful. Accordingly, the principles aggregation, specialisation, instantiation, and analogy are presented in this chapter.

Initially, as a theoretical background, the concept of reuse in reference modeling is introduced. This allows an analysis of preliminary works leading to a closer specification of this study's research focus and methodology. On that basis, new design principles are introduced and analysed according to their potential for reference modeling. Finally, a conclusion is drawn and perspectives for future research are suggested.

Foundations of Design Principles for Reference Modeling

The Concept of Reuse in Reference Modeling

In order to learn how to build reference models according to specific needs, a deeper understanding of essential elements of these particular kinds of models is required. This chapter outlines how these essential elements lie in the intention of building information models which can easily be reused in the design of other models. In addition, relevant dimensions of reusing information models are presented, serving as a framework for this work.

A Reuse-Oriented Concept of Reference Models

According to reviews on reference modeling literature (vom Brocke, 2003, p. 31 ff.), which are predominantly written in German, the concept of reference modeling is introduced on the basis of special characteristics of models. In particular, a certain degree of validity and quality are highlighted. Thus, reference models are meant to describe a sort of best (or common) practice of business in a creation application domain. This approach enables a sophisticated understanding of the idea of reference modeling. However, certain limitations are obvious. Considering the problem of measuring characteristics, for instance, there is no objective reason for awarding or rejecting best practice to a model. At the same time, it may even be questionable in how far this discussion helps to learn about principles of building reference models so that they finally prove to be best practice.

For further work, it seems to be reasonable to ground the concept of reference modeling on the intention of reusing information models. To give a definition, reference models are referred to as special information models that serve to be reused in the design process of other information models (vom Brocke, 2003, p. 38). According to a recent study (Thomas, 2005), this concept is increasingly applied in reference modeling. A process-oriented view on the design and usage of reference models enables a deeper understanding of the concept (see Figure 1).

Modeling is referred to as a design process in which a designer is in charge of building a model according to a user's needs. Due to different mental models of people carrying out these roles, co-ordination is vital for both effectiveness and efficiency of the process. Whereas effectiveness measures the users' satisfaction due to the appropriateness of model quality, efficiency takes into account the ratio of in- and output coming along with the process.

Considering the reuse-oriented concept of reference models, a kind of support process for information modeling is added. This support lies essentially in providing information models that serve to be incorporated in other models. Specifically, reuse is conducted by taking parts

Figure 1. Reuse-oriented concept of reference modeling

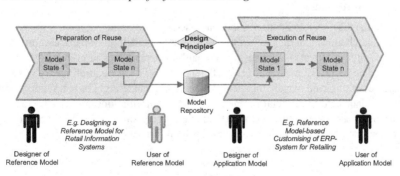

of one or more original models and adapting and extending them in the resulting model. That way, both efficiency and the effectiveness of the modeling process may be fostered.

Taking reference models as models to support design processes, reference models have to be differentiated from meta-models (Karagiannis & Kühn, 2002) that are commonly used for the definition of modeling languages. Following a wider understanding, further types of meta-models, for example, may well be distinguished that describe the procedure of conducting the modeling process. In contrast to reference modes, these models are "used," but not "re-used," as their content is not incorporated in the resulting model. Thus, whereas meta-models define rules for conducting modeling, reference models offer content to be reused.

Regarding the reuse-oriented concept, different types of models are candidates for being reference models. Models can vary widely, regarding, for example, the type of application, the level of implementation or the type of organisational setting. In addition, reference models might also be classified by supplementary criteria. By looking at relevance and rigor, for example, a special subset of reference models may be identified serving as scientific artefacts. However, the term "reference" does not indicate a sort of "high quality" model in general. The decisive factor is the user's view about the suitability of the model for a special purpose. Thus, reference models have to be considered from at least two perspectives (vom Brocke, 2003, p. 32):

- **Supplier perspective:** The designer may plan to supply a reference process model under consideration of the purpose of reusability in other design processes. This however, does not guarantee that reuse will take place in practice.
- **Customer perspective:** The decision on reusing a model is in fact taken by the customer. Thus, models might either be planned to be reused but fail on the customer side or the customer decides to reuse models that have not been designed for that purpose.

Reference modeling as a research discipline intends to discover means to coordinate both perspectives: The analysis of the customer side is essential in order to learn about requirements. For that purpose an insight into relevant domain knowledge of various fields of application as well as in people's behaviour in reusing artefacts is required. In addition, work on the designer's side mainly aims at finding means to fulfil these requirements. Furthermore, research is necessary on the interchange of models comprising work on institutional and technical infrastructures.

Thanks to the reuse-oriented concept, the wider scope of reference modeling gives way to indicate research areas that may contribute to reference modeling. In particular, in the area of reuse-oriented (software) engineering, a wealth of experiences in principles of reusing artefacts can be found (H. Mili et al., 1995; Peterson, 1991). Hence, preliminary work from various fields of this kind may be transferred to reference modeling. For that scope, findings have to be adapted to the special problem of reusing information models. The following examines basic aspects of reuse techniques in engineering and assembles them in order to present a picture of relevant dimensions of reuse in reference modeling.

Figure 2. Framework for relations reusing information models

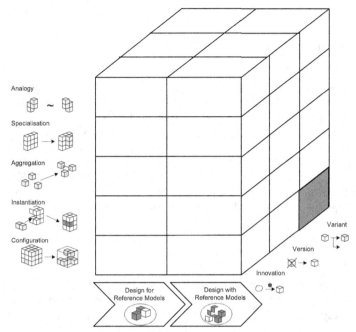

Dimensions of Reuse in Reference Modeling

In former studies on reference modeling, the design of configurative reference models was focussed on in order to support the derivation of multiple variants of a reference model for a certain application (Becker et al., 2004; Meinhardt & Popp, 2006; Recker et al., 2005); for a review on German literature (see vom Brocke, 2003, pp. 95-158). That way, this research is concentrated on a rather special field of reusing information models. Figure 2 gives an overview of the relevant dimensions of reuse in reference modeling.

The differentiation visualised in Figure 2 provides a three-dimensional framework for the identification of model relations in the context of reuse.

Stage in Value Chain

In reuse-oriented software engineering, technical issues of reuse are covered in two stages in the value chain: the development "with" reuse that is carried out in application engineering and the development "for" reuse that is subject to domain engineering (Gomaa, 1995; Kang et al., 1998; Mili et al., 2002, p. 27). Correspondingly, the design of reference and application models may be distinguished. The content shipped with the reference model needs to be adapted regarding the requirements of the empirical application. In addition, the design of reference models may be supported by reuse itself. That way, a kind of reference model-based modeling may be established.

Degree of Innovation

In particular, when considering industrial engineering and configuration management (Conradi & Westfechtel, 1998, p 238ff.), constructions may be differentiated by degrees of innovation. Correspondingly, both innovations and modification of models can be distinguished. While modifications offer a solution for a specific type of problem by changing initial models, innovations come up with solutions for other types of problems for the first time. If the modification is carried out in order to tap a new shaping of a problem, a so-called variant is constructed. If the adaptation, instead, brings in a new solution to a problem that has already been dealt with, a new version is available. This assessment is taken subjectively considering the relevant application domain and mental model of the recipient.

Principle of Construction

In order to facilitate reuse, design principles are applied. Design principles provide rules describing the way in which the content of one model is reused in constructing another. The rules describe ways of taking over contents as well as of adapting and extending them in the resulting model. With each design principle, specific sets of rules are differentiated. Apart from configuration as a parametric approach, a great variety of principles are discussed in software engineering that are originally referred to as adaptive principles (Karhinen et al., 1997; Peterson, 1991). In recent works, these principles have been evaluated for use in reference modeling (vom Brocke, 2003, pp. 259-319). In particular, the principles of instantiation, aggregation, specialisation, and analogy seem to offer promising means for extending the set of design principles for reference modeling. According to instantiation, general aspects of a domain are designed as a framework providing generic placeholders for plugging in models considering special requirements of an application. Specialisation enables the takeover of entire contents of a general model into a specific model allowing modification and extending individually. Aggregation enables the takeover of contents delivered by various part models that are composed and extended according to special requirements of an application. Analogy, finally, employs seemingly similar solutions in a creative way to tackle new problems.

Whereas much research has been carried out on configuration, little attention has so far been paid to instantiation, specialisation, aggregation, and analogy. Thus, these design principles will be introduced in more detail with this contribution. As for configuration, an introduction can be taken from literature. Having introduced the principles, questions of selecting the right principle will be addressed. This discussion will again include configuration.

Preliminary Work and Focus of Research

In the previous chapter, reference (information) modeling was introduced for the essential idea of reusing artefacts in information modeling. Hence, the significance of a wide range of work in the field of reuse-oriented software engineering (McIlroy, 1968) becomes obvious. For this study, insight into various types of principles for reusing information systems artefacts can be gained in particular. Figure 3 gives an overview of the impact of principles from reuse-oriented software development on those for reference modeling.

Early works on reuse-oriented software engineering have been carried out in structuring programs by means of modules (Jones, 1984). In particular, the concept of generic packages (Slater, 1995) provides inspiration for the construction technique of instantiation. Generic packages allow reusing a unique data structure for various data types by means of deriving instances of the package for concrete data types. The idea of reuse is essentially incorporated in the object-oriented paradigm (Coad & Yourdan, 1991; Cox, 1990). Within this context, information systems are composed of co-operating objects that are entirely specified regarding their properties and behaviour. The way in which objects share these descriptions by inheritance serves as an example and gives clues for the principle of specialisation. The idea of composing information systems out of rather independent fragments is further developed in the concept of component-based software engineering (George & Heineman, 2001; Szyperski, 1998). The leitmotif of combining off-the-shelf components that are ready to be used in a new context gives an example for the principle of aggregation. Apart from these rather formalised concepts, pattern-based software engineering aims at providing artefacts that can be reused free-handedly by the designer (Alexander et al., 1977; Gamma et al., 1995; Hay, 1996). This approach gives stimuli to the construction principle of analogy for reference models (Spanoudakis & Constantopoulos, 1993).

In reuse-oriented software engineering, the concepts described above have also been covered in the phase of requirements engineering and, thereby, in the design of information models (Coad et al., 1997; Kruchten, 2003; Raumbaugh et al., 1991). The principles of aggregation, specialisation, and partly instantiation are incorporated especially in most modeling languages like the unified modeling language (UML) (Kruchten, 2003; Rumbaugh et al., 2004). The implementation of these principles, however, takes place "within models." In a class diagram, for example, classes may well be linked by aggregation or specialisation symbols. For reference modeling, in contrast, these principles are to be applied to linkages "between models." These kinds of relations are rarely covered, except in pattern-oriented software engineering. In particular, work on analysis patterns (Fowler, 1997) fits well with the kind of abstract conceptional models that have predominantly been subject to reference modeling research so far. However, due to the type of reuse principles, little information is given about rules of how to take over, adapt and extend the model's content with respect to certain applications.

Figure 3. Deriving design principles for reference modeling from reuse-oriented software engineering

Branch in Reuse-Oriented Software Engineering (SE)	Major Contribution to Design Principles for Reference Modeling
Module-oriented SE	Instantiation
Object-oriented SE	Specialisation
Component-based SE	Aggregation
Pattern-based SE	Analogy

In addition to the general contribution of reuse-oriented software engineering, special studies can be found that address problems of specifying information system artefacts for the purpose of reuse. Apart from work in the field of configurative reference modeling (Becker et al., 2004; van der Aalst et al., 2005) that is not focused on here, works on further principles of reuse can be found (D'Souza, 2000; Melton & Garlan, 1997; Remme, 1995). Altogether, these studies are characterised by the approach of introducing extensions to notations that are used in order to describe relevant artefacts. These contributions give examples of the implementation of certain design principles in modeling languages. However, each approach is limited to merely one specific modeling language. Reference modeling, however, is characterised by a pluralism of languages especially substantiated by the focus on contents of models that are to be constructed. The linguistic representation of the contents, instead, needs to be adapted to specific preferences of the addressee.

Thus, design principles for reusing information models in reference modeling should be introduced in a way that they are independent of special languages. Such an approach is presented in this chapter. It aims at enabling the incorporation of reuse by instantiation, aggregation, specialisation and analogy in various languages according to the same principles.

A Language-Independent Approach for Introducing Design Principles

For reference modeling, design principles should be specified on a general methodological level. In particular, a specification of essential rules for each design principle is required that remains independent of special modeling languages. This specification can then be transferred to a great variety of specific languages. This approach will be referred to as language independency in the following section. A methodological approach for developing language independent design principles can be drawn from reference meta-models (vom Brocke, 2003, pp. 85, 263-269); similarly (Axenath et al., 2005, pp. 50-51). With reference meta-models, essential rules for specific construction purposes are specified in a way that they can be incorporated by various other languages (application languages).

Applying this approach, the construction of aggregation, specialisation, instantiation and analogy will be introduced on the basis of reference meta-models. For further illustration, workflows for conducting them on the basis of case tools as well as examples are given. According to the reference meta-models and the examples, relevant assumptions are introduced in the following.

Reference Meta-Models for Design Principles

On the basis of reference meta-models, design principles can be introduced according to their essential rules, in order to be transferred to a number of modeling languages. For this purpose, assumptions about characteristic language constructs of application languages have to be made so that the scope of reference languages can be determined. The assumptions refer to the type of modeling languages as well as to the types of elements the languages may consist of.

- **Type of modeling languages:** Languages serving the description of a system's behaviour and properties have to be differentiated. Models describing the behaviour of a system show possible adaptations to the system's state. Thus, these models are characteristically described by statements given in both a temporal and logical order. Languages, consequently, provide constructs for placing and relating corresponding statements. With models describing the properties of a system, the characteristics of the various states of the system have to be specified. Therefore, statements referring to sets of attributes and relations between these states are relevant. Languages for the description of properties, hence, provide according constructs.

- **Type of elements of the language:** For the purpose of abstraction, modeling languages are considered to consist of the following general elements: Languages are sets of *rules* that present language constructs by means of which language statements can be made. Language statements about construction results are referred to as model statements by means of which the contents of a model can be described. If model statements of a particular purpose are combined, these statements are referred to as a representation of a model. Design principles are formalised by sets of rules that describe how model representations and model statements can be put into relation to one another for the purpose of transferring, adapting and extending contents of an original model into a resulting model.

Rules of design principles are specified in a way that extensions of application languages can be derived. In reference meta-models, characteristic language constructs are introduced that are necessary for incorporating a certain design principle in reference modeling. Transferring these rules to application languages, either adaptations or the extensions of already existing constructs, have to be carried out, or new constructs are introduced.

Examples for the Design Principles

With this chapter, the design principles are illustrated by means of examples. Selecting the examples, a couple of requirements have to be considered:

- **Languages:** Models should be represented in languages like ERM (Chen, 1976) and EPC (Keller et al., 1992; Scheer, 1994) as these languages are widespread in reference modeling and therefore serve as a good example for illustrating how to apply the design principles.
- **Domain:** Models should be taken from a domain that is of relevance for a wide range of applications.
- **Suitability:** The contents of the models should be suitable for demonstrating the various principles of reuse.
- **Focus:** The models should be proven in order to focus the discussion on changes in design due to the application of the design principles.

Figure 4. Data model "Accounts Payable" as major source for demonstrating design principles with ERM

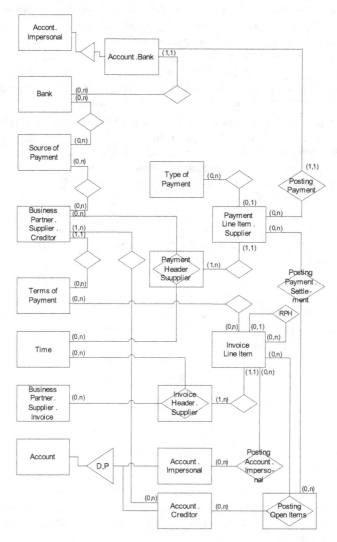

In order to fulfil most of the requirements, examples were chosen from the field of *accounting* that are described in both the reference models of Scheer (1994) and Becker/Schütte (Becker & Schütte, 2004). With respect to ERM, the examples show how rather detailed descriptions of "Accounts Payable" in Becker/Schütte (Becker & Schütte, 2004, p. 389) might be designed reusing parts of the models given in Scheer. The entire model of "accounts payable" is given in Figure 4.

Figure 5. Process model "Handling of Payments" as major source for demonstrating design principles with EPC

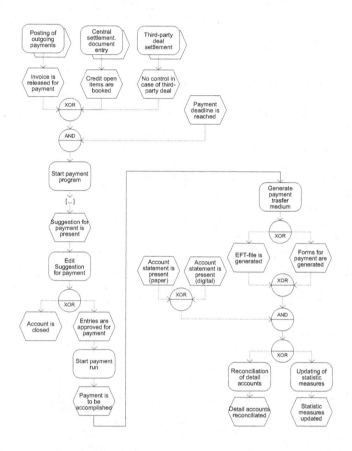

According to EPC, the process "Handling of Payments" (Becker & Schütte, 2004, pp. 392 ff.) is examined correspondingly (see Figure 5). In the model of Scheer, a description of the process is given on a textual basis (Scheer, 1994, p. 417 ff.).

In order to illustrate the design principles, minor modifications to the models are made in the examples. The models of Becker/Schütte have been translated considering the terminology applied in Scheer. Applying the reference meta-models, it is intended to use language constructs that are available in the ERM und EPC as far as possible. Additional annotations are made using constructs that are common in the unified modeling language (UML) (Rumbaugh et al., 2004).

Introduction of New Design Principles
for Reference Models

Instantiation

The principle of instantiation is characterised by the creation of a resulting model "I" by integrating one or several original models "e" into appropriate generic place holders of the original model "G." The resulting model "I," therefore, incorporates the integrated construction results of "e" in "G." The corresponding meta-model is presented in Figure 6.

Instantiation offers the opportunity to construct models for which both the theoretical frame as well as the statements required for appropriation can be reused. For this purpose, generic statements have to be produced in one of the original models. Step by step, they are then replaced by the integrative model representation in the process of instantiation. For integrating the statements in the resulting model, a special construct of modeling language is needed. This language construct serves to describe how the generic statements in G have to be linked with statements in e during the construction process of I. The integration is completed if all relations of the generic statement in G are updated correspondingly in I.

The principle of instantiation is illustrated by extending the data model "Accounts Payable" (Becker & Schütte, 2004, p. 389) to incorporate different types for sources of payments. For

Figure 6 . Metamodel for the design principles of instantiation

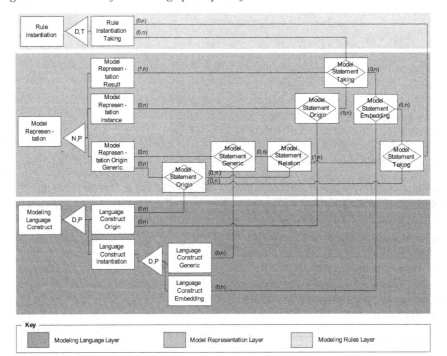

Figure 7. Example for applying the design principles of instantiation in ERM

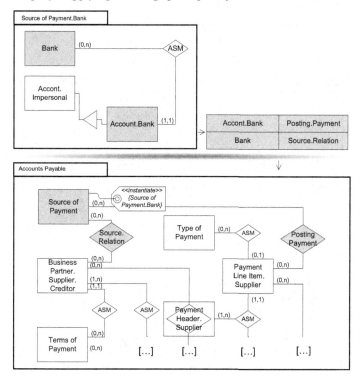

that purpose, a generic placeholder, "Sources of Payments," is used that serves to integrate various data models to specify relevant structures of each kind of source. In the example, a concrete source of payment, "Bank," is embedded that has been extracted from Scheer (1994, p. 611). The entity type "Source of payment," which is extended by the stereotype "«*instance*»," marks the relation between both data models. At the time of the instantiation, the interfaces of the resulting model and the model to be integrated have to be indicated. The example in Figure 7 reveals the relation between the entity type "bank" and the entity type "Business Partner Supplier Creditor" in the process of which the entity type "bank account" adopts the relation "Posting Payment" with the entity type "Posting Line Item Supplier." The opportunity of creating specific grades of abstraction appropriate to the needs of the addressee has a positive impact on clarity and relevance of the model.

In order to conduct an instantiation with EPC, process interfaces can well be used. In contrast to aggregation, the integration of part processes is conditional in case of instantiation. This means that different concrete processes can be plugged into the interface that serves as generic place holder. In contrast to data models, the relations of the generic place holder do not have to be updated specifically. The proper linkage is assured by the process interface construct. An additional specification can be made on the criteria for embedding different processes.

Figure 8. Example for applying the design principles of instantiation in EPC

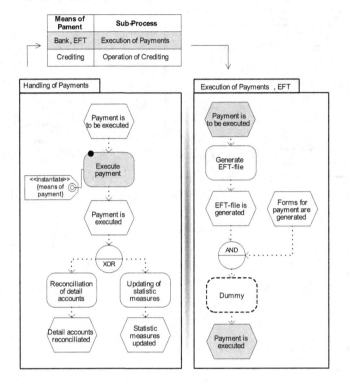

In Figure 8, the principle of instantiation is applied for considering various types of payments in the process of "Handling of Payments." Therefore, the execution of payments has been implemented as a generic place holder. Accordingly, specific sub-processes can be designed for each source of payment and plugged into the process of "Handling of Payments" (Becker & Schütte, 2004, p. 392). In the example, the process of bank payment by EFT (electronic funds transfer) is described (Scheer, 1994, p. 417) and plugged in.

The design by instantiation requires realisation of the following work steps:

1.   Select the generic model (e.g., in a tree-view).

2.   Select generic statement within the model (e.g., by mouse-click).

3.   Select a model to be integrated in place of the generic statement (e.g., in a tree-view).

4.   For each relation of the generic statement, specify an equivalent statement in the model to be integrated to take over the relation (e.g., in a table).

5.   Either select or create a resulting model; the model to be integrated is embedded in the generic model according to the rules (e.g., in a routine).

Figure 9. Meta-model for the design principle of aggregations

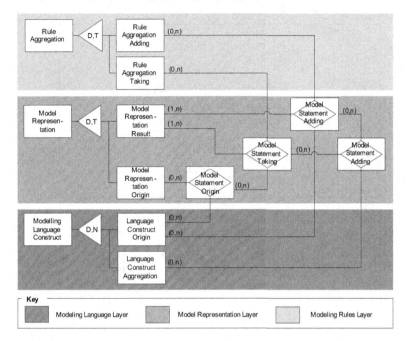

Aggregation

The principle of aggregation is characterised by the combination of one or more original models "p" that build "a" resulting model "T," with the models "p" forming complete parts of "T." The meta-model for incorporating the principle of aggregation in modeling languages is presented in Figure 9.

Aggregations offer the potential of combining model statements of original models in new contexts. For this purpose, a language construct for connecting statements of separate models has to be provided for in a modeling language. Statements of aggregated models can be taken over in the resulting model. That way, supplementary statements can be replenished and statements of integration can be positioned.

An example for the application of aggregation in ERM is given in Figure 10. In the example, the essential account structures described by Scheer (1994, p. 611), are referred to from the model for "Accounts Payable" by Becker and Schütte (2004, p. 389). As a result, the content of the data model "Account Structure" can be resorted back to without modeling redundantly. In ERM, the relation between model messages is basically supported by using identical entity types. That way, the relation is carried out by the entity type "Account." For a more explicit relation, the stereotype "«*aggregate*»" is added, that might also be specified regarding the target of reference in case different entity types are to be linked for aggregation.

Figure 10. Example for applying the design principle of aggregations in ERM

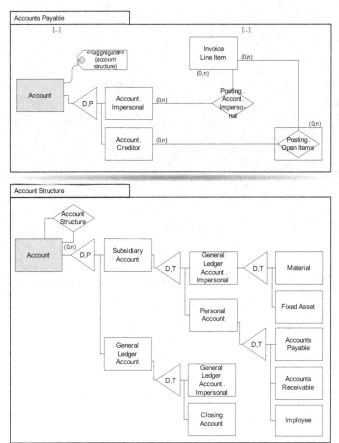

In order to demonstrate an application of aggregation in EPC, the process of "Handling of Payments" (Becker & Schütte, 2004, p. 392) has been decomposed and interlinked with other processes. For incorporating the principle, language constructs can be used that already exist in the EPC syntax. In order to aggregate entire processes, the interface for detailing functions by processes can be used. In addition, aggregation can be carried out by interlinking local steps of processes by means of the interface for linkage. Both examples are displayed in Figure 11. The examples show that in applying aggregation the events have to be handled properly. Flexibility of reuse is raised when the various events that possibly trigger a process are not modelled locally in the model of the sub-process itself but in the processes calling the sub-process. Then, an accumulation of events has to be handled. For that purpose, a dummy function was added in the example that serves to bridge events properly.

In the example, the process "Payment Program" is fully aggregated in the process "Handling of Payments" (Becker & Schütte, 2004, p. 392). In addition, one resulting event from the

Figure 11. Example for applying the design principle of aggregations in EPC

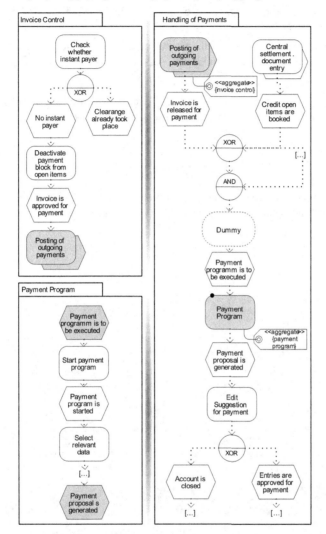

process "Invoice Control" is integrated in the process "Handling of Payments" as one trigger of this process, in the same way triggers from the processes of "Invoice Control" and "Central Settlement Document Entry" can be modelled according to aggregation.

For each model to be aggregated, the following steps need to be conducted:

1.   Select model to be aggregated.
2.   Select modeling messages to be integrated in the aggregated model.

3.   Select or create the resulting model.

4.   Iterate the process for each model to be aggregated; the messages will be transferred to the resulting model.

5.   Integrate aggregated messages in the resulting model by additional messages according to the (new) scope of the resulting model.

The process may as well be executed top down. In that case the resulting model is selected at first and original models to be aggregated are selected on demand.

Specialisation

The specialisation is characterised by the derivation of a resulting model "S" from a general model "G." That way, all modeling messages in "G" are taken over in "S" and can either

Figure 12. Meta-model for the design principle of specialisation

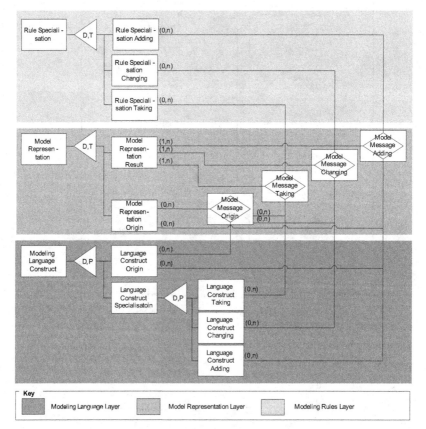

Figure 13. Example for applying the design principle of specialisation in ERM

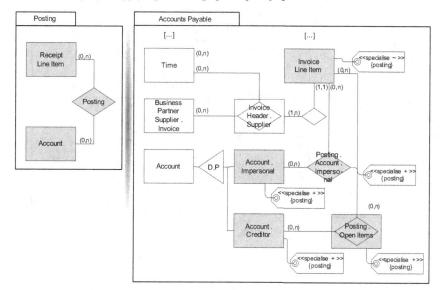

be changed or extended. Deleting messages, however, is not provided in the general case. Figure 12 shows the corresponding meta-model.

The specialisation allows the taking over of general construction results and adapting them to specific demands. In order to preserve the relation between the general and the specific model during amendments, constructs are required that help documenting which construction results have been both assumed and added. On a methodological level, rules can be provided according to which modeling messages, for example, do not necessarily have to be marked individually in the standard case.

In order to illustrate the specialisation, a model for posting was generalised from the structure for the purchasing process given by Scheer (1994, p. 420). The general model was then reused twice for describing special posting structures in the model of "Accounts Payable" by Becker and Schütte (2004), p. 389). Modeling messages that have been amended like "Invoice Line Item" and "Posting Open Items," are characterised by the stereotype "*«specialise ~ »*." For messages that are added, the stereotype "*«specialise + »*" is used (see Figure 13).

In order to show how to conduct reuse by specialisation on the basis of EPC, a general model was generated that describes essential preconditions for payments to be executed. The model is based on Scheer (1994, p. 621) and Becker and Schütte (2004, p. 392). This model is reused by specialisation in the process of "Handling of Payments." The special model considers "Central Settlement" and "Third-Party Deal Settlement" so that additional statements were added. Furthermore, changes were made as a payment program is executed in the special model (see Figure 14).

In order to conduct model-reuse by specialisation, the following workflow has to be carried out:

Figure 14. Example for applying the design principle of specialisation in EPC

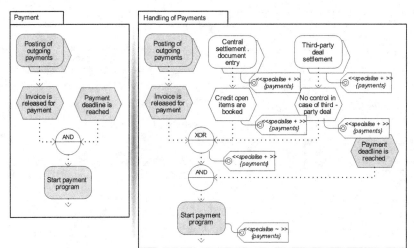

1.   Select a general model (e.g., in a tree view).

2.   Run a specialisation service (e.g., in a context menu).

3.   Either select or create a special model (e.g., in a tree view); the content of the general model may be transferred to the special model; the takeover may either be carried out by reference or a new instance of the model can be generated.

4.   Adapt the special model by both changes and extensions (e.g., by standard features); the adaptations may be tracked automatically and displayed on demand.

Analogy

The principle of analogy is characterised by an original model "A" serving as a means of orientation for the construction of a resulting model "a." The relation between the models is based on a perceived similarity of both models regarding a certain aspect. The according meta-model is presented in Figure 15.

The relatively high degree of freedom in reusing contents of an original model comes along with relatively little regulation on the model quality as opposed to other principles. Although no real means of formalisation between the model statements are required, a methodological support of the principle seems to be adequate. According to the principle of analogy, constructs may be introduced that serve to document the similarity relation perceived by the constructor. Standardisation of documentation can be realised by forms or text-based descriptions. In addition, a classification-based approach can be applied (vom Brocke, 2003).

The application of analogy in ERM is illustrated by incorporating a common structure for accounting documents in the data model of "Accounts Payable." The general structure can be found either by Scheer (1994, p. 616) or by Becker and Schütte (2004, p. 386). The

Figure 15. Meta-model for the design principle of analogy

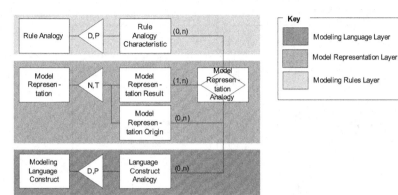

Figure 16. Example for applying the design principle of analogy in ERM

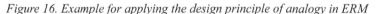
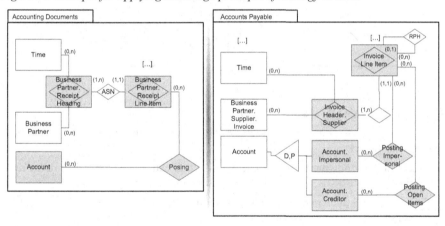

similarity of the models is evident in both content and structure. Both data models describe properties that are necessary for the booking of receipts. In the example, given in Figure 16, the structure is applied by analogy for posting an invoice on both the impersonal account and the open item list of creditors account. For documentation purpose, it may be indicated which statements refer to the reference model. Therefore, the stereotype "«*analogy*»" is used.

Also with EPC, the analogy can be carried out rather free-handedly. In the example given in Figure 17, a pattern for final assessment of processes in accounting is described (Scheer, 1994, pp. 619). The content of this model is partly reused, designing the final branch of the process "Handling of Payments" (Becker & Schütte, 2004, p. 392). As one major modification, the functions for reporting results and recording lessons learned are dropped out in the special model.

In order to conduct a construction by analogy, essentially the following steps have to be carried out:

Figure 17. Example for applying the design principle of analogy in EPC

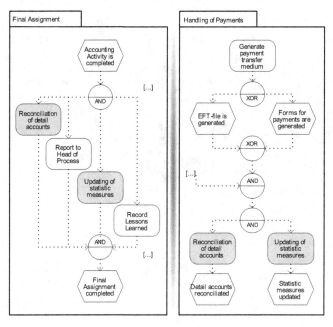

1. Select or generate the resulting model.

2. Select a model to be reused by aid of analogy; the entire model is transferred to the resulting model.

3. Adapt the resulting model free-handedly; all modifications are admissible in the resulting model.

4. Document construction by describing the similarity perceived between both models, in order to raise comprehensiveness.

Having introduced the new design principles, a larger variety in reference modeling is apparent. The following chapter will discuss how far this variety might contribute to success in reusing information models.

Potentials of the New Design Principles for Reference Modeling

The wider set of design principles makes it possible to consider different requirements of the application domain in reference modeling. As each principle implements a special technique

Figure 18. Addressing diverse modeling situations by multiple design principles

Principle	Situation	Technique
Configuration	The application domain can be described fully in design time including all relevant adaptations that have to be considered in various applications.	Adaptation by selection
Instantiation	The application domain can be covered by a general framework; this framework, however, has to be adapted in regard to selected aspects that can not be fully described while building the reference model.	Adaptation by embedding
Aggregation	The application domain can be described partly; each part can be fully specified whereas their contribution for replenishing the entire coverage of an application cannot be forseen when building the reference model.	Adaptation by combination
Specialisation	The application domain can be covered by a core solution, which has to be extended and modified (without deleting) in an indefinite manner for various applications.	Adaptation by revising
Analogy	The application domain can be described by certain patterns recurring in each application; the entire solution, however, has to be replenished in an indefinite manner.	Adaptation by transfer

of reusing content, typical situations can be identified that call for the application of certain principles (see Figure 18).

For the appropriate principle selection, an estimation of the effect on the modeling process brought about by each principle is relevant. Such an estimation can be grounded on a transaction cost-based assessment (Coase, 1937; Williamson, 1985), similar to those in reuse-based software engineering (Mili et al., 2000). In this respect, transaction costs are

Figure 19. Estimated derivation of the costs of building and applying reference models driven by design principles

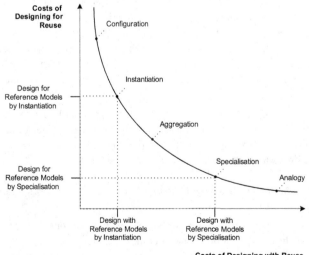

considered additional costs that come along with reusing contents in modeling. Depending on the design principles, these "costs of reuse" essentially comprise costs of designing "for" reuse and costs of designing "with" reuse. Further transaction costs (e.g., for exchanging models; vom Brocke & Buddendick, 2004), are omitted as they are not significantly driven by the choice of construction construct.

In Figure 19, a rough estimation of these "costs of reuse" is given that may be taken as a hypothesis for further empirical studies. The graph is rather simplified in order to highlight the essential relations between the costs coming along with each principle. In particular, both plot and positioning of each principle within this plot vary depending on a certain modeling situation. The principles discussed in this chapter are marked by spots as they represent stereotypes for reuse. Further principles as well as adaptation of the principles may as well be added in between the spots.

Looking at the derivation of costs, it becomes apparent that configuration and analogy form two opposite principles for reference modeling. Whereas configuration implies that most of the work on reusing the content is done by building the reference model, this work is left for the application using analogy. Consequently, configuration comes along with relatively high costs for building the reference model, but with low costs for applying it. The principle of analogy, on the contrary, causes a minimum cost on building the model but a maximum on applying it. The other principles gradually lie in-between the two. Applying instantiation, prospective applications do not need to be specified entirely while building the reference model, but at least certain generic aspects have to be identified and specified for embedding special solutions. In aggregation, only certain parts of the application domain have to be described definitely that may be combined and extended in various ways. However, modifications of each part model to be aggregated are not provided. This is possible with the principle of specialisation which gives way to rather flexible modifications except eliminating parts of the reference model. With the principles of analogy, finally, unlimited ways of adapting the content are given.

With the different ways of reusing the content, not only consequences related to costs have to be taken into account. Since the shape of the later model is determined in different stages of the value chain, implications on the model quality come along with the choice of principle. However, no general suggestion can be given on the choice. An early determination of the model's shape, for example, facilitates quality assurance as individual modifications are restricted. In some cases, however, these modifications might as well be necessary to meet the specific requirements of a single application. In practice, these various factors have to be weighed regarding the special purpose of the model (e.g., customising and knowledge management).

Apart from the purpose, general decision support can be given with respect to the characteristics of the application domain. The interdependences described above show that the efficiency of the principles depends on how far it is possible to foresee relevant requirements of the application domain when building the model. The degree in how far requirements cannot be foreseen may be captured by the complexity of the application domain. Then, a basic estimation of the overall costs of reuse in relation to the complexity can be drawn. Figure 20 gives a brief insight.

The derivation of costs reflects that configuration is best in situations that can be foreseen rather clearly. Then, the easily adapting benefits comes into play and may rather compensate

Figure 20. Estimated derivation of costs reuse driven by design principles in relation to complexity of the modeling situation

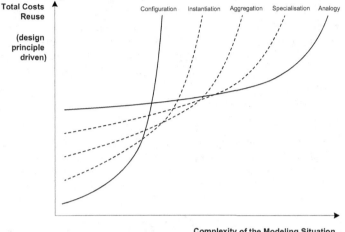

the efforts of designing variants. However, with growing complexity, either the costs of design explode or the models tend to cover the relevant cases too little and are, therefore, inadequate. Analogy, on the contrary, causes relatively high costs in situations that are characterised by low complexity. This is because of the generally high costs of design with reuse that are not justified by the degree of complexity. Although with growing complexity, analogy appears to be of raising efficiency. In addition, there might even come a degree from which analogy might be the only reasonable way of reusing artifacts.

Due to the great variety of modeling situations, a selective use of multiple design principles in reference modeling seems to be most adequate. Apart from choosing one principle for a modeling project that appears to be most suitable, also combinations of principles can be aimed at.

- **Model-specific combination:** The application domain of the model may consist of areas that show different characteristics with respect to the appropriate design principle. The level of complexity serves as an example: When modeling a retailing system, core processes may be rather standardised whereas additional processes for special cooperation can hardly be foreseen. In these cases, the entire reference model can be structured in partial models each applying special design principles.

- **Aspect-specific combination:** Also within a single representation of a model, the complexity of the modeling situation might differ with respect to special aspects of the model. Even in models with a rather high average complexity, for example, there are mostly some elements that can well be standardised, like those describing account characteristics and posting services. For these cases also, a combination of design principles within one representation of a model may be useful. Rules for the combination have to support the consistency of the model.

- **Time-specific combination:** Design principles may also be combined in time during the entire value chain of modeling. Opposed to configurative reference modeling, the principles can either support the application or the design of the reference model. First, the principles may be used in order to make further adaptations to a model that has been applied by configuration. Second, the principles serve as well to deliver reusable models that can be composed and adapted (Mili, et al., 1995, pp. 552-557) in the design of configurative reference models. For some applications, these techniques may as well be used in order to adapt the reference model in the field of application right away. In Figure 21, these situations are specified in more detail including the preconditions for time-specific combination.

Applying an appropriate mix of design principles might significantly contribute to both efficiency and effectiveness of reference modeling.

Conclusion

With this chapter, new design principles have been introduced to reference modeling. In particular, the principles of instantiation, aggregation, specialisation and analogy are supplied offering alternatives to principle of configuration that have been focussed on so far. The extended set of design principles provides greater flexibility in reference modeling. This also contributes to the evolution of models. New design principles allow the design of specialised fragments of models (e.g., by analogy) in order to combine them (e.g., by aggregation or instantiation) and to adopt them (e.g., by specialisation). Due to an increasing exchange of models, particularly positive effects on the model quality can be expected. Consequently, either configurative reference models may be fostered or part-models may be combined and adapted directly in the application domain. Especially with respect to an increasing dissemination of component-based and service-oriented information systems, this may be a promising means for future reference modeling.

References

Alexander, C., Ishikawa, S., & Silverstein, M. (1977). *A pattern language*. New York.

Axenath, B., Kindler, E., & Rubin, V. (2005). *An open and formalism independent meta-model for business processes*. Paper presented at the First International Workshop on Business Process Reference Models (BPRM'05), Nancy, France.

Becker, J., Delfmann, P., Dreiling, A., Knackstedt, R., & Kuropka, D. (2004). *Configurative process modeling: Outlining an approach to increased business process model usability*. Paper presented at the Proceedings of the 2004 Information Resources Management Association Conference, New Orleans, LA.

Becker, J., & Schütte, R. (2004). *Retail information systems (in German)* (2. vollst. überarb., erw. u. akt. Aufl. ed.). Frankfurt a. M.

Chen, P. P.-S. (1976). The entity-relationship model: Toward a unified view of data. *ACM Transactions on Database Systems, 1*(1), 9-36.

Coad, P., North, D., & Mayfield, M. (1997). *Object models: Strategies, patterns, and applications*. NJ: Yourdon Press.

Coad, P., & Yourdan, E. (1991). *Object oriented analysis* (2nd ed.). Saddle Brook, NJ: Prentice Hall.

Coase, R. H. (1937). The nature of the firm. *Economica, 4* (11), 386-405.

Conradi, R., & Westfechtel, B. (1998). Version models for software configuration management. *ACM Computing Surveys (CSUR), 30*(2), 232-282.

Cox, B. (1990). Planning the software industrial revolution. *IEEE Software, 7*(8), 25-33.

D'Souza, D. (2000). Relating components and enterprise integration: Part 1. *JOOP, 13*(1), 40-42.

Fettke, P., & Loos, P. (2003). Classification of reference models: A methodology and its application. *Information Systems and e-Business Management, 1*(1), 35-53.

Fowler, M. (1997). *Analysis patterns: Reusable object models*. Menlo Park, CA: Addison Wesley.

Gamma, E., Helm, R., Johnson, R., & Vlissides, J. (1995). *Design patterns: Elements of reusable object-oriented design*. Menlo Park, CA: Addison-Wesley.

George, W. T. C., & Heineman, T. (2001). *Component-based software engineering: Putting the pieces together*. New York.

Gomaa, H. (1995). Domain modeling methods and environments. *ACM SIGSOFT Software Engineering Notes, 20*(SI), 256-258.

Hay, D. C. (1996). *Data model patterns: Conventions of thought*. New York: Dorset House Publishing.

Huschens, J., & Rumpold-Preining, M. (2006). IBM insurance application architecture (IAA): An overview of the insurance business architecture. In P. Bernus, K. Mertins, & G. Schmidt (Eds.), *Handbook on architectures of information systems* (2nd ed., pp. 669-692). Berlin: Springer-Verlag.

Jones, T. C. (1984). Reusability in programming, a survey of the state of the art. *IEEE Transactions on Software Engineering, 10*(5), 488-493.

Kang, K., C., Kim, S., Lee, J., Kim, K., Shin, E., & Huh, M. (1998). FORM: A feature-oriented reuse method with domain-specific reference architectures. *Annals of Software Engineering, 5*, 143-168.

Karagiannis, D., & Kühn, H. (2002). *Metamodelling platforms*. Paper presented at the Proceedings of the Third International Conference EC-Web, September 2-6, 2002, LNCS 2455, Dexa, Aix-en-Provence, France.

Karhinen, A., Ran, A., & Tallgren, T. (1997). *Configuring designs for reuse*. Paper presented at the Proceedings of the 19th International Conference on Software Engineering, Boston.

Keller, G., Nüttgens, M., & Scheer, A.-W. (1992). Semantische Prozeßmodellierung auf der Grundlage Ereignisgesteuerter Prozeßketten (EPK). *Veröffentlichungen des Instituts für Wirtschaftsinformatik der Universität des Saarlandes,* (89).

Kittlaus, H.-B., & Krahl, D. (2006). The SIZ banking data Model. In P. Bernus, K. Mertins, & G. Schmidt (Eds.), *Handbook on architectures of information systems* (2nd ed., pp. 723-743). Berlin: Springer-Verlag.

Kruchten, P. (2003). *The rational unified process: An introduction* (3rd ed.). Boston.

McIlroy, M. D. (1968). Mass produced software components. In P. Naur & B. Randell (Eds.), *Software Engineering, Report on a Conference by the NATO Science Committee* (pp. 138-150). Brussels: NATO Scientific Affaris Division.

Meinhardt, S., & Popp, K. (2006). Configuring business application systems. In P. Bernus, K. Mertins, & G. Schmidt (Eds.), *Handbook on architectures of information systems* (2nd ed., pp. 705-721). Berlin: Springer-Verlag.

Melton, R., & Garlan, D. (1997). *Architectural unification.* Paper presented at the Proceedings of the 1997 conference of the Centre for Advanced Studies on Collaborative research, Toronto, Ontario, Canada.

Mili, A., Fowler, S., Gottumukkala, R., & Zhang, L. (2000). *An integrated cost model for software reuse.* Paper presented at the Proceedings of the ACM, ICSE 2000, Limerick, Ireland.

Mili, H., Mili, A., Yacoub, S., & Addy, E. (2002). *Reuse-based software engineering.* New York.

Mili, H., Mili, F., & Mili, A. (1995). Reusing software: Issues and research directions. *IEEE Transactions on Software Engineering, 21*(6), 528-562.

Peterson, A. S. (1991). Coming to terms with software reuse terminology: A model-based approach. *SIGSOFT Softw. Eng. Notes, 16*(2), 45-51.

Raumbaugh, J., Blaha, M., Premerlani, W., Eddy, F., & Lorensen, W. (1991). *Object-oriented modeling and design.* Englewood Cliffs: Prentice Hall.

Recker, J., Rosemann, M., van der Aalst, W. M. P., & Mendling, J. (2005). *On the syntax of reference model configuration.* Paper presented at the First International Workshop on Business Process Reference Models (BPRM'05), Nancy, France.

Remme, M. (1995). *Systematic development of informations systems using standardised process particles.* Paper presented at the 3rd European Conference on Information Systems—ECIS '95, Athens, Greece.

Rumbaugh, J., Jacobson, I., & Booch, G. (2004). *The unified modeling language reference manual* (2nd ed.). Addison-Wesley Longman.

Scheer, A.-W. (1994). *Business process engineering: Reference models for industrial enterprises.* New York: Springer-Verlag.

Scheer, A.-W., & Nüttgens, M. (2000). ARIS architecture and reference models for business process management. In W. M. P. van der Aalst, J. Desel, & A. Oberweis (Eds.), *Business process managemen: Models,techniques, and empirical studies* (pp. 376-389). Berlin: Springer.

Slater, P. (1995). Output from generic packages. *ACM SIGAda Ada Letters, XV*(3), 76-79.

Spanoudakis, G., & Constantopoulos, P. (1993). *Similarity for analogical software reuse: A conceptual modelling approach.* Paper presented at the Proceedings of Advanced Information Systems Engineering.

Szyperski, C. (1998). *Component software. Beyond object-oriented programming* (Vol. 2). New York: ACM Press and Addison-Wesley.

Thomas, O. (2005). *Understanding the term reference model in information system research.* Paper presented at the First International Workshop on Business Process Reference Models (BPRM'05), Nancy, France.

van der Aalst, W. M. P., Dreiling, A., Gottschalk, F., Rosemann, M., & Jansen-Vullers, M. H. (2005). *Configurable process models as a basis for reference modeling.* Paper presented at the First International Workshop on Business Process Reference Models (BPRM'05), Nancy, France.

vom Brocke, J. (2003). *Reference modelling, towards collaborative arrangements of design processes.* Berlin: Springer. [in German]

vom Brocke, J., & Buddendick, C. (2004). Organisation theory in reference modelling: Requirements and recommendation on the basis of transaction cost economics . *Wirtschaftsinformatik, 46*(5), 341-352. [in German]

Williamson, O. E. (1985). *The economic institutions of capitalism.* New York: Tree Press.

Endnote

[1]   As the special subject of "reference modeling" has until now been discussed predominantly in German literature, some sources that are considered in this chapter are written in German. Apart from major pieces, reviews on the subject's works have been referred to as far as possible. In addition, the reuse-oriented concept of reference modeling that is introduced in this chapter gives way to a discussion of the subject against the background of international works in the field of reusing artifacts in information systems.

Section II

Reference Modeling
Methods

Chapter IV

Process Model for an Empirically Grounded Reference Model Construction

Frederik Ahlemann, Universität Osnabrück, Germany

Heike Gastl, Univerität Osnabrück, Germany

Abstract

This chapter stresses the importance of integrating empirical evidence in the construction process of reference models. With reference to the authors' underlying epistemological beliefs, requirements for an empirically grounded process model are derived. Based on a literature review of existing process models and experience gained from three research projects, an advanced process model is proposed in order to provide concrete instructions that show how these requirements can be met. Real-life examples from completed and ongoing research projects are continuously integrated so as to contribute to the practicability of the proposed model for the reader.

Introduction

In recent years, reference modeling has gained increasing relevance in information systems research and information systems development. The benefit of reference modeling is documented by a growing number of researchers working in this area and the large number of reference models that are available (Fettke & Loos, 2004a, pp. 17, 30). At the same time, a differentiation of reference modeling techniques can be observed, which explains the wide spectrum of recommendations and tools available for reference modeling (cf., for example, Rosemann & Schütte, 1999; Becker et al., 2001; Becker et al., 2002). According to Schütte (1998, p. 69), a reference information model is defined as a construction created by a modeler who declares universal elements and relationships of a system as a recommendation so that a center of reference is created. In this context, reference models are used for the design of information systems, and are typically documented using semi-formal or formal languages.

To a large extent, however, the analysis of the hitherto developed reference modeling techniques and methods shows a disregard for empirical inquiries as the basis for reference modeling. The authors of the well-established process models for reference modeling indeed refer to the necessity to integrate potential reference model users and domain experts into the construction process. The question of how this integration can be brought about, however, is typically left unanswered (Fettke & Loos, 2004a, p. 20).

Moreover, the construction process is normally not documented in reference modeling projects. It does not become clear how the modeler arrives at his or her models. Very often, the empirical evidence for the reference model construction is not properly recorded. This lack of documentation and empirical evidence makes it difficult to validate the research results. Furthermore, the discourse on the research results and the incremental refinement and improvement of reference models is unnecessarily complicated (e.g., Scheer, 1995; Becker & Schütte, 1996; Schlagheck, 2000).

This chapter therefore proposes a process model for empirically grounded and validatable reference model construction and documentation. This process model is derived from existing research results and has already been validated in three reference model construction projects. It contains instructions on how potential model users and domain experts can be involved in the construction process and how the construction results can be documented so that a high degree of intelligibility and validatability can be achieved. Moreover, it contains recommendations on how to set up advanced empirical research designs (e.g., with regard to the necessary number of domain experts involved and the planning and conducting of interviews).

The use of this process model (and process models for the construction of reference information models in general) has several benefits: First and foremost, it reduces the effort and costs required to develop a proprietary research process and research design, respectively. Furthermore, the user of a process model can profit from the experience of those who have developed it. This leads to higher research quality and reduced risk of project failure. Of course, a structured and well-elaborated research process also facilitates comprehensible and reproducible research results.

The chapter is structured as follows: In the first section, the state of the research on reference modeling is analyzed with respect to process models that comprise recommendations for the integration of potential model users or domain experts. Subsequently, common requirements for an empirically grounded and reliable research design are explained. These requirements are then used to elaborate an advanced process model. At the end of the chapter, the findings are summarized and some remaining research questions are discussed.

Existing Process Models for Referencing Information Modeling

In the following, the prevalent process models for reference modeling are introduced and reviewed with regard to the degree to which they integrate aspects of empirical evidence in the construction process. Provision of a detailed introduction of representation techniques and tool support options is avoided, since these research fields play a subordinate role with regard to the question of the empirical foundation of reference model construction (vom Brocke, 2003, p. 95; Fettke & Loos, 2004a).

In the field of reference modeling, process models have a twofold focus on construction and application processes. The term "construction process" pertains to all activities which are relevant to the development of a reference model. The term "application process" refers to all the steps required for developing enterprise-specific information models on the basis of reference models (Fettke & Loos, 2004a, p. 18). In the existing approaches, both construction and application processes are usually integrated into one process model (cf., e.g., Schütte, 1998; Schlagheck, 2000; Becker et al., 2002). Since the focus of this work lies on the construction process, aspects of application will be neglected in the remainder of the chapter.

Although a wide variety of process models exists, all representations can be reduced to a similar basic structure (vom Brocke 2003, p. 133; Fettke & Loos, 2004a, p. 18). In analogy with systems engineering, the overall construction process is based on a cyclic structure to allow for model corrections on preceding construction stages via feedback-loops (Schütte, 1998, p. 187; Schlagheck, 2000, p. 77). Four commonly presented core process steps can be identified:

- **Problem definition:** At the beginning of the construction process a project's key data are to be specified. These data include a definition of scope, a brief outline of the problem domain, a description of the intended purposes of use, as well as the selection of the modeling language and further modeling conventions (e.g., glossary including technical terms; Schütte, 1998, p. 189; Schlagheck, 2000, p. 79).
- **Construction of a frame of reference:** The starting point for the modeling activities is the development of a frame of reference, the major purpose of which is to support navigation within the problem domain. This is sometimes also called conceptual information system architecture, and can be regarded as a highly condensed version of the reference model on a high level of abstraction. An early start in the development of the frame of reference in parallel with the problem definition can be advantageous, since it can help with the definition of the project's scope (Schlagheck, 2000, p. 79).

With regard to the core construction phase, the frame of reference has two functions: On the one hand, it supports a systematic identification of single model elements; on the other hand, the gradual processing of its structure guarantees the completeness of the finished reference model (Schlagheck, 2000, p. 81).

- **Core Construction:** The reference model is gradually refined on the basis of the frame of reference and the selected modeling language.

- **Validation:** Finally, the finished reference model is examined with regard to consistency and the fulfillment of user requirements (Schlagheck, 2000, p. 77; Frank, 2000; Fettke & Loos, 2003).

Substantial differences between existent process models result from different emphases. The process models created by Becker et al. (2002), Rosemann and Schütte (1999) or Schlagheck (2000) can be taken as examples. Becker et al. (2002) have developed a process model for configurative reference modeling to satisfy special requirements of variant management. Hence, the core issue of this approach is to find out which mechanisms have to be integrated into the construction process in order to facilitate the subsequent adjustment of reference models to specific application contexts. Special requirements addressing subjectivity-management are considered in the process model for multi-perspective reference modeling by Rosemann and Schütte (1999). Schlagheck's (2000) process model is finally characterized by transferring concepts of the object-oriented paradigm to the construction process. The guiding idea is to increase reusability, expandability and, thus, the flexibility of reference models.

Approaches to integrate empirical evidence into the construction process are generally recognizable in those parts of the process models where the importance of multiple user participation is stressed. Schütte (1998, p. 184), for example, emphasizes the participation of users in the problem definition phase in order to avoid reference models being constructed for problems that are not recognized as such by the users. Both Rosemann and Schütte (1999, pp. 28, 38) and Schlagheck (2000, p. 83) emphasize the participation of users in the core construction phase, as the users are the subject-matter experts of the problem domain. With regard to the validation phase, the authors commonly recommend an intensive exchange with users as a quality-assurance and thus an acceptance-heightening measure. Detailed recommendations on which persons should be involved as experts are included in the above-mentioned work on multi-perspective reference modeling. According to this approach, people should be selected based on their ability to adopt a specific perspective that corresponds to one of the intended model uses. In effect, all perspectives should be sufficiently represented by the group of users involved (Schütte, 1998, p. 201; Rosemann & Schütte, 1999, p. 25).

Although the existing process models recommend user participation, there is insufficient information on how participation should be arranged while taking into account economic criteria. For example, there are no concrete statements about the number of users who should be involved, nor about suitable research methods. Moreover, existing process models are lacking instructions regarding how the results of user participation and their effects on the model construction should be documented. Since the quality of documentation affects the inter-subjective comprehension and validatability of research results, process models should pay more attention to recommendations that allow for the necessary level of quality. A corresponding quality framework, especially for reference information models, has been developed by Schütte (1998). Other approaches are discussed by Maier (1996) or Krogstie, et al. (1995).

Derivation of Requirements for a Process Model Based on Emperical Evidence

Starting from a moderate constructivist epistemology that stresses subjectivity in perception, this work is based on a consent-oriented concept of truth (Lorenz, 1995, p. 599). Accordingly, a common perception of reality among observers of a system requires them to exchange and discuss the results of their individual cognitive processes. In a methodically controlled way, they are able to develop complex suggestions for human action by means of constructive criticism and purpose-means discussions. A declaration is considered to be truthful if each member of the group of experts grants their acceptance (Becker et al., 2004, p. 8). The ultimate proof is not striven for (Schütte, 1998, p. 21; Kneer, 1999, p. 300).

Applying this concept to the field of reference modeling raises the claim that all propositions contained in a reference model are to be scrutinized with regard to their acceptance in a group of subject-matter experts. Grounding a reference model's validation on an empirical foundation becomes an imperative. In this context it needs to be clarified which persons can be considered subject-matter experts and how many of them need to be involved to satisfy a certain degree of universality (total universality cannot be achieved), while taking into account aspects of economic efficiency. Moreover, in order for experts to be able to discourse on a reference model's proposition, the inter-subjective comprehensibility of these propositions first needs to be guaranteed. First, to fulfill this prerequisite, the reference model documentation must be based on a common linguistic system, since the exchange of linguistic artifacts ultimately presents the foundation for every validation effort (Becker et al., 2004, p. 11). Second, the explication of the construction process on the grounds of which the reference model was obtained contributes to inter-subjective comprehension. Third, single reference model elements should be linked with corresponding theoretical and empirical references. Finally, the validation process itself, namely the discourse and its implications for the modeling process, needs to be documented appropriately.

The Process Model

The suggested process model for empirically grounded reference modeling consists of five phases. Although these are to be dealt with sequentially, they may contain cyclic sub-processes (Figure 1).

The *first phase* covers the planning of the reference model. This phase is concerned with defining the subject matter of the reference model, defining which methods to use, orga-

Figure 1. Process model at a glance

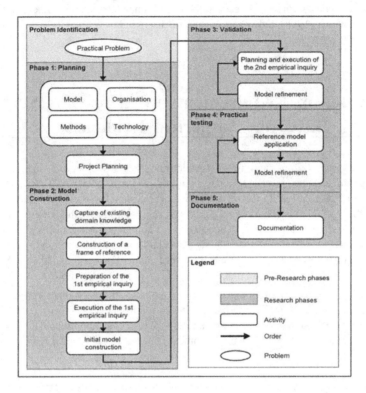

nizing the project and choosing the required software tools. The *second phase* comprises the construction of the reference model based on the know-how of selected subject-matter experts. The *third phase* is intended for the validation of the results. The *fourth phase* involves testing the reference model by applying it to solve a practical problem. Complete documentation is carried out in the *fifth phase*.

While the first two phases are designed to set up and construct the reference model, the following phases are meant to "stabilize" and refine it. On the one hand, this is achieved by discussing and enhancing the model in a discourse with the subject-matter experts. On the other hand, the reference model should ideally be used in an information system project in order to confirm its applicability and practical benefits.

The process model largely complies with common suggestions for qualitative research designs in systems analysis and social sciences. Guiding ideas can be found in Krallmann et al. (2002, p. 49) or Patton (2002).

In the following, the process phases are discussed in detail. The explanations are illustrated by examples from three different reference modeling projects that have been undertaken by the authors of this chapter: one project concerns the construction of a reference model for enterprise-wide project management (EPM project), the second deals with enterprise-wide e-learning management in large corporate groups (EL project) and the third is a universal information model for project management data (PMD project).

Phase 1: Planning the Reference Modeling Project

The first phase of the process model covers the planning of the reference modelling project. According to vom Brocke (2003, p. 52), four different aspects of reference modelling can be distinguished: (a) the model itself, (b) the methods used to create the reference model, (c) the (software and hardware) tools deployed, and (d) the organization of the reference modelling. The aspects that need to be planned in the first phase will be described below.

Model-Related Planning

Problem Definition

In the first place, model-related planning stands for the clear and precise definition of the reference model domain. Schütte (1998, p. 184) refers to this as problem definition, and postulates an agreement between the model creator and future model users so that errors of the third kind can be avoided.

The problem definition should be done in collaboration with domain experts to prevent such errors. The model creator and domain experts initiate a collective discourse on the definition and characterization of the problem to be solved by the reference information model (Schütte, 1998, p. 185).

The problem definition is typically conducted in the form of workshops that apply advanced moderation and creativity techniques by surveys or Delphi studies. A consensus on the problem can be stated if (a) each expert has accepted the documented problem definition as valid, and (b) the development of a reference model is regarded as a promising means to solve the problem.

Inter-Model Relationships

This aspect is especially relevant with respect to the increasing number of standards and norms that are developed and publicized by professional associations and official institutions for standardization (e.g., DIN, EN and ISO) and are frequently presented as models. The least of these norms are oriented toward the design of information systems. However, they need to be considered during the reference model construction process, since they often provide basic definitions and define requirements for information systems. Consequently, reference information models that are compatible with such standards and norms are very often regarded as high quality. Compliance with standards and norms can only be proved by a direct mapping of reference information model elements to standard or norm elements. Such mapping can be established easily when relevant standards and norms are identified at an early stage of the model construction. Two consequences therefore exist for the planning of a reference model project: (a) relevant standards and norms have to be identified; (b) it needs to be investigated whether a proof of compatibility is necessary.

- **Example A:** For the EPM project, the standards of the Project Management Institute (PMI) were of special relevance. PMI's project management body of knowledge (PMBOK) is a standard that is accepted worldwide and that consists of numerous definitions and elementary process descriptions. It was therefore desirable to prove compatibility with PMBOK. This was achieved by mapping all PMBOK elements to EPM elements.

- **Example B:** In the EL project, e-learning standards like SCORM play an important role. Data structures describing learning materials are designed to be compatible with this standard.

Method-Related Planning

The method-related aspect covers the selection of appropriate problem-solving and model representation techniques. A problem-solving technique consists of rules that affect the temporal and logical sequence of tasks to accomplish the model construction (vom Brocke, 2003, p. 60). Representation techniques comprise rules that affect the representation of the construction result (vom Brocke, 2003, p. 61).

The process model presented in this chapter can be interpreted as a problem-solving technique. It is used to control the model construction by specifying how the interaction between model creators and model users, or subject-matter experts, has to be arranged. Usage of this process model does not preclude the application of other problem solution techniques (e.g., such as for the construction of configurable reference models). Thus, it can be said that this process model is a partial problem-solving technique that needs to be complemented by other techniques for special purposes.

In each case, a representation technique has to be selected in addition to the process described here. It is possible to choose from a large repertoire of modelling languages and concepts. The most common are the unified modelling language (OMG, 2003a, 2003b), event-driven process chains (Keller et al., 1992) and entity relationship models (Chen, 1976).

- **Example:** The UML was used as the representation technique in the EPM, the EL and the PMD projects. For each of the projects, a specific sub-set of UML 2 was defined that was considered adequate for the project scope and environment. For instance, the modelling skills of the subject-matter experts were taken into consideration.

Organizational Planning

Organizational planning covers the definition of the subject-matter experts who take part in the model construction and the coordination of construction activities. For instance, organizational planning leads to the elaboration of rules for the synchronization of simultaneous modelling activities when several persons or organizations are involved (vom Brocke, 2003, p. 91).

The process model presented here describes to a large extent how the reference modelling process has to be organized. However, a process model will rarely be used completely and without modifications in real modelling projects. This is because specific circumstances of the problem domain or the project environment may require adjustments. For this reason, organizational planning (a) requires the adaptation of a process model or rather the definition of a research design and (b) its proper documentation.

- **Example:** In the EPM project, the reference model construction was not only based on interviews with subject-matter experts. Since there are numerous commercial software applications available for the problem domain, the research design also contained the analysis of these products. It included a review of the database schema as well as an examination of the user interface and the corresponding documentation.

Technological Planning

Technology-related planning deals with technologies supporting the construction process (mainly software systems). Here, tools have to be developed or purchased, and media have to be defined to create, store and process the reference information models. CASE tools (computer-aided software engineering) play an important role. Such tools can help to automate some activities related to the reference information model (e.g., the generation of documentation). Furthermore, they support specific problem-solving and representation techniques, and can hence streamline the construction process (vom Brocke, 2003, p. 88).

Technological planning requires decisions on what software and hardware systems are to be used during reference model construction. With regard to the process model presented here, three types of systems in particular have to be taken into consideration: (a) modelling tools or CASE-Tools for the model construction, (b) text processing systems for the documentation of the reference model and (c) audio systems for the recording and analysis of subject-matter expert interviews.

- **Example:** In the EPM project, three different CASE tools were thoroughly tested before the reference modelling commenced. It could be shown that only two tools were stable and scalable enough to handle the number of diagrams necessary. Of these two, only one offered the necessary functionality to create UML 2 diagrams according to the needs of the project.

Project Planning

In addition to the four planning aspects described above, reference information modelling initiatives, like any other initiatives, require classic project planning. This covers at least work breakdown structure planning, resource planning, scheduling, risk and cost planning. Project planning is influenced by preceding decisions regarding models, methods, organization and technology.

- **Example:** Our experience with the EPM, EL and PMD projects shows that the devel-opment of an empirically grounded and completely documented reference information model for a medium-complex problem domain (like e-learning management or project management) on a medium level of abstraction (e.g., 90 UML classes and 10 activity diagrams with 100 actions) requires an effort of approximately 1.5-2 man-years.

Phase 2: Model Construction

Capture of Existing Domain Knowledge

The model construction should always begin with an analysis of current domain knowledge. On the one hand, this is to make sure that a reference modelling project makes sense and to ascertain that such a reference model is not already available. On the other hand, existing research work can be incorporated into the reference model construction. In this context, scientific publications, practice reports, case studies or product descriptions can be used as appropriate sources. It is important to (a) identify, (b) catalogue and (c) prioritize these sources.

- **Example:** In the EPM project, we were able to profit from a large number of publica-tions on project management processes. These publications allowed us to construct a first version of the reference model without having to interact with the subject-matter experts, who were subsequently involved for a discourse on this first version of the model.

Construction of a Frame or Reference

A first analysis of the problem domain is achieved by constructing a frame of reference. This frame of reference represents a high-level perspective on the problem domain, and is used for structuring the expert interviews, the reference model documentation and the reference model itself. It can be used for navigating the problem domain and is typically the result of a deductive, theoretical breakdown of the subject matter into smaller sub-units that are further refined and described in the reference model. The structuring is done using criteria that preferably have a high degree of clearness, intelligibility and comprehensibility on the one hand and practical and theoretical relevance on the other. Typical criteria for structuring the problem domain are, for example:

- A differentiation of static (data) and dynamic aspects (processes, functions) of the reference model (e.g., Becker & Schütte, 1996, p. 10; Scheer, 2001, p. 33),
- A breakdown according to processes (e.g., Ahlemann, 2002, p. 31),
- A differentiation of management levels (e.g., Ahlemann, 2002, p. 28), or

Figure 2. Frame of reference in the EPM project

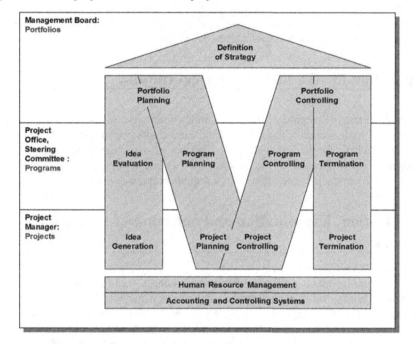

- A differentiation of different levels of abstractions regarding information technology, such as a specification, design and implementation level (e.g., Scheer, 2001, p. 38).

The deductive construction of the frame of reference needs to be followed by an inductive, empirical validation. Here, the structure of the frame of reference is mapped and compared to real structures. This verification can be carried out on the basis of existing case studies and in a discourse with domain experts. If sufficient existing research results are available, a literature-based verification should be undertaken first. A discourse with experts should then be the next step. The frame of reference should be examined with regard to the following aspects:

- **Completeness:** Are all aspects of the problem domain represented?
- **Disjoint elements:** Are the elements of the frame of reference disjointed or do they overlap?
- **Comprehensibility:** Is the frame of reference intuitively comprehensible? Can it be understood in a short period of time? Although this is not an obligatory quality criterion for high-quality research, a high degree of comprehensibility is very useful for the successive discourse with domain experts. It increases the *acceptance* of the project results.

- **Example:** In the EPM project the so-called M-Model was developed as a frame of reference. The M-Model was completely derived from theoretical considerations and was discussed with researchers and practitioners before being used as the basis for empirical inquiries and the reference model construction.

Preparation for the First Empirical Inquiry

Preparation for the first empirical inquiry can commence as soon as the first version of the frame of reference is available. The first inquiry is carried out to capture the experts' domain knowledge as a basis for the first cycle of the reference model construction. Primarily, two tasks need to be accomplished: (a) the identification, examination and selection of interview partners, and (b) the preparation of an interview guide or questionnaire.

Identification, Examination and Selection of Interview Partners

As a prerequisite for gaining interview partners, it is necessary to describe the reference model project briefly and to explain the role the interview partner is going to play in the construction process. The document should also contain details on how the interview partner can prepare himself for the survey. It can be delivered to the interview partner for general information in advance so that time-consuming explanations can be avoided in the first meeting. In some projects, it has also proven useful to give the potential interview partner an incentive for his participation. A typical incentive is to grant free access to the research results (e.g., by sending a free copy of the reference model documentation). In doing so, the interview partner can directly profit from his or her support of the project; he or she can use the results of the project for his or her own purposes.

Generally, there are two possible approaches of making contact with a potential subject-matter expert: On the one hand, (mass) media (e.g., journals or newsletters) can be used to contact a large number of experts anonymously. On the other hand, an existing network of contacts can be used to identify such experts. The latter approach, which is called *chain sampling,* has the advantage of being very economical and efficient (Patton, 2002, p. 237). One disadvantage, however, is the dependence on a contact network. In contrast, the first approach offers the opportunity to gain a much larger number of interview partners. Furthermore, it is guaranteed that the interview results are not affected by personal relations to the reference model creator. The drawback, however, is that higher costs are incurred to gain interview partners.

In order to decrease the risk of unsuccessful interviews, it is recommended to contact the interview partner by telephone prior to the first meeting. This is done in order to ascertain whether the contact partner can really be regarded as a subject-matter expert with knowledge that is useful for the reference model construction. The frame of reference can be helpful here: The potential interview partner is asked to outline his or her experience and domain knowledge for each element of the frame of reference. The resulting information can be used both in order to decide whether an interview is generally promising and to find out which elements of the frame of reference have to be discussed in the subsequent interview. It is reasonable to concentrate on those parts of the frame of reference in which the interview partner is most experienced and has most knowledge.

The initial empirical data collection should comprise as many interviews as necessary in order to identify reoccurring processes and data structures. It is advisable to ask different experts from the same company so that different perspectives regarding the problem domain can be included. Usually 10 to 15 case studies with one to three interviews each need to be carried out.

- **Example:** In the EPM project, 13 experts were interviewed and 28 software systems were analyzed. In the EL project, 16 experts from 11 organizations served as interview partners. In both projects, the experts were gained using chain sampling.

Preparation of an Interview Guide and Questionnaire

The preparation of an interview guide or questionnaire is essential to obtain a structured interview. It guarantees a comprehensible and goal-oriented interview process covering all necessary aspects of the problem domain.

We suggest an interview guide with at least three sections:

1. The first section covers the interview partner's working environment, his or her experience and general understanding of the problem. This section usually contains closed questions. It includes general information about the interviewee's organization (information about organizational structure, the governance structure, the interviewee's department, a job description, etc.), about basic terms and definitions (are fundamental terms defined equally or similarly?) and about his or her problem consciousness (which concrete problems, challenges and critical points does the interviewee perceive?).

2. The second section deals with their detailed domain knowledge and specific experience. The questions asked here are typically open. The second part includes questions regarding the problem domain and the design of the reference model. The reference model itself is not discussed here, however. Instead, the interviewee's domain knowledge and the experience he or she has in their working environment are of interest. In this context, the frame of reference can be used to structure the interview. Ideally, each element of the frame of reference is discussed with regard to processes, corresponding data needed or produced, exception rules, organizational competencies, etc. According to the ARIS-concept, the following aspects can be brought up for discussion:

    - **Functions/processes:** Which activities are carried out in what order?
    - **Organization:** Who is responsible for these activities?
    - **Data:** Which input data are needed? Which output data are produced?

If a validation of the frame of reference has not yet taken place, this can be brought up during the interview. The results can be used for an incremental improvement of the frame of reference.

3.   General questions regarding the interviewee's person are the subject of the third section, where his or her experience background is of special interest. It can be determined by discussing curriculum vitae, past project experience and any advanced training programs attended.

The interview partner should receive the interview guide/questionnaire a few days prior to the interview date so he or she has the opportunity to prepare. Sending the interview guide long before the date, however, often leads to improper and incomplete preparation, since the expert may have forgotten about the interview guide by the time of the interview.

The process model described here includes two interview rounds. While the objective of the first interview round is to collect basic data for the initial reference model construction, the second round is meant for discussing and improving the reference model. All interview partners should participate in both the first and second round, since an analysis of the results of the second round is easier if the interviewee and their organization are already known.

•   **Example:** In the EL project, all interviewees are met twice. The aim of the first meeting was to learn about the specific processes and structures of the interviewee's organization. The data collected are used to create a preliminary version of the reference model. The second interview round, which is carried out six months later, is characterized by an in-depth discourse on the model created.

Execution of the First Empirical Inquiry

After completion of the preparatory phases, the interviews can be executed using the interview guide/questionnaire. We recommend recording the interviews, since it is difficult to conduct the interview and write down the results simultaneously.

After the interview, the results can be transcribed and summarized. If necessary, the results may need to be dealt with anonymously. If possible, simple information models on a high level of abstraction can be used to illustrate the domain knowledge captured. This eases the initial construction of the reference model.

In either case, documentation of the interview results has to be approved by the interviewee. Written authorization is useful for later publication. Since authorization may take awhile, we recommend requesting it as soon as possible.

•   **Example:** In the EPM project, the interviews were carried out within a period of six months. The last authorization for publication was given 12 months after the last interview.

Initial Model Construction

The domain knowledge captured in the first inquiry is now used for the initial construction of the reference model. For this purpose, the model creator can apply some of the well-known problem solution and representation techniques (e.g., configurative reference modelling techniques).

The model construction is based on five sources of data:

- **Interview results:** The model construction can be based on specific findings of the first inquiry.
- **Standards and norms:** As mentioned above, standards and norms may play an important role in the construction of the reference model.
- **Existing research results:** A thorough review of any existing literature may reveal valuable research results that could be of use in the model construction.
- **Own domain knowledge:** In many cases, a reference model creator will already have profound domain knowledge that can be used in the reference model construction process.
- **Other data sources:** Sometimes other data sources are also available (e.g., in the EPM project, the analysis of commercial software products was also considered).

In order to facilitate the validation of the reference model, it is important to continuously document the construction process. We suggest immediately assigning empirical evidence to each new reference model element. This is basically achieved by mapping interview results or excerpts from literature to model elements. In doing so, other researchers, model creators or model users can easily reconstruct the reference model based on the empirical inquiries that have been carried out.

Phase 3: Validation

Planning and Execution of the Second Empirical Inquiry

Regarding the choice of the interview partners, it is recommended to involve the same persons who participated in the first interview round. The advantage of this procedure is that the interviewees' areas of expertise and organizational context are already known so that their respective statements can be more easily qualified with respect to each other. Another advantage is the reduction of interview planning effort, since the activities of initial contact and introducing the research project no longer apply. Finally, the second interview can be used to reconcile the minutes of the first interview, thus allowing a swift publication clearance. If a reconciliation of previous interview minutes is intended, the documentation should be made available to the interviewee well in advance for preparation purposes. The course of the interview should be structured accordingly into two main parts (i.e., settlement of documentation and validation of the refined reference model). In any case, the settlement process should be started as early as possible, since firm specific permission processes may cause delays.

A core issue to be determined in connection with the second interview round again regards the necessary number of interviewees. Since the process of constructing a reference model with the participation of different subjects cannot be compared with traditional quantitative empirical inquiry methods (e.g., based on a questionnaire), this issue cannot be resolved by means of corresponding calculations for computing the size of samples. Instead, this decision requires agreement on certain conditions, by the fulfillment of which the continuous cycle of discussing, correcting and refining the reference model can be terminated. This work follows the approach by Lincoln and Guba (1985, p. 234), who refrain from further interviews if insights gained from preceding interviews are diminishing. The approach being conveyed to the field of reference modelling implicates that the interview cycle terminates if the reference model stabilizes. On the occurrence of this situation, the conclusion is drawn that consent has been reached among subject-matter experts regarding the reference model's propositions. This procedure, however, also implies that additional interviewees need to be gained if no convergence of opinions is recognizable after having interviewed all interviewees in the first inquiry round.

As with the first interview round, for the benefit of a higher inter-subjective comprehension, the interviews should be recorded and subsequently transcribed. As an integral part of each interview's documentation, a list of model correction proposals is to be compiled. Again, all written documentation should be reconciled with and authorized by the respective partner before publication.

- **Example:** In the EPM project, 13 interviews were sufficient to "stabilize" the reference model. In the PMD project, 11 interviews proved to be sufficient to gain a consensus.

Model Refinement

Each single list of model correction proposals derived from an interview provides the basis for the revision or refinement of the reference model. A major challenge in this context is the evaluation of different suggestions with respect to each other. For example, before a correction is integrated it has to be determined whether the proposal can be characterized as being universally valid or whether it is tied to a specific corporate context and therefore not suitable for model refinement. Furthermore, it is possible that improvement suggestions made by different persons are quite contradictory. There are two main options to resolve such a situation: First, one proposal can be preferred to the other if the wealth of experience of one interviewee in this matter can be judged as significantly greater compared to the other. This evaluation will be substantially facilitated if the interviewee's experience background has already been detected in detail during the first interview round. The advantage of questioning the same interview partner twice becomes obvious. Second, it is possible to consider both suggestions by integrating configuration techniques.

In general, each incorporated model correction based on an interviewee's proposal should be denoted with the appropriate cross-reference to ensure a greater level of inter-subjective comprehension.

- **Example:** In the EPM project, an average of approximately five to ten suggestions for reference model corrections or refinements emerged in a two-hour interview with a subject-matter expert.

Phase 4: Practical Testing

Acceptance of a reference information model can be improved by a practical application. Furthermore, insights from this application can be used to further refine and improve the model.

Reference Model Application

In this phase, the reference model is used to solve a practical problem within an organization. This means that the reference model forms the basis of the design of an information or organizational system. In such a project, the reference model does not necessarily need to be used as a whole–very often only selected parts of the model are of relevance. The model creator should act as a consultant and accompany the project by helping to:

- Specify the organization's requirements
- Identify the relevant parts of the reference model
- Customize (configure) the reference model according to the organization's requirements

Following the completion of the project, the practical benefit of the reference model should be evaluated by both the model users and the model creator. The model creator is very likely to identify new limitations and deficiencies of the model that can be eliminated during a new incremental model refinement and improvement. In any case, model users should be asked how the weaknesses can be overcome in order to provide initial hints for the next model improvement.

- **Example:** The reference model resulting from the EPM project has already proved its applicability in several projects. It has been used in an organizational project for the definition of a standardized project initiation process, it served as the basis for the definition of software requirements and was also used as input for the PMD project.

Model Refinement

The results from the practical application form the basis of a new incremental refinement and improvement of the reference information model. Moreover, the experience gained can be used to develop a process model for the step-wise application and customization of the reference model. This facilitates subsequent reference model application projects for which the model creator will not be available as a consultant.

Phase 5: Documentation

Appropriate documentation of research results is a prerequisite for inter-subjective comprehension and validity, and thus a subject of great importance.

In previous reference modelling projects, the following documentation structure has proved valuable:

- **Description of construction process:** In order to evaluate the suitability of a reference model for a certain application setting, the user will stipulate which sources of knowledge and research methods from which the reference model has been developed. For this reason, the construction process should be delineated to a degree that is sufficient to be comprehended by the user along general lines.

- **Annotations of model elements:** Each model element represented by means of the chosen modelling language is to be clarified with annotations that include theoretical and empirical references. For example, if the design of a certain model element can be attributed to an interview outcome, that particular case study should be referred to in the corresponding annotation. In favor of a coherent flow of text, it is recommended to place references in footnotes.

- **Documentation of case studies:** Case study documentation should be made available in the appendix so that references to case studies are easily viewable (Figure 3). In this connection, it is important for the clearance of the respective interview partner to be obtained before publishing any documentation. Publication of the interview guide also presents part of a comprehensive case study documentation.

- **Table of model elements:** In the case of extensive reference models, the provision of a table of model elements in the appendix is recommended. The user can flexibly start navigating the model at any diagram because explanations about model elements that have already been introduced can easily be found and referred to via that table.

Figure 3. Excerpt from a case study documentation in the EPM project

---

C.4.   *Infineon Technologies AG*   *305*

C.4.4   Contributions to the Improvement and Refinement
of the Reference Model

The presentation and discussion of the reference model led to the
following suggestions for improvement:

- Even small projects should never be initiated without a check of
  strategy compliance. Otherwise there is the risk that large projects
  are split into several small projects in order to avoid the strategy
  check.
- The function "portfolio controlling" should also cover an
  organisational budget controlling.
- Ideas that can be approved immediately should not be implemented
  as a project but in the realm of normal line activities.
- ...

Conclusion

This chapter demonstrates how reference modelling projects can be based on an empirically grounded and verifiable process. The proposed process model represents an attempt to improve existing recommendations by:

- Proposing a research design for an inquiry that serves as the basis for the model construction,

- Showing how the inquiries can be planned and organized with the help of a frame of reference, interview guides and questionnaires,

- Giving advice on how many subject-matter experts are required to develop a reference information model, and

- Outlining how reference models can be documented so that their construction process is comprehensible.

The explication of the construction process, the documentation of empirical analyses and the mapping of model elements to empirical evidence allows the justification to use both the modelling of single model elements and the construction as a whole. Hence, it becomes easy to assess the quality of the resulting reference model.

The process model has already been tested in two reference model construction projects that were completed at the end of 2004 (EPM project) and at the end of 2005 (PMD project), respectively. In a revised version, the process model is currently being used for a further reference model project (EL project).

References

Ahlemann, F. (2002). *The M-model: A conceptual information system architecture for the planning, controlling and coordination of projects.* Research Report of the Chair for Business Administration/Organization and Information Systems. Osnabrück: University of Osnabrück [in German]

Becker, J., Delfmann, P., Knackstedt, R., & Kuropka, D. (2002). Configurative reference modelling. In J. Becker & R. Knackstedt (Eds.), *Knowledge management with reference models: Concepts for the eesign of software and organisational systems* (pp. 25-144). Heidelberg: Physica-Verlag. [in German]

Becker, J., Knackstedt, R., Kuropka, D., & Delfmann, P. (2001, November 1-3). Subjectivity management for reference modelling: Process model and tool concept. In *Referenz-modellierung 2001. 5. Fachtagung Neue Messe Dresden, 2. November 2001*, Katalog zur Tagung IFM, COMTEC, KnowTech, Dresden. [in German]

Becker, J., Niehaves, B., & Knackstedt, R. (2004). Framework for the epistemological positioning of reference modelling. In J. Becker & P. Delfmann (Eds.), *Referenz-modellierung. Grundlagen,techniken und domänenbezogene Anwendung* (pp. 1-17). Münster: Physica-Verlag. [in German]

Becker, J., & Schütte, R. (1996). *Retail information systems.* Landsberg, Lech: Verlag Moderne Industrie. ([in German]

Chen, P. P. (1976). The entity relationship model. Toward a unified view of data. *ACM Transactions on Database Systems, 1*, 9-36.

Fettke, P., & Loos, P. (2003). Classification of reference models: A methodology and its application. *Information Systems and E-Business Management, 1*(1), 35-53.

Fettke, P., & Loos, P. (2004a). *Reference modelling research. Long version of a paper* (Rep. No. 16). ISYM: *Information Systems & Management.* Mainz: Universität Mainz. [in German]

Frank, U. (2000). Design of a reference model for trading platforms in the Internet. *Tagungsband der fachtagung KnowTech (CD-ROM).* Leipzig. [in German].

Keller, G., Nüttgens, M., & Scheer, A.-W. (1992). *Semantic process models on the basis of event-driven process chains (EPC).* Veröffentlichungen des Instituts für wirtschafts-informatik. Heft 89. Saarbrücken: Universität Saarbrücken [in German]

Kneer, G. (1999). Constructivism. In P. Prechtl & F.P. Burkard (Eds.), *Metzler philosophie lexikon* (2nd ed., pp. 299-300). Stuttgart: Metzler. [in German]

Krallmann, H., Frank, H., & Gronau, N. (2002). *Systems analysis in enterprises. Process model, modelling techniques and design options* (4th ed.). München: Oldenbourg. [in German]

Krogstie, J., Lindland, O.I., & Sindre, G. (1995). Defining quality aspects for conceptual models. In *Proceedings of the International Conference on Information System Concepts (ISCO3). Towards a consolidation of views* (pp. 216-231). Marburg: Chapman & Hall.

Lincoln, Y.S., & Guba, E.G. (1985). *Naturalistic inquiry*. Beverly Hills, CA: Sage.

Lorenz, K. (2004). Theories of truth. In J. Mittelstraß (Ed.), *Enzyklopädie philosophie und wissenschaftstheorie* (pp. 595-600). Stuttgart; Weimar: Verlag J. B. Metzler. [in German]

Maier, R. (1996). *Quality of data models*. Wiesbaden: Dt. Univ.-Verlag [in German]

OMG. (2003a). *Unified modeling language (UML) specification: Infrastructure*. Version 2.0. Final adopted specification. Retrieved: December 8, 2005, from http://www.omg.org/technology/documents/modeling_spec_catalog.htm

OMG. (2003b). *Unified modeling language (UML) specification: Superstructure*. Version 2.0. Final Adopted Specification. Retrieved December 8, 2005, from http://www.omg.org/technology/documents/modeling_spec_catalog.htm

Patton, M. Q. (2002). *Qualitative research & evaluation methods* (3rd ed.). Thousand Oaks, CA: SAGE.

Rosemann, M., & Schütte, R. (1999). Multi-perspective reference modelling. In J. Becker, M. Rosemann, & R. Schütte (Eds.), *Referenzmodellierung. State-of-the-art und entwicklungsperpektiven* (pp. 22-44). Heidelberg: Physica-Verlag. [in German]

Scheer, A.-W. (1995). *Business informatics. Reference models for industrial business processes*. Berlin: Springer. [in German]

Scheer, A. W. (2001). *ARIS—from business processes to application software* (4th ed.). Berlin: Springer. [in German]

Schlagheck, B. (2000). *Object-oriented reference models for process and project controlling. Foundation—construction—fields of application*. Wiesbaden: Deutscher Univ.-Verlag. [in German]

Schütte, R. (1998). *Principles of methodical reference modelling. Construction of configurative and adaptable models*. Wiesbaden: Gabler. [in German]

vom Brocke, J. (2003). *Reference modelling. Design and distribution of construction processes*. Dissertation, University of Münster. [in German]

Chapter V

Business Modeling in Process-Oriented Organizations for RUP-Based Software Development

Francisco J. Duarte, Blaupunkt Auto-Rádio Portugal, &
Universidade do Minho, Portugal

João M. Fernandes, Universidade do Minho, Portugal

Ricardo J. Machado, Universidade do Minho, Portugal

Abstract

Several organizations nowadays are not particularly comfortable with their internal structuring based on a hierarchical arrangement (sub-divided in departments), where collaborators with a limited view of the overall organization perform their activities. Those organizations recognize the need to move to a model where multi-skilled teams run horizontal business processes that cross the organization and impact suppliers and clients. To develop software systems for any organization, the development process must always be appropriate and controlled. Additionally, for organizations that want to migrate to a horizontal business processes view, it is required to model the organizational platform where the organizational processes will run. This necessity is also true when the organization under consideration is a software house. In this chapter, a proposal of a generic framework for process-oriented software houses is presented. The way of managing the process model and the instantiation of their processes with the rational unified process (RUP) disciplines, whenever they are available or with other kind of processes, is recommended as a way to control and define the software development process. To illustrate the usefulness of the proposal, the chapter presents how the generic reference framework was executed in a real project called "Premium Wage" and shows, in some detail, the created artifacts (which include several UML models) during the development phases following the RUP disciplines, especially the artifacts produced for business modeling.

Introduction

A generic reference framework for process-oriented organizations is presented in Fernandes and Duarte (2004). Here, that framework is specialized to the specific case of organizations that develop software (software houses) and we describe its main characteristics. From now on, the term "target organization" is used to refer to those organizations where the software is deployed and installed. The term "software house" is used to refer to the organization that develops software to run in the target organizations.

The main objective of this chapter is to present a reference framework based on processes and RUP disciplines for software houses and to show its usage in a real software development project, as a demonstration case to illustrate the applicability of the proposed model.

With the proposed framework, a holistic view of any software house is straightforward to obtain, allowing a more accurate definition of those processes directly related with the software development, without disregarding the management and support processes.

Process-Oriented Organizations

The concept of a process-oriented organization is a way of focusing the activities of an organization toward the clients needs (Hammer, 1996). These activities are oriented toward and validated by the clients, whose necessities must be satisfied efficiently and with quality. Reengineering, and its process orientation, must be applied to anticipate change and not as a corrective procedure when bad business indicators occur. In process-oriented organizations, clients' needs must be continuously satisfied, which mandates an easy and fast adaptation to changes. This favors and forces the continuous improvement of every aspect of the enterprise, being it process-, product- or organizational-related.

Information technologies are among the principal factors to permit a process-based restructuring of a given organization (Spurr, 1994). The development of a software application for organizations of this kind must consider their process framework. Thus, the software engineering processes must take into account the organization structure. With this model, the application becomes more useful to the target organization, and maintenance is facilitated since no major modifications and adaptations to the process framework are needed.

A process framework inside an organization contains processes, and these can be viewed as a set of activities that has as inputs and outputs a set of services and/or materials. This view must be oriented toward the necessities of the client and to the creation of added-value. This implies that the clients' requirements must always be considered, both in the design and in the performance of the system. In an organization, there are other processes rather than those that provide added-value to the clients. The existence of different types of processes is necessary to assure, for example, the strategic planning for the organization, the recruitment of the human resources or the fiscal duties. As illustrated in Figure 1, these processes are instantiated in Management and Support Processes.

Within an organization, the management by processes requires a structure that differs from the typical functional hierarchy. It is mandatory to synchronize the processes among them and to fulfill the strategic objectives of the organization. For a process-oriented organization, a structure with the following elements should exist:

- **Process management top team:** This team includes the top managers, all process owners and, if existing, the process management structural responsible. Its mission is to revise all the processes according to the strategic objectives of the organization, to analyze the effectiveness of the process-oriented management and to decide about unsolved problems at the processes' interfaces.

- **Process sponsor:** The mission of this top manager is to help and instruct the process owner, to decide when there is a problem of interface among processes, to determine the strategic orientation of the process and to assure that the process is uniform within the organization.

- **Process owner:** For each process, its owner must have know-how on managing processes and persons and competency in the areas associated with the process. His mission is to lead the process' multi-disciplinary team.

- **Multi-disciplinary team:** This team must be created for each added-value process, since they represent the most important processes for the clients. The mission of this team is multi-fold: to monitor its process, to define and analyze the key indicators and the process objectives, to ensure that the process documentation is updated, to decide when and how to use improvement teams and to coordinate them and to manage the process execution teams.

- **Execution teams and team leaders:** These teams and their leaders represent the instances of a given process (Scheer & Nüttgens, 2000). Therefore, during the execution of a process, some teams will use it with a specific focus. For example, for a given production process, one team may be responsible for producing parts for industrial clients, while another team may produce them for individual clients.

To align a process-based organization with its strategic objectives, it is crucial that the goals are based on the organization mission and vision, and also on its principles and values. Based on those strategic objectives and in the business plan, the priority when deciding the key business processes within the organization can be perceived and included in the process landscape. This action may imply that some processes, activities or tasks can be eliminated if they do not add any value to the clients or to the organization. These eliminated (or redefined) processes, activities and tasks, and their respective consequences in terms of reorganization and impact in human resources, are the essence of re-engineering (Hammer, 1996).

Demonstration Case

The proposals made in this chapter were tested in a real industrial environment, more specifically in the first author's organization.

The project, titled "Premium Wage," consists of the development of a software application to calculate the payment of extra money to employees, based on their productivity, quality and absenteeism (Fernandes & Duarte, 2004). This project was considered critical, since it is likely to have important social and behavioral impacts on the organization, namely, if the amount is badly calculated or if it is impossible to explain how it was obtained. This premium was introduced with the aim of ameliorating the organization's overall productivity and quality, and to return the excellence to the workers.

Besides its criticality, the business process is also complex since it depends on other processes. In this case, the payment of a premium depends on three main factors: individual absenteeism, quality of the products made in the employee's line and individual performance. The first two sub-processes were extended in order to support new functionalities. For the third, a complete reengineering was carried out. Finally, a new process was designed, modeled and implemented to the premium wage calculation.

In the project, the proposed reference framework, namely RUP's business modeling discipline, is extensively used and we evaluate the capacity of the process to cope with complex organizations.

Structure of the Chapter

This chapter is structured in five main sections. The second section presents the main characteristics of the reference framework for Process-Oriented software houses, namely the processes they are composed of. In the third section we describe RUP's business modeling core discipline, which implements an added-value process. In the fourth section we describe and discusses in detail the produced artifacts for the demonstration case during the execution of the business modeling discipline. In fifth section, future trends and work along with the conclusions are presented.

Reference Framework for
Process-Oriented Software Houses

A reference framework, also called PSEE (process-centered software engineering environment), does not support the notion of a predefined process model that is supposed to be applied in every development project, but instead supports a wider variety of processes based

Figure 1. Reference framework for software houses

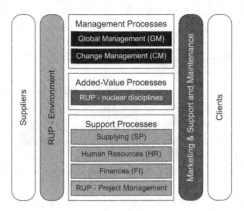

on parameterization (Engels et al., 2001). SPADE (Bandinelli et al., 1994), EPOS (Conradi et al., 1994), MELMAC (Gruhn & Jegelka, 1992), OIKOS (Montangero & Ambriola, 1994), OPEN (Henderson-Sellers, 2000), ESF (Gasch et al., 1987) and APPL/A (Sutton et al., 1995) are well-known examples of PSEE systems or process modeling formalisms.

A reference framework for process-oriented organizations is presented and justified in Fernandes and Duarte (2005). In this chapter, an updated version of this particular framework (Figure 1) includes a new process, called *change management,* that allows a more explicit management of continuous improvement and changes. This framework has some of its processes consubstantiated with RUPs disciplines. Since RUP is a process meta-model, we can obtain a specific process model by tuning some of the parameters, allowing our reference framework to be tailored for each kind of project.

According to the classification described in Fettke et al. (2005), the framework in Figure 1 has the following main characteristics:

- **Construction:** domain differentiation (institution), domain description (software houses), modeling language (graphical, UML activity diagrams and RUP business use cases), modeling framework (yes) and evaluation (demonstration case)
- **Application:** method (procedure model), reuse and customization (customization of model contents)

The reference framework intends to cope with all issues related to software development processes and potentially can be used with the following purposes: documentation, analysis and improvement of software process models (Bandinelli et al., 1993), software process improvement (Avrilionis et al., 1996) and software process execution (Deiters & Gruhn, 1998).

Figure 1 represents a top-level view of the process landscape, which is useful to show and discuss with top managers and process owners. Afterwards, this view must be further refined by the process owner and the multidisciplinary team, to present the process at the appropriate level of detail for each software house professional.

It is also important to notice that Figure 1 corresponds to a specialization of the general framework presented in Fernandes and Duarte (2005) for the particular situation of organizations whose main activity is to develop software. The execution of the TTM process by the software house produces an instance of the general framework that models the organization where the software will run. This fact makes the general framework valuable in two senses: (1) as a reference for the software house to model itself, and, (2) as a reference for the software house to model the target organization.

In software houses, we propose the business processes to be organized into two different groups: (1) the first one includes processes that exist in any organization independently of its relation to the software development business; (2) the second group includes processes that present specific characteristics due to the fact that the organization's main activity is the development of software-based solutions.

Management and Support Processes

We can observe several processes in the context of the management and support issues that are common to any type of organization.

The *global management* process includes the sub-processes *global strategy* (GS), *policy deployment* (PD) and *business plan* (BP). This process is equivalent to that of any other organization, although we must take into account the particularities of the software market, such as the rapid changes in technology and the competition in worldwide markets when defining, for instance, an organizations' business and vision.

Once stable process models have been obtained, they should be released and afterwards it is desirable to manage their changes, according to the change requests made by process stakeholders (Gruhn & Wellen, 2000). The *change management* (CM) process allows the software house to collect, organize and manage the output data and experiences that are the basis for processes self improvement. This new process should exist in any software house aiming to reach the highest CMM (*capability maturity model*) levels (Paulk et al., 1995). To reach the highest CMM levels, the concern about the constant improvement of the development processes must be part of each process, instead of being only a matter of the CM process. CMM level 3, which is considered the minimum when discussing the software process (Henderson-Sellers, 2000) is reachable with RUP if it is extended accordingly, for example, to the proposals made in Manzoni and Price (2003). Also, rules and procedures should be defined previously to cope with the introduction of significant changes in the organization.

The *supplying* (SP) process consists essentially in creating copies of an application. In contrast with more traditional industries, where it represents probably the most important process, in software, due again to its intangible nature, this is a trivial process. The usual outsourcing of this process comes from the fact that it is considered to be secondary for an organization that develops software. Therefore in this kind of organization, this process is a support one.

The *human resources* (HR) process for software factories is the same as for other types of organizations. We must, however, point out that software development requires highly specialized people, making their hiring a critical issue for the success of the organization. It is impossible to produce quality software without skilled people.

The *finances* (FI) process is the typical fulfillment of the fiscal obligations, which is common to all types of organizations and may also include controlling activities.

The processes *marketing* and *maintenance and support,* represent the typical *customer relationship management* (CRM) process. This ensures that when a software application is delivered to the final clients, its life-cycle does not end at that time, but instead continues by incorporating changes and corrections, providing training to the users, while the application is being used by the clients. Hotline support activities can also exist as an included sub-process.

Added-Value Processes

In the context of added-value processes, the proposed reference framework is influenced by the fact that RUP constitutes a systematic approach to assign tasks and responsibilities to its members. The main aim of RUP is to construct quality software that meets the requirements of the stakeholders, within a typical engineering context (Machado et al., 2005). RUP identifies and defines the activities needed to map user requirements into a software application and is accepted to be a generic/customizable process that can be adapted for a wide range of contexts, namely organizations with distinct CMM levels, different skills and tools and unequal number of team members.

Since software is an intangible product, it is obvious that no raw materials are needed to produce it. For organizations that develop software, RUP's *environment* discipline can instantiate the *supplier relationship management* (SRM) process, since it furnishes the working environment (e.g., development tools) and the development guidelines to be followed by the teams.

The RUP's core disciplines (*business modeling, requirements, analysis and design, implementation, test and deployment*) represent the most critical activities for an organization that develops software and can be seen as the *time-to-market* (TTM) process of the organization. This set of activities, or sub-processes, run in parallel for the same development project.

The RUP's discipline *project management* implements the *data management* (DM) process. In this discipline, some activities lead to the production of indicators of the project status. Its existence is the foundation to take decisions based on facts, related to the advance of the project aiming to adjust and improve the software development process.

3. Business Modeling in RUP

RUP's core disciplines implement added-value process. These disciplines are sub-divided in activities, which can be viewed as sub-processes. The description of those sub-processes is made with UML activity diagrams, complemented optionally with other kinds of diagrams, such as interaction and business object diagrams.

This representation is also valid for all other processes of a generic organization. Any time a software house starts a new project, the TTM process is executed. Since we propose this process to be implemented by the six RUP's core disciplines, it implies that *business model-*

Figure 2. Activity diagram to help the execution of RUP's business modeling discipline in TTM process

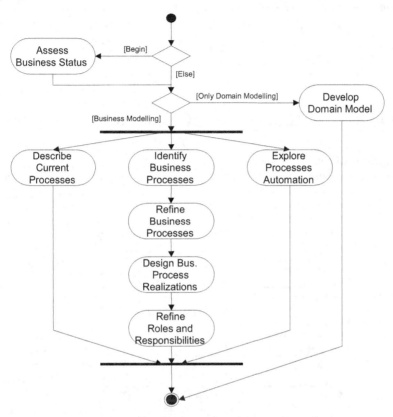

ing will also be executed. Among the recommended diagrams by this discipline for modeling purposes are included activity diagrams. Thus, a target organization will be modeled also by a collection of these diagrams. Additionally, within the software house, the discipline *business modeling* itself can also be modeled by activity diagrams, since it is a sub-process of the TTM process (Figure 2).

During software development, all the stakeholders must have a common understanding of the business processes that exist in the target organization. This reality is not circumscribed to the obvious organizational information systems. If the development of applications does not take into account the current business processes (or those to be implemented), the result will be probably unsuccessful. This may be caused by the fact that end users do not employ correctly the application, since it does not support directly the activities under their responsibility.

The main activities of *business modeling* are centered on the identification, refinement and realization of the business processes and in the definition of the roles of people associated to the business. Each role in this RUP's discipline has under its responsibility the execution of several activities that will have as deliverables several artifacts (Table 1).

The activities of Table 1 are at a detailed level than those of Figure 2. For example, the activity *refine business processes* includes the activities *structure the business use case model*, *review the business use case model* and *detail business use cases*.

Among all the activities and their respective artifacts, only some are mandatory. This flexibility permits the configuration of RUP, so that it can be adapted to a specific project executed in a given organization.

Business Artifacts for the Demonstration Case

Nowadays, the technology-planning horizon for big companies is a synthesis of software and process engineering (Smith & Fingar, 2002). Additionally, the success of a project de-

Table 1. Roles, activities, and main artifacts for business modeling in RUP

Role	Sub-Activity	Activity (Figure 2)	Main Artifacts
Analyst of the Business Process	Assess target organization	Assess Business Status	Business rules
	Set and adjust goals		Business use case model
	Capture the business vocabulary		Business glossary
			Business object model
	Find business actors and use cases	Describe Current Processes	Business vision
			Supplementary business specification
	Maintain the business rules	Assess Business Status & Identify business processes	
			Target organization verification
	Structure business use case model	Refine Business Processes	
			Business architecture
	Define the business architecture	Identify Business Processes	
Reviewer of the Business Model	Review the business use case model	Refine Business Processes	
	Review the business object model	Refine Roles and Responsibilities	
Designer of the Business	Detail business use cases	Refine Business Processes	Organizational units
	Find business workers and entities	Describe Current Processes	
	Define the automation requirements	Explore Processes Automation	
	Detail business entities	Refine Roles and Responsibilities	
	Detail business workers		

pends heavily on the correct perception of the business process to be modeled. Taking into account these two aspects, the RUP's *business modeling* discipline assumes a critical role in the software development process. The artifacts that can be generated by this discipline have the following objectives:

- To understand the structure and dynamics of the organization where the system will be executed
- To comprehend the current problems of the target organization and to identify potential improvements
- To assure that clients, final users and developers have a common understanding about the target organization
- To capture/deduct the requirements of the system necessary to support the target organization

RUP can be parameterized and used both in small and complex projects; next we discuss what artifacts were produced for the demonstration case. For this parameterization to occur, it is necessary, during project execution, to choose which artifacts to use and their level of detail. This choice was validated by quality assessments contained in the process model as milestones between phase transitions. Thus, both the subset of used artifacts and also its degree of detail can not be anticipated with rigor, but must be selected based on experience and knowledge of the development team in relating the characteristics of each project with the functionalities offered by the artifacts. The criteria to fulfill this choice are related with:

- Characteristics of the project itself (e.g., criticality of the modeled business processes, type of target organization)
- Characteristics of the organization that develops software (e.g., team size, level of knowledge about internal rules)
- Temporal restrictions. Since resources are limited in engineering projects, it is always a necessary balance between the quantity and detail of the produced artifacts and the deadlines for implementing the project.

The produced artifacts result from a set of activities that occur inside those disciplines. In this demonstration case, we identified the need for the artifacts to represent two distinct situations in terms of business: One part of the project represents reengineering activities of some business processes, while the other part represents the introduction of a new business process. In several diagrams (e.g., business use case model), the standard UML is augmented with the stereotypes defined by RUP, thus allowing the creation of RUP-like artifacts.

Business Rules

The business rules correspond to policy statements and conditions that should be fulfilled from the business perspective. They are similar to systems requirements, but they focus on

Table 2. Business rules examples for Premium Wage

Rule #	Description
1	**If** worker_has_conflict_inside_team **or** worker_is_under_disciplinary_process **then** premium(worker) = 0

2	**Switch** absenteeism(worker)
	    case = 0h: premium(worker) = premium(worker) * 1
	    case]0-4h]: premium(worker) = premium(worker) * 0.75
	    case]4-8h]: premium(worker) = premium(worker) * 0.5
	    case >8h: premium(worker) = premium(worker) * 0

3	**If** line_productivity_not_available **or** absenteeism_not_available **or** quality_factor_not_available **then** premium(worker) = 0

the business core, expressing rules related to business, and also its architecture and style. Its modelling must be rigorous, one possibility being the use of the object constraint language (OCL) as specified in UML. Alternatively, business rules can be modeled with structured English, using some fixed constructors (Odell, 1998).

The usage of structured natural language with fixed constructs and with a pseudo-programming language syntax was chosen due to the necessity to validate directly with key users the perception of the development team about stated business rules, and also because key users have a generic engineering background. This way, in the particular situation of the demonstration case, the usage of natural language was preferred over OCL.

Table 2 shows, as examples, three rules for Premium Wage system.

Rule 1 describes a situation where no premium payment is due when the worker has conflicts in its team or is under a disciplinary process, even though productivity, quality and absenteeism are at good levels for that worker. Rule 2 assigns a weight factor to the final premium based on the worker's absenteeism. Rule 3 states that if there is no information available from one of the three premium factors, no payment will be made for that worker.

Business Use Case Model

The main goal of this artifact is to show how the business is being perceived and run by stakeholders. This is achieved by modeling the business processes and their interactions with external parties, based on business use case diagrams (with stereotypes for business use cases and business actors) (Fernandes & Machado, 2001; Machado & Fernandes, 2002).

Business processes models should specify how added value is created for the business actors. Activity diagrams, possibly extended with the representation of organizational units interfering in the business process and with the distribution of the activities by those organizational units, can support this modelling. The knowledge about "who is doing what" should be obvious when reading this model.

Figure 3. Business use case model: As-Is situation

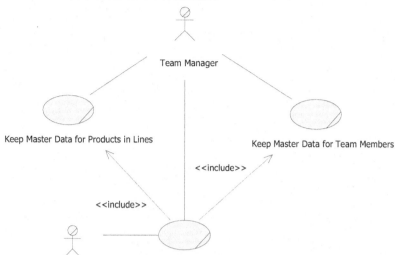

Business use case model is the first description of the business functionalities and actors inside the target organization. For Premium Wage, one artifact was created to model the current situation (Figure 3) and another for the desired future situation (Figure 4).

The existence of these two models shows to all stakeholders, using the same notation and same detail level, the first perspective of effort amount needed to reach a future situation, and more important, acts as a base for the target organization's management to decide on business re-engineering and improvement. A special emphasis should be given to explain to the target organization's management that an information system is not the complete business reality, but an abstraction of it. Real business processes, such the ones stated in *business modeling* discipline, are far more extent than the ones implemented inside the information system. This may be caused by people's activities because they do not act similarly every day, and mainly because people like to have their own special information systems (e.g., spreadsheets or personal databases) to make decisions and cause the *starvation* of the organization business information system with missing data. This is a crucial success factor at the present time because the work is no longer only individual or departmentally related, but exists through horizontal business processes that cross the entire organization and reaches external partners.

Figure 3 shows the current situation, where only three business use cases exist and only two business actors take part. The line productivity is calculated by the controller-based master data lines' team member and products maintained by the team manager. This situation shows that no information was available on how and where to collect quality data and absenteeism. Next, in Figure 4, the desired extensions and new business use cases can be seen. For the future situation, six business actors are needed, and special care should be put on this situation because some of them may not be directly related with project activities and may not understand the business value of the new activities (stated in the business use cases) if no proper involvement and education is provided.

Figure 4. Business use case model: To-Be situation

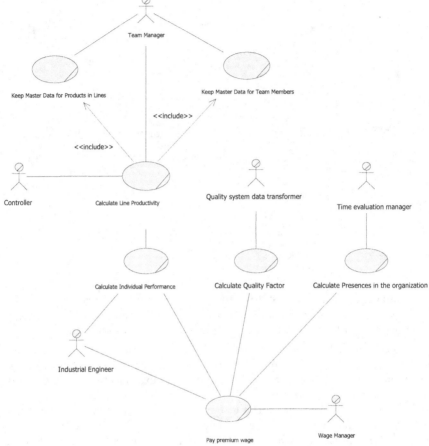

In this situation, line productivity is *triggered* also by the controller, but to be useful, it first has to be transformed into individual performance (because one employee can work in several production lines for the premium calculation time frame). Additionally, the remaining two premium factors (quality and absenteeism) are stated, thus allowing the industrial engineer to calculate the final values and the wage manager to handle them.

Organizational Units

This artifact is used to reduce the complexity and structure of the business object model by dividing it into smaller parts. For the demonstration case, five organization units where created (Figure 5), each one representing a collection of business workers, business entities, relationships, business use-case realizations, diagrams and other organization units.

The organization unit *line productivity* includes the re-engineered activities for the productivity calculation, *quality* and *presences in the organization* where extended to cope

Figure 5. Organizational units

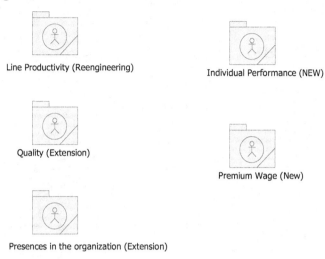

Line Productivity (Reengineering)

Individual Performance (NEW)

Quality (Extension)

Premium Wage (New)

Presences in the organization (Extension)

with premium calculation. The *individual performance* and *premium wage* calculation organizational units were newly created in the organization, because none of the existent capabilities could handle it.

Business Object Model

This artifact is an object model describing the realization of business use cases. It serves as an abstraction of how business workers and business entities need to be related and how they need to collaborate in order to perform the business. In Figures 6 and 7 the realiza-

Figure 6. Business object model: Calculate presences in the organization

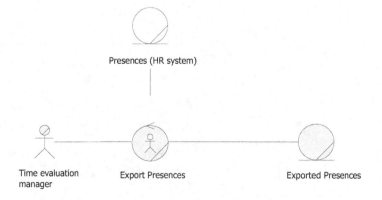

Presences (HR system)

Time evaluation manager

Export Presences

Exported Presences

Figure 7. Business object model: Pay premium wage

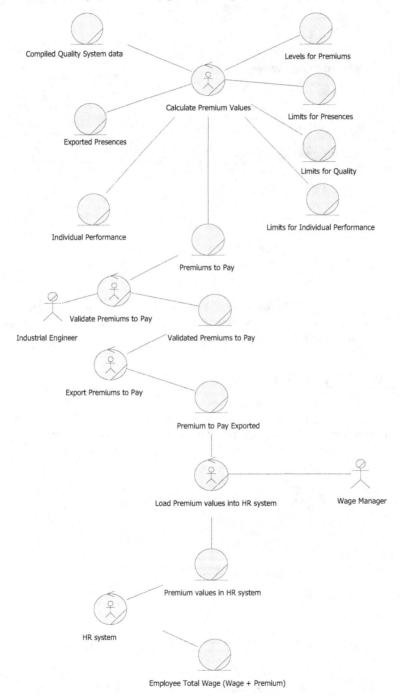

tions of some To-Be situation business use cases are presented, namely *Presences in the organization* and *Pay premium wage.*

The importance of this artifact comes also from it being a basis for identifying future information system actors and use cases, and in addition, to identifying classes for analysis and design models. First modelling the business and afterwards the information system is a crucial practice to correctly align the business reality with the abstraction the information system implements. If the software information system development only starts with the modelling of a software system, a quality software product can be obtained (being the quality perceived as the degree of correctly implementing requirements) but that may fail completely to cope with the business reality of the organization in which it will run. Although business information systems implement a large percentage of the business practices, there are always some parts of the organization's business processes that are not implemented in software systems. The modeling of such business practices by the software development team is a wise and safe procedure to avoid future inconsistencies when introducing the information system in the organization.

To calculate the presences in the organization (Figure 6), the business worker *Time evaluation manager* uses business entity *Export presences* to pick the business object *Presences* available in the HR system and generate a new business object *Exported presences* containing the presences in the organization in a proper format to use inside the Premium Wage information system.

In Figure 7, business entity *Calculate Premium Values* uses several business objects representing final premium factors, such as *Compiled Quality System data, Exported presences* (generated in Figure 6, business object model) *Individual Performance* and also business objects representing levels and limits (acting as data supports to implement business rules (Table 2) to generate the business object *Premium to Pay.* Afterwards, this business object will be used and transformed by several business entities, with and without the intervention of business actors, until the final Employee Total Wage (Wage + Premium) is loaded and calculated in the HR system, as shown in Figure 7.

The business object model exposed in Figure 7 is not fully contained in Premium Wage information system. The business object Premium to Pay Exported is generated by Premium Wage to be used inside the organization's HR system. This is an example where some of the business actors, business entities and business objects will not be part of the information system required by the software development team, but they were modeled to guarantee a proper integration of current information systems (e.g., HR system) with newly developed ones (e.g., Premium Wage).

Other Business Artifacts

From all of the proposed artifact in RUP for business modeling, some were not used in the Premium Wage demonstration case. Next, we present the reason why they were not needed in the instance of the RUP we used for this project:

- **Business glossary:** In this artifact all business terms and expressions are kept. They are necessary for a good understanding among all project stakeholders. In our situation, the business terms are common to the target and to the software developing organization because they both are sub-organizations of the same organization.

- **Business vision:** This artifact captures the goals of a particular business modeling activity, stating what is to be modeled and the reasons why. It also serves as an oracle to all future high-level decisions. We did not use business vision because it is common to the target and software development organization due to the same reasons as those of business glossary.

- **Supplementary business specification:** No need for extra-detail than that available in the business use case and the business object models.

- **Target organization verification:** The target organization is perfectly known by the software developers. The current processes are modelled by the business use case model, As-Is situation.

- **Business architecture document:** The detail level presented in the business use case model and in the business object model is sufficient to understand the business architecture.

Conclusion and Future Trends

In this chapter, we have presented a revised version of a reference framework for process-oriented software houses which serves as a foundation to model organizations. This specific framework is based on a more generic one, which is also used as a template to model the target organization in which the software product is to be executed. Additionally, we also show the way of managing the framework and the instantiation of its processes with RUP disciplines whenever feasible.

We also discuss in detail the usage of the framework within a demonstration case, and more particularly, the produced artifacts during the execution of the RUP's business modelling discipline. The modeling capabilities of a graphical modelling language (such as the UML) and the understanding that it gives to all the stakeholders was a crucial factor in the demonstration case to avoid communication and interpretation errors and to improve the solution utility and correctness.

As future work, we plan to model the reference framework with UML (Fettke et al., 2006) and formalize the processes of the framework by using colored Petri nets (Jensen, 1992). Similar approaches also based on Petri nets were also experienced with results (Gruhn & Wellen, 2001; van der Aalst, 2003).

By adopting a formal language, it is possible to model, animate, simulate and formally verify the properties of each single process. Additionally, we intend to explicitly model the interfaces between the business processes in our reference framework, which allows the complete framework to be analyzed, verified and validated.

We intend to automatically generate CPN skeletons from business requirements models. A semantic layer in the Arena environment (Kelton et al., 2002), capable of accepting CPN-based business specifications, will also be developed to allow the stochastic execution of workflow scenarios as a complement to some current validation approaches based on CPN/Tools (Beaudouin Lafon et al., 2001).

After formally describing the reference framework processes, we can use them in every organization (in this case, software houses) to compare with current processes. This comparison (based on the same Petri net formalism) should allow a quick assessment of the organization against world-class processes and consequently permit the re-engineering and improvement of its own processes. In this way, the reference framework acts as a To-Be model to be compared with the As-Is model of the software house. The detected mismatches show the improvement areas for the software house to proceed accordingly within the organization vision and mission.

References

Avrilionis, D., Belkhatir, N., & Cunin, P.-Y. (1996). Improving software process modelling and enactment techniques. In C. Montangero (Ed.), *The 5th European Workshop on Software Process Technology*, Nancy, France (LNCS 1149, pp. 65-74).

Bandinelli, S., Fuggetta, A., & Grigolli, A. (1993). Process modelling in-the large with SLANG. In *Proceedings of the 2nd International Conference on the Software Process: Continuous Software Improvement*, Berlin, Germany (pp. 75-83). IEEE.

Bandinelli, S., Fuggetta, A., Ghezzi, C., & Lavazza, L. (1994). SPADE: An environment for software process analysis, design, and enactment. A. Finkelstein, J. Kramer, & B. Nuseibeh (Eds.), *Software process modeling and technology*. London: Research Studies Press.

Beaudouin-Lafon, M., Mackay, W. E., Andersen, P., Janecek, P., Jensen, M., Lassen, M., et al. (2001). CPN/Tools: A post-WIMP interface for editing and simulating coloured Petri nets. In *Application and Theory of Petri Nets 2001, Proceedings of the 22nd International Conference (ICATPN 2001)*, Newcastle upon Tyne, UK.

Conradi, R., Hasgaseth, M., Larsen, J.-O., Nguyên, M. N., Munch, B. P., Westby, P. H., et al. (1994). EPOS: Object-oriented cooperative process modeling. A. Finkelstein, J. Kramer, & B. Nuseibeh (Eds.), *Software process modeling and technology*. London: Research Studies Press

Deiters, W., & Gruhn, V. (1998). Process management in practice: Applying the FUNSOFT net approach to large scale processes. *Automated Software Engineering, 5*, 7-25.

Engels, G., Schäfer, W., Balzer, R., & Gruhn, V. (2001). Process-centered software engineering environments: Academic and industrial perspectives. In *Proceedings of the 23rd International Conference on Software Engineering*, Toronto, Canada (pp. 671-673). IEEE CS Press.

Fernandes, J. M., & Duarte, F. J. (2005). A reference framework for process-oriented software development organizations. *Software and Systems Modeling (SoSyM), 4*(1), 94-105. Springer-Verlag.

Fernandes, J. M., & Duarte, F. J. (2004). Using RUP for process-oriented organisations. In F. Bomarius & H. Iida (Eds.), *Proceedings of the 5th International Conference on Product*

Focused Software Process Improvement (PROFES 2004) (LNCS 3009, pp. 348-362). Springer-Verlag.

Fernandes, J. M., & Machado, R. J. (2001). From use cases to objects: An industrial information systems case study analysis. In *Proceedings of the 7th International Conference on Object-Oriented Information Systems (OOIS '01)* (pp. 319-328). Springer-Verlag.

Fettke, P., Loos, P., & Zwicker, J. (2005). Business process reference models: Survey and classification. In *Proceedings of the Workshop on Business Process Reference Models (BPMR 2005)*, Nancy, France (pp. 1-15).

Fettke, P., Zwicker, J., & Loos, P. (2006) Using UML for reference modeling. In P. Rittgen (Ed.), *Enterprise modeling and computing with UML*. Hershey, PA, USA: Idea Group Inc.

Gasch, B., Kelter, U., Kopfer, H., & Weber, H. (1987). Reference model for the integration of tools in the EUREKA software factory. In *Proceedings of the 1987 Fall Joint Computer Conference on Exploring Technology: Today and Tomorrow* (pp. 183-189). IEEE Computer Society Press.

Gruhn, V., & Jegelka, R. (1992). An evaluation of FUNSOFT nets. In *Proceedings of the 2nd European Workshop on Software Process Technology (EWSPT '92)* (LNCS). New York: Springer-Verlag.

Gruhn, V., & Wellen, U. (2000). Structuring complex software processes by "Process Landscaping." In *Proceedings of the 7th European Workshop on Software Process Technology (EWSPT 2000)*, Kaprun, Austria (LNCS 1780, pp. 138-149). Springer Verlag.

Gruhn, V., & Wellen, U. (2001). Process landscaping: Modelling distributed processes and proving properties of distributed process models. *Unifying Petri nets* (LNCS 2128, pp. 103-125). Springer-Verlag.

Hammer, M. (1996). *Beyond reengineering: How the process-centered organization is changing our work and our lives*. New York: Harper Collins.

Henderson-Sellers, B. (2000). The OPEN framework for enhancing productivity. *IEEE Software, 17*(2), 53-58.

Jensen, K. (1992). Coloured Petri nets: Basic concepts, analysis methods and practical use, Vol. 1: Basic concepts. In *EATCS monographs in theoretical computer science*. Springer-Verlag.

Kelton, W. D., Sadowski, R. P., & Sadowski, D. A. (2002). *Simulation with ARENA* (2nd ed.). New York: McGraw-Hill.

Machado, R. J., & Fernandes, J. M. (2002). Heterogeneous information systems integration: Organizations and methodologies. In M. Oivo M. & S.K. Sirviö (Eds.), *Proceedings of the 4th International Conference on Product Focused Software Process Improvement—PROFES '02*, Rovaniemi, Finland (LNCS 2559, pp. 629-643). Springer-Verlag.

Machado, R. J., Ramos, I., & Fernandes, J. M. (2005). Specification of requirements models. In A. Aurum & C. Wohlin (Eds.), *Engineering and managing software requirements* (pp. 47-68). Berlin: Springer-Verlag.

Manzoni, L. V., & Price, R. T. (2003). Identifying extensions required by RUP (rational unified process) to comply with CMM (capability maturity model) levels 2 and 3. *IEEE Transactions on Software Engineering, 29*(2), 181-192.

Montangero, C., & Ambriola, V. (1994). OIKOS: Constructing process-centered SDEs. A. Finkelstein, J. Kramer, & B. Nuseibeh (Eds.), *Software process modeling and technology*. London: Research Studies Press.

Odell, J. (1998). *Advanced object-oriented analysis & design using UML*. Cambridge University Press.

Paulk, M. C., Weber, C. V., Curtis, B., & Chrissis, M. B. (Eds.). (1995). *The capability maturity model: Guidelines for improving the software process*. Reading, MA: Addison-Wesley.

Scheer, A. W., & Nüttgens, M. (2000). ARIS architecture and reference models for business process management. In W. van der Aalst, J. Desel, & A. Oberweis (Eds.), *Business process management, models, techniques, and empirical studies* (LNCS 1806, pp. 376-389). Springer.

Smith, H., & Fingar, P. (2002). *Business process management: The third wave*. Tampa, FL: Meghan-Kiffer Press.

Spurr, K., Layzell, P., Jennison, L., & Richards, N. (1994). *Software assistance for business re-engineering*. New York: John Wiley & Sons.

Sutton, S., Heimbigner, D., & Osterweil, L. (1995). APPL/A: A language for software process programming. *ACM Transactions on Software Engineering Methodology, 4*(3), 221-286.

van der Aalst, W. M. P. (2003). Challenges in business process management: Verification of business processes using Petri nets. *Bulletin of the European Association for Theoretical Computer Science, 80*, 174-198.

Chapter VI

Evaluation of Reference Models

Ulrich Frank, University of Duisburg-Essen, Germany

Abstract

Evaluating a reference model is a demanding task. Not only do reference models inherit the problems well known from the evaluation of conceptual models in general, but furthermore, their claim for general (re-) usability implies the ability to take into account the possible variety of requirements and specific constraints within the set of potential applications. This Chapter presents a method that is aimed at fostering a differentiated and balanced judgement of reference models. For this purpose, it takes into account various perspectives—among others, economic, engineering and epistemological. It also includes a process model that demonstrates how to organize a specific evaluation project.

Evaluation of Reference Models
as a Multi-Faceted Challenge

Reference models are a reification of a very attractive vision: They promise higher quality of information systems at less cost. This vision goes along with two pivotal claims. On the one hand, reference models are intended to provide appropriate *descriptions* of an application domain. On the other hand, reference models are aimed at delivering *blueprints* for a distinctively good design of information systems and related organizational settings. Thus, they are descriptive and prescriptive at the same time. While many conceptual models include descriptive and prescriptive elements, reference models should fit the specific needs of a whole range of organizations. Since the idea of reference modeling is emphasizing the improvement of quality, evaluating them is a core issue: From the perspective of prospective users, it can hardly be taken for granted that a particular reference model is of superior quality. However, evaluating reference models is a major challenge. This is for various reasons. Not only that reference models inherit the problems well known from the evaluation of conceptual models in general, but furthermore, that their claim for general (re-) usability implies a takeing into account the possible variety of requirements and specific constraints within the set of potential applications. Another source of complexity is the variety of objectives related to the use of reference models. They include economic goals, such as increase of productivity, or goals related to specific analysis, design or implementation tasks. In addition to that, testing the claim for excellence faces deep and subtle epistemological problems.

Against this background, the paper will propose a *method* for evaluating reference models. It consists of a conceptual framework that serves to structure the overall evaluation problem, which is supplemented by a prototypical process model that demonstrates how to organize a specific evaluation project.

Related Work

While reference models are arguably of pivotal importance for the IS discipline, the idea of reference models has not been around for too long. This is even more the case for actual reference models. In a recent survey focussed on German speaking countries, Fettke and Loos identified only 33 reference models of various kinds, 22 of which were accessible (Fettke & Loos, 2004). Therefore, it does not come as a surprise that there have been only a few approaches that focus explicitly on the evaluation of reference models. However, there is other work which is directly related to this topic: approaches to the evaluation of conceptual models and approaches to the evaluation of modeling languages.

Evaluation of Conceptual Models

Reference models are conceptual models. A conceptual model is an abstraction that stresses the core terms or concepts which characterize an application domain, while neglecting technical aspects that are related to the implementation of corresponding software systems. Hence, they should contribute to a better understanding of a domain and foster the communication between the various stakeholders involved in a particular project. In a definition that has been quoted frequently, conceptual models are regarded as "... descriptions of a world enterprise/slice of reality which correspond directly and naturally to our own conceptualizations of the object of these descriptions" (Mylopoulus & Levesque, 1984, p. 11). However, describing reality is only one facet of a conceptual model. Usually, a conceptual model is a (re-) constructing description of a domain that also includes prescriptive elements. This is for two reasons. First, it will often make no sense to leave a domain the way it is if one wants to foster the introduction of efficient software systems. Instead, it will usually be required to re-organize patterns of action, such as business processes. Second, the development of software has to take into account the limitations of implementation level languages. In order to support a seamless transformation of conceptual models into implementation level documents, it is not advisable to completely neglect the concepts used on the implementation level.

There is a widespread consensus that conceptual modeling is pivotal for the professional development of information systems. But only if conceptual models are of high quality themselves, will they foster the implementation of high quality software. Therefore, the evaluation of a conceptual model's quality is an important topic in IS. With respect to designing information systems, there have been several attempts to guide the evaluation of a model's quality. They all stress the necessity to use a multi-criteria approach for conceptualizing the notion of quality. Moody and Shanks suggest six criteria to evaluate entity relationship models: *simplicity, understandability, flexibility, completeness, integration and implementability* (Moody & Shanks, 1994). In a textbook on data modeling, Batini et al. suggest similar criteria (Batini, Ceri, & Navathe, 1992). Lindland et al. emphasize, among other things, the need for using a modeling language that is appropriate for the problem domain and for the expected audience (Lindland, Sindre, & Sølvberg, 1994).

To validate a particular model, evaluators differentiate syntactic, semantic and pragmatic quality. While syntax and semantics are considered on a formal level, among other things, "inspection" and "explanation" are suggested as instruments to foster pragmatic quality. In addition to syntax, semantics and pragmatics, Krogstie et al. (1995) propose "knowledge quality" explicitly as an evaluation criterion. It refers to the knowledge of people who participate in a modeling project. Therefore, they suggest "perceived semantic quality" as a further criterion. They do not, however, discuss how this aspect could be used for the overall evaluation of a conceptual model. A later refinement of this approach (Krogstie, 1998) does not answer that question either. Becker et al. (Becker, Rosemann, & Schütte, 1995) suggest six principles for appropriate conceptual modeling: *correctness, relevance, economics, clarity, comparability*, and *systematic construction*. Later, this approach was refined by Schütte—mainly based on epistemological considerations. Among other things, he replaced "correctness" with *constructive fitness*. In a recent review of quality frameworks, Moody demands a unification of existing frameworks and stresses the need for disseminating them into practice (Moody, 2005). Weber suggests a focus on the question of how well a model represents a user's conception of the real world (Weber, 1997, p. 72). While this important question is difficult to answer—unless you favour a naive realism—it is not sufficient for many conceptual models either. Since conceptual models often describe future domains, they cannot be evaluated against a user's perception of reality only. In a recent article, Shanks et al. suggest to use ontologies for validating conceptual models (Shanks, Tansley, & Weber,

2003). However, they mainly discuss how a philosophical ontology could contribute to the selection of an appropriate modeling language.

To summarize, research on evaluating the quality of conceptual models has resulted in various frameworks that suggest criteria which cover—and sometimes mix—a wide range of quality aspects from language concepts and syntactical features to user perception. Since reference models are special kinds of conceptual models, all of these criteria could be applied to them, as well.

Evaluation of Modeling Languages

The quality of a conceptual model depends on the suitability of the modeling language being used. Hence, it implies taking into account the quality of modeling languages as well. There are not many publications on evaluating the quality of modeling languages. They can be differentiated into three categories: approaches that focus on formal requirements, approaches that focus on pragmatic aspects concerning the use of a modeling language and approaches that make use of ontologies.

In software engineering, the purpose a modeling language should serve is mainly restricted to formal aspects: It should provide a suitable basis for the implementation of correct and reliable software. Hence, formal properties like *completeness*, *simplicity* and *correctness* (for instance, Süttenbach & Ebert, 1997) are of outstanding importance for the evaluation of a language. In addition to that, the analysis of languages in computer science is sometimes related to their expressive power, for instance, by referring to a particular layer of the Chomsky hierarchy. While both aspects, formal rigour and expressive power, are relevant for a number of purposes models may have to serve, they neglect entirely the users' perspectives and those purposes that are not directly related to the implementation of software. Notice also that such approaches to evaluate modeling languages do not allow for discriminating between a set of modeling languages that are complete and correct and share the same expressive power.

Partially, approaches to a more pragmatic evaluation of modeling languages were motivated by the need to compare modeling languages. Some of the approaches are not focussed on modeling languages alone, but at entire modeling methods (e.g., De Champeaux & Faure, 1992; Hong & Goor, 1993; Monarchi & Puhr, 1992). As part of a comprehensive analysis of Petri nets, Zelewski (1995) has developed a framework for evaluating modeling languages. While his focus is primarily on Petri nets, the criteria he suggests can be applied to other modeling concepts/languages as well. He differentiates between general language features (like expressive power) and features that are helpful for specific applications of a language. In order to support the evaluation of the latter, he introduces a number of criteria. Among other things, they include concepts to express causality, temporal semantics, to coordinate tasks, sequential and parallel processes, etc. In addition to approaches that are aimed on the conceptualisation of quality, there have been attempts to detect quality aspects through empirical studies. They are focused mainly on the perception of language users. Two studies, Goldstein and Storey (1990) and Hitchman (1995) found evidence that many prospective users have difficulties understanding and hence using entity relationship models. However, the studies suffer from two shortcomings. First, they were not representative—both with respect to prospective users and the selected modeling languages. Second, they did not take into account how the level of training for applying a particular language would influence a user's judgement.

Referring to the philosopher Bunge, Weber recommends to regard the level of "ontological completeness" (Weber, 1997, p. 94) as essential for the quality of a modeling language (he speaks of a "grammar"). A language is ontologically complete if it provides concepts to represent each class of phenomena in the real world. Despite the formal definition he introduces for ontological completeness, Weber admits that there is hardly a complete list of phenomena everybody could agree on. To be more concrete, he suggests a number of features a modeling language should provide in order to be ontologically complete. They include concepts to express "things," "properties of things," "types," "states," "laws" (comparable to constraints), "lawful states" (comparable to invariants) and events. By applying his criteria to the entity relationship model, Weber establishes that the ERM is not ontologically complete. Opdahl and Henderson-Sellers use Bunge's ontology for the evaluation of an object-oriented modeling language (Opdahl & Henderson-Sellers, 2005). Fettke and Loos apply the same ontology to a language for enterprise modeling (Fettke & Loos, 2003). Ontologies can foster a better understanding of modeling languages. However, they are not a sufficient reference for evaluating modeling languages or models on the object level: Both modeling languages and models are abstractions that should serve a certain purpose. This does not imply that they have to be complete in an ontological sense. There is only one exception where an ontological evaluation makes sense: in the case of (meta) modeling languages that come with the claim of covering all possible modeling purposes related to information systems, such as the UML. It is common practice in IS research to use Bunge's ontology as a reference without questioning it. Such an attitude is hardly acceptable. Bunge's ontology—like any other—is an artifact in itself. While it is elaborated and Bunge has a remarkable reputation as a philosopher, it is certainly not appropriate to take it for granted.

Evaluation of Reference Models

There are hardly any specific approaches to the explicit evaluation of reference models. In order to foster a systematic description, Fettke and Loos propose a method to guide the classification of reference models (Fettke & Loos, 2003d). With respect to the evaluation of reference models, the same authors suggest a multi-perspective approach (Fettke & Loos, 2003c). For this purpose, they outline various research approaches to study the quality of reference models (e.g., "feature-based evaluation," "ontology-based evaluation" and "cognitive psychology-based evaluation"). In a further publication, they demonstrate how to use the "Bunge-Wand-Weber Model," which is based on Bunge's ontology, for the evaluation of reference models (Fettke & Loos, 2003b). However, they mainly apply the ontology to conceptual models and modeling languages in general. Mišic and Zhao present a "linguistic-based comparison framework" for evaluating reference models and apply it to a few selected models. Their notion of reference model is slightly different from the one outlined above, since they put more emphasis on system architecture: "...a conceptual framework for describing system architecture" (Mišic & Zhao, 2000, p. 484). They extend the framework proposed in Lindland, Sindre, and Sølvberg (1994) by a few criteria (e.g., "level of stratification"—does a model offer different levels of abstraction—or "orientation"—technology or business). However, they do not discuss any feature that would be specific to reference models.

A Multi-Perspective Framework for Evaluation

Our brief overview of the state of the art in evaluating reference models reveals a number of peculiarities. First, there has been only little work on the explicit evaluation of reference models. The majority of related work is concentrated on evaluating conceptual models or—to a lower extent—on evaluating modeling languages. Most authors suggest a *multi-perspective* approach. Perspectives are often inspired by linguistic categories (syntax, semantics and pragmatics), sometimes extended by a more differentiated consideration of users' perception or a model's relationship to reality. While most frameworks include the judgment of language features, some lack an explicit differentiation of meta- and object levels. The use of ontologies is a valuable contribution to a more comprehensive and obliging evaluation. However, usually the ontology that serves as a reference is taken for granted, thereby terminating the course of reasoning in a somewhat ideological way.

In part, the framework presented in the following section makes eclectic use of the work discussed so far. Therefore, it stresses a multi-perspective approach. It also takes the burden of these approaches: that an objective evaluation is hard to accomplish. Hence, the idea is to get closer to objectivity by fostering a more differentiated and balanced judgment. In this sense, the structure that is suggested here is an attempt, not the solution—or, following Wittgenstein—*a* structure, not *the* structure. The conceptual framework includes four main perspectives, which are structured in a number of specific aspects. The perspectives are not necessarily independent. Their differentiation is mainly motivated by analytical reasons. The *economic perspective* is aimed at discussing criteria that are relevant for judging costs and benefits related to the use of reference models. Among other things, it takes into account protection of investment, possible effects on information quality and competitiveness. The *deployment perspective* is focused on criteria that are relevant for those who work with the models. It stresses criteria such as comprehensibility, compatibility with other representations being used in an organization, availability of tools, etc. Reference models are artifacts that have been designed for a certain purpose. Also, they will usually be related to the analysis and design of information systems. The *engineering perspective* is aimed at evaluating a reference model as a design artifact that has to satisfy a specification—including the support for analysis and transformation. With respect to their claim for general validity, reference models resemble scientific theories. The *epistemological perspective* is aimed at evaluating reference models as the results of scientific research. For this purpose, it focuses on criteria for evaluating scientific theories as they are discussed in Philosophy of Science. In order to differentiate between conceptual models in general and reference models, features that are more specific to reference models will be marked as such. Note, however, that the borderline between a conceptual model and a reference model cannot be drawn precisely. The evaluation of a reference model depends also on its type (e.g., an object model, a data model, a business process model, etc.). However, due to the limited space of this chapter, specific features of particular model types will be widely abstracted in form. The suggested criteria are intended to provide guidance for evaluating reference models. They do not imply a specific scale level. Most of them will allow for classification, some for applying an ordinal scale only (e.g., a Likert scale). If there is need for calculating aggregated evaluation measures, one could define corresponding higher order scales. However, this would cause a distortion of the evaluation result.

These suggestions are based on previous work on the evaluation of modeling languages. In Frank and Prasse (1997), a framework for the evaluation of object-oriented modeling languages is presented. It includes 33 criteria which are applied to a comparison of the UML and the OML (Firesmith, Henderson-Sellers, Graham, & Page-Jones, 1996). Frank (1998) suggests a multi-perspective framework for the discursive evaluation of modeling languages. Frank and Schauer (2006) are aimed at languages for modeling business processes. It presents a comprehensive analysis of requirements for these kinds of languages.

The Economic Perspective

Both, the construction and the (re-) use of reference models chiefly depend on economic aspects. We will mainly take the viewpoint of a potential model user rather than that of a model developer. The type of user depends on the purpose a reference model is deployed for. Some will take a reference model as a foundation for developing software (*pre-development use*—referred to as type 1 in the table that illustrates the framework). For other users, a reference model serves mainly as a documentation of existing software (*post-development use*—referred to as type 2). Both pre- and post-development use can be applied to object models (or data models respectively) or business process models. In the case of post-development use, component models or application models—which would mainly focus on interfaces—are an option as well. In order to illustrate their deployment, they should be integrated with business process models. A third group of potential users is primarily interested in organisational or strategic issues (*business (re-) design*-referred to as type 3). Reference models that represent corporate strategies or organisations (e.g., business processes and organisational charts) are suitable for this category of use. In a particular case, different approaches to using a reference model may be combined, for instance pre-development use and business (re-) design. During the following discussion of economic aspects, we will at first abstract from these different types of uses. Only later, they will be taken into account again. For the evaluation of primarily economic issues, three main categories are suggested: *costs*, *benefits*, and *protection of investment*.

Focus on Costs

While reference models are aimed at reducing costs, their use will cause costs, too. The following criteria serve to guide the estimation and evaluation of costs to be expected with the use of a reference models. Sometimes, they depend on features of a model that are the subject of other perspectives. The aspects are differentiated into three main categories: *introduction, transformation and analysis and maintenance*. Costs for introducing a reference model include acquisition or license costs as well as costs for training, adaptation, strategic re-design, organisational re-design and integration. Transformation costs are caused by transforming a model into other representations, such as implementation level documents.

Table 1. Introduction

Aspect	Relevant for type of use	Criteria	Comment	Specific to reference model?	Related to
Acquisition	1, 2, 3	Cost of purchasing, licensing model Cost of inhouse development Economies of scale	Cost of inhouse development is often hard to determine; the more prospective users, the higher the economies of scale	Yes	
Training	1,2, 3	Familiarity of own staff with modelling language, terminology Inhouse modelling expertise Availability of training offers Overall complexity of model	Training costs depend heavily on the complexity of a model and the expertise of prospective users	Yes	Deployment -> understandability, attitude
Adaptation	1, 2, 3	Concepts that support adaptation in a safe and convenient way Availability of tools Cost of tools Cost of integrating with existing tools/ systems	Adaptation costs are often hard to estimate in advance; if available, one should look at costs caused in similar projects	Yes	Engineering -> Technical model features
Strategic Re-Design	1, 2, 3	Model recommends/ requires strategic adaptation Degree of change required	Strategic adaptation can be a chance, but also a threat. In any case, it will usually require major investments.	Yes	
Organisational Re-Design	1, 2, 3	Model recommends/ requires organisational adaptation Degree of change required	Depending on the degree of change, estimating related costs can require an extensive analysis.	Yes	
Integration	1, 2	Integration with existing models Integration with business partners Amount of integration required Compatibility of modelling concepts	Here, the focus is on modelling languages and on concepts (semantics) being used in already existing models.	No	Benefits -> Openness

Table 2. Transformation and analysis

Aspect	Relevant for type of use	Criteria	Comment	Specific to reference model?	Related to
Suitability	1, 2	Modelling concepts allow for automatic transformation into implementation level documents Modelling concepts support required types of analysis If necessary: cost for adapting model for transformation/ analysis	If the suitability of a model is not satisfactory, there is no chance to deploy tools; hence, high costs can be expected.	No	Engineering -> Technical model features
Tools	1	Availability of tools that feature transformation/ analysis functions Cost of tools Cost of integrating tool with existing software development environment	For handling complex models, tools are almost mandatory.	No	Benefits -> Openness
Training/ Support	1, 2	Skills required for performing transformation/analysis tasks available Cost of training Cost of external support	This is especially relevant for models that serve as vehicles for analysis or transformation.	No	Deployment -> understandability, attitude

Table 3. Maintenance

Aspect	Relevant for type of use	Criteria	Comment	Specific to reference model?	Related to
Conceptual support	1, 2, 3	Concepts that support adaptation in a safe and convenient way	In case a model lacks these concepts, adaptation becomes risky and expensive.	Yes	Engineering -> Technical model features, Language features
Tools	1, 2, 3	Availability of tools that support model management (versions, users) Cost of tools	This includes multi-user access.	No	Engineering -> Technical model features Benefits -> Openness
Skills	1, 2, 3	Cost of internal skills Cost of external skills	These costs depend on the complexity of maintenance tasks and the spreading of a model.	Yes (external skills)	Benefits -> Openness

Analysis costs result from analysing a model with respect to a specific purpose (e.g., using a business process model for detecting bottlenecks or for running simulations). Maintenance refers to costs that are required for keeping a model up to date in the long run, which includes small and major changes.

Focus on Benefits

Using a reference model promises a number of benefits. While the ex ante quantification of these benefits has to face a number of severe obstacles, differentiating the overall potential benefit in a number of aspects can contribute to an evaluation that supports a comprehensive comparison with alternatives—such as developing a corresponding model on one's own or doing without conceptual models. Three categories are proposed for this purpose: *efficiency*, *flexibility* and *coordination/communication*.

Figure 4. Efficiency/effectiveness

Aspect	Relevant for type of use	Criteria	Comment	Specific to reference model?	Related to
Software Development and Maintenance	1	Improvement of productivity Improvement of software quality Functionality and maturity of available tools Compatibility with existing abstractions Skills of software developers Willingness to use reference model	These are core promises of reference models. Evaluating them requires taking into account relevant requirements, model features and user competence.	Yes	Deployment -> understandability, attitude Engineering -> technical model features
Business/ Management	1, 2, 3	Increased efficiency of affected business processes Cost reduction within business processes Support for specific decision scenarios Familiarity with model based decision making Willingness to use model within decision scenarios Improved customer-orientation	These are crucial criteria for the benefits to be expected from a model. They require a thorough analysis.	No	Benefits -> coordination Deployment -> understandability, attitude

Figure 5. Flexibility/integration

Aspect	Relevant for type of use	Criteria	Comment	Specific to reference model?	Related to
Dependence from IT-vendors	1, 2	Number of relevant IT-vendors that support model Number of users Degree of customization Standardisation Level of industry commitment	Dependence does not have to be avoided, if there is a satisfactory level of trust.	Yes	Openness Protection of Investment -> spreading/ commitment Deployment -> understand-ability
Openness	1, 2	Compatibility to relevant standards Integration with further reference models Coverage of possible future business models	This includes standards both for modelling languages and models.	Yes	Protection of Investment -> Spreading/ Commitment
Expressive Power	1, 2, 3	Degree of (ontological) completeness of modelling language	This requires analysing the actual need for expressive power.	No	Engineering -> language features
Relationship to other IT Artifacts	1, 2	Concepts that foster integration/transformation into other relevant representations	For instance: ER to Relational Model, business process models to workflow schema	No	Cost -> tools

This aspect serves to analyse whether a reference model contributes to an organisation's ability to respond to change.

Coordination/Knowledge Management

A conceptual model should serve as a medium to foster communication between stakeholders with different professional backgrounds, such as software users, managers, software developers, consultants, etc. At the same time, it can be regarded as object and reification of corporate knowledge management: A conceptual model represents knowledge about a firm and supports people who want to learn how a company works. A reference model can provide additional support for coordination and knowledge management, since it may increase the number of people/institutions to communicate with, and it may incorporate knowledge from external sources that adds to the corporate knowledge base.

Table 6. Coordination/knowledge management

Aspect	Relevant for type of use	Criteria	Comment	Specific to reference model?	Related to
Coordination	1, 2, 3	Helps to overcome communication barriers within company Fosters communication with external partners Improves coordination of business processes Fosters the establishment of inter-organisational coordination	While this is an aspect that applies to conceptual models in general, reference models promise to amplify the corresponding effects.	No	Deployment -> understandability Openness Protection of Investment -> Spreading/ Commitment
Knowledge Management	1, 2	Contributes to internal dissemination of relevant knowledge Supports development of relevant skills of employees Contributes to cross-organisational exchange of knowledge Incorporates relevant, external knowledge Decreases time to bring new employees, business partners up to date Contributes to a unified, enterprise-wide terminology	Makes knowledge available to people who formerly had no access	Yes	Deployment -> understandability, attitude

In case a more detailed analysis of benefits is required, the deployment of a reference model can be analysed in association with related business objectives. If, for instance, the reference model is an enterprise-wide object model, models of relevant business processes could be used to study the potential effects on important goals associated with these processes. If the reference model itself is a business process model, it could be evaluated using a model of the corporate strategy: The strategic goals can then be used to analyse the contribution of a certain process type. For an example of how to relate features of business processes to strategic plans, see Frank and Schauer (2006).

Figure 7. Protection of investments

Aspect	Relevant for type of use	Criteria	Comment	Specific to reference model?	Related to
Spreading/ Commitment	1, 2, 3	Number of organisations that use the model Number of vendors and service providers that support the model Standardisation of modelling language Standardisation of model	Corresponding statements of vendors should be tested thoroughly.	Yes	Benefits -> openness
Technological Change	1, 2	Independent from a particular technology Supports technologies that can be expected in near future	This requires identifying the core concepts of a technology.	No	Engineering -> technical model features

Focus on Protection of Investments

Taking into account that using a reference model can cause substantial investments, the question of how these investments are protected is a core issue.

The Deployment Perspective

The success of a reference model depends heavily on its users. This includes their ability as well as their willingness to deal with the model. Within this perspective, the framework includes the following aspects: *understandability*, *appropriateness* and *attitude*. In order to foster communication between the involved stakeholders, a model should be understandable. In other words, it should correspond to concepts, the prospective model users are familiar with. A reference model should stress an appropriate level of abstraction in detail—with respect to the purpose, a model is supposed to fulfil. If prospective users are not willing to make use of the model or if there are any objections against the model's usability, this lack of attitude can become a critical success factor. Therefore, it should be taken into account, even if it does not necessarily correspond directly to certain model features.

The Engineering Perspective

A reference model is a design artifact that can be regarded as a specification of possible solutions to a range of problems. From an engineering viewpoint, two questions are pivotal:

Figure 8. Deployment perspective

Aspect	Relevant for type of use	Criteria	Comment	Specific to reference model?	Related to
Understand-ability	1, 2, 3	Elaborate structure for documentation (e.g., with design patterns) Comprehensive documentation Scenarios and examples Familiarity with modelling language Familiarity with terminology Intuitive access to graphical representation Views for different groups of stakeholders	A modelling concept is the more understandable, the more it corresponds to concepts/terms, an observer is familiar with.	No	Engineering -> explanation
Appropriateness	1, 2	Amount of support for purposes relevant for users Supports technologies that can be expected in near future	Implies requirements analysis	Yes	Benefits -> suitability
Attitude	1, 2, 3	"Not invented here"-syndrome Reputation of model developers Resistance to organisational change Cultural barriers	If resistance is to be expected, it can help to get developers involved in time.	Yes	

Does the model fulfil the requirements to be taken into account? Is the specification suited for supporting the intended purposes of the model? To analyse these questions, four aspects are differentiated: *definition, explanation, language features, model features.*

Testing a model against requirements implies the requirements are to be made explicit in a comprehensive and precise way. Requirements include a definition of the intended application domains as well as a definition of the purposes to be satisfied. In the ideal case, these definitions should allow for deciding whether the model fits a particular application area or whether it supports a certain purpose. Note, however, that this does not only depend on the quality of the requirements documentation. Furthermore, every prospective user should know the requirements and purposes of the application he has in mind. In addition to merely defining the requirements, the model should also be explained in the sense that a potential user is supported in understanding and judging it. This includes an assignment of model elements to requirements as well as a substantiation of major design decisions that the model

Figure 9. Engineering perspective

Aspect	Relevant for type of use	Criteria	Comment	Specific to reference model?	Related to
Definition	1, 2, 3	Comprehensive description of intended application domains Comprehensive description of intended purposes	In both cases definitions should allow for deciding whether a reference model fits specific needs	No	Deployment -> understandability Epistemological -> general principle
Explanation	1, 2, 3	Assigning model elements to requirements Justification/substantiation of design decisions Discussing design compromises and resulting drawbacks Discussion of alternative approaches	An elaborated explanation of this kind is a tremendous support for model evaluation.	No	Epistemological -> general Principles
Language Features	1, 2, 3	Level of formalization, extensibility, supported conceptual views, integration of views, tool support, concepts to support the adaptation of models, concept to foster model integrity	The modelling language is essential for the engineering use of a model.	No	Benefits -> expressive power Epistemological -> critical distance
Technical Model Features	1, 2, 3	Formal correctness/ consistency Model architecture Use of classes Use of generalisation/ specialisation Use of modularisation/ encapsulation	Here, it has to be analysed, whether the concepts provided by the modelling language have been used appropriately to achieve integrity and flexibility.	No	Language Features

is based on. Often, design decisions require a compromise. This should be discussed including the resulting drawbacks. With respect to a modeling language, the following criteria are relevant: *level of formalization, extensibility, supported conceptual views, integration of views, tool support* and concepts to support the *adaptation of models.* Technical features of a model include *formal correctness, model architecture* and *adaptability.*

From an engineering point of view, adapting a reference model to individual requirements in a safe and convenient way is a core challenge. A key idea to accomplish adaptability of this kind is *abstraction.* It recommends differentiating between invariant parts of the model and those parts that are subject to change and adaptation. This differentiation can be reflected in the architecture of a model. In the ideal case, changing variant parts should not cause any side effects on other parts of the model. Abstraction requires corresponding concepts within the modeling language as well as their adequate use in the reference model. Important concepts to foster abstraction are classes, generalisation/specialisation and modularisation/encapsulation. The concept of a class allows for abstracting from single instances. As a consequence, changes can be applied to all instances of a class at one place. Generalisation allows for abstracting from special features of subclasses. Changes that are applied to a superclass are transparently effective in all subclasses as well. On the other hand, adding a further subclass does not affect the semantics of existing classes. Encapsulation is an abstraction of internal structures of a class (in case of modularisation: of a module). It allows for adapting the implementation of a class to individual needs without changing its interface.

The Epistemological Perspective

This perspective serves to enrich the evaluation of reference models with epistemological considerations. They are differentiated into four interrelated aspects: the *evaluation of theories*, *general principles of scientific research*, *critical reflection of human judgement* and *reconstruction of scientific progress*.

Reference models reveal similarities to scientific theories. Like theories, they are supposed to provide representations not just of a single instance (an enterprise, an application, etc.), but of an entire class. Also, they can be regarded as contributions to the body of knowledge within a certain domain of interest. Therefore, it makes sense to apply criteria that are used for the evaluation of theories to the evaluation of reference models. There is, however, one major difference between theories and reference models. A theory is aimed at describing the world as it is. Hence, a key criterion for assessing theories is truth, or rather: a certain concept of truth, such as the correspondence, coherence or consensus concept. A concept of truth is only of limited use for evaluating reference models, since they are usually aimed at intended systems or future worlds: They are not only descriptive, but also prescriptive. Nevertheless, also with reference models, the claim for truth cannot be entirely neglected— we could speak of "relaxed truth": A reference model does not have to fit reality entirely; however, it should not contradict evidence. Hence, the descriptive parts of the model and the assumptions underlying the prescriptive parts can be evaluated according to the judgement of theories.

The correspondence concept of truth recommends testing a hypothesis against reality. This requires a precise description of the model and its intended applications as well as testing procedures that allow for comparing a statement with perceptions of reality. The coherence concept of truth recommends that a new hypothesis should be in line with an established body of knowledge (e.g., with research results and opinions found in acknowledged publications).

Applied to reference models, this implies that assumptions underlying the design of a model should not contradict accepted knowledge (e.g., established accounting principles—notice that this is just one notion of truth). From the viewpoint of truth as result of a consensus, emphasis is on discursive judgement by experts. This would recommend getting acknowledged people involved who should discuss and eventually confirm the assumptions a reference model is based on.

Despite the ongoing discussion on concepts of truth and corresponding research methods, there are three generic principles that allow for differentiating scientific research from other sources of knowledge: *abstraction*, *originality*, and *judgment*. While not necessarily with the same rigour, they should apply to reference models, too. A high quality reference model should abstract from peculiarities of single instances and from changes that may occur over time. Abstraction, however, does not simply mean to arbitrarily fade out parts of the domain. Instead, abstraction should be made explicit and should include hints of how to turn it into a concrete description that applies to a particular case. With reference models, originality is hard to judge. Nevertheless it is certainly important. This is especially the case for reference models that result from scientific research (see "progress"). Judgement in science means that there has to be given comprehensive reason/justification for any hypothesis. For this purpose, one will usually refer to the preferred concept of truth and the related testing procedures. This can be applied to the descriptive parts of a reference model, too. With respect to decisions that motivate prescriptive elements of a reference model, this is different, because truth is not the issue. In order to provide reasons for design decisions, reference could be made to the accepted state of the art (following the coherence concept) or to discursive judgement by experts (following the consensus concept). In any case, judgement implies that every non-trivial assumption that design decisions are based on should be made explicit and reasons given for the choice.

Epistemology deals with the study of scientific judgements or, in other words, with the limits of human knowledge. Despite the ongoing debate, a critical or even sceptical evaluation of our perception and ability to judge prevails. There are many kinds of deception. With respect to the social sciences (or the humanities), perception and judgement are often biased by social/cultural constructions one is not entirely aware of. With respect to reference models, there is even more reason for epistemological scepticism. Reference models are linguistic artifacts: They are described using a language and—on another level of abstraction—they represent a language themselves. Although we are able to reflect upon language, for instance by distinguishing between object and meta-level language, our ability to speak and understand a language is commonly regarded as a competence that we cannot entirely comprehend. Therefore, any research that aims at inventing new "language games" (i.e., artificial languages and actions built upon them), has to face a subtle challenge: Every researcher is trapped in a network of language, patterns of thought and action he or she cannot completely transcend, leading to a paradox that can hardly be resolved.

Understanding a language is not possible without using a language. At the same time, any language we use for this purpose will bias our perception and judgement or, as the early Wittgenstein put it, "The limit of my language means the limit of my world" (Wittgenstein, 1981, §5.6). If one has to judge a reference model specified in UML and happens to dislike UML, an objective evaluation of the model will be hardly possible. Also, if a reference model of an accounting system makes use of terms that are different from those we use for accounting, it is very likely that we do not find it comprehensive—although it might be superior with respect to consistency or adaptability.

While it seems impossible to entirely overcome these obstacles, they can be met with certain precautions. Everyone involved in the evaluation of a reference model should name the modeling languages he or she is familiar with as well as preferences for modeling languages and technical languages. Then, everyone should reflect upon the question how his or her

Figure 9. Epistemological perspective

Aspect	Relevant for type of use	Criteria	Comment	Specific to reference model?	Related to
Evaluation of theories	1, 2, 3	Precise description of core concepts with respect to corresponding real world concepts; precise description of underlying assumptions	Precision in this case does not require formalization. Instead, the description should allow for testing against reality.	Yes	Engineering -> definition Deployment -> understandability
Generic Principles	1, 2, 3	Abstraction Originality Judgement	Different from theories, judgement does not have to relate to truth.	Yes	Engineering -> explanation
Critical Distance	1, 2, 3	Subjective nature of underlying decisions Bias through familiarity with modelling language High degree of spreading may be mistaken for high quality	The main purpose of this aspect is to motivate a critical reflection on the constraints an evaluation has to face.	Yes	
Scientific Progress	1, 2, 3	Discussion of long-term goals of research Elaborate documentation of model with respect to generic principles and long-term research goals Comparison with alternatives	While this is mainly an aspect that is of concern for scientific research, developing a notion of progress in reference modelling can also help with evaluation in practice.	Yes	

language background could influence their judgement. This could contribute to a more critical distance and a more objective judgement.

Taking into account their similarity to theories, reference models are an ideal subject of design-oriented research. If reference models are regarded as results of scientific research, there is need for identifying or reconstructing progress in the field. This requires reference models to be compared with respect to their contribution to the discipline's body of knowledge. Usually, that does not happen. Hevner et al. suggest that an artifact "may extend the knowledge base or apply existing knowledge in new and innovative ways" (Hevner, March, Park, Ram, 2004, p. 87). They do not, however, discuss how this could be accomplished. While there is no objective measure of progress with regard to reference models, there is only one approach to foster the identification of progress: documentation and competition. Reference models need to be documented in a way that makes them comparable. This requires a common structure—comparable to structures being used for the documentation of design patterns. In addition to documentation, it is necessary that everyone who presents a reference model compares it thoroughly with existing similar models—which in turn demands the definition of design goals. Such elaborated comparative documentation could then be used for presenting the body of knowledge of the field and for reconstructing progress.

Applying the Framework: Outline of a Process

The rationale behind the framework presented here is to emphasize the need for considering a complex object such as a reference model from different perspectives in order to contribute to a more balanced judgement. The complexity of this task recommends the definition of a project. The generic process model that accompanies the framework is intended to guide the management of evaluation projects. The process consists of five major stages. Each stage is described using a common structure (see Figure 1).

The introduction of a reference model can be a major investment with implications that last for a long time. If this is the case, the process should start with a strategic analysis. It is aimed at studying the effect of a reference model on a company's competitiveness, which includes its ability to cope with change, to reduce cost, to improve its customer orientation, etc. Only if this stage results in a potential benefit to be expected from a reference model, does it makes sense to continue. In addition to the generic criteria presented in the framework, it is necessary to define concrete requirements that are related to the specific purpose of the model. The level of detail requirements analysis should cover depends on the assumed degree of peculiarities to be dealt with. Although the framework includes four perspectives, it might not be appropriate to use all of them in every project. The epistemological perspective especially requires a certain mindset and competence that is not always available. Also, one may want to do without the deployment perspective. Therefore, the perspectives that are regarded as relevant—and affordable, have to be selected. Furthermore, it is possible at this stage to modify the criteria assigned to a perspective. The following step is focussed on the evaluation of the reference model using the (customized) framework. Finally, the perspective-specific evaluations have to be integrated in order to accomplish an overall, balanced judgement.

The method (i.e., the framework and the process model) should not be mistaken as clear directions. Instead, they are only a guideline to structure the overall problem. The identification and interpretation of specific model features requires a competent and thorough analysis. For this reason, staffing is a key success factor. This is the case for those who are taking certain perspectives and even more so for those who moderate the process of balancing the perspectives.

Figure 1. The generic process model and excerpt of documentation

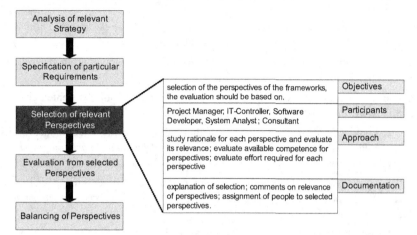

Conclusion

For a number of reasons, the evaluation of reference models is a challenging, yet important task. For a business firm, the deployment of a reference model is not only a substantial investment but it changes the process of software development and may affect the motivation and productivity of software developers. This recommends a thorough and elaborated evaluation as it is fostered by the method presented in this chapter. However, such an evaluation does not come for free. While one can expect the overall judgement to improve with the effort put into the evaluation, there will be a point when the cost caused by an evaluation overcompensates for its benefit. This implies that there is need for evaluating the evaluation from a controlling perspective. Especially in cases where no experiences with similar projects are available, estimating costs and benefits of an evaluation project in advance is hardly possible. Nevertheless, it is a good idea to reflect upon these aspects before defining a particular project.

While the motivation for evaluating reference models in academia is different, the challenges are similar. From a scientific point of view, it would make sense to study the effects produced by a reference model in the long run. Often, this is no option, since it would require resources that are not available to research institutions. If the evaluation is based on a method only, a scientific approach recommends a critical analysis of the method itself—again an evaluation of the evaluation. If this is done by deploying a further (meta) framework, one would finally produce an endless regress. Therefore, similar to controlling, a pragmatic solution is required. It could include the evaluation of the framework by peers and prospective users as well as empirical studies that focus on the use of the framework—or the method respectively.

References

Batini, C., Ceri, S., & Navathe, S.B. (1992). *Conceptual database design: An entity relationship approach*. Redwood City: Benjamin Cummings.

Becker, J., Rosemann, B., & Schütte, R. (1995): Guidelines for modeling. In *Wirtschaftsinformatik, 37*(5), 435-445. [in German]

De Champeaux, D., & Faure, P. (1992). A comparative study of object-oriented analysis methods. In *Journal of Object-Oriented Programming, 1*(5), 21-33.

Fettke, P., & Loos, P. (2003a). Ontological evaluation of the semantic object model. In E.J. Sinz, M. Plaha, & P. Neckel (Eds.), *Modellierung betrieblicher Informationssysteme. Proceedings of the MobIS Workshop* (pp. 109-129). Bamberg, Germany. [in German]

Fettke, P., & Loos, P. (2003b). Ontological evaluation of reference models using the Bunge-Wand-Weber-model. In *Proceedings of the 9th Americas Conference on Information Systems*, Tampa, FL (pp. 2944-2955).

Fettke, P., & Loos, P. (2003c, October 13). Multiperspective evaluation of reference models: Towards a framework. In M. A. Jeusfeld & Ó. Pastor (Eds.), *Conceptual modeling for novel application domains: ER 2003 Workshops ECOMO, IWCMQ, AOIS, and XSDM*, Chicago (LNCS 2814, pp. 80-91). Berlin, Germany: Springer.

Fettke, P., & Loos, P. (2003d). Classification of reference models: A methodology and its application. In *Information Systems and E-Business Management, 1*(1), 35-53.

Fettke, P., & Loos, P (2004). *Systematic survey of reference model: Preliminary results*. Working Papers of the Research Group Information Systems & Management. Paper 19, Mainz, Germany. [in German]

Firesmith, D., Henderson-Sellers, B., Graham, I., & Page-Jones, M. (1996, December 8). *OPEN modeling language (OML). Reference manual, Version 1.0*. Retrieved from http://www.csse.swin.edu.au/OPEN/comn.html

Frank, U. (1998). *Evaluating modelling languages: Relevant issues, epistemological challenges and a preliminary research framework*. Arbeitsberichte des Instituts für Wirtschaftsinformatik der Universität Koblenz-Landau/Germany.

Frank, U., & Schauer, C. (2006). E-MEMO: A method to support the development of customized electronic commerce systems. *Information Systems and E-Business Management, 4*(4).

Frank, U., & Prasse, M. (1997). *A framework for evaluating object oriented modeling languages: Exemplified by the examples of OML and UML*. Arbeitsberichte des Instituts für Wirtschaftsinformatik der Universität Koblenz-Landau, No. 7. [in German]

Frank, U., & Van Laak, B. (2003). *Requirements for business process modeling languages*. Arbeitsberichte des Instituts für Wirtschaftsinformatik, Nr. 34, University of Koblenz-Landau, Germany. [in German]

Goldstein, R. C., & Storey, V. (1990). Some findings on the intuitiveness of entity-relation-ship constructs. In F. H. Lochovsky (Ed.), *Entity-relationship approach to database design and querying* (pp. 9-23). Amsterdam, NL: Elsevier Science.

Hevner, A.R., March, S.T., Park, J., & Ram, S. (2004). Design science in information systems research. *MIS Quarterly, 28*(1), 75-105.

Hitchman, S. (1995). Practitioner perceptions on the use of some semantic concepts in the entity-relationship model. *European Journal of Information Systems, 4*, 31-40.

Hong, S., & Goor, G. (1993). A formal approach to the comparison of object-oriented analysis and design methodologies. In J. F. Nunamaker & R. H. Sprague (Eds.), *Information systems: Collaboration technology, organizational systems, and technology. Proceedings of the 26th International Hawaii International Conference on System Sciences*, Los Alamitos (pp. 689-698).

Krogstie, J. (1998). Integrating the understanding of quality in requirements specification and conceptual modeling. *Software Engineering Notes, 23*(1), 86-91.

Lindland, O. I., Sindre, G., & Sølvberg, A. (1994). Understanding quality in conceptual modeling. *IEEE Software, 11*(2), 42-49.

Mišic, V. B., & Zhao, J. L. (2000, October 9-12). Evaluating the quality of reference models. In A. H. F. Laender, S. W. Liddle, & V. C. Storey (Eds.), *Conceptual modelling. ER 2000—19th International Conference on Conceptual Modeling*, Salt Lake City, UT (pp. 4484-498). Berlin.

Moody, D. L. (2005). Theoretical and practical issues in evaluating the quality of concep-tual models: Current state and future directions. *Data and Knowledge Engineering, 55*(3), 243-276.

Monarchi, D. E., & Puhr, G. (1992). A research typology for object-oriented analysis and design. *Communications of the ACM, 35*(9), 35-47.

Moody, D. L., & Shanks, G. G. (1994). What makes a good data model? Evaluating the qual-ity of entity relationship models. In *Proceedings of the 13th International Conference on the Entity-Relationship Approach (ER'94)* (pp. 94-111). Manchester, UK.

Mylopoulus, J., & Levesque, H. J. (1985). An overview of knowledge representation. In M. L. Brodie, J. Mylopoulos, & J. Schmidt (Eds.), *On Conceptual Modelling. Perspec-tives from Artificial Intelligence, Databases and Programming* (pp. 3-17). Berlin; Heidelberg, Germany: Springer.

Opdahl, A .L., & Henderson-Sellers, B. (1999). Evaluating and improving OO modelling languages using the BWW-model. In *Proceedings of the Information Systems Founda-tions Workshop* (Ontology, Semiotics and Practice). [digital publication]

Shanks, G., Tansley, E., & Weber, R. (2003). Using ontology to validate conceptual models. *Communications of the ACM, 46*(10), 85-89.

Süttenbach, R., & Ebert, J. (1997). *A booch metamodel*. Fachberichte Informatik 5/97, Universität Koblenz-Landau.

Weber, R. (1997). *Ontological foundations of information systems*. Melbourne: Coopers & Lybrand.

Wittgenstein, L. (1981). *Tractatus logico-philosophicus*. Englewood Cliffs, NJ: Routledge Kegan Paul.

Zelewski, S. (1995). Petrinet-based modeling of complex production systems. Vol. 9: Evaluating the concept of Petrinets. *Arbeitsbericht des Instituts für Produktionswirtschaft und industrielle Informationswirtschaft, Nr. 14*, University of Leipzig/Germany. [in German]

Chapter VII

Using Reference Models in Enterprise Architecture:
An Example

Ovidiu Noran, Griffith University, Australia

Abstract

This chapter presents a way to use reference models in enterprise architecture (EA) by (a) assessing and organising them into a structured repository using a generalised architecture framework (ISO15704:2000 Annex A) and (b) providing guidance for the selection of refer-ence models that are suitable for specific EA tasks. A brief introduction to EA and current issues in using reference models in this domain is followed by sample mappings of several reference models from the company networks and virtual enterprises area onto the chosen framework. This is followed by a brief description of the meta-methodology guiding the selection of the reference models and by an example of reference model selection for a real situation. The chapter closes with reflections on improving reference models' quality and conclusions on the usefulness of the framework and meta-methodology used to structure and select reference models for EA tasks.

Introduction

The survival of a business nowadays depends essentially on its *agility*, that is, its capability to change (Goranson, 1998) in response to environmental factors such as suppliers, clients, prices, new business entrants, laws, and so forth. Thus, business analysis and architectural design, also known as *enterprise engineering* (EE), is always present, although often only in a tacit form. Note that within this chapter, enterprise architecture (EA) is used as a term synonymous to EE, although EA can also refer to the architecture of an enterprise as an artifact (hence the end result of the architectural design/re-design activities). Such differences will be emphasized in context where relevant.

Currently, EA as a discipline is still in its early phases. Although several EA research directions exist, the ontology of EA is not yet widely agreed upon. For example, current EA publications and advertised EA positions in the industry reflect a variety of perceptions about the meaning of EA and about the role of "enterprise architects" in an organisation. In addition, EA is not yet fully supported by established "school(s) of thought" espousing formal theoretical foundations and associated paradigms; as a result, the EA researcher needs to find "best matches" in paradigms and research methods from related disciplines, notably social sciences and IS.

Typically, the scope of EA cuts across several disciplines and requires significant resources. The success of EA projects typically depends on the maturity of the methods and models used and on the extent of knowledge capture and reuse. Knowledge management (to understand the current state of the business) and change management (to control business transition from current to future states) are presently main drivers of EA.

A comprehensive introduction to the EA discipline and research is beyond the scope of this chapter, whose focus is on illustrating the use of reference models in EA.

Creating and Using Reference Models in Enterprise Architecture

The reuse of EA knowledge can be achieved by identifying commonalities in enterprise models (EMs), grouping them accordingly and abstracting common features into *partial* enterprise models that act as a *reference* for all the models they represent. Here, the term "partial" suggests that the model obtained by abstraction is not necessarily a complete model of anything. Thus, a partial model needs to be detailed, specialised, instantiated and/or combined with other models in order to create a complete model. EA standards, such as ISO15704:2000 (ISO/TC184, 2000), use the terms *partial* enterprise models (PEMs) or *reference* enterprise models. For simplicity, in this chapter PEMs will be called "reference models" (RMs). RMs in EA can take various forms, such as fill-in templates or patterns (verified solutions to typical EA problems) and can be represented using several languages.

In the context of EA, RMs can perform several functions. Their main purpose is to speed up the modeling process by providing templates and thus avoiding the need to start from scratch every time an EM is needed (provided that a suitable enough RM exists for the EA task in question). An important aspect of using reference models for creating particular models of individual systems is that they have a *common referent* and thereby exhibit some level of commonality; thus, RMs can be used to enforce some consistency among models. RMs may also support the EA education process by providing a "learn by example" approach.

Current Issues in Using Reference Models in Enterprise Architecture

RMs are useful artifacts but they do present drawbacks, as described below. For example, RMs come in various degrees of specialisation. A specialised RM has a narrow area of application, while a more generic RM may need to be customised before being used for a specific EA task. Thus, an assessment of the RMs in terms of their scope, specialisation level and life cycle phase applicability in respect to a suitably expressive reference would help prospective RM users estimate the amount of effort needed to use a specific RM.

Typically, users need significant knowledge of the RMs used—either to know when and where to apply them (for the specialised RMs), or to know how to customise them (for the more generic RMs). This problem could be solved by providing a method that could recommend various RMs based on user knowledge of the specific EA task (application domain knowledge) rather than on knowledge of the multitude of available and usable RMs.

RMs are developed to encapsulate reusable knowledge about various domains of the modelled enterprise; thus, RMs are typically focused on specific aspects (e.g., function, information, decision, etc.) or on a combination thereof. The scope of an RM is not always published or otherwise obvious. In addition, RMs developed for a particular domain are often applicable in other domains as well. The user needs to know the coverage of the various RMs in order to make an informed decision on whether one, several or perhaps no existing RMs are suitable for the enterprise modeling exercise in question. This aspect can be addressed by assessing the RMs against a fixed reference (able to contain all RM aspects) and mapping their universe of discourse (UoD) coverage.

In conclusion, the users needing to perform EA tasks could be significantly helped by (a) evaluation of the RMs in respect to their specialisation and scope using a fixed and comprehensive reference, and (b) guidance on *which* RMs (if any) to use for their specific EA problem and *how* to use the selected RMs. These two aspects are addressed within the efforts to design a method describing how to construct customised methods guiding specific EA tasks—a *meta-methodology* for EA (Noran, 2004a). One of the main meta-methodology components is a repository containing elements of several architecture frameworks (including RMs), assessed in respect to a common reference and attached rules containing selection criteria. The term "architecture framework" (AF) is understood within this chapter as an artifact defining the types of elements needed to support the creation of an object, from the identification of the need to create it, to its ultimate decommissioning. Note that, beside the obvious modeling framework component, elements such as RMs, methods, tools and theoretical foundations such as ontologies and metamodels are also considered as necessary within an AF, in line with the requirements set out in ISO15704:2000.

The meta-methodology uses the repository content to build ranked lists of AF elements recommended for specific EA tasks. Therefore, the meta-methodology can provide sound advice to non-expert users regarding RMs suitable for a particular EA project, also taking into account the specific life cycle phase (see GERA structure) of that project. In addition, the creation of a new RM is supported: The methods produced by the meta-methodology application can be grouped into classes and abstracted into RMs for EE methods.

The Scope of this Chapter

This chapter aims to exemplify the use of RMs in EA by (a) organising RMs relevant to EA into a structured repository (SR) using ISO15704:2000 Annex A as a framework, and (b) by providing guidance for the selection of suitable RMs for specific EA tasks using meta-methodology described in Noran (2004a, 2005).

Note that the two artifacts used in this example do not *prescribe* the use of any specific AF or AF elements (modeling frameworks, methods, languages, tools, etc.). They rather provide means to assess AFs and their elements (including the RMs) and guidance on their suitability for specific EA tasks. Therefore, this example could be reused by EA practitioners to evaluate their AFs, RMs and methods of choice in view of their specific EA needs.

Evaluation Tools for Architecture Framework

A Structured Repository of Architecture Framework Elements

In addition to the RM issues previously highlighted, a significant problem in EA practice is the lack of *specific* guidance, such as for the selection of AF elements (e.g., RMs) for specific

Figure 1. Meta-methodology environment showing the structured repository

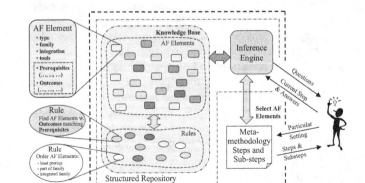

EA tasks. Similar to available RMs, the existing guidance (methods) is either very specialised (and often proprietary), or quite generic and requiring significant customisation to become useful. The research question addressing this problem was whether it was possible to build a *method to create methods* guiding various specific EA tasks (thus, a *meta-methodology*) and also assisting the user in selecting suitable AF constructs including RMs, modeling languages, tools, and so forth.

Following the research question, the existing AFs needed to be investigated for relevant components, such as modeling frameworks (MFs), RMs, generic modeling concepts (such as metamodels, ontologies, etc.), modeling methods, languages, tools, and so forth. Therefore, a critical literature review (Noran, 2003a) was performed, mapping the elements of several mainstream AFs against the reference described in the next section. This exercise has led to the creation of a *structured repository* (SR) organising AF elements by several criteria, such as family, type, integration, tools and, importantly, associating prerequisites and outcomes to each AF element (see the repository concept in Figure 1, left). In the case of RMs, this task has allowed representation by type, whether they belonged to a set of RMs, if the set was integrated (e.g., by a meta model) and whether the RMs were supported by any available tools. The most important attributes of an RM representation were the *outcomes* provided by the use of that RM and the *requirements* (prerequisites) that had to be satisfied before using the RM in question.

The Reference Model Assessment Framework

The ISO15704:2000 standard, "Requirements for Enterprise Reference Architectures and Methodologies," has been developed to supply a generic set of criteria for testing the ability of existing AFs to provide "complete" assistance for EA tasks. Annex A of the standard, namely *GERAM* (the Generalised Enterprise Reference Architecture and Methodology), is a generic AF compliant with ISO15704, obtained by generalising concepts present in several mainstream AFs and in EA best-practice.

GERAM provides guidance on the collection of AF elements (tools, methods, reference models, languages, etc.) to be employed in EA tasks. In addition, GERAM can be used as a tool for establishing the completeness and suitability of a proposed selection of AF elements for a particular EA task, and to recommend suitable artifacts for addressing any identified gaps in the coverage of the AF elements composing that solution. Note that GERAM only specifies *requirements* for tools, methods and models; it does not enforce any particular choices to satisfy these requirements. The expressiveness of GERAM's components (such the multitude of views present in the MF of its reference architecture) ensured that all features present in an AF element (such as an RM) could be represented and thus made GERAM an appropriate choice for the proposed assessment.

GERAM Components Relevant to Reference Modeling

Although the acronym "GERAM" suggests a structure composed only of a reference architecture and a methodology, Figure 2 reveals several other important AF components such

Figure 2. A GERAM metamodel (Source: ISO/TC184, 2000) (greyed areas not addressed in this chapter)

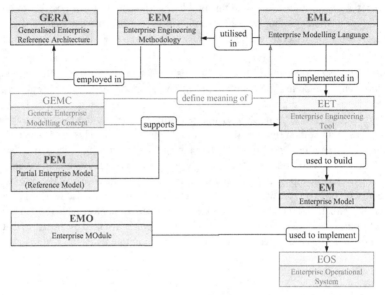

as modeling languages, tools, generic modeling concepts, and so forth. Note that only the components relevant to the present study are covered in this introduction to GERAM.

An essential component of GERAM is its reference architecture (GERA), whose MF features a three-dimensional structure containing several views that may be used to structure the knowledge in various interrelated models (refer to Figure 3). GERA does not enforce the presence of all views, and other view types can also be added. The condition, however, is that the views that *are* present must together cover the intended UoD of the specific EA task. GERA is described separately in the next section.

Enterprise engineering methodologies (EEMs) guide the user in the EA activity. Thus, in GERAM terms, the proposed meta-methodology application provides EEMs (expressed via models) customised for particular EA tasks.

Enterprise modeling languages (EMLs, or *grammars* in Wand and Weber's framework, 2002) provide the necessary constructs to describe the various artifacts present within GERAM. For example, EEMs represent the models of engineering processes by means of EMLs. Typically, a *combination* of EMLs has to be used to describe the various modeling aspects (e.g., information, function, behaviour, etc.) necessary for an EA project.

In GERAM, partial enterprise models (PEMs) represent reusable templates for human roles (organisational), processes (common functionality) or technology (resources, e.g., IT). The proposed meta-methodology recommends the use of suitable existing RMs depending on the application domain and supports the creation of new EEM RMs (abstracted from the EEMs created by the meta-methodology).

Enterprise models (EMs, called *scripts* by Wand and Weber (2002)) are the main vehicle for structuring the knowledge existent in the enterprise (e.g., by modeling the AS-IS state) but are also essential enablers of the change processes that may have prompted their creation (by modeling potential TO-BE states). A typical set of EMs as described by GERAM should include enterprise operations, organisation, IS and resources, and clearly show the human role within the control and production systems. Further detail such as hardware/software may also be required depending on the models' purpose (see the GERA views below).

Enterprise modules (EMOs) are implemented RMs, usable as "plug-and-play" components. For example, if a design has used certain RMs, the EMOs corresponding to those RMs can be directly used in the implementation of that design.

GERA Structure

GERA is a *life cycle* generalised reference architecture (i.e., an architecture that can model activities involved in the implementation of a project spanning over a part or the entire life of an entity). For example, in contrast, a *system* architecture models the structure of an entity (system) at a given point in time (similar to a snapshot). GERA contains an MF (represented in Figure 3) and other concepts such as life history, entity recursiveness, and so forth.

A modeling framework is a structure containing placeholders for artifacts needed in the modeling process. Depending on the structure of the framework, the type of these artifacts may be limited to models, or may extend to other construct types such as RMs, meta-models, glossaries, and so forth. The GERA MF, for example, contains placeholders for artifacts whose type is described in the GERAM meta-model (Figure 2). The life cycle representation capability of the GERA MF is reflected in its vertical geometrical dimension, containing typical life cycle phases (see Figure 3). This dimension was contributed by the Purdue En-

Figure 3. The GERA modelling framework (Source: ISO/TC184, 2000)

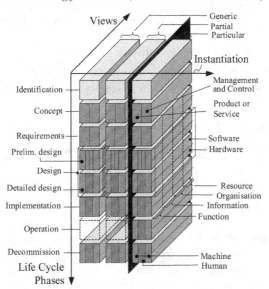

terprise Reference Architecture (PERA) (Williams, 1994) and the open system architecture for CIM (CIMOSA) (CIMOSA Association, 1996).

The GERA MF allows the practitioner to focus on certain aspects of complex EMs by using *views* defined by several criteria, as further described.

The *model content* criterion provides four views describing the functional, information, resource and organisation aspects of an enterprise. These views were contributed to GERA MF by CIMOSA and GRAI-GIM (Doumeingts, Vallespir, Zanettin, & Chen, 1992). It is to be noted that the organisation view may be obtained by mapping part of the resource view (human side) onto a subset of the functional view (the human-implemented functions).

The *purpose* criterion divides the EE artifacts into production (or customer service) and control (or management). In this study, this division is used when representing the relation between the life-cycle phases of various enterprise entity types in the business models used in meta-methodology application.

The *implementation* criterion provides a way to distinguish between the production/service and the management/control aspect of an enterprise, while at the same time allowing representation of the extent of the human roles in both aspects ("humanisability"). The human role is an essential success factor in EA, although it is typically overlooked or only marginally covered in the AFs and RMs currently available.

Finally, the *physical manifestation* criterion provides a finer subdivision, setting apart hardware and software aspects of EA artifacts. It is usually used in conjunction with views derived from other criteria.

The GERA MF also contains the concept of *genericity*, which allows representing all of the above enterprise aspects at the generic, partial and particular levels. The partial level of GERA was used in the assessment since it can represent RMs with various degrees of specialisation.

Other concepts in GERA (residing outside its MF) may be used to model additional aspects. For example, the concept of life *history* can be used to model process concurrency. In GERA, life "history" implies a time dimension and represents the collection of life-cycle phases that the entity has gone (or *will* go) through during its life. In contrast, life *cycle* abstracts from time and is a collection of life-cycle phases that the entity *could* go through during its life.

In conclusion, GERAM provides a suitable reference for assessing and structuring the pool of AF elements needed for the meta-methodology application, including RMs.

GERAM Assessment Example:
Wand and Weber's Research Framework

Wand and Weber (2002) define a research framework for conceptual modeling in IS, which is used to identify shortcomings and research opportunities in several main areas of conceptual modeling.

In the framework's terminology (Figure 4 right), modeling *grammars* provide constructs and rules on how to use them to represent the desired UoD. Modeling *methods* provide guidance on how to use grammars, while modeling *scripts* are the result of using grammars

Figure 4. Mapping of the conceptual modelling research framework components described by Wand and Weber (2002) on GERAM elements and EA concepts

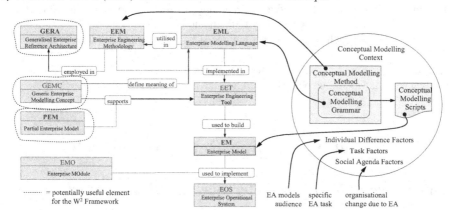

to model the UoD. In GERAM terms, "grammars" are languages and "scripts" are models created using the grammars.

Wand and Weber's framework (hereafter called the W^2 framework for simplicity) also describes the main types of influence factors within the modeling context. One of the factor types is "individual difference," such as stakeholder experience, training, and so forth; in an EA view, this represents the proficiency and background of the audience of the EA models and methods. "Task"-type factors model the suitability of the resulting "scripts" (models) to various tasks; this is reflected in the adopted AF (GERAM) where the task factors are the specific EA tasks (or task types) requiring customised methods and models. The framework also identifies "social agenda"-type factors, dealing with organisational change brought about by the resulting models. This is reflected in the adopted AF, which recognizes that the ultimate (stated or implicit) purpose of EA is *change*. A high-level mapping of the W^2 framework on GERAM's elements and other concepts in shown in Figure 4.

The assessment value of the adopted AF can now be demonstrated. Thus, in Figure 4 it can be seen that some elements present in GERAM are not covered by the W^2 framework. The next step would be to determine whether such elements are indeed needed within the W^2 framework. Such an analysis could find gaps in the W^2 framework coverage and could propose suitable elements of other frameworks to fill in the gaps if needed. It must be noted that such an analysis is typically performed in the context of the particular task and corresponding task-type factors. In this case, it can be argued that the addition of *generic modeling concepts* such as ontologies, meta-models and glossaries to the W^2 framework could be warranted for formalisation purposes. Similarly, the presence of RMs would enrich the W^2 framework, reference modeling being an essential facilitator of conceptual modeling.

The presence of a reference architecture (such as GERA in GERAM, see Figure 3) containing a MF with placeholders for artifacts such as models, methods, and so forth would allow for consistent description of artifacts of interest to the W^2 framework using various criteria. Again, the usefulness of such classifications must be considered in the context of the applicable task factors (i.e., the specific application of the scripts).

GERAM can be used to support the research agenda based on the W^2 framework by representing many of the future research directions described by Wand and Weber. Most of these directions are also applicable to reference modeling, such as method efficiency, methods to identify types of phenomena and classify them and how (and if) the values and beliefs underlying various modeling methods are embraced by the practitioners of those methods. The meta-methodology research design described in Noran (2004a, 2004c) addresses the last issue by presenting and justifying a selection of ontological and epistemological choices reflecting specific values and beliefs underlying the EA methodological research.

Evaluating Existing Reference Models

Some Previous Work on Reference Model Assessment

Reference (or partial) models in the GERA sense may be prototypes, abstract models or models of classes of enterprises which must be specialised, completed and/or instantiated in order to obtain the model of a particular enterprise (i.e., moving to the right-hand side on the instantiation axis in Figure 3). Human role, process and technology are specified as possible RM domains, with emphasis on RMs covering technology-oriented systems and *integrating services*, since this type of RM is similar for most enterprises and thus may be widely reused. RMs may exist at the policy level (i.e., at the GERA Concept life cycle phase), requirements level, architectural design level and even on the detailed design level, where RMs might describe detailed views of a *type of* product.

The critical literature review performed as part of the meta-methodology research effort (Noran, 2003a, 2004a) has investigated mainstream AFs for components according to the GERAM structure and has mapped those components against GERAM elements. Thus, the MF of GERA has been used to scope the identified RMs in order to determine their usability for the intended and *potential* applicability domain(s). Such RMs have included the CIMOSA Integrating Infrastructure Services (IIS), the GRAI Grid (Doumeingts, Vallespir, & Chen, 1998), the CIM reference model of PERA (Williams, 1988), a Zachman sample reference model (Popkin Software, 2001), the C4ISR Universal Reference Resources (C4ISR Architectures Working Group, 1997) and the ARIS partial model for CIM (Scheer, 1994).

The assessed and mapped RMs have then been stored in the SR as shown in Figure 1. The interested reader is directed to Noran (2003a) for details of other RM mappings using GERA, the full presentation of which is beyond the scope of this chapter.

The following sections will exemplify the use of GERAM and the meta-methodology to assess several RMs belonging to the company networks and virtual enterprises domain.

A Reference Model for Virtual Enterprises

In the current global market, enterprises worldwide must often come together for the purpose of tendering, executing and servicing large scale, one-of-a-kind or repetitive projects requir-

Figure 5. Company network and virtual enterprise model (Source: Globemen, 2000-2002; Tølle & Vesterager, 2002)

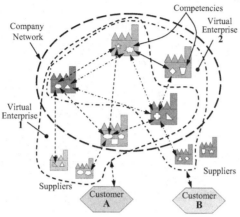

ing competencies and resources beyond those existent in any of the participants alone. The resulting organisations, although composed of various participants, appear as an indivisible entity to the outside environment (service providers, clients, etc.)—hence their name of *virtual* organisations (VOs) or virtual enterprises (VEs). Several conceptual and reference models of VOs are currently available in order to guide their prompt formation in response to business opportunities. However, in the formation of VEs, there is a multitude of issues to be resolved such as human processes (trust building, learning about the knowledge and culture of other potential partners, etc.), the agreement on a stable common ICT infrastructure (Camarinha-Matos & Afsarmanesh, 1999) and the establishment of commonly understood RMs, all of which are crucial requirements for effective interoperability of the VO participants.

Such processes typically need time and cannot be rushed. A possible solution is *breeding environments* (BEs), which help establish *preparedness* (Bernus, Noran, & Riedlinger, 2002) of potential VO partners for the quick establishment of a VO in response to a business opportunity. Thus, companies (or departments of larger companies) become collaborative networked organisations (CNO) that form a *collaborative network* (Camarinha-Matos, 2004) or *company network* (CN) (Globemen, 2000-2002) (see Figure 5) that provides the necessary BE for future VOs and capitalises on the knowledge (competencies) and market power existent in the network partners.

VERA (Virtual Enterprise Reference Architecture) has been developed by the Globemen Consortium (Globemen, 2000-2002) as a specialisation of the GERA reference architecture for CNs and VEs. The *particular level* of VERA constitutes a reference model showing the relations between enterprises participating in a CN, the VE(s) set up by the network and the product(s) of those VE(s) in the context of their life cycles (Figure 6). VERA is described in more detail by Vesterager, Tølle, and Bernus (2002). Previous research (Hartel, Billinger, Burger, & Kamio, 2002; Hartel, Kamio, & Zhou, 2002) has validated the applicability of this RM to the after-sales services sector, while the case study described by Noran (2004b) confirmed its applicability for VOs in higher education.

Figure 6. VERA-based reference model (Source: Globemen, 2000-2002; Vesterager et al., 2002)

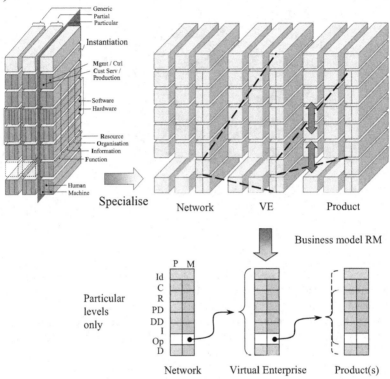

Figure 7. Generic GRAI-Grid with mapped organisational roles

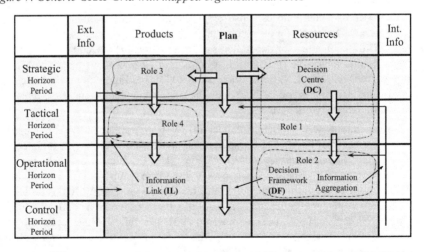

Figure 8. Decisional reference model for CN, participants and VEs (Source: Bernus et al., 2002;Olegario & Bernus, 2003)

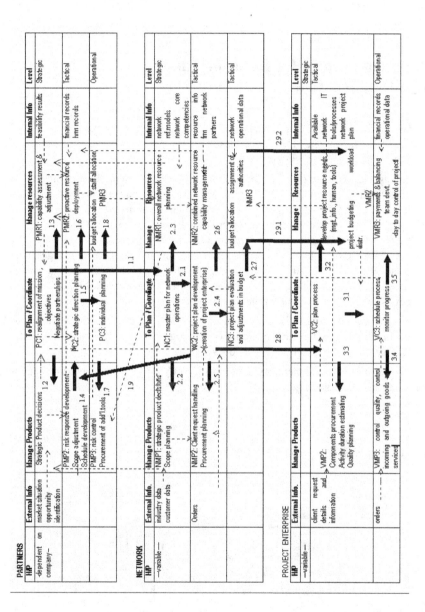

The VERA RM has been mapped against GERAM and included in the SR. One of its main outcomes is the possibility to assist with CN and VE business analysis, for example, allowing the life cycle-based assessment and selection of the preferred TO-BE (future) CN and VE states.

A Reference Model for Decisional and Organisational Aspects

Olegario and Bernus (2003) have created a reference model for the management of CNs and of the VEs they create. This model describes the decisional system of the CN, CN participants and its VEs (see Figure 8).

The formalism used to describe the model is the GRAI (Graphs with Results and Activities Interrelated) Grid (Doumeingts et al., 1998), which is in essence a generic RM for decisional modeling. The GRAI Grid describes types of decisional functions defining decision *centres* (DC) that send decision *frames* (DF) to lower DC echelons. DCs (in fact, *job descriptions*) are shown in a GRAI Grid as intersections of decision functions and levels (Figure 7). The functions of the DCs can be further scoped by using activity modeling languages such as Integration DEFinition for function modeling (IDEF0) (IEEE, 1998), unified modeling language (UML) activity diagrams (Rumbaugh, Jacobson, & Booch, 1999) or GRAI nets. This shows the close relationship of the decisional and functional aspects.

Moreover, once a GRAI Grid is completed, it is possible to map the enterprise's human resources on its DCs (see the areas covering DCs in Figure 7) in order to obtain the *organisational* structure of the enterprise ("who does what").

The RM shown in Figure 8 can also be used to identify present or potential management problems in an organisation generated by over-managed hierarchies, conflicting roles, nar-

Figure 9. Mapping of the decisional RM on the GERA partial level (dashed lines and lightly shaded areas represent implicit mapping)

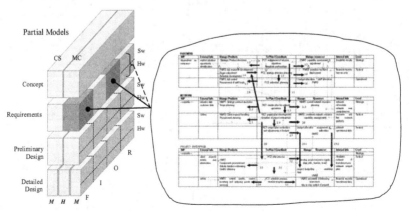

row/paternalistic management, and so forth as shown by Bernus (2003).

The RM maps onto the GERA partial level on the functional, organisational and (implicitly) resources views at the Requirements life cycle phase, on the Management and Control side as shown in Figure 9. This is because the aspect depicted by the RM is primarily functional, but it can be used to derive an organisational aspect by using the resources aspect; for example, resources may appear as mechanisms in functional models of the DCs, in which case the consistency of the resource representation across models must be ensured.

The RM outcomes represented in the SR in this case will contain decisional and organisational modeling for CN and VE or similar settings (e.g., extended enterprise, integrated supply chain, etc.). Thus, the RM may be reused for similar settings and further customised and/or even translated into another modeling language if desired. Another outcome of the RM is the identification of management problems, such as previously shown.

A Reference Model for the Functional Aspect

The functionality of an enterprise is typically regarded as an essential aspect in analysing, designing/re-designing and operating a business and as a result, it is almost always modelled.

This section briefly presents the assessment using GERA of a functional reference model created for CNs, their participants and the VEs created by them. The model was created using IDEF0 (NIST, 1993)—a functional modeling language commonly used for concept definition and requirements engineering. In IDEF0, each activity is described as a box with attached ICOMs (inputs, controls, outputs and mechanisms) as shown in Figure 10.

IDEF0 activities are decomposable. These decompositions are represented at different levels, allowing control of the complexity of the IDEF0-based models and RMs and thus enabling the presentation of the same model/RM to various audiences (e.g., management, technical personnel, etc.). In addition, the layered feature of IDEF0, whereby the models/RMs become increasingly specific at lower levels, facilitates the use of RMs in EA practice.

Figure 11 presents the second level (A0) of the functional RM, with activities describing the set-up and part operation of the CN and the VE(s) created by it. The activities present in the RM at this level also reflect typical life cycle phases of the CN and VEs described

Figure 10. Generic IDEF0 model, level A-0 (context)

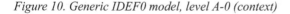
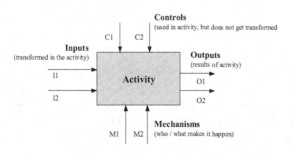

Figure 11. Functional reference model for CN, participants and VEs: Second level shown (Source: Bernus et al., 2002)

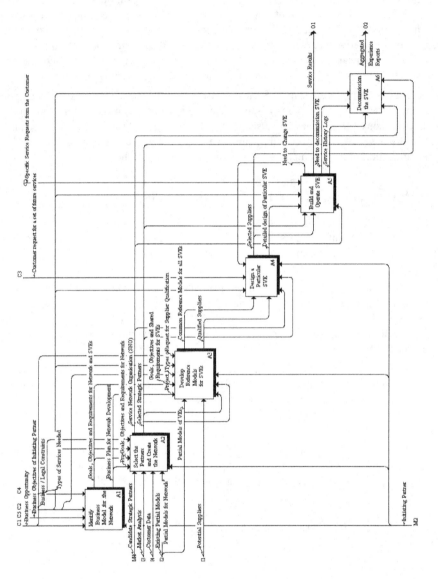

and thus can be used together with the VE RM previously presented.

The mapping of the functional RM on the GERA partial level is presented in Figure 12. The main result of this mapping in the RM outcomes (represented in the SR) is that the RM provides a template for modeling the functional view of the target enterprise(s) at the Concept and Requirements, and to a lesser degree at the Preliminary and Detailed Design

Figure 12. Mapping of the functional reference model on GERA (dashed lines and light shading show implicit coverage)

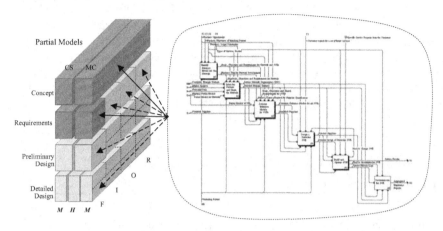

life cycle phases. However, warnings must be present (possibly as prerequisites) stating that the consistency of models needs to be checked if modeling of the information, resources and organisation views is also performed. This is because although this RM represents functional aspects, it will also refer the information, resources and organisation of the enterprise through the descriptions of the ICOMs present for each activity. This highlights a potential overlap if RMs of information, resources or organisation aspects of the same enterprise are used, and brings about the need to ensure consistency in the overlapping areas. Although IDEF0

Figure 13. The people process map (Gratton, et al., 1999) and Keidel's organisational patterns and profile RM (1995) mapping on GERA partial level

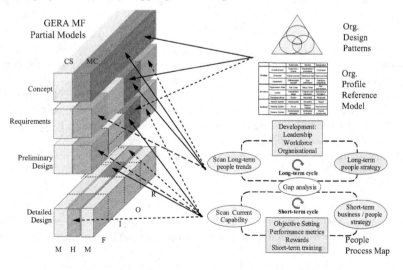

belongs to a family of languages, that family does not currently have a published meta model (Noran, 2003b) and thus, consistency between RMs or particular models created with IDEF languages is not inherent; current enterprise modeling tools supporting IDEF do enforce some degree of consistency, which however should be checked by the user.

The EA practitioner can reuse this RM for a different but similar setting (e.g., extended enterprise, integrated supply chain, etc.) by identifying the degree of similarity to the RM and subsequently customising it accordingly. The user may be assisted in this endeavour by the inference engine of the meta-methodology environment, as previously described. The knowledge required for reuse, apart from the concepts within the reference framework and the language used (which does not have to be IDEF0), is moderate.

Reference Models for Organisational Change and Human Resources

As previously shown, decisional RMs can be used for high-level modeling of the enterprise organisation by mapping the human resources to the decisional structure expressed in the RM (see Figure 7).

The organisational design effort can also be significantly assisted, for example, by RMs describing organisational types (such as Keidel's organisational patterns, 1995) and by RMs usable for requirements gathering (such as the gap analysis described by Ansoff, 1965, and Mintzberg, 1994). Such theories are in fact templates/patterns (hence RMs) that need to be customised/completed and/or fully instantiated for a particular organisation.

Once the present (AS-IS) and future (TO-BE) organisational states have been modelled as needed (Uppington & Bernus, 2003) and agreed upon with the stakeholders, methodological assistance is needed on how to proceed to achieve the TO-BE state. Such assistance is offered in this regard by change management methods and approaches such as the eight-stage change process described by Kotter (1996), the people process map (Gratton, Hope Hailey, Stiles, & Truss, 1999) and the behavioural change scenarios described by Mackay (2003). Such methods offer guidance for *types* of EA organisational tasks and hence they are considered RMs (of methods) within this chapter.

Typically, the customised EE method created by the meta-methodology will also cover the creation/management of the organisation, thus providing guidance for organisational change and proposing suitable methodological RMs such as previously described. Figure 13 shows a possible mapping of the people process described by Gratton et al. (1999) using the gap analysis method described by Ansoff (1965) and Mintzberg (1994) on the GERA MF. Keidel's (1995) organisational design patterns and profile RMs are also mapped in the same figure. As can be seen, although the main emphasis is on the organisational requirements and design, human resources and functional aspects are present as well due to the nature of the organisational aspect. This is reflected in the dashed lines and lighter shading in Figure 13.

These mappings allow for the outcomes definition of the RMs in question. For example, Keidel's Organisational Design Patterns are referring to the Organisational aspects of the GERA Concept, Requirements and Architectural (or Preliminary) Design life cycle phases.

Note that in GERA it is considered that the Concept level only contains the purpose views (i.e., management vs. production/service), being too early a phase to contain content views such as information, function, and so forth.

Conclusions from the Evaluation of Reference Models

The mappings of the RMs on GERAM and GERA have revealed that typically, several RMs may cover a particular area. However, the dimensions offered by the assessment framework such as the set of views, the specialisation and especially the life cycle dimension have allowed differentiation between the *ability* of RMs to cover specific aspects at given life cycle phases. For example, the functional RM previously described can cover the functional aspect at Concept, Requirements, Architectural and Detailed Design, however, its coverage is the strongest at Concept and Requirements life cycle phases. For that reason, the meta-methodology would create *ranked lists* of matching RMs for a specific task, with the user being able to select specific RMs and thus test several scenarios. In this case, the RM previously described would rank high for Concept and Requirements but lower for the other applicable life cycle phases.

Selecting Suitable Reference Models

A Meta-Methodology for Enterprise Architecture

A meta-methodology is being developed to support the development of methods for specific EA tasks. It is based on the concept of "reading" the life cycle phases of the target enterprise(s) in the context of its relations with other entities, using a life cycle-based business model. The meta-methodology contains the following main steps (see Figure 14):

- Identify entities relevant to the specific EA task.
- Construct a business model showing these entities and their relations, in the context of their life cycles.
- "Read" the life cycle diagrams of the entities to be designed phase by phase, noting the relations of each phase with phases of other entities and constructing a list of activities expressing these relations.

This chapter only describes the meta-methodology aspects relevant to RMs. Full details on the meta-methodology development and testing are beyond the purpose of this chapter and are available in Noran (2004a).

Figure 14 and Figure 1 show how the AF elements in the SR are used in the meta-methodology. Thus, the inference engine (or an artifact with similar functionality depending on the implementation) shown in Figure 1 selects RMs and other AF elements from the SR

Figure 14. Meta-methodology concept (Source: Noran, 2004a)

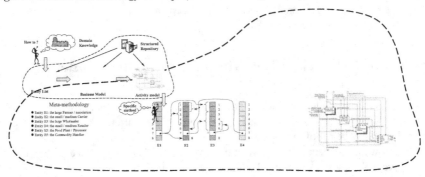

for the specific step, based on how well their outcomes match the modeling needs of the specific EA task. This assists the user in selecting an RM which, although suitable, may not have been an obvious choice in the absence of the meta-methodology and the associated SR. Also, the EA practitioner needs to be informed that the selection of an RM can call for certain prerequisites, such as the need to use particular modeling languages, methods, tools, MFs, and so forth, that are necessary or can significantly facilitate the use of the selected RM(s). Such artifacts are typically included in the proposed selection of AF elements for the specific EA task.

Hence, the SR is holding an organised collection of RMs, from which the meta-methodology engine extracts and proposes suitable RMs depending on the particular situation. In a decision support system implementation type (similar to Figure 1), the "particular setting" is gathered interactively from the user (the owner of domain knowledge—see Figure 14).

Other factors, such as staff proficiencies in particular modeling languages or available/legacy enterprise modeling tools in the participating organisations, are also considered in order to rank the lists of RMs proposed.

Reference Model Selection Example: Company Networks and Virtual Enterprises

The meta-methodology and SR have been used in several case studies to produce specific methods for the creation and operation of CNs and VEs. For example, in the case of creation of a CN and VEs in the after-sales services sector (see Figure 15) (Hartel, Billinger, et al., 2002; Hartel, Burger, et al., 2002), the meta-methodology has guided the selection of RMs based on matching the requirements gathered from the user and inferred by the meta-methodology steps with the outcomes provided by the RMs.

Here, the requirements called for the modeling of the creation and operation of a specific type of CN and VEs produced by it. Based on the interaction with the user, the meta-methodology has recommended modeling of the decisional, organisational and functional aspect at a minimum, taking into account management aspects, all in the context of the CN, VE and participants' life cycles. Once these propositions were confirmed by the user, RMs were

Figure 15. Collaborative service model (Source: Hartel et al., 2002)

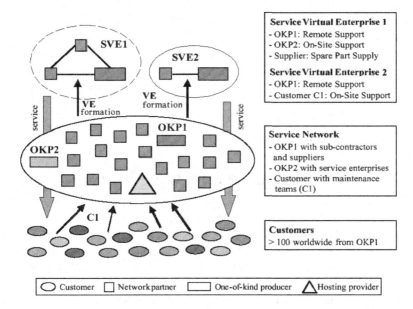

sought matching the decisional, organisational and functional modeling requirements; in addition, RMs were sought to build the business model, preferably in the context of life cycle and taking into account management aspects. This has led to the selection of the RMs previously described, from the SR. Full details on the application of the meta-methodology in this case study are described in Noran (2004a).

Reflections on Building "Better" Reference Models

The process of evaluating/mapping and selecting RMs for EA tasks has also led to several reflections on building "better" RMs, which could significantly help the EA practitioner. Thus, it has been found that RMs can be constructed in EA practice by either "adapting" (e.g., specialising or abstracting) an existing RM or by abstracting particular models into a new RM. In either case, some essential aspects should be observed, such as:

- The resulting RMs should be validated in practice by using them to create other particular models and assessing the quality and usefulness of the RMs and the models produced.
- There is a balance between the level of detail (specialisation) of an RM, its applicability and its usability. For example: A highly specialised RM may have narrow applicability but it would be easy to use in that restricted domain, provided that reasonable knowledge of the particular RM is available. A more generic RM may have wide

applicability; however, significant customisation will be necessary to make it usable to a particular domain. That customisation may require significant knowledge of the RM. The knowledge requirement may be somewhat avoided if methods are available to use and customise the RMs.

- The language used to create the RM may significantly assist the EA practitioner. For example, complexity management would make the RM usable for a wider range of users and audiences. If the language belongs to an integrated set, it would help create a *consistent* set of RMs (e.g., for functional. information, decision, etc.), typically, a major issue when modeling several (and typically related) aspects.

Conclusion and Further Work

This chapter has attempted to show that existing but currently scattered knowledge contained in RMs for EA and other domains referred by EA (IS, IT, manufacturing, social, etc.) can be put to better use in EA by (a) organising the RMs in a structured way in respect to a common reference, and (b) providing a method to assist the users in selecting the appropriate RMs based mainly on their *domain* knowledge.

Often, RMs have overlapping domain coverage; in addition, RMs developed for a particular domain may be applicable beyond their intended area after moderate changes. Such aspects may be confusing or not obvious to the non-expert user. Therefore, in order to make better use of RMs, the users should be offered assistance in selecting and customising RMs for a broader area of EA tasks. This should lead to a set of RMs and a customised EE method for a particular EA task and for specific host organisation proficiencies and needs. The proposed meta-methodology would achieve this, making use of an SR containing AF elements (such as RMs) that have been assessed and classified/formalised in respect to a common reference (in this case GERAM).

Future research efforts in this area will be focused towards the mapping of additional RMs against the chosen reference; in addition to enriching the SR, this will also lead (as it did in the past) to the discovery of new application domains for existing RMs, which will be coded in the repository rules. Another future work direction relates to the formalisation of the meta-methodology environment (the SR and the rules associated to the meta-methodology steps). Finally, further field testing and refinement of the meta-methodology is needed in order to improve its accuracy and usefulness.

References

Ansoff, H. I. (1965). *Corporate strategy*. New York: McGraw-Hill.

Bernus, P. (2003). Organisational design. In P. Bernus, L. Nemes, & G. Schmidt (Eds.), *Handbook on enterprise architecture* (pp. 575-594). Heidelberg: Springer Verlag.

Bernus, P., Noran, O., & Riedlinger, J. (2002). Using the globemen reference model for virtual enterprise design in after sales service. In I. Karvoinen, R. van den Berg, P. Bernus, Y. Fukuda, M. Hannus, I. Hartel, & J. Vesterager (Eds.), *Global engineering and manufacturing in enterprise networks (Globemen). VTT Symposium 224* (pp. 71-90). Helsinki, Finland.

C4ISR Architectures Working Group. (1997). *Command, control, communications, computers, intelligence, surveillance, and reconnaissance—C4ISR*. Retrieved from http://www. cisa.osd.mil

Camarinha-Matos, L. M. (Ed.). (2004). *Virtual enterprises and collaborative networks, Proceedings of IFIP 18th World Congress—TC5/WG5.5 (PROVE 04): 5th IFIP Working Conference on Virtual Enterprises*. Toulouse, France: Kluwer Academic.

Camarinha-Matos, L. M., & Afsarmanesh, H. (1999). *Infrastructures for virtual enterprises,* Dordrecht: Kluwer Academic Publishers.

CIMOSA Association. (1996). CIMOSA: Open system architecture for CIM, Technical baseline, ver 3.2. *Private Publication.*

Doumeingts, G., Vallespir, B., & Chen, D. (1998). GRAI grid decisional modelling. In P. Bernus, K. Mertins, & G. Schmidt (Eds.), *Handbook on architectures of information systems* (pp. 313-339). Heidelberg: Springer Verlag.

Doumeingts, G., Vallespir, B., Zanettin, M., & Chen, D. (1992). *GIM-GRAI integrated methodology: A methodology for designing CIM systems.* Bordeaux: Version 1.0, Unnumbered Report, LAP/GRAI, University Bordeaux 1.

Globemen. (2000-2002). *Global engineering and manufacturing in enterprise networks (IMS project no. 99004 / IST-1999-60002).* Retrieved January 20, 2006, from http:// globemen.vtt.fi/

Goranson, H. T. (1998). Agile manufacturing. In A. Molina, A. Kusiak, & J. Sanchez (Eds.), *Handbook of life cycle engineering: Concepts, models and methodologies.* Dordrecht: Kluwer Academic Publishers.

Gratton, L., Hope Hailey, V., Stiles, P., & Truss, C. (1999). *Strategic human resource management.* New York: Oxford University Press.

Hartel, I., Billinger, S., Burger, G., & Kamio, Y. (2002). Virtual organisation of the after-sales service in the one-of-a-kind industry. In L. Camarinha-Matos (Ed.), *Collaborative business ecosystems and virtual enterprises. Proceedings of the 3rd IFIP Working Conference on Infrastructures for Virtual Enterprises (PROVE '02)* (pp. 405-420). Sesimbra, Portugal.

Hartel, I., Kamio, Y., & Zhou, M. (2002). Collaborative service in global manufacturing: A new paradigm. In DIISM (Ed.), *Proceedings of the 5th International Conference on Design of Information Infrastructure Systems for Manufacturing (DIISM 2002)* (pp. 225-232). Osaka, Japan.

IEEE. (1998). *IEEE Std 1320.1-1998: Standard for function modelling language: Syntax and semantics for IDEF0.*

ISO/TC184. (2000). Annex A: GERAM. In *ISO/IS 15704: Industrial automation systems: equirements for enterprise-reference architectures and methodologies.*

Keidel, R. W. (1995). *Seeing organizational patterns: A new theory and language of organizational design*. San Francisco: Berrett-Koehler Publishers.

Kotter, J. P. (1996). *Leading change*. Boston: Harvard Business School Press.

Mackay, H. (2003). Leadership: Better relationships through better communication. In P. Bernus, L. Nemes, & G. Schmidt (Eds.), *Handbook on enterprise architecture* (pp. 255-279). Heidelberg: Springer Verlag.

Mintzberg, H. (1994). *The rise and fall of strategic planning*. New York: Free Press.

NIST. (1993). *Integration definition for function modelling (IDEF0)* (No. 183: Federal Information Processing Standards Publication): Computer Systems Laboratory, National Institute of Standards and Technology.

Noran, O. (2003a). A mapping of individual architecture frameworks (GRAI, PERA, C4ISR, CIMOSA, Zachman, ARIS) onto GERAM. In P. Bernus, L. Nemes, & G. Schmidt (Eds.), *Handbook of enterprise architecture* (pp. 65-210). Heidelberg: Springer Verlag.

Noran, O. (2003b). UML vs IDEF: An ontology-oriented comparative study in view of business modelling. In I. Seruca, J. Filipe, S. Hammoudi, & J. Cordeiro (Eds.), *6th International Conference on Enterprise Information Systems (ICEIS 2004)* (Vol. 3, pp. 674-682). Porto, Portugal: ICEIS.

Noran, O. (2004a). *A meta-methodology for collaborative networked organisations*. Unpublished doctoral thesis, School of CIT, Griffith University.

Noran, O. (2004b). A meta-methodology for collaborative networked organisations: A case study and reflections. In P. Bernus, M. Fox, & J. B. M. Goossenaerts (Eds.), *Knowledge sharing in the integrated enterprise: Interoperability strategies for the enterprise architect. Proceedings of International Conference on Enterprise Integration Modelling and Technology—ICEIMT'04*. Toronto, Canada: Kluwer Academic Publishers.

Noran, O. (2004c). Towards a meta-methodology for collaborative networked organisations. In L. Camarinha-Matos (Ed.), *Virtual enterprises and collaborative networks. Proceedings of the 5th IFIP Working Conference on Virtual Enterprises (PROVE '04)* (pp. 71-78). Toulouse, France: Kluwer Academic Publishers.

Noran, O. (2005). A meta-methodology prototype for collaborative networked organisations. In L. Camarinha-Matos (Ed.), *Collaborative networks and breeding environments. Proceedings of the 6th IFIP Working Conference on Virtual Enterprises (PROVE '05)* (pp. 339-346). Toulouse, France: Kluwer Academic Publishers.

Olegario, C., & Bernus, P. (2003). Modelling the management system. In P. Bernus, L. Nemes, & G. Schmidt (Eds.), *Handbook on enterprise architecture* (pp. 435-500). Heidelberg: Springer Verlag.

Popkin Software. (2001). *Building an enterprise architecture: The popkin process*. Retrieved October 2002, from www.popkin.com

Rumbaugh, J., Jacobson, I., & Booch, G. (1999). *The unified modelling language reference manual*. Reading, MA: Addison-Wesley.

Scheer, A.-W. (1994). *Business process engineering: Reference models for industrial enterprises*. Berlin: Springer-Verlag.

Tølle, M., & Vesterager, J. (2002). VEM: Virtual enterprise methodology. In I. Karvoinen, R. van den Berg, P. Bernus, Y. Fukuda, M. Hannus, I. Hartel, & J. Vesterager (Eds.), *Global engineering and manufacturing in enterprise networks (Globemen). VTT Symposium 224*. Helsinki, Finland.

Uppington, G., & Bernus, P. (2003). Analysing the present situation and refining strategy. In P. Bernus, L. Nemes, & G. Schmidt (Eds.), *Handbook on enterprise architecture* (pp. 309-332). Heidelberg: Springer Verlag.

Vesterager, J., Tølle, M., & Bernus, P. (2002). VERA: Virtual enterprise reference architecture. In I. Karvoinen, R. van den Berg, P. Bernus, Y. Fukuda, M. Hannus, I. Hartel, & J. Vesterager (Eds.), *Global engineering and manufacturing in enterprise networks (Globemen). VTT Symposium 224*. Helsinki, Finland.

Wand, Y., & Weber, R. (2002). Research commentary: Information systems and conceptual modeling: A research agenda. *Information Systems Research, 13*(4), 363-376.

Williams, T. J. (1994). The Purdue enterprise reference architecture. *Computers in Industry, 24*(2-3), 141-158.

Williams, T. J. (Ed.). (1988). *CIM reference model committee: A reference model for computer integrated manufacturing (CIM): A description from the viewpoint of industrial automation* (2nd ed.). Research Triangle Park, NC: Instrument Society of America.

Section III

Reference Models

Chapter VIII

A Reference Model for Industrial Enterprises

August-Wilhelm Scheer, IDS Scheer AG, Germany

Wolfram Jost, IDS Scheer AG, Germany

Öner Güngöz, Institute for Information Systems (IWi) at the German Research Center for Artificial Intelligence (DFKI), Saarbrücken, Germany

Abstract

The introduction of the CIM concept approximately 20 years ago paved the way for holistic examination of logistical and engineering processes alongside the integrated support of information technology within the industrial sector. With the advent of new business management ideas and technological developments, CIM has gradually been developed further and become more integrated with complementary and contemporary concepts. Reference models are developed for the aim of using the CIM concept. The Y-CIM reference model is now established and recognised as a standard reference model within the industrial sector. Furthermore, other sectors are increasingly having success with the Y-CIM reference model in order to benefit from improved competences acquired in the industry during the last few decades. In recent years the Y-CIM reference model has gradually transformed into a comprehensive reference model that can be applied in a number of sectors. This chapter focuses on the development of business process concepts within the industrial sector and critically discusses the changes made to them over time. There is particular emphasis on the development of CIM and its implementation using the Y-CIM reference model. The article also illustrates the features of the Y-CIM reference model and discusses its applicability in service industries.

Development of CIM

At the beginning of the 1980s, CIM was the catchword for an apparent revolution of industrial business process management. It refers to the integrated information processing requirements for the technical and operational tasks of an industrial enterprise. It is the computerized handling of integrated business processes among all different functions in an industrial enterprise, the consistent application of information technology, along with modern manufacturing techniques and new organizational procedures. Industrial enterprises rationalized their production and development processes in order to increase process efficiency. The support of business processes with information technology led to an essential boost in process efficiency. At first, the use of information technology for well-defined and isolated business fields by enterprises led to isolated applications solutions. The introduction of the CIM approach prompted industrial enterprises to adopt an integrated view of logistic and development processes coupled with integrated information technology support. CIM embraced integrated information processing for business and technical tasks in industrial enterprise. It therefore aimed to unite logistical processes with the research and development processes (R&D) within an industrial firm and to support them with integrated information systems. The CIM concept was a logical further development of both high process competences in industrial firms for the development of new products and of manufacturing at factory level. The importance and complexity of such products meant that a high level of competence was necessary in both fields. In order to develop industrial products such as cars or machines, up to several thousand employees may be required: for research and development departments, for constructive improvement, building prototypes, planning production and factory building.

In no other branch has business process been so formally thought-out (a DIN[1]-norm is even defined for it). The creation and testing of production processes lasted a number of decades. The revolutionary idea of depicting product structures without redundancies using bills of materials made the complexity of industrial processes transparent and comprehensible. A bill of material is an itemized listing of the parts of a product with material quantities (Stewart, 1991, p. 93). Thus, bills of materials record the structure and quantitative composition of end products from intermediate products and raw materials (see the following product tree). For the description of bills of materials Gozintographs are used. A Gozintograph presents each part and each structural relationship only once in order to avoid redundancy (Scheer, 1991, p. 189). Work schedules were also used to develop a business process description for the production of individual components of the list. Industrial engineering methods originating from the USA and the production planning and work preparation methods that were developed in Germany have gained much recognition. Reducing an entire business process description to descriptions of product structure and work schedules remains exemplary for other sectors. Through strong structuring of products (bills of materials can for example include several thousand components in the motor industry or in mechanical engineering) each business process description (work schedule) is reduced to a small sub-process. Put simply, the entire business process description from the raw material to the final product is divided into a description of product structure and work schedules. The complicated flow of material is contained in the product structure. The work schedules simply give the sequential working steps between two product stages. Work schedules for specific parts in

Figure 1. Product and process model (Source: Scheer, 1999, p. 59)

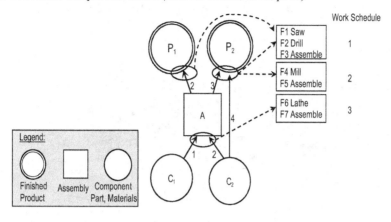

manufacturing processes are detailed documents, since process descriptions are not only used to support fundamental organizational rules, but also to implement processes directly (Scheer, 1999, p. 59). Bills of materials and work schedules describe the composition between product and process models effectively.

Figure 1 depicts a bill of material and work schedule describing the composition and production of finished products (P1, P2). P1 and P2 consist of assemblies (A) and component parts (C1, C2). The work schedules that reflect the working stages which have to be carried out contain the production processes. In the work schedule, manufacturing processes are

Figure 2. Bill of material list (Source: Knox, 1984, p. 266)

Figure 3. Industrial production system (Source: Scheer, 1999, p. 110)

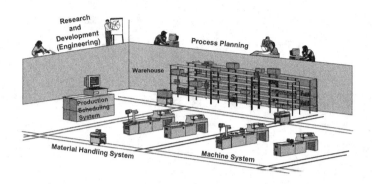

allocated to every part to be manufactured. In order to set up a work schedule it is necessary to know the product model. The work schedule comprises the operations (functions) to be executed in order to assemble the materials, parts, components, etc. into a finished product. The process model can therefore be derived to an extent from the product model. The manufacturing of the product model requires the execution of the process model. Bills of material show the structural and quantitative assembly of the final product, semi-manufactured products and basic materials. The numbers on the arrows reflect the production coefficients. For bills of materials Gozintographs are employed to avoid redundancies. The construction of parts from their components can be represented diagrammatically by means of a Gozintograph. It shows which lower level parts are used in what quantity to construct a given higher level part. Figure 2 shows a common type of bill of materials list used in an industrial enterprise.

As later illustrated, the Y-CIM reference model uses bills of materials and work schedules to connect logistic and engineering processes used from both fields.

Development Stages of CIM

Production within the industrial sector is highly developed, not only due to product and process descriptions, but also because of the structuring of the production system itself. Figure 3 depicts both aspects—the structuring of products and processes as well as systems.

The system is divided into sub-systems: stockrooms for those components still to be processed, a processing system consisting of machines and employees and the link between both via a transport system reduces the complexity and increases the transparency of the system. A control panel ensures that the respective process status is known and will be used for controlling the system.

The CIM concept aimed to transfer this high competence of process description and control to all areas within an industrial enterprise. Both the planning processes and the processes involving external partners of the enterprise (i.e., suppliers and customers) are included. The basis for this was pre-existing product and process documentation in the form of work schedules and bills of materials. These form the connection between the R & D process and logistic planning. The bills of materials show the prognosticated demand of the final products and are therefore required to ascertain which external materials are needed for the procurement process. The work schedules form the connection between the planned production quantities and the required capacities. In this respect, CIM also met the demand for an integrated database, since it placed the research and development function, the planning requirement calculations and the capacity considerations on one unified database. Although data are distributed among various components of a CIM system, it should be logically centralized in order that the whole system can be found within a single database. The information from the bills of materials and the work schedules is generated in the research and development process, so that there is an automatic connection to IT-supported construction systems, such as computer aided design (CAD) and computer aided engineering (CAE). CAD offers the designer information technology support in order to design and create products. In the process he can call up drawings, for example, of already existing parts from a database and amend them or combine them with other drawings to create new drawings. The call-up and further processing of previously stored drawings secures a considerable rationalization (Scheer, 1991, p. 201). CAE offers functions to support engineering tasks. In addition to graphical CAD capabilities, the possibility of developing prototypes within the computer can largely replace the creation of real prototypes. Thus, there is a huge possibility to cut costs.

Moreover, the data can be easily accessed during the implementation stage. At factory level, the production control information, derived from logistic applications, runs alongside the product information. A machine controlled by numeric control (NC) needs to know how many units it has to produce (information from the order chain) and which geometric contours it should process (information from the product description of a CAD-system). In general, CIM can connect the automation technologies of manufacturing processes, such as robotics and NC machine tools, with the computerized product and process design, and automated planning and control (Rainey, 2005, p. 402).

Y-CIM Reference Model

The implementation of CIM requires a reference model that can meet industry-specific requirements. In general, the most important requirement for such a reference model is its ability to consider and allow the integration of logistic systems, including all of its sub-systems (procurement, production and distribution logistic are some examples). Full integration of all logistic systems from planning level up to product scheduling is required. An integrated perspective between the logistic and engineering fields is also essential, since there are close links between these two core areas. Moreover, there are interdependencies between logistics and engineering. As regards the former, bills of material and information concerning work schedules (produced during product planning) are needed for production planning aspects, such as requirement planning, time and capacity management, etc. The initial tasks of capacity management are to carry out capacity scheduling, in which production orders and work schedules are combined (Scheer, 1994, p. 25). The production planning depends to an extent on product planning. As regards engineering, product manufacturing depends to some extent on production scheduling, since this is used to control manufacturing. Interdependencies can occur mutually between both fields. The reference model should take account of this approach and ensure that pre-existing bills of materials and work schedules can be used to attempt to link the core industrial functions—logistic and engineering. It should also be considered that logistic and engineering processes can be affected, for example, by information and coordinating processes, accounting, etc.; an effective reference model is one that takes this into account also. In order to set up an integrated and holistic industry-specific beneficial solution, the reference model must be able to cope with the described requirements. There should be guidelines on how to set up an appropriate solution that is capable of handling computer-based processes in an integrated way within all of the various functions in an industrial enterprise.

The Y-CIM reference model fulfils all described requirements. By interlinking business and engineering related tasks, it offers a conceptually outstanding frame for CIM (Ferstl & Sinz, 2001, p. 233). The Y-CIM reference model is renowned for its unique ability to implement CIM in practice. Considered to be the industrial standard reference model for implementation of CIM, the Y-CIM reference model was developed by Professor Scheer in 1980. It illustrates the integration of and relationship between the core industrial fields in a clear and graphical form. The Y shape reflects the core industrial functions by illustrating the business and engineering related components and the relationship between them. The integration concept aims to integrate business and engineering related functions in an industrial enterprise. The left side depicts business related functions whilst the right side

Figure 4. Y-CIM reference model (Source: Scheer, 1998, p. 93)

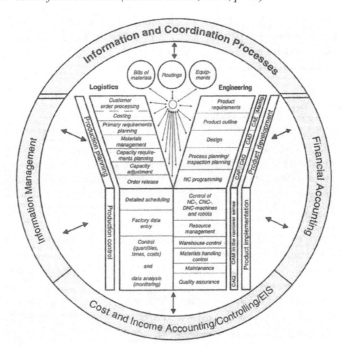

relates to engineering. The bottom of the Y stands for the integration of both fields. This reference model can be used to integrate business and technology oriented information systems within an industrial enterprise (Fischer & Herold, 2002, p. 81). The integration of logistic and engineering systems, as well as processes, is the main objective. It has been used successfully in many enterprises as a guideline for the development of their own integration strategies. Y-CIM is one of the most popular reference models to define CIM (Jost, 1993, p. 7). It remains valid nowadays and is used in many industrial enterprises. There are a wide range reference models available. An overview is provided by Fettke and Loos's reference model catalogue (Fettke & Loos, 2004). Moreover Y-CIM is transferable even in other domains such as service industry and public administrations. This issue will be discussed at a later point in the paper. Figure 4 illustrates the Y-CIM reference model.

The left part of the Y-CIM reference model concerns mainly business related issues. It describes production planning and control systems (PPC), primarily from the business-oriented planning view. PPS is able both to take over planning functions and also administer bills of materials, work schedules and manufacturing facilities. The upper left part focuses particularly on production planning, while the lower left part refers to production control. This is important due to the high quantity and complexity of the data to be managed. The left side concerns functions which are controlled by the flow of the customer order processing via requirements planning, time management, manufacturing control, industrial data capture and shipping. The production logistic therefore consists of the functions of order processing and distribution logistic shipping. At the same time requirements planning includes procurement logistic. In general, PPS deals with the entire process of planning and execution of production orders such as material logistics, production planning and production control. Sub-systems of production planning and control are interlinked apart from each other with other operative systems and technical components such as CAD, CAP and CAM (Stahlknecht & Hasenkamp, 2005, p. 360). One area of any CIM system is the linking of CAD and CAM (Waters, 1996, p. 7). Between each of these functions information exchanges can be based on a common basic data management or, in best case, an integrated database (Alpar et al., 2002, p. 216). In chemical, pharmaceutical and food industries, the production planning and control require a different approach since they focus more on recipes and charges instead of parts (Stahlknecht et al., 2005, p. 356).

The upper right part of the Y-CIM reference model focuses mainly on engineering-related objectives. It reflects output and product development processes, including all necessary documentation. It includes technical support components such as CAD, computer aided planning (CAP) and computer aided manufacturing (CAM). CAD includes computer aided compositions, drafts and constructions of products. The CAP task is to support conventional work scheduling and NC controlled manufacturing facilities (Alpar et al., 2002, p. 218). By contrast, CAM deals with computer-based manufacturing and improvement of internal material logistics. The loose connection of the upper part (logistics and engineering) of the Y-CIM reference model is based on commonly used data (logistics and engineering) such as bills of materials and work schedules, which arise or are generated through the product development.

The lower right part of the Y-CIM reference model contains computer-based resources that are required for product engineering. The control of these systems demands the description of the products which they produce. Apart from the informational relationship between product development and implementation, there is also a close short-term relationship between manufacturing control and feedback system of the industrial data capture. The production orders that are defined within the production logistic are merged with the description data of the output development and carried out using the manufacturing facilities. Due to the close relationship between the short-term manufacturing control and manufacturing resources, the description of them is processed at that point as far as necessary to establish understanding for business issues. There is also a relationship through the description data of output purchased and distribution required by procurement and distribution logistic processes. The right part of the Y-CIM reference model contains technical systems but also possesses high business meaning. It deals with economical issues and technical alternatives in order that an efficient solution may be set up (Alpar et al., 2002, p. 218).

Various systems inter-linked with the business and technology related systems or processes (logistic and engineering fields) are depicted in the area surrounding the Y-CIM reference model. The business and engineering based information systems' alignment to the corporate objectives through the information and coordinating systems is illustrated. The operative data from the primary processes are used as input information for information and coordinating systems. The operative systems are concurrently data suppliers for the financing, cost and activity accounting systems and for information management, too. Financial accounting reflects the business processes of the corporation with its environment from the value view. Thus, it is also called external accounting. By contrast, internal accounting focuses on the value of used input resources in order to check and control output production. The information management develops concepts for the provision of resources, applications systems and their operation.

The demand for integration and computer-based support of business and engineering-related functions of CIM is fulfilled by the Y-CIM reference model. The interlinking of administration and disposition systems in particular (e.g., financial, cost and activity accounting and order processing with product planning and control through the use of technical oriented systems (CAD, CAM, CAP) and the access to an unified data pool of a common database) leads to the aimed integration purpose (Alpar et al., 2002, p. 218). Thus, the integration takes place mainly via commonly used basic data such as bills of material, work schedules and operating resources (Hansen & Neumann, 2005, p. 89). That means that the conjunction between logistic and engineering is established through description data such as bills of materials and work schedules. The integration is achieved mainly via function and data integration (Fischer et al., 2002, p. 378). Data integration is realized because different functions and components of the Y-CIM reference model use the same database. This leads to the avoidance of redundancies (Blazewicz, Ecker, & Pesch, 2001, p. 425). The information interrelationship between production planning and product engineering is carried out via product data descriptions. They are used by NC-based control of manufacturing facilities. Moreover, there is also an information connection between the short-term manufacturing control and feedback system. The integration of the Y-CIM reference model demands willingness on the part of enterprises to agree on organisational integration requirement challenges. Just-in-Time, kaizen and lean production are some of the challenges that are partially, but not completely, included in the CIM approach (Stahlknecht et al., 2005, p. 354). The Y-CIM reference model is able to meet these challenges since its holistic and integrated view on enterprises enables enterprise to implement innovative concepts more efficiently and effectively. Beside that, it is also able to identify the processes that need to be changed for successful implementation of such concepts (Kirchmer & Scheer, 2003, p. 6).

Generally, it is possible to incorporate and support emerging new business or engineering concepts using the Y-CIM reference model.

The various interdependencies between corporate processes and the different quantity and value-oriented views make it difficult to depict the design of the Y-CIM model simply. The Y-CIM model, with its basic and enhanced version (which ensures integration of information and coordination systems), should therefore be understood as a raw graphical guideline. Despite the handling of sub-processes, it contains an integrated and holistic view on processes. An outline of the development process using Y-CIM follows next.

Example: Output Design Processes with Y-CIM

The design of new products is one of the most challenging topics in industrial companies. Due to globalisation, industrial over-capacity, shift from vendors to customer market and shrinking product lifecycles, enterprises are under pressure to design and introduce new innovative products into the market (Bussmannm, Jennings, & Wooldridge, 2004, p. 41). At the same time, the development time of products is one of the most important factors for success in the market. Product development is increasingly becoming the most important decision centre of an industrial enterprise. Product development predefines important parameters for the proceedings of the logistic chain and expense situation of an enterprise. Concepts that are developed for product design cannot be realised efficiently without in-

Figure 5. Extract of the Y-CIM reference model (Source: Scheer, 1998, p. 532)

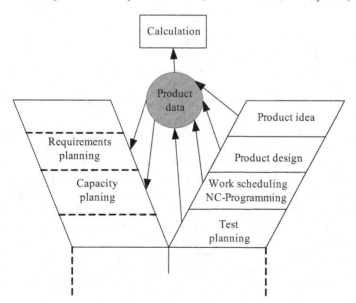

tegrated information technology support. The close interrelationship between organisation and information technology is evident (see Figure 5).

Product development is illustrated on the right side of the Y-CIM reference model. The figure indicates that product development can be described from different views. The marketing view defines the product requirements within the product idea phase. Marketing mainly involves finding out about customers' attitudes towards product features. The product design phase has the task of developing the technical features of the product and describing them with topological-geometrical data. The manufacturing unit plans the procedures that are necessary in order to produce the product using work schedules. Quality assurance describes the quality features of the product. Defined test procedures and test plans should ensure that the target quality level will be met.

Descriptions related to products that are produced during product development are called product data. As far as bills of materials are concerned, product data controls the requirements explosion within the requirements planning. It also controls capacity planning where work schedules are concerned. At the same time, these data are fundamental for product calculation. It is therefore clear that product development belongs to the main "data production centre" within an industrial enterprise.

The terms used in the previous figure relate to manufacturing industries. They are, however, also relevant for process-oriented manufacturing, including chemical and food industries, since these process procedures are mostly analogue. In these sectors, the term "product design" is replaced by the term "research and development," while "work schedules" are called "production specifications." They are also named together with the product composition as "recipe." The production team should consider the entire product lifecycle when developing the product. During the product development phase, the following stages in the product lifecycle must all be considered, so that the later effects of decisions made at this point can be predicted. Considering these effects during product development phase avoids expensive and time consuming product corrections.

Lack of Preconditions in the Past for the Implementation of CIM

Unfortunately, the term CIM fell into disrepute in the past. This is not unusual. A new catchword often rouses expectations which cannot be fulfilled in a short period, with the result that optimistically drafted projects end in failure. This was the case with CIM. At that time, the use of databank systems to integrate logistic and product-related information systems, as well as production support, was not widespread. Furthermore, there existed no corresponding networking possibilities that were developed enough for the system. Even integrated standard software wasn't available for all areas. The CAD software system had an independent existence and those responsible for system development generally had no competence for logistic systems and for the real-time requirements of carrying out production. The planning and logistic applications were entrusted to suppliers of commercial software systems. These suppliers too had little or no competence for the product development processes and carrying out production, and the CIM-large projects were unsuccessful. This was also the case with the MAP-Programme (manufacturing automation protocol) developed by General Motors, which aimed to standardise the CAD-system. The standardisation of networking various production systems (quality assurance, checking system, production management, CNC, DNC, etc.) should have been hugely successful, since the "crème de la crème" of information technology and industrial customer power were combined. These developments made it difficult to exploit the potential of CIM in practice. There was therefore no opportunity for the potential of the Y-CIM reference model to be exploited at that time.

The lack of success of these projects demonstrates how the enterprises of that time were overwhelmed by their vision. The failure of a vision doesn't, however, mean that it was not correct. Thus, many approaches from the CIM-conception of that time have become highly significant in today's business and industrial world. Similar ideas with different names have been introduced.

Connecting planning functions and the execution level through hierarchical production planning- and control-systems using client/server architectures, whilst not a complete success, has achieved near success. The inclusion of customers and suppliers in the processes is being developed further through the concepts of customer relationship management (CRM). In contrast to that, CIM was mostly concerned with intra-enterprise interactions (Vernadat, 1996, p. 3). The major idea of CIM was the effort to define and develop large, monolithic software systems that could manage many points of internal manufacturing process integration. The inability to do this was the main weakness of the CIM concept (Blazewicz et al., 2001, p. 116). Put simply, the extensive CIM concept has been broken down into small concepts for sub-processes, whereby even their integration will continue to be tracked. This leads to a potentially new field of application for the Y-CIM reference model. The importance of complete integration can even be seen in market developments. Initially successful software suppliers for sub-solutions such as CRM or supply chain management (SCM), for example Siebel, were being forced back by suppliers of enterprise resource planning (ERP) software. In the case of SAP, this was because their solutions also include the integration of these sub-processes with the backbone-processes of internal order processing, commercial systems of financial accounting and controlling. The basic idea of CIM was taken up into ERP systems without being explicitly mentioned (Mertens et al., 2005, p. 354).

Applying Y-CIM in the Service Industry

Service engineering describes approaches, methods and tool support for systematic planning, development and realisation of services products and processes. The object of this engineering approach is to increase effectiveness and efficiency of the development process and the quality of service itself. In contrast to this, product engineering focuses on the systematic development and planning of physical products from the first idea until the realisation of the finished product. One of the core differences between industrial and service enterprises is in the type of production planning process. In industrial enterprises, production planning is mainly based on customer orders. In general, this is not the case in service industries because services are normally not storable. Services usually are simultaneously produced and supplied. The production planning is based to an extent on estimations that can be derived from former experiences and prognoses. The production planning of services, which do not contain material elements, are usually designed independently from the existence of customer orders.

Received customer orders only influence production control because of the integration necessity of external factors into the creation process. In consideration of the customer relationship, there is a close analogy between system structure of an information technology-supported service process and the structure of production process in an industrial enterprise. In service industries the production of service is strongly supported by information technology. The information technology used corresponds approximately to the machines employed within an industrial company. The data which is necessary for service engineering is stored and managed in a data warehouse which is reminiscent of the storage system of an industrial enterprise. The link between the data objects and the processing functions as software modules is established in a service factory via a workflow management system which is like a transporting system in the industrial sector. The transparent control of single process executions is also achieved through a monitoring and analysis system. The transfer of industrial concepts and methods in order to get a more transparent control of processes in the service sector requires on the one hand the systemization of the service structure, and, on the other, the documentation of the processes that are necessary to produce the service components. Beside that, there is a need to organize the integration of external factors into the service production process. Up to now, the implementation of the systematic and information technology supported development of services that are bases to some extent in difficulties to describe output, processes and potential dimensions of services. In order to cope with these challenges, there is a need for a methodical concept that deals with the issues. These challenges can be met using the Y-CIM model as described in the following paragraph.

The integrated and holistic issue of business processes remains highly topical and exciting. Not only does the Y-CIM concept help to shape business processes in industrial firms, but also many of the ideas related to it are being communicated to and discussed in other areas—from services enterprises to public administrations. Twenty years of CIM and business process optimisation in industrial firms is producing its fruits now, and will define the future of organisations and information processing in other branches too. The industrial competencies (developed during the last decades) concerning integrated product and process design can be transferred to business processes of other branches because of existing analogies. The Y-CIM reference model is also applicable within sectors apart from the industrial one. The basic concepts derived from the running of typical industry processes can in principle be transferred to any organisational structure. The analogy becomes clear when using terms such as "service engineering," where the industrial development of new products can be transferred to service enterprises such as banks, insurance companies and even—to some extent—to public administrations. Even service enterprises are increasingly falling under pressure to quickly develop new variations of an existing product or to create new, innovative ones. Until now it has rarely been customary for these enterprises to therefore define departments and formal procedure methods. This is, however, becoming necessary due to the short lifecycle of products and higher diversity of variants. For this reason, the experiences and organisation concepts such as simultaneous engineering and concurrent engineering are valuable information sources for the reorganisation of service enterprises. The term "credit factory" even refers to the fact that banks are behaving increasingly like industry enterprises. There is a close analogy between the system structures of an IT-supported service process and the structure of an industrial firm (see Figure 6).

Although service enterprises structure their products more strongly and document the processes required to generate product components, they have the same initial situation as industrial enterprises for the transparent control of processes. In service enterprises, the

Figure 6. Service industry product and process design

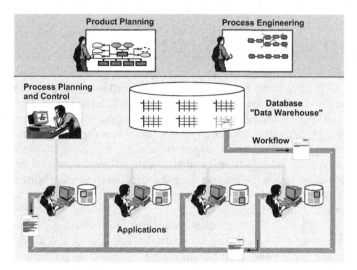

"factories" are shaped to a large extent by electronic information systems. Computer systems form a quasi machine level for supporting the execution of functions. The data objects to be processed (i.e., documents) are administrated in databases. Here, the term "data warehouse," understood in a somewhat different sense, can build up an analogical relationship. The link between the data objects and the process functions in the form of application software modules is created by a workflow system in the form of a transport system. The transparent control of individual processes is also achieved using a monitoring and analysis system as described above.

As a result of the analogous utilisation of industrial experiences, expertise within the field of service engineering has increased in recent years. It is beneficial to use industrial approved methods and approaches in order to achieve systematic and efficient production of services. IT support of the service engineering process is necessary in order to exploit partially unused success potentials. Software supported service engineering can be carried out systematically with adopted industrial methods and approaches. Company-wide unified documentation of product (service) and process structures, and their storage in a centralized database, allow the work of service suppliers to be standardised. The aim is an information technology-based holistic and integrated support of service engineering and the supply of services. The Y-CIM reference model is applicable in the service industries with a few modifications (Herrmann & Klein, 2004, p. 182). There are close analogies between both fields. The service industry can learn from long term experiences in planning, control of production as well as development and implementation of products from the industrial sector. The amount of experience gained using the Y-CIM reference model is useful in enhancing the efficiency of service engineering. Service enterprises are behaving increasingly like industrial ones. The analogies between industrial and service sectors enable the use of the Y-CIM reference model within the service industry and thus provide an opportunity to achieve comparable benefits like those found in the industrial sector (Krämer & Zimmermann, 1996, p. 555).

Unified BPM Supported by Y-CIM

Thus, the circle comes to an end: At first the industry required structuring of the development process for areas in which the processes are particularly crucial because, for example, their optimisation helped to amortise high sums in mechanical facilities investment, and the high complexity of products demanded stronger structuring in order to reduce complexity. The competences developed during the last few decades are now being transferred to all business process types in order to benefit and accelerate progress. Industrial enterprises also carry out service processes. This means that the concept illustrated in Figure 6 is valid for administrative business processes such as procuring, sales and commercial support in industrial enterprises. A unified concept can therefore be used within industrial firms for supporting business processes. Service enterprises are behaving increasingly like industrial enterprises. We are on the way to achieving a unified business process management concept. The Y-CIM reference model makes a great contribution towards implementation of this type of concept. Y-CIM stands for an integrated process view which is the requirement for business process excellence (Jost & Kruppke, 2004, p. 13). The first results of such a solution can be seen in the ARIS-HOBE approach (Scheer, 2000, p. 3).

References

Alpar, P., et al. (2002). *Application-oriented information systems: Strategic planning, development, and utilization of information systems* (3rd ed.). Wiesbaden: Vieweg. [in German]

Blazewicz, J., Ecker, K., & Pesch, E. (2001). *Scheduling computer and manufacturing processes.* Berlin: Springer.

Bussmannm, S., Jennings, N., & Wooldridge, M. (2004). *Multiagent systems for manufacturing control. A design methodology.* Berlin: Springer.

Ferstl, O. K., & Sinz, E. J. (2001). *Foundations of information systems* (4th ed.). München: Oldenbourg. [in German]

Fettke, P., & Loos, P. (2004). Reference modeling research. *Wirtschaftsinformatik, 46*(5), 331-340. [in German]

Fischer, J., & Herold, W. (2002). Components of information systems. In J. Fischer et al. (Ed.), *Bausteine der Wirtschaftsinformatik* (3rd ed., pp. 49-146). Berlin: Erich Schmidt. [in German]

Hansen, H.-R., & Neumann, G. (2005). Information Systems I: Foundations and applications (9th ed.). Stuttgart: Lucius&Lucius. [in German]

Herrmann, K., & Klein, R. (2004). Method-based visualization of services. In A.-W.Scheer & D. Spath (Eds.), *Computer Aided Service Engineering : Informationssysteme in der Dienstleistungsentwicklung* (pp. 93-119). Berlin: Springer. [in German]

Jost, W. (1993). IT-based CIM-planning. Wiesbaden: Gabler. [in German]

Jost, W., & Kruppke, H. (2004). Business process management. In A.-W.Scheer, F. Abolhassan, H. Kruppke, & W. Jost (Eds.), *Innovation durch Geschäftsprozessmanagement* (pp. 13-23). Heidelberg: Springer.

Kirchmer, M., & Scheer, A.-W. (2003). Change management: Key for business process excellence. In A.-W. Scheer, F. Abolhassan, W. Jost, & M. Kirchmer (Eds.), *Business process change management: ARIS in practice* (pp. 1-14). Heidelberg: Springer.

Knox, C. (1984). *Engineering documentation for CAD/CAM applications*. New York: CRC Press.

Krämer, W., & Zimmermann, V. (1996). Public service engineering--Planning and realization of innovative government solutions. In A.-W.Scheer (Ed.), *Rechnungswesen und EDV: Kundenorientierung in Industrie, Dienstleistung und Verwaltung* (17. Saarbrücker Arbeitstagung 1996 ed., pp. 555-580). Heidelberg: Springer. [in German]

Mertens, P., Bodendorf, F., et al. (2005). Foundations of information systems (9th ed.). Heidelberg: Springer. [in German]

Rainey, D. (2005). *Product innovation leading change through integrated product development*. Cambridge: Cambridge University Press.

Scheer, A.-W. (1991). *Principles of efficient information management*. Heidelberg: Springer.

Scheer, A.-W. (1994). *CIM: Towards the factory of the future* (3rd ed.). Heidelberg: Springer.

Scheer, A.-W. (1999). *ARIS: Business process frameworks* (3rd ed.). Berlin: Springer.

Scheer, A.-W. (2000). *ARIS: Business process modeling 67* (3rd ed.). Berlin: Springer.

Scheer, A.-W. (1998). *Information systems* (2nd ed.). Berlin, Heidelberg: Springer. [in German]

Stahlknecht, P., & Hasenkamp, U. (2005). *Introduction to information systems* (11th ed.). Heidelberg: Springer. [in German]

Stewart, R. (1991). *Cost estimating (new dimensions in engineering)* (2nd ed.). New York: John Wiley & Sons.

Vernadat, F. (1996). *Enterprise modeling and integration*. London: Chapman & Hall.

Waters, F. (1996). *Fundamentals of manufacturing for engineers*. London: Taylor & Francis.

Endnote

[1]   German Institute for Standardization (DIN)

Chapter IX

Reference Model for Retail Enterprises

Jörg Becker, Westfälische Wilhelms-Universität Münster, Germany

Reinhard Schütte, Dohle Handelsgruppe GmbH & Co. KG, Germany

Abstract

In order to provide a structural framework for information systems that serves as a basis for understanding the organizational structure and the information systems of the retail sector, we present an architecture, the "retail-H," that outlines the various facets of trade information systems. The framework encompasses two further criteria, the types of businesses and the differentiation of goods. This architecture and its graphical representation aim at enhancing the orientation within the heap of information models applied in the retail sector. These information models are crucial for the management of information systems and organizational processes.

Retailing:
A Multifarious Field for Reference Modeling

Over the years, the percentage of service industries has continuously increased with respect to manufacturing industries and, therefore, the development of a reference model for retail enterprises has become more important in order to enhance the efficient use of information systems for this sector.

When looking for the significant trends in trading with consumer goods, the trend to size may well initially predominate. On the one hand, mergers and acquisitions of other companies mean that the retailing companies themselves become ever larger—the growth of the German Metro, for example, is primarily based on acquisitions, but also mergers and mutual purchases of large department stores show this. On the other hand, sales areas are also growing. Large self-service department stores are being built on greenfield sites; specialized shops, such as do-it-yourself centers (e.g., Home Depot), are being established successfully, and department stores are also striving to expand their size. Retailing chains are increasingly supplanting independent retailers. The trend toward shopping centers, which has long been established in the USA, is also coming to Europe. One of the largest centers in the USA is the Mall of America in Bloomington, Minnesota. The Mall of America, which was opened

Figure 1. Characteristic forms of retailers

Characteristic	Characteristic form			
Business level	Retailer		Wholesaler	
Extent of trading	Within the country		Outside the country	
Horizontal cooperation	Retailers	Wholesalers	Other cooperation	
Vertical cooperation	Retail and wholesale	Wholesale and industrial companies	Retail and industrial companies	Retail, wholesale and industrial companies
Contact orientation	Stationary	Itinerant	Mail order	
Sales contact form	Sales person	Self-service	Catalog	Vending machine
Beneficiary	Investment goods trade		Consumer goods trade	
Range extent	Wide and deep range	Wide and shallow range	Narrow and deep range	Narrow and shallow range
Price policy	Active		Passive	
Purchase initiation through	Visit to store	Letter / fax	Telephone (caller center)	Internet	Push (e.g., Clubs)
Logistics handling	By the customer (collect)	By the retailer / intermediary (delivery)	Through the Internet (for digital products)	

in 1992, today comprises over 520 stores, employs more than 12 thousand people and has between 35 to 42 million visits yearly—more than Disney World, Graceland and Grand Canyon have together (www.mallofamerica.com). The most prominent German example is the CentrO in Oberhausen that opened on September 12, 1996. Two hundred businesses offer their goods under a single roof in this shopping mall with a sales area of 70,000 square meters. A car park with space for 10,500 vehicles surrounds the shopping complex and ensures problem-free logistics.

The Internet and, based on the opportunities it provides, electronic commerce form a further trend. Increasingly, products can be ordered with just a click of the mouse from the personal computer at home. In principle, anything can be bought over the Internet: from books, CDs, travel and cars, through jam and fresh vegetables. Many pundits who see the future of retail in the Internet, predict an elimination of stationary retailers and foresee a direct logistics chain from the producer to the final customer.

However, countercurrents are becoming apparent. The corner shop that had encountered a drastic fall in sales and was considered to be threatened by extinction has experienced a renaissance in the form of service station shops (now with professional management and completely organized logistics). The ease of shopping just around the corner has also experienced a comeback, as has saving at any price at food discount stores or in self-service department stores. A relativization of the absolute pursuit of size states itself in the shop-within-a-shop concept, which, within a larger unit, promotes the "familiarity" of a small, sometimes independently operated, unit.

These observations show that there is no distinct trend in consumer goods trading. A focusing on specific types of selling or business segments is not taking place—quite the reverse: The range of different retailing forms is increasing and none of these forms appears to have long-term advantages. This results in one paramount requirement for retail information systems: the need for flexibility. Consequently, a (standard) retail information system must be capable of handling many characteristics of retailing companies as shown in Figure 1.

A large range of functions and flexibility of standard application systems in retailing is necessary because some retailing companies (at any one time) exhibit several forms of a characteristic and over the course of time change their characteristic forms. Thus, it is not unusual that a single company has wholesalers and retailers, engages in stationary and mail order trading, follows active price policies in one range of goods and a passive price policy in another. And, in the course of time, this particular company complements its classic structures by electronic commerce over the Internet and goods distribution of music albums and videos over this medium. A widening of the range can be observed, for instance, at IKEA (augmenting the furniture range with a wide range of day-to-day products) and even the German ALDI, the classic provider of a "restricted range of products and producers," has added refrigerated and frozen goods to its assortment of dry goods. An expansion of logistics and customer contact can be found at many grocery retailers, which, in addition to the classic branches, also offer Internet sales with direct delivery, for example Albertsons (www.albertsons.com) and Asda (www.asda.com). Also the European leader in the drugstore sector, the German company Schlecker, offers Internet sales with direct delivery service for Germany, Austria and The Netherlands with Schlecker Home Shopping (www.schlecker.de).

The realization of adequate data processing support for all characteristics listed in Figure 1 represents a major challenge for providers of retail information systems. In addition to the diverse types of retail companies, various recent developments, such as the increasing decentralization of merchandise management, the expansion of merchandise information systems to become decision support systems or the trend to point-of-sales acquisition (cf. Ahlert, 1997, p. 31), must be taken into consideration. Furthermore, a retail information system must have a structural form that allows it to be adapted to future requirements with an acceptable effort.

Most of the large trade companies tend to use individualized software systems for selling, purchasing and inventory control, probably due to the variety of business types. However, since trade companies do not usually transform their products, which would doubtlessly require individualized software, it appears that preconditions for standardized software systems already exist. The reference model for retail enterprises, which is described in the following, was developed inductively by abstracting data from several company-specific models and by deducing from theoretical findings (e.g., organizational rules deduced from a company's goals. In this chapter we focus on the general structure of this reference model).

Development and Application of an Architecture for the Retail Domain

Architectures, also known as grouping frames, have achieved great importance in providing an understanding of information systems at the process design level. An architecture structures a particular section of the real world at an abstract level using the selected structuring paradigm and thus emphasizes relationships and possible time-related sequences between independent parts of the frame. Closely connected to the architectures are *modeling languages*, which provide the fundamental means of description for information systems. The

Figure 2. ARIS architecture (Source: Scheer, 2000, p. 1)

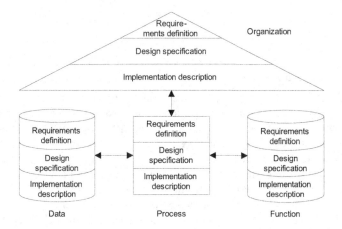

Figure 3: Y-CIM reference model (Source: Scheer, 1990, p. 2)

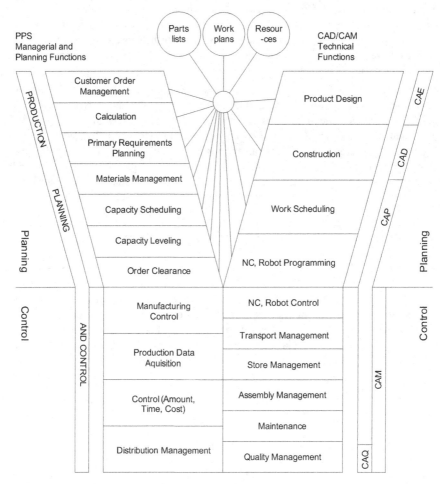

language meta models must integrate with the respective views of the architecture; in many practical cases architectures are tightly coupled with specific modeling languages.

Domain independent architectures, such as the Architecture of Integrated Information Systems (ARIS), provide the classification of information models into a generic framework (cf. Scheer, 1999, 2000), thus structuring results of information system construction. These architectures support different views and layers based on certain model aspects (such as structural or behavioral) or on the model's position in the information system development life cycle (e.g., analysis or design). Domain independent grouping frames however do not support model classification in respect to business semantics, for they abstract from specialized domain knowledge to provide a generic instrument for structuring complex information models. The intention is to provide methodical guidance for model development by structuring the extensive sets of related models resulting during the process.

In accordance with Scheer's ARIS architecture (architecture of integrated information systems, see Figure 2), a differentiation can be made between *functions* within tasks, namely the subtasks to be performed, *data*, namely the structure of the tasks and *processes*, namely the behavior of these areas (cf. Scheer, 1999, 2000). However, function and process are not completely distinct. A process contains the temporal sequence of individual transactions, alternatives in the procedure and parameters on which these alternatives depend.

Domain specific architectures specialize in a smaller application area in order to provide utilie knowledge for their practical use. An early domain-specific architecture for the manufacturing industry has been introduced by Scheer with the Y-CIM model (cf. Scheer, 1990; see Figure 2-2). Another example for a domain-specific architecture is the CIM-OSA, which specializes in manufacturing as well (cf. ESPRIT 1993).

The intention of the reference model for retail enterprises introduced in this paper is to provide a domain-specific architecture for the retail domain. It further intends to structure the set of models according to retail business semantics (cf. section 3) as well as to combine methodical aspects introduced with the views of the ARIS architecture (cf. section 4).

The main purpose of reference models is to provide recommendations that are applicable in a multitude of development projects. The required practical relevance is ensured by both an *inductive approach* on the model construction as well as successful instantiations of the model in real-life projects. The model discussed in this paper has been developed by abstracting from specific information models of several companies and therefore represents a "best practice" solution. *Deductive* attempts to enhance models by deriving from theoretical findings are utilizable in reference modeling as well. The applicability of model aspects so constructed, however, can only be verified by their practical use.

As mentioned above, reference models are based on a particular modeling language. The conceptual grounding of the model introduced in this paper concerning the utilized description languages as well as the supported model views is provided by the ARIS architecture (cf. section 4).

The successful application of a reference model is a significant phase in the model's lifecycle. For there is no possibility to prove the correctness or applicability of reference models in a formal manner; feedbacks from model instantiation in several real-world scenarios are crucial to provide important information for further model improvements.

Reference models can be used for two distinct generic purposes (Schütte, 1998). The first area of application is the *analysis* of an organization's actual state and its respective evaluation in relation to the recommendations stated in the reference model. Another purpose for reference models is their utilization as *construction support*. Therefore, the model is customized for the specific needs of a particular organization while designing an organizational or application system.

The retail-H architecture has been applied in several projects (e.g., in the context of development for retail applications as means of documentation and functional enhancement for an existing software system). The gained experience and knowledge has been integrated into the over 100 detail models that perpetually refine the reference model.

Architecture for Business Processes of the Retail-H Reference Model

The architecture of integrated information systems in retailing companies forms a pictogram of an H, which represents the principal tasks. To derive the H, let us consider the major tasks executed by retailing companies:

Goods-related requirements planning, logistics and billing functions ensure that goods flow from the supplier to the retailing company, and from the retailing company to the customer. The business-administrative tasks refer to the value-related sphere of the company in terms of cost accounting from the internal viewpoint, billing functions of the external accounting and all tasks associated with personnel accounting, employee information, career planning and employee administration. In addition to these operative tasks, further necessities arise from tactical and strategic business, controlling and company planning.

Interfaces to upstream and downstream operations in the same company, as well as to suppliers and customers, must ensure the complete, integrated, consistent and fast communication with marketing partners. The structure of these tasks depends on the types of retailing business. The classic warehousing business covers more tasks and consequently also requires more functionality from the merchandise management system compared to a third-party business or a pooled payment business. Special sales promotions and service business provided in retailing additionally require other functions.

The Merchandise Management System

Greatly simplified, a retailing company must perform three principal tasks: procurement, storage and distribution of goods. The trading objects are goods (i.e., physical products). The terms service companies, brokers or agents are used when non-physical products are involved. The actual manufacturing of products does not belong to the task scope of retailing; in this case, the term industry company would be used. However, there are companies that call themselves retailing companies (retailing in the institutional sense) and perform functions beyond retailing in the functional sense (procurement, storage and distribution). Similarly, there are retailing companies that do not perform certain retailing tasks in the functional sense. An example of the former is a retailer entering a service business, examples of the latter are the third-party business and the pooled payment business.

Merchandising thus covers the goods-oriented planning tasks, as well as logistical and billing-related tasks that a retailing company needs to perform.

The *merchandise management system* is the information system that supports and controls these goods-oriented planning tasks, the logistical and the billing-related tasks of a retailing company using value- and quantity-related transaction data.

Considering the central tasks of retailing in more detail, we can identify the following merchandise management subtasks:

Contracting

Contracting makes the basic procurement decisions and updates the relevant base data. Central tasks are determining suppliers with which the retailing company will enter a business relationship, goods to be obtained from these suppliers, negotiating the price and conditions framework for these goods (often in annual meetings) and possibly determining value and quantity contracts or delivery schedules.

Order Management

Order management involves placing orders by determining the quadruple: supplier, article, quantity and time. As subtasks it includes the following calculations: limit requirements, and purchase order quantity as well as the stock allocation and order transfer and monitoring.

Goods Receipt

Goods receipt is the quantity-related logistical equivalent to the purchasing order. The goods receipt must be planned; this requires notifying the supplier such that an efficient ramp assignment planning can be performed. Goods acceptance, sometimes also without having been ordered, and quantitative as well as qualitative goods control follow. The goods receipt also covers the physical goods storage, recording the goods receipt and analyzing the delivery notes with the assessment of the goods receipt, an update of the inventory and, finally, if need be, the handling of returns to the supplier. The administration of reusable packaging and goods on deposit are also tasks of the goods receipt.

Invoice Auditing

The value-based equivalent to the goods receipt task are the invoice arrival and auditing with the subtasks invoice acquisition, checking, release, subsequent invoice processing and processing of subsequent conditions. On the one hand, the invoiced quantities must be compared with the order (the request to deliver), the delivery note (the delivered quantity from the supplier's viewpoint) and the goods receipt slip (the delivery quantity from the retailer's viewpoint). On the other hand, the invoiced values must be compared with the agreed price and conditions scheme.

Accounts Payable

The major task of the accounts payable task is handling payments (i.e., the payment of open items resulting from the supplier's invoice). This requires updating the creditor master data. Unless an invoice is passed on automatically from the invoice auditing, an entry is made for this particular invoice (e.g., material cost entry). Credit notes and subsequent billings may need to be booked. The payment can take place through an automatic payment run or by means of manual payment. If the creditor is also a debtor (e.g., for subsequent payments), the accounts payable may also include sending reminder notices and interest calculation tasks.

Marketing

In the context of monitoring the retailing processes and tasks, only operative marketing is considered as marketing; strategic marketing is considered as being a task within the company planning (see Meffert, 1998, or Lilien, Kotler, & Moorthy, 1992, for a comprehensive description of the marketing tasks). Here, subtasks of the (operative) marketing are updating of customer master data, assortment and product policies (including goods planning), in particular assortment planning, sales planning and turn-over planning, as well as article lists. These subtasks require customer groupings and time-dependent article-customer assignments. The sales condition policy and sales advertising also belong to the marketing task.

Sales, goods issues, billing and accounts receivable are analog concepts to the corresponding tasks on the goods receipt side (contracting, order management, goods receipt, invoice auditing and accounts payable).

Selling

Selling includes the subtasks of customer query processing, customer offer processing, creation of order records, order processing, possibly customer complaint processing and, finally, support for sales representatives with customer contact, sales support and sales processing by the sales representatives.

Goods Issue

Subtasks of the goods issue activities involve route planning, planning and execution of order picking, goods issue acquisition—either at the (central) warehouse or in the branch–and entering the inventory. The shipping activities and, if need be, the processing of customer returns and the management of reusable packaging are also part of the goods issue.

Billing

Billing tasks include, in particular, the evaluation of a customer delivery note, various forms of invoicing the customer (e.g., individual invoices or collective invoices) and calculation of subsequent reimbursements, combined with the generation of any required credit and debit notes.

Accounts Receivable

The central task of accounts receivable is the administration of debtor accounts and the monitoring of payments. The major activities are updating the accounts receivable master data, booking of invoices, credit notes, subsequent sales conditions and the collection including debiting, booking of payment arrivals and perhaps the handling of reminder notices, and, last but not least, credit management (i.e., determination of credit limits and monitoring a debtor's credit worthiness).

Warehousing

Warehousing performs the bridging function between the procurement side and the sales side. This bridging is done with regard to time, quantity and logistics. Warehouse subtasks involve updating the warehouse master data, stock transfers and posting transfers, stocktaking in the warehouse or in the branch and warehouse control.

When all tasks related to suppliers are placed on one leg, all tasks associated with customers are assigned to the other leg and the logistical functions with goods receipt, warehousing and goods issue are arranged horizontally across, the merchandising management-related areas of a retailing company to form an H (see Figure 4).

The above-mentioned tasks of procurement, distribution and logistics do not occur exceptionally in retailing companies, but also in industrial enterprises. However, retailing has some unique features that affect the particular structure of the tasks and consequently the supporting information systems.

- **Contracting:** Comprehensive requirements arise for the central object of any merchandise management system (i.e., the article). The way of establishing an article (which should be as simple as possible due to the large number), the time dependency of the article master data resulting from special promotions of limited duration or prices and conditions, the multi-stage organizational structures typical in retailing (in particular

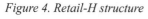

Figure 4. Retail-H structure

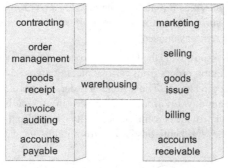

with regard to purchasing bureaus) and the determination of sources for a special article are unique to merchandise management systems.

- **Order management:** The multi-stage form of retailing companies largely determines the operative procedures. For example, order management must take into account both local and central order quantity planning. Thus, pull strategies, where sales at the cash desk form the starting point for requirements planning at both the branch and the central warehouse, constitute a specific requirement of multi-stage retailing.

- **Goods receipt:** While inventories at a wholesaler or in a central warehouse of a multi-stage retailing company are listed based on quantity, this is often not possible at retailers due to technical and organizational restrictions. In order to control the assortment, article stocks are listed value-based with purchasing and selling prices at the merchandise category level (or some similar system of grouping). The difference between the purchasing value and the selling value corresponds to the gross profit of the retailing company and provides the basis for determining the retailing margin.

- **Invoice auditing:** The number of invoices to be processed requires a high degree of division of labor in the invoice auditing. Accordingly, the invoice auditing is normally separated from the financial accounting in retailing. Delivery notes and invoices (normally only the invoice total) form the input to separate work steps. Invoices are then automatically matched to the processed delivery notes.

- **Warehousing:** The warehousing functions are especially dependent on the retailing level. As mentioned before, retailers normally value the stock based on the selling price. Handling seasonal articles in the central warehouse, which are meant to be sold at the end of the season, requires the transfer between picking and reserve warehouse areas. There might also be a change in the assignment of fixed picking locations to articles, if, for instance, summer season goods are no longer stocked in the picking warehouse in fall.

- **Marketing:** Articles must be assigned to branches or customers in the marketing area (so-called listing). The article assignment is the result of policies based on the assortment. The usually large number of articles and the heterogeneity of sales transactions indicates that classifications of articles and customers must be made in order to achieve the fastest and most efficient assignment of articles to customers. Another issue in marketing involves the support for sales promotions. Besides different logistical procedures, promotions require special billing techniques which, for example, affect the granting of conditions in both debtor and creditor contexts. The promotion business provides a suitable starting point to create processes that transcend business levels—up to today promotion activities initiated by the industry and promotion activities from retailing companies suffered from insufficient information sharing. In other words, integration potential remains unused.

- **Goods issue:** Goods issue covers the logistical processes from picking goods through to shipping them. Picking orders from various picking areas have to be grouped and loaded in special shipping zones. Those picking orders are normally derived from the route plan for a certain day. Enormous fluctuations in picking loads require that the capacity management provides profiles for capacity demand and capacity availability as used in industry. Several heuristics known from industry can be used for this sub-problem.

- **Billing:** Billing involves invoicing the customer for the provided goods and services. Many wholesale companies demand support for the pooled payment business form. This requires the combination of supplier and customer invoices.

Business Administrative Systems

The goods-oriented planning, logistical and billing tasks of merchandise processing are augmented with business-administrative systems of the general accounting and asset management, cost accounting and human resources management. Whereas the merchandise management tasks relate either to the supplier, the customer or are of a logistical nature, business-administrative systems do not have a delimitable focus.

General Accounting

General accounting combines the subledgers of accounts payable, accounts receivable and materials accounting. It summarizes them in order to produce the general ledger accounts. Tasks of general accounting involve maintaining the general ledger account master data, booking of the general ledger accounts, bank transactions and preparations for financial statements, the creation of financial statements and financial planning.

Asset Management

In addition to maintaining the fixed-assets master data, fixed-assets accounting includes entry bookings for fixed-assets, bookings for depreciation, entry postings, transfer postings and issue postings together with final statements and fixed-assets controlling.

Cost Accounting

While the financial accounting is primarily associated with external accounting, cost accounting is used for internal purposes. Since key figures used in controlling build on the results (e.g., cost and profit types) from cost accounting, it provides the informational basis for controlling purposes. The cost accounting tasks involve master data administration, including the management of supplementary cost and profit types as well as reference quantities and objects. Additionally, they comprise cost and profit planning proceeded by sales forecasts, the goods resource costs and inner-company services and the acquisition of the actual data for analysis and monitoring purposes—in particular, profit margin calculations and business comparisons. Central profit margin calculations in retailing are the merchandise category profit margin calculation, the supplier profit margin calculation and the customer profit margin calculation.

Human Resources

In addition to various accounting tasks, human resources management also includes planning tasks. Maintaining the personnel master data covers the creation and updating of employee master data (e.g., personal data, working form and bank account details) and the assignment of employees to organizational units (e.g., the employee is purchaser for a specific purchasing organization or the planning officer in a branch or a warehouse). The accounting-based task of human resources management is personnel payment. Planning tasks involve determining personnel requirements using a personnel requirement, acquisition and possibly personnel allocation, combined with personnel assignment and cost planning. The personnel evaluation and the personnel development planning are further associated tasks.

Since the architecture of the retail-H model groups all supplier-related tasks in one "leg" of the H and all customer-related tasks in the other "leg," accounts payable and accounts receivable are on the supplier-related side and the customer-related side, respectively. This complies with the definition of a merchandise management system that combines goods-related planning, logistical and billing functions. In contrast, the grouping of bookings in the general ledger accounting is assigned to the "foot" of the H. However, in many data processing solutions, accounts payable and accounts receivable are integrated with general accounting and asset management in the financial accounting system.

Strategic Planning, EIS, and Controlling

The previously listed tasks have a rather operative nature, describing the day-to-day retailing business, whereas strategic planning, EIS and controlling involve strategic tasks of retailing management. For support purposes, the appropriate data are required in a highly aggregated form that supplies the relevant operating numbers. These, then, form the basis for company decisions. The aggregated data are extended with external data (e.g., from market research companies such as GfK or Nielsen). Technically, data warehouse systems (i.e., large databases optimized for rapid data retrieval analysis of large data volumes, are often used for this purpose).

The difference between controlling systems, executive information systems and systems for company planning is somewhat fuzzy. The tasks arising in a controlling system are usually cyclical analyses for price and sales control or logistics control. Furthermore, there are profit-related breakdowns, such as controlling specific sales promotions or determining the success of an advertisement campaign. Operations type and competition comparisons as well as market data analyses can more appropriately be assigned to the executive information systems area, while tasks of the business area planning, location planning and strategic logistical planning belong to the area of strategic planning.

Figure 5. Retail-H model

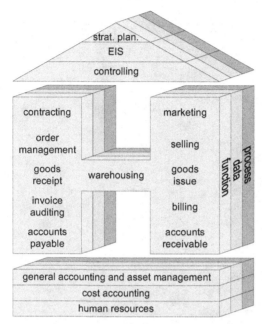

Views of the Retail-H Reference Model

As shown before, a retailing company has to engage in more than purely merchandise management tasks. Of particular importance are business administrative tasks as well as general controlling and company planning tasks. Therefore, a merchandise management system cannot account for all required IT-support and additional information systems and applications are usually necessary. An information system, which covers all these tasks, will be called a *retail information system*. Logically, and maybe also physically, the merchandise management system is part of the retail information system.

The variety of retailing tasks and, as such, the functionality of retail information systems, can be structured based on the retail-H. For a differentiated picture, though, there are different viewpoints which have to be considered. These views (process, data and function) have been derived from the domain-independent ARIS architecture (cf. section 2).

The retail-H model summarizes the tasks of a retailing company and the different viewpoints (see Figure 5).

Functions

The functional view lists all (basic) functions related to activities in the fields of procurement, warehousing, distribution, business administration and strategic decision making. This view

Figure 6. Functional model of invoice auditing

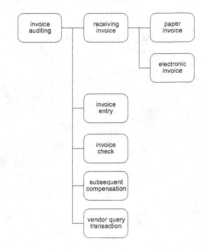

Figure 7. ERM of the product

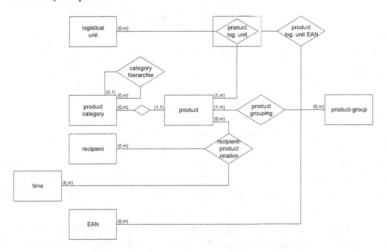

has a documenting and classifying function and is, within each "enterprise-goods-transaction type" class, usually consistent (an example of such a class might be a three-way combination of "wholesaling-groceries-settlement" business). Figure 6 shows a functional view of the invoice auditing sector for instance.

Data

Representations of static structures are created through data modeling (Chen, 1976; Elmasri & Navathe, 1994). Examples of common situations where this technique can be applied

Figure 8. Process model of invoice entry

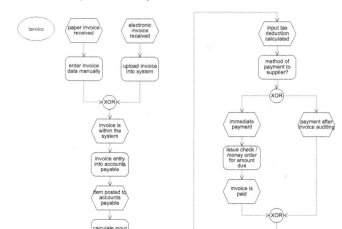

include: setting prices and terms, managing multi-level supplier hierarchies (e.g., foreign distributors), allocating stocks (determining quantities to be delivered to recipient, e.g., based on past sales) or tracking promotions (e.g., promotional theme, extent of validity, terms for supplier and customer, articles to be included, internal and external logistics). The "product" data model plays a central role in Merchandise Information Systems (see Figure 7).

Processes

Processes determine the temporal and logical sequence of functions. A typical instance of this is the two-level process of entering data from received invoices and invoice auditing which, due to the large number of transactions involved, allows for the achievement of a substantially digressive cost effect. When invoices are drawn up, it will often happen that only the total amount due is entered. During invoice auditing, the auditor will naturally attempt to reconcile this invoice total with the total value of goods received. However, if the system makes all three documents available for simultaneous examination (which it rarely does), apparent discrepancies can be found with the help of the system. The need for laborious manual comparisons of invoice positions and value of goods received positions can thus be eliminated. The process of feeding invoices into the information system is depicted in Figure 8.

A complete description of functions, data and processes for retail information systems can be found in Becker and Schütte (2004).

Figure 9. Reduced retail-H model for retailers

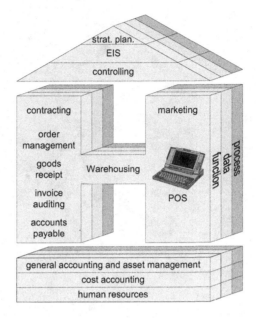

Variants of the Retail-H Reference Model

At first glance, it might appear that the retail-H model applies primarily to wholesalers in which the tasks on the supplier side and the customer side have similar structures. In contrast, stationary retailing involves some tasks from the right hand side at the point of sale (i.e., at the cash desk). This results in a reduced retail-H model.

However, the retail-H model for retailers shown in Figure 9 applies only to "classic" stationary retailing. If the retailing company issues customer credit cards, then the retailer knows the debtor, and billing and accounts receivable become evident again as tasks. Mail order

Figure 10. Classic third-party business

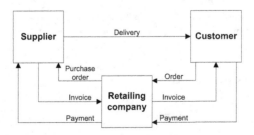

Figure 11. Retail-H model for third-party business

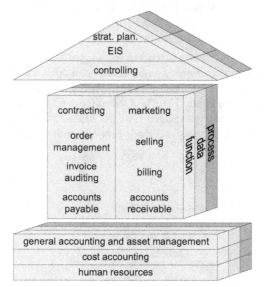

(also a form of retailing) and Internet trading require all functions of the complete retail-H model. Thus, the model covers a superset of retailer and wholesaler's tasks. It can be "shortened" appropriately for specific situations.

The classic type of retailing business is warehousing business with procurement, storing and distribution functions described in the retail-H model. In addition to the classic warehousing business, third-party business and the pooled payment business have emerged and, orthogonal to these, promotional and service types of business that can occur in conjunction with the first three types of business.

Third-Party Business

In a classic third-party business, a customer places orders with the retailing company, which in turn forwards the order to the supplier. The different step is that the delivery is made di-

Figure 12. Store-based third-party business

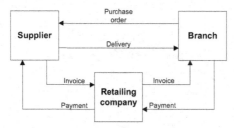

rectly from the supplier to the customer. The supplier invoices the retailing company, which independently invoices the customer (Figure 10). The logistics take place directly between supplier and customer. The associated Retail-H model for classic third-party business is reduced to the functions shown in Figure 11.

A second form of third-party business occurs in retailing with branches. The branch orders directly from the supplier (sometimes without entering an order into the information system). The supplier then delivers to the branch and sends the invoice to the head office and eventually to the branch (see Figure 12). The head office is responsible for monitoring the process. This transfer handling is executed similarly to the first case when the orders are entered into the system and the transfer is made centrally to the supplier.

Figure 13. Retail-H model for pooled payment business

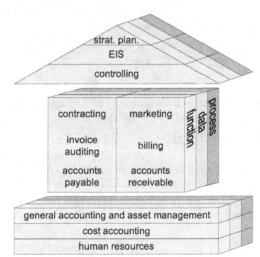

Figure 14. Pooled payment business

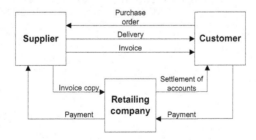

Pooled Payment Business

The tasks a retailing company needs to perform in the case of pooled payment business are reduced to an even greater degree (see Figure 13). The handling of both the logistical and the planning functions takes place directly between supplier and customer, while the retailing company is only involved in billing tasks.

The customer places orders with the supplier, who then delivers directly to the customer who also receives the invoice from the supplier. The supplier sends a copy of the invoice to the retailing company. The retailing company settles the invoice and sends an account statement for payment to the customer (see Figure 14). Since the creditor invoice flows immediately into a debtor account statement, accounts payable and accounts receivable are closely connected. The master data for creditors and debtors should also be closely coupled, when, for example, the creditor has agreed to specific terms bilaterally with the debtor (payment terms, immediate rebate, etc.).

In the case of pooled payment business, the retailing company normally provides a default guarantee for its customers' purchases (acceptance of the factoring discount)—it acts primarily as bank (i.e., a paying agent for the customer's debts). The specific central settlement contract can be either a contract with guarantee character or a form of *factoring*. Factoring in this context is understood to be the contracted continuous purchase of debt claims (normally before they become due) from deliveries and services through a factor while assuming certain service functions and often bearing the risk of default (cf. Perridon & Steiner, 1995, p. 401). The feature of the handling of a pooled payment business is the coincidence of

Figure 15. Retail-H model for promotion business

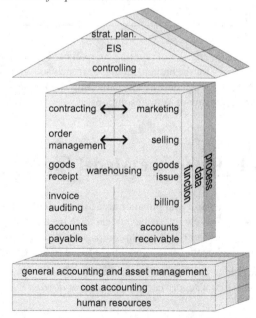

invoice payment and billing (in the sense of presentation of the invoice). In the legal sense, the pooled payment business transaction is *one* business transaction, whereas the third-party business represents *two* separate business transactions.

Promotion Business

Promotion and service processes can occur during warehouse, third-party and pooled payment business (for detailed information about promotions refer to Merrilees & Miller, 1996, p. 261ff.). Promotions are purchasing and/or sales measures that take place over a limited amount of time and make use of favorable conditions and other terms of the suppliers and/or serve to increase sales. Especially in consumer goods retailing, and in particular in food retailing, sales promotions have a large importance. To attract off-the-street customers, prices of a range of products are sometimes drastically reduced in periodic intervals, sometimes even weekly. In the promotion business, the tasks of the sales side are more closely coupled with the tasks of the purchasing side than is the case of traditional warehousing business. If a promotion is planned, the head office negotiates the quantities of the promotion articles to be ordered with the branches. This allows a preorder to be defined. The identified quantities then serve as a basis for price negotiations with the suppliers. In this case, there is no normal stocking in the warehouse, but often a direct transfer from the goods receipt to the goods issue (transshipment or cross-docking). Because promotional goods are billed separately, this requires a time-related control of prices, a non-trivial problem for merchandise processing systems.

Figure 15 shows the typical retail-H model for the promotion business in which the coupling of the procurement and sales sides causes the two sides of the H to move together.

Service Business

Service business completes the activities of retailing companies. The head office, wholesaler and franchiser perform services for the branch, retailer or franchisee with regard to business and tax consultancy, data processing consultancy, marketing support and recommendations for entering the market or provision of system solutions.

The Retail-H Reference Model in Comparison

Retail enterprises represent a rewarding application area for the reference modeling approach (cf. Fettke & Loos, 2004). Only few reference models have been developed covering that particular type of business. This section intends to compare the different concepts of existing approaches, emphasizing the benefit of the model introduced in this Chapter.

Reference models in the field of information systems can be classified into two main categories (cf. Vering, 2002). The first category comprises *business domain reference models* that represent state-of-the-art knowledge covering a particular business domain (i.e., a particular type or sector of business). The second category, referred to as *software reference models*, groups models that describe features of software products in a conceptual manner.

Business Domain Reference Models

Existing business domain reference models for the retail business are the retail reference model by Marent (1995), the reference model for digital commerce by Luxem (2000) and the retail logistics reference model by Remmert (2001). Fettke and Loos proposed a framework for the evaluation of reference models specifically addressing retail enterprises (cf. Fettke & Loos, 2004) and applied it respectively to the models specified above.

The reference model proposed by Marent focuses on retail and wholesale enterprises in the food and luxury sector. It comprises a data view as well as a functional view.

Remmert discusses the interface between manufacturers and retailers giving special attention to the food industry sector as well. He provides a procedure model to derive reference models from the organizations context in four steps: goal definition, process identification, process design and the analysis of alternative process designs. The author utilizes event-driven process chains (EPC) as means of visualization. The reference model is restricted on the process view.

The reference model for digital commerce is based on the retail-H and specializes on the trade of fully digitizable goods (e.g., music, books and software) over the Internet, explicitly excluding traditional distribution channels. The model is limited to a functional view and does not provide data or process-oriented aspects.

The reference model for retail enterprises discussed in this paper provides a significantly more exhaustive as well as a higher detailed knowledge base for the retail domain (cf. Fettke & Loos, 2004). Additionally, it is both applicable to organizational as well as application systems design.

Software Reference Models

As an exponent for software reference models, the IBM retail application architecture (RAA) is focused on the specialized class of application systems employed in retail business (cf. Stecher, 1993). It is intended to support the introduction of such DP-systems in respective enterprises. The architecture comprises functional and data models. The functional view consists of decomposition diagrams, which visualize the hierarchical structure of identified processes, and flow charts representing functional sequences.

The Association for Retail Technology Standards (ARTS) proposed a standardized data model for retail enterprises. It is intended to support system development projects for retail applications focusing on store and point-of-sale specifics. It comprises models representing standard data structures and flows in three hierarchically ordered views, classified by their level of abstraction concerning technical detailing (business and logical view, near-physical model) but is limited on a data view.

Both reference models are focused on the development of software systems for the domain in question. The RAA model, especially, has been developed completely by an inductive approach aiming at application development and integration. The applicability of organizational design independent of information technology is considered as being a by-product of the reference architecture, although abstractions of modeling results from real-life reengineering projects are not explicitly included. RAA intends to be a generic framework for application integration and basically provides modeling concepts for the retail domain, giving only few examples that explain the use of the architecture.

The numerous models provided with the introduced architecture, however, contain usable knowledge that is applicable directly in respective development or reengineering projects and represents a comprehensive repository for the various business types of the retail domain.

Conclusion and Outlook

Highly abstract graphical representations run the risk of being dismissed as too iconographic, but a somewhat abstract structure of the retail information system as presented in the paper can be of great help to understand "real world" retailing. It is now possible to place existing knowledge and current research projects into this framework in order to structure the field of retailing. Having thus obtained an overview of the field, it is possible to focus on specific areas of research to gain further insight into more detailed aspects of the retailing business.

The framework presents views, business processes and other processes as well as criteria for differentiation as they apply to retail business information systems. Any reference model for trade businesses or enterprise-specific trade business information model can find its appropriate place in this architecture.

References

Ahlert, D. (1997). Merchandise information systems and controlling of consumer goods distribution. In D. Ahlert & R. Olbricht (Eds.), *R. Integrierte Warenwirtschaftssysteme und Handelscontrolling* (3rd ed., pp. 3-113). Schäffer-Poeschel, Stuttgart.

Becker, J., & Schütte, R. (2004). *Retail information systems* (2nd ed.). Frankfurt am Main-Verlag: Moderne Industrie. [in German]

Becker, J., Uhr, W., & Vering, O. (2001). *Retail information systems based on SAP products.* Berlin: Springer.

Chen, P.P.-S. (1976). The entity relationship model: Toward a unified view of data. In *ACM Transactions on Database-Systems, 1*(1), 9-36.

Elmasri, R., & Navathe, S. (1994). *Fundamentals of database systems* (2nd ed.). Redwood City: Addison-Wesley.

ESPRIT 1993. (n.d.). *ESPRIT Consortium AMICE: CIMOSA: Open System Architecture for CIM* (2nd ed.). Berlin: Springer.

Fettke, P., & Loos, P. (2004). Reference models for retail enterprises. In *IT-Lösungen für den Handel, Praxis der Wirtschaftsinformatik HMD 235. dpunkt* (pp. 15-25). Heidelberg: Verlag. [in German]

Lilien, G. L., Kotler, P., & Moorthy, K. S. (1992). *Marketing models*. Englewood Cliffs, NJ: Prentice-Hall.

Luxem, R. (2000). *Digital commerce: Electronic commerce mit digitalen produkten*. Köln: Eul, Lothmar.

Marent, C. (1995). *Tool-based reference modeling for retail enterprises*. Dissertation Wirtschafts-universität Wien, Wien.

Meffert, H. (1998). *Marketing: Foundations of marketing policy* (8th ed.). Wiesbaden: Gabler.

Merrilees, B., & Miller, D. (1996). *Retailing management: A best practice approach*. Victoria: RMIT Press.

Perridon, L., & Steiner, M. (1995). *Public finance* (8th ed.). Munich:Vahlen. [in German]

Remmert, J. (2001). *Reference modeling for retail logistics*. Wiesbaden: DUV. [in German]

Scheer, A.-W. (2000). *ARIS: Business process modeling* (3rd ed.). Berlin: Springer.

Scheer, A.-W. (1999). *ARIS: Business process frameworks* (3rd ed.). Berlin: Springer.

Schütte, R. (1998). *Guidelines for reference modeling*. Wies-baden: Gabler. [in German]

Stecher, P. (1993). Building business and application systems with the retail application architecture. *IBM Systems Journal, 32*(2), 278-306.

Vering, O. (2002). *Systematical software selection for retail enterprises*. Berlin: Logos. [in German]

Chapter X

A Reference Model
for Savings Banks

Annett Mäuser, IBM Global Business Services, Germany

Abstract

With approximately 17,490 well-defined modeling objects, the SKO[1]-Datenmodell[2] is probably the most extensive reference data model in German for the banking area. So far, this reference data model has been used in about 30 projects describing different subject areas. The detailed project data models that have been derived from these projects have been reintegrated into the generic reference data model, as far as the results are applicable to the entire Sparkassenorganisation. The SKO-Datenmodell was initially developed approximately 15 years ago. It is derived from the financial services data model[3] (FSDM), which has been provided by IBM. The FSDM is a reference data model which is generally valid for the banking area. In contrast to the FSDM, the SKO-Datenmodell is specialized for the requirements of the Sparkassenorganisation. The basic elements of the reference data model are a conceptual design of data model abstraction levels, an extensive methods and procedures handbook with precise quality requirements and an integrated tool support by m1[4] and Rochade.[5] The different levels of the SKO-Datenmodell and the use of these levels in practice are described in this chapter.

Figure 1. The levels of the SKO-Datenmodell

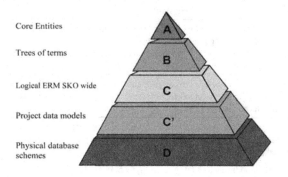

The Conceptual Design of Levels of
the SKO-Datenmodell
==

The *SKO-Datenmodell* covers approximately 80% of the business data that are required by application development projects in the Sparkassenorganisation. The data model is subdivided into the five levels A, B, C, C' and D (Figure 1). The A-Level is a very compact level with business data. This level covers the architecture view. The following levels become more extensive and the contents become more and more detailed in the direction of a technical view.

The content of the levels A, B and C are developed and maintained by a central group hosted by the SIZ.[6] The models of these three levels are available for all members of the Sparkassenorganisation. The C'- and D-level contents are developed by the various projects of the joint use centers of the Sparkassenorganisation.

The A-Level (Architecture View)
==

The *A-Level* of the SKO-Datenmodell consists of nine *core entities* (Table 1). These core entities represent containers for the business terms in the banking area. The business terms are assigned to their proper places on the highest level. Each term belongs only to one of the nine core entities. Each core entity has a detailed definition and description as well as examples to support the classification.

The nine core entities are a useful instrument at the beginning of application development projects. During the definition of requirements, the project contents can be delimited by assigning the business terms to the core entities. However, the A-Level is also a good place to define responsibilities in a project. In one of the last application development projects with the SKO-Datenmodell, the project teams had been organized by the core entities. The "customer relationship management" team was responsible for the core entities involved

Table 1. The core entities of the A-Level

Core Entity	Definition	Example
Involved Party	An involved party is an individual, an organization, an organization unit or a community of involved parties about which the financial institution wishes to maintain information to enable a good cooperation.	Individual, organization
Event	An event is an activity or an occurrence about which the financial institution wishes to keep information as a part of managing its business.	Order, booking, advisory talk
Business Direction Item	A business direction item is an externally or internally caused regulation which helps to regularize the business of an involved party and to define its framework for action.	Enterprise objective, legal guidelines
Classification	A classification is a definition of dividing features for business information and their structure.	Account, unit of measure, market segment
Condition	A condition is a single requirement or a combination of requirements, which are necessary for the processing of the businesses of a financial institution.	Fee, maturity, interest rate
Location	A location is a bounded area or a point where something is addressed to or where something can be found.	Town, address
Product	A product is a service which is offered or sold by the financial institution or its competitors. It can also be a service which is offered to the financial institution.	Consumer loan, custodianship in a safe deposit box
Resource Item	A resource item is every object which is owned, managed and/ or used for the business of the financial institution or which is of special interest for the financial institution.	Building, manual
Arrangement	An arrangement is a potential or a real conclusion of a contract between two or more Involved Parties.	Product arrangement, employment arrangement

party, location and resource item. Arrangement and account (classification) had been covered by the "arrangement management" team and product and condition by the "product management" team.

In this case of having several teams, close communication between the data modelers of each team is important during the development of the project data model.

The B-Level (Business View)

The *B-Level* of the SKO-Datenmodell is a specialization of the A-Level. Each of the nine core entities is decomposed into a *tree of terms*. Such a tree of terms at the B-Level consists of a *classification hierarchy*, a *description hierarchy* and a *relationship hierarchy*. This hierarchical structure allows the detailed classification of business terms. With this specialization of the nine core entities, it is possible to cover the demand for information in a financial institution. The actual version of the SKO-Datenmodell contains 7,500 objects at the B-Level.

Figure 2. Extract of the description hierarchy of the core entity involved party with the tool m1

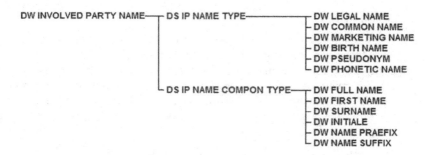

The construction elements of the B-Level are *scheme* and *value*. Each B-Level-hierarchy starts with a value. Then, schemes and values alternate. Figure 2 shows a part of the description hierarchy of the core entity involved party (IP). The abbreviation DW stands for description value. DW marks the term as a value of a description hierarchy. In the same way, the schemes are marked with DS. This abbreviation stands for description scheme. The example shows two schemes for the classification of "involved party name." The scheme "DS IP NAME TYPE" distinguishes between several kinds of names like "birth name," "marketing name" or "legal name." The second scheme, "DS IP NAME COMPONent TYPE," shows the different components of names like "first name," "surname" or "full name." The name "Max Miller" can be the legal name of an involved party as well as the marketing name. Furthermore, "Max Miller" can be filed as first name "Max" and surname "Miller" or as full name "Max Miller." The example shows that a term, found by the modeling, can be described by several categories.

On the B-Level, the same rule as on the A-Level applies: Every value and every scheme has to be described by a definition and some examples. This is necessary to enable the correct classification of terms and to avoid synonyms and homonyms. The given examples especially facilitate the use of the model for business professionals.

After an analysis of the context, each term is put in its proper place in one of the hierarchies by using suitable modeling principles. If a business term is a specialization of a core entity, it belongs to the classification hierarchy of this core entity. An "entry" is a specialization of an event and therefore belongs to the classification hierarchy of the core entity event. All the values that describe or identify a core entity—like the "involved party name" or the "account number"—are part of the description hierarchy of the corresponding core entity. Therefore, the "involved party name" belongs to the description hierarchy of the core entity involved party. "Account number" belongs to the description hierarchy of the core entity classification, because account is a subtype of classification. The relationship hierarchy contains all terms, which describe relationships within a core entity as well as relationships between two core entities. The relationship "involved party is customer of an involved party" is part of the relationship hierarchy of the core entity involved party. The relationship "involved party is supplier of resource item" is included in the relationship hierarchy of the core entity involved party as well as in the relationship hierarchy of the core entity resource item.

The model of the B-Level is a very good assistance for conversations with the business department. The simple construction also allows a business professional without modeling knowledge to find business terms very fast. The model also facilitates the navigation within the SKO-Datenmodell.

In application development projects, the model of the B-Level supports the definition of requirements. Moreover, the trees of terms support the clarification of business terms. The selection of terms of the B-Level model allows a simple and fast definition of the project scope. Because the reference model is already filled with terms and definitions, the specification process of a concrete project will be sped up. This definition of the project contents is the basis for the development of the project data model with the C-Level model of the SKO-Datenmodell.

The B-Level is not only useful in projects that develop new applications. The B-Level model also supports package integration, migration and re-engineering projects. Migration projects use the model as a neutral medium. The data models of applications that have to be migrated get an association to the B-Level model to define derivation rules from old to new.

The C-Level (Logical ERM Organization-Wide)

The *C-Level* of the SKO-Datenmodell consists of a logical *entity relationship model* (ERM). This level considers structural aspects. The actual SKO-Datenmodell version 3.1 contains the following elements on the C-Level:

- 1,023 entities
- 2,100 attributes
- 938 domains
- 5,014 domain values
- 704 relationships
- 215 subtype sets

Figure 3. Extract of the C-Level model with the tool Rochade (core entity event)

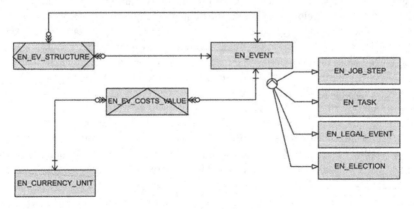

The business content of the entity relationship model is mainly derived from the B-Level hierarchies. A number of rules define the derivation mechanism. Each element of the model has a detailed description as well as examples.

Also, on the C-Level business aspects are decisive. Technical considerations do not influence the modeling. Generic structures, which cover a large area, help to reduce the complexity of the model.

This extensive entity relationship model is primary a communication basis for data modelers and developers. The user should be familiar with the data model based application development techniques. Application development projects use the model as a basis for the development of the project data models. The elements of the B- and C-Level models are linked with a so-called level trace. This trace allows the tool-supported selection of the data model extract that is relevant to the project, based on the scope definition on the B-Level. This C-Level extract is the basis for the project data model.

However, this is not the only use of the C-Level. The entity relationship model of the SKO-Datenmodell can also be the foundation for the development of an own enterprise-wide data model. For example, the German savings bank Hamburger Sparkasse has developed their enterprise-wide data model based on the SKO-Datenmodell.

The C'-Level (Logical ERM Subject Area View)

The logical data models of the different application development projects are located on the *C'-Level* of the SKO-Datenmodell. These project data models are parts of the C-Level model that are either extended specifically to the business or reduced. In contrast to the C-Level, which has the emphasis on structure, the C'-Level concentrates on the modeling of a specific subject area or of one project. Because of this strong orientation on a special subject area, C'-Level models are much more detailed than the entity relationship model of the C-Level. Not only data modelers and developers can use the models of the C'-Level. In addition, business professionals with modeling knowledge can use these models, because of the subject area view.

During the development of a C'-Level model, application-specific and/or technical aspects will be added to an extract of the C-Level model. One example for the modeling of technical aspects on the C'-Level is the modeling of a special concept for historical data.

Most of the project data models on the C'-Level are entity relationship models. However, they do not have to be entity relationship models just because this notation has been used for the model on the C-Level of the SKO-Datenmodell. The use of the notation depends on the modeling standards and the application development standards in the projects as well as on the project type.

In a card management project, experiences with object-oriented application development using the SKO-Datenmodell have been made. To also cover the modeling of systems for planning purposes, the project "OLAP modeling with the SKO-Datenmodell" was realized. The results of this project have been integrated in the *Methods and Procedures Handbook* of the SKO-Datenmodell.

The outcomes of the A-, B- and C-Levels are created and maintained by a central data administration group. But the models of the C'-Level are results of the application development projects of the various joint use centers. Experienced SKO data modelers support these projects.

The SKO data modelers collect new findings into a database during the project work. The entries of this database are used for revision and extension of the B- and C-Level models of the SKO-Datenmodell. If generally applicable, these findings are included in the SKO-Datenmodell during a so-called maintenance project. The result of such a maintenance project is always a new version of the SKO-Datenmodell. The members of the Sparkassenorganisation each get a new version. In order to follow the changes made between the versions of the model, a history and version trace will be delivered in addition. The trace helps to understand the deviations between the two model versions.

The D-Level (Physical Database Scheme)

All the previous levels of the SKO-Datenmodell have a very strong business view. Technical aspects have hardly been covered during the modeling on these levels. Now, the *physical database schemes* of the *D-Level* take the technical requirements of the database design into consideration. These technical requirements depend very much on the guidelines of the joint use centers as well as on the hardware used, database management system and the underlying application architecture. Therefore, instructions for the step from the logical to the physical database scheme are not included in the SKO-Datenmodell.

Overall Concepts (Level Independent)

In order to support communication between the logical concepts of the SKO-Datenmodell and the business community, *overall concepts* irrespective of level have been introduced, for instance, account or customer. The SKO-Datenmodell distinguishes between two different kinds of overall concepts:

*   Overall concepts based on the core entities of the A-Level
*   Overall concepts which include—in addition to the core entities—modeling principles for the design of semantic connections

The core entities with their definition and relationships are the basis for the nine overall concepts, which are based on the core entities, such as involved party or arrangement.

Additional overall concepts of the SKO-Datenmodell are customer, account, managerial account, segment and trading object. All overall concepts have detailed descriptions. Table 2 shows a short definition of the additional overall concepts.

Overall concepts help the analyst and the data modeler to put the business terms and facts in their proper places. In this way, the overall concepts support the uniform comprehension

Table 2. Overall concepts of the SKO-Datenmodell

Overall concept	Definition
Customer	A customer is a connection between two involved parties. One of these involved parties has an existing or a potential business relation with the other involved party.
Account	An account is a two-sided calculation of the financial institute about requests and liabilities toward third parties based on business relations.
Managerial Account	A managerial account is an aggregation or a compacting of data of internal accounts and/or customer accounts. This data has been made available for controlling purposes of the financial institution. It can be used for further evaluation.
Segment	A segment is a specific group of objects. These objects are interesting to the financial institution in any combination because they support the institution and its business functions.
Trading Object	A trading object is a resource item, which is offered for sale or arranged to be sold by the financial institution or another involved party.

of facts within the Sparkassenorganisation. They are, together with the structural criteria, a way for standardization. The overall concepts should also support the delimitation of different aspects of complex business facts.

Methods and Procedures Handbook and Tool Support

As pointed out in the previous section, there are several guidelines and instructions available in a methods and procedures handbook accompanying the SKO-Datenmodell. This section will introduce the *Methods and Procedures Handbook* and will describe the tools around the SKO-Datenmodell and the model management.

The Methods and Procedures Handbook of the SKO-Datenmodell

The *Methods and Procedures Handbook* covers precise modeling instructions for all model components. It describes in detail the objectives and the use of each level of the SKO-Datenmodell. Furthermore, it defines which modeling elements belong to a level and how they have to be created and described.

However, the *Methods and Procedures Handbook* not only includes guidelines, which relate to one level, but also detailed instructions to the associations between the levels. The interaction of the modeling elements of the different levels and versions of the SKO-Datenmodell is defined with the help of so-called traces. These traces completely document the connection between the objects of the model. Moreover, they facilitate the navigation between the levels and the versions of the SKO-Datenmodell. The objects of the B- and C-Level are linked by a level trace. For instance, the classification value "involved party" of the B-Level model is linked with the entity "involved party" of the entity relationship model on the C. Therefore, you can see that this classification value is modeled as an entity in the C-Level model. "account number" is modeled on the B-Level as the value of the description hierarchy and on the C-Level as attribute of the entity "account."

Traces also connect different versions of the SKO-Datenmodell. The objects of the B- and C-Level models of the SKO-Datenmodell Version 3.1 are linked via traces with the objects of the previous version 3.0.

The detailed instructions in the *Methods and Procedures Handbook* of the SKO-Datenmodell allow a homogeneous modeling with high quality standards. In addition, SKO-Datenmodell newcomers have a comprehensive reference book.

Model Management

Such an extensive reference model like the SKO-Datenmodell cannot be administered and expanded without *tool support*. At present, three tools are used for the work with the SKO-Datenmodell. *Rochade* and *m1* are used for modeling and administration of the model. Whereas the SKO-Datenmodell Meta model and specialized model management applications are implemented on base of the *Rochade repository* by the model management team, the *ml* tool is being used on an "as is" basis without modifications. Moreover, a task database supports the maintenance process.

For a long time, the *Rochade tool* was used "just" as repository for the administration of the different versions of the SKO-Datenmodell and for the tool-supported quality assurance of the models. Since 2001, *Rochade* is also used for the further development of the SKO-Datenmodell because the supplier has not supported the modeling tool any longer.

A very good support for the use of the A- and B-Level of the SKO-Datenmodell in application development projects is provided by the *ml* tool.

The "FrameWork Window" of m1 allows a simple navigation between the different levels of the model (Figure 4). So *ml* relieves a simple entry in the SKO-Datenmodell, especially for users who have no or only limited experience with the model.

However, the tool m1 is not suited as modeling tool for the maintenance of the B- and C-Level of the SKO-Datenmodell. The strengths of this tool are the fast navigation between levels, very good search- and trace-functions and the function to define scopes.

In projects, the active work with the A- and B-Level of the SKO-Datenmodell usually takes place with the *ml* tool. At the beginning of a project, the project contents will be set at the B-Level. The relevant C-Level part will be extracted based on the B-Level scope of the project contents. This step is fully supported by the *ml* tool. Then the C-Level extract will be transferred in the respective modeling tool, where the development of the project data model takes place. At present, the projects use *Rochade* as the modeling and model management tool.

Figure 4. The FrameWork Window of m1

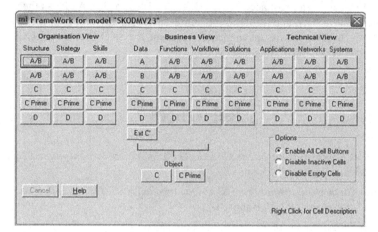

The *task database* is a Lotus Notes database. It has been developed to support the maintenance process for the SKO-Datenmodell. All change requests concerning the B- or C-Level of the SKO-Datenmodell are collected in this database. Each request has a reference to the application development project, which has made the request. Every maintenance project is planned in the task database. In addition, all changes made in such a project are documented in the database. Therefore, it is possible to reproduce which changes have been made in the new version of the SKO-Datenmodell and which application development project has made the change request.

Development of the Data Model

In 1991, the Sparkassenorganisation bought the financial services data model (FSDM) of IBM. In the following years, the model has been customized and enhanced. A mixed team of FSDM consultants and various representatives of the SKO has adapted and enlarged the tree of terms of the B-Level and the entity relationship model of the C-Level to meet the special requirements of the SKO. The A-Level of the FSDM with the nine core entities has been retained. However, the overall concepts have been developed in addition to the three levels of the FSDM. In parallel to the customization, the marketing process for the new model has been started. Moreover, scenarios for the introduction of the model have been developed and a lot of conviction work has been done. In 1995, the first release of the SKO-Datenmodell was ready for the use in the SKO.

So far this reference model has been used in about 30 projects with the following subjects: "statement analysis, booking, clearing and settlement, (sale-) controlling, derivatives/trades, real estate consultation, lending business, customer relationship management, marketing, market research, micro geography marketing, internal organization, personnel, audit, risk control and management, cost accounting" (Kittlaus, 1999, p. 31). As far as the results of these projects have been applicable to the entire Sparkassenorganisation, the integration into the SKO-Datenmodell has taken place. At present, the SKO-Datenmodell Version 3.1 is the most recent version of the model in use.

References

Kittlaus, H.-B. (1999). *Bankfachliche Modelle für die Sparkassenorganisation. [Conceptual models savings banks]*. Bonn: SIZ.

SIZ. (2001). *Methodenhandbuch zum SKO-Datenmodell V2.3. [Method handbook for the SKO-Datenmodell V2.3]*. Bonn: SIZ.

SIZ. (2004). *SKO-Datenmodell Version 3.1*. Bonn: SIZ.

Endnotes

[1]   SKO stands for Sparkassenorganisation (savings bank organization in Germany).

[2]   Datenmodell = data model

[3]   FSDM is a trademark of the company IBM.

[4]   M1 is a trademark of the company Modelware.

[5]   Rochade is a trademark of the company asg.

[6]   SIZ stands for Informatikzentrum der Sparkassenorganisation GmbH (For detailed information on the SKO-Datenmodell please contact the SIZ: SIZ, Simrockstraße 4, 53113 Bonn (Germany); Internet: www.siz.de, E-Mail: info@SIZ.de).

Chapter XI

A Reference Model for Strategic Supply Network Development

Antonia Albani, Delft University of Technology, The Netherlands

Nikolaus Müssigmann, University of Augsburg, Germany

Johannes Maria Zaha, Queensland University of Technology, Australia

Abstract

Based on rapidly changing market conditions and increasing pressure on cost and productivity, companies in different industries have started to concentrate on their core competencies and to decrease vertical range of manufacture. This resulted in an increasing dependency between the producing companies and their suppliers. Enterprise networks are formed creating the necessity to focus on the strategic development of supply network partners. While currently strategic purchasing mainly deals with direct suppliers, future strategic purchasing needs to deal with flexible and dynamic supply networks. This results in a paradigm shift in the domain of strategic sourcing from a supplier-centric to a supply network scope. In order to support the paradigm shift, the development of a reference model specifying the organizational and functional implications is necessary. This chapter therefore introduces a reference model for the domain of strategic supply network development extending the traditional frame of reference in strategic sourcing to a supply network perspective.

Introduction

Driven by drastically changing market conditions, companies are facing an increasingly complex competitive landscape. Decisive factors such as globalization of sales and sourcing-markets, shortened product life cycles, innovative pressure on products, services and processes and customer requests for individual products are forcing companies to undergo a drastic transformation of business processes as well as organizational and managerial structures (Burtler et al., 1997). The shift from a function-oriented to a process-oriented organization with a strong customer focus is essential in order to better adapt to fast changing market requirements and to become more flexible while meeting individualized customer demands (Osterloh & Frost, 2003, pp. 28-31). Within an enterprise, the core business processes (Prahalad & Gary, 1990) need to be identified, improved and (partly-) automated, while at the same time other processes are outsourced to business partners. As a consequence, business processes concerning, for example, product development, market research, sales, production, delivery and services, are affected and have to be adjusted and integrated not only within a single company but also with external partners, spanning multiple tiers of suppliers. As already recognized by Malone (Malone & Lautbacher, 1998, pp. 151-152), "the boundaries between enterprises will become much less important. Transactions within organizations will become indistinguishable from transactions between organizations and the business processes, once proprietary, will freely cross organizational boundaries." Companies recognize that the source of their competitive strengths does not only lie in their core competences, but also in the cooperative relationships with their business partners (Jarillo, 1988, p. 31). To an increasing degree, traditional organizational structures are nowadays evolving towards *hybrid* and *network structures* (Malone & Lautbacher, 1998, p. 166; Picot et al., 2003, p. 289), taking advantage of complementary competences of their external partners.

In *hybrid organizational structures*, cooperation (Picot et al., 2003, pp. 303-304) describes the dependency between two firms, which are coequal and collaborate in order to exchange or share information, products or services. Cooperation has a symbiotic character, can take a variety of forms, such as strategic alliances, strategic partnerships, strategic cooperations, operative cooperations and joint ventures and occurs across vertical and horizontal boundaries. Cooperation mainly occurs as a result of outsourcing nonspecific activities—necessary for the production of a product or service—which are of medium strategic relevance. If instead, idiosyncratic activities with low strategic relevance are outsourced to business partners, the degree of autonomy between the partners may change, depending on the level or importance of the single enterprises.

If two or more companies are involved in inter-organizational collaboration, an *enterprise network structure* is created. Enterprise networks are formed to better fulfill specific customer requests providing customized products on time in the right quality and for a competitive price. Such networks can span over several tiers, especially in large manufacturing companies (e.g., in the automotive industry). Even if enterprise networks have been introduced many years ago by Jarillo, Malone and Miles, (Jarillo, 1988; Malone et al., 1987; Miles & Snow, 1984; Thorelli, 1986), there is no single, broadly accepted definition of an enterprise network today. Several expressions exist to define different, or sometimes similar, types of enterprise networks. Terms such as *strategic networks* (Gulati et al., 2000), *alliance networks* (Gulati, 1998), *economic webs* (Hagel III, 1996), *business webs* (Tapscott et al., 2000), *value webs* (Herman, 2002), *virtual networks* (Malone & Lautbacher, 1998) or *dynamic networks* (Pine et al., 1993), can be found in the literature. As defined by (Gulati et al., 2000, p. 203), "*strategic networks* potentially provide a firm with access to information, resources, markets, and technologies; with advantages from learning, scale, and scope economies; and allow firms to achieve strategic objectives, such as sharing risks and outsourcing value-chain stages and organizational functions." Gulati uses strategic networks in a quite general manner, assigning several types of networks—which are composed of inter-organizational ties—for example, strategic alliances, joint ventures and long-term buyer-supplier partner-ships to this term. More precisely, Gulati defines *strategic alliances* (Gulati, 1998, p. 293) as "voluntary arrangements between firms involving exchange, sharing, or co-development of products, technologies, or services." The authors of economic webs, business webs, value webs, virtual networks and dynamic networks all discuss the same basic idea of sup-porting enterprises by means of information and communication technology, primarily the Internet, in order to "shed functions in which they are not competitive to service providers and partners that may have far greater expertise, scale or geographical reach" (Herman, 2002, p. 35). Malone (Malone & Lautbacher, 1998, pp. 146-148) mainly sees the increasing importance of "ad-hoc structures," where single business units join together into *virtual and temporary network-companies* in order to produce or sell goods and services, and as soon as such projects finish, the temporary companies would become obsolete. Hermann (2002, p. 31) envisions, that "the traditional value chain, which optimized as sequence of functions for one business, is transforming into a global *value web*, which can optimize the supply, demand, and product design activities for an entire network of partners. (...) Rather than think in terms of a linear value chain, we think of a value web where material, information, and money flow in parallel, taking multiple separate path through a complex network of suppliers, service providers, distributors, and customers." Pine additionally adds a *dynamic* aspect to the enterprise networks in order to make mass customization work, say-ing that "companies must break apart long-lasting, cross-functional teams and relationships and form dynamic networks" (Pine et al., 1993, p. 114). In mass-customization, where, for example, processes, technology and products need to be reconfigured in order to fulfill the individualized demands of customers, the corresponding enterprise networks cannot remain fixed, but need to be adjusted dynamically.

Considering the network definitions introduced above, we use the term *strategic supply network* in this chapter in order to define in the manufacturing industry (e.g., in the automo-tive industry) a network of *suppliers* spanning over several tiers and communicating among each other using the Internet. The network has a *fixed* part, namely the original equipment manufacturer (OEM), and a *dynamic* part, the suppliers, allowing *flexible* extension and modification of the network when additional competencies are needed. The OEM has a *higher degree of autonomy*, since it is the requestor for specific products and therefore the initiator of the identification of the network partners. The network has *strategic* relevance and focuses only on long-term relationships.

Supply networks are gaining more and more importance, especially in the automotive industry. For example, Dodel (2004) cites in his research on the logistic criticality in the automotive industry a logistics manager of DaimlerChrysler AG, who states that "the processes and skills of the direct suppliers are well known. What is missing is the transparency on the complete supply network, which serves behind the direct suppliers. If a supply problem occurs, great efforts have to be taken to identify the cause of the problem." Additionally, in spring 2004 DaimlerChrysler had to call back 1.3 million cars due to problems with the integration of system modules provided by different supply partners. Jürgen Schrempp, CEO of the company, stated during an interview prior to the annual general meeting, "the company underestimated the complexity of networking partners, who deliver complete system modules."

In order to gain competitive advantage in such supply networks, the selection, development, management and integration of respective suppliers, located not only in tier-1 but also in the subsequent tiers, are of major relevance. Modern information and communication technologies—like the Internet, semantic standards, distributed applications, component based, and respectively service-oriented architectures—are necessary in order to sustain the creation and management of supply networks (Kopanaki et al., 2000). However, at present IT-enabled networks can be largely found in form of rather small, flexible alliances of professionalized participants. The support of large networks with multiple tiers of suppliers still causes considerable difficulties. The high degree of complexity resulting from dynamic changes in supply networks is the main reason for the lack of practical implementation that is connected with the identification of supply network entities and the modeling of the supply network structure, as well as with the high coordination effort, as described by Lambert and Cooper (2000). Despite the fact that those are basic principles in order to succeed in supply networks, many research efforts have been based on more operative tasks primarily focusing on the optimization of forecast and planning accuracy and the optimization of material flows over the whole supply chain (Houlihan, 1985; Jones & Riley, 1985). Current enterprise resource planning (ERP) systems build the fundamentals for the management and controlling of supply networks but there is a lack of functionality to support dynamic identification, evaluation and qualification of competent partners (Angeli, 2002).

In order to analyze the basic principles, such as network modeling, it is necessary to focus primarily on strategic tasks such as long-term supplier development before dealing with operative tasks of supply chain management. Strategic tasks have not been widely discussed in a network perspective yet, even if current research work, such as Carr and Smeltzer (1999), give an extended interpretation of supply chain management partly considering supplier relationships as part of that management. Therefore, the domain of *strategic supply network development (SSND)*, which extends the traditional frame of reference in strategic sourcing from a supplier-centric to a supply-network scope, has been developed and described in a *reference model*, specifying the implications for the construction of the supporting IT-infrastructure.

According to vom Brocke (2004, p. 390), a reference model is understood as an information model, which is developed or used to support the construction of application models. Since this definition gives a very wide description of the reference model concept, a classification is needed in order to better understand the development and the purpose of a concrete reference model. The classification provided in Fettke and Loos (2004, p. 332), differentiates between reference models describing existing real world business aspects and reference models describing theoretical constructs of business challenges. The paradigm shift from a supplier-centric to a supply network perspective is an implication which became necessary due to massive changes in current markets. As described above, existing information models and systems do not sufficiently support the basic principles of the network perspective. The SSND reference model, as a *theoretical construct*, provides the relevant information for modeling complex and dynamic changing supply networks and builds the basis for the development of information systems for those value networks. Fettke and Loos (2004, p. 332), divides the class of reference models as a theoretical construct additionally into several sub classes. One of the sub classes defines *reference models as a technique* used for building supporting information systems in order to improve business efficiency such as increasing product quality and reducing costs and product development time. The SSND reference model is a contribution to this sub class since it describes functional, data and process aspects in strategic sourcing in order to optimize the purchasing function in a network perspective. The SSND reference model is therefore not based on empirical studies, but, as a first step, the efficiency of the model is evaluated by a prototype implementation.

The work presented in this chapter summarizes different aspects of the SSND reference model, which have already individually been published in Albani et al. (2004a), Albani et al. (2003a, 2003b), Albani and Müssigmann (2005), Albani et al. (2004b), and focuses on two functional aspects, the *strategic demand planning* and the *modeling of strategic supply networks*. An overall description of the domain is introduced and an extract of corresponding process models and data diagrams of the functions mentioned is given. Additionally, the prototype implementation of SSND is shortly described.

The Domain of Strategic Supply Network Development

The relevance of the purchasing function in enterprises has increased steadily over the past two decades. Until the 70s, purchasing was widely considered an operational task with no apparent influence on long term planning and strategy development (McIvor et al., 1997, p. 166). This narrow perspective was broadened by research that documented the positive influence that a targeted supplier collaboration and qualification could bring to a company's strategic options (Ammer, 1968). In the 80s, trends spurred the recognition of the eminent importance of the development and management of supplier relationships for gaining competitive advantages. Such trends were, for example, the growing globalization, the focus on core competencies in the value chain with connected insourcing and outsourcing decisions, as well as new concepts in manufacturing. As a result, purchasing gradually gained strategic relevance on top of its operational and tactical relevance (Kaufmann, 2002).

Based on these developments, purchasing has become a core function in the '90s. Current empirical research shows a significant correlation between the establishment of a strategic purchasing function and the financial success of an enterprise, independent from the industry surveyed (Carr & Pearson, 1999, p. 513). One of the most important factors in this connection is the buyer-supplier relationship. At many of the surveyed companies, a close cooperation between buyer and supplier led to process improvements and resulting cost reductions that were shared between buyer and suppliers (Carr & Pearson, 1999, p. 516).

In practice, supplier development is widely limited to suppliers in tier-1 (i.e., the direct suppliers). With respect to the superior importance of supplier development, as mentioned above, we postulated the extension of the traditional frame of reference in strategic sourcing from a supplier-centric to a supply-network-scope (Albani et al., 2004a; Albani et al., 2003b; Albani

Figure 1. Functional decomposition diagram for strategic supply network development

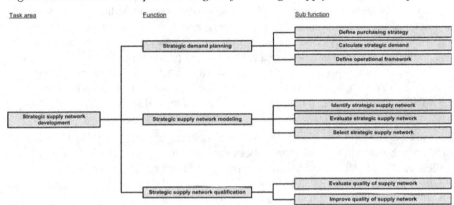

et al., 2004b). That means the further development of the strategic supplier development to a strategic supply *network* development. This shifted the perspective in the field of strategic sourcing to analyze multi-tier supplier networks instead of single suppliers.

The tasks within the strategic supply network development can be grouped into three main areas as illustrated in Figure 1: S*trategic demand planning, strategic supply network modeling* and *strategic supply network qualification* (Albani et al., 2004a).

Those tasks are derived from the main tasks in strategic sourcing. The most evident changes apply for functions with cross-enterprise focus. Within the function *strategic demand planning,* a corporate framework for all purchasing-related activities is defined. This framework consists of a consistent and corporate-wide valid purchasing strategy (*define purchasing strategy*), a strategic demand planning and demand bundling function (*plan strategic demand*) and the definition of methods and tools to control performance and efficiency of purchasing and to establish a conflict management concept (*define operational framework*).

The function *strategic supply network modeling* provides a methodology for the *identification* (identify strategic supply network), *evaluation* (evaluate strategic supply network) and *selection* (select strategic supply network) of potential suppliers, not only located in tier-1 but also in the subsequent tiers. Using evaluation criteria such as lowest cost, shortest delivery time or best quality, and corresponding evaluation methods, the identified supply networks are evaluated. If there is a positive result on the evaluation, the supply network is selected and contractually linked to the company.

Within the function *strategic supply network qualification*, the quality of a performing supplier network is evaluated using evaluation criteria and evaluation methods (*evaluate quality of supply network*). Dependent on the result of the evaluation, sanctions may be used to improve the quality of the supply network (*improve quality of supply network*).

Figure 2. Function decomposition diagram of the function strategic demand planning

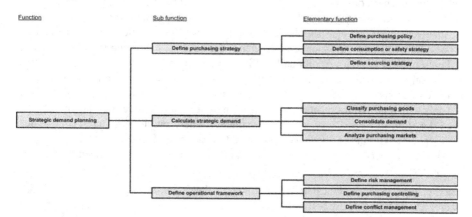

Strategic Demand Planning

Due to the positive effect that long-term and high-quality supplier relationships contribute to the success of a company (Ammer, 1968), the purchasing function was divided into a strategic and an operational domain. The field of responsibility of strategic purchasing comprises not only the selection and qualification of strategic suppliers but also the long-term strategic activities for demand planning. The paradigm shift in strategic purchasing has influenced the strategic tasks and led to different characteristics in the area of strategic supply network development.

Figure 2 shows the sub- and elementary-functions of *strategic demand planning* which are described in detail in the following sub-sections.

Define Purchasing Strategy

The purchasing strategy (a) describes the purchasing policy of the company, (b) determines whether consumption-oriented or safety-based purchasing will be accomplished and (c) declares the basic principles of the purchasing and sourcing strategy respectively (see elementary function in Figure 2).

The corporate *purchasing policy* defines responsibilities and approaches, which need to be followed by the entire purchasing organization of a company (Strache, 1983, p. 76). This policy consists of the specification of a corporate purchasing organization, the definition of a consistent approach for (e.g., demand consolidation) and the adoption of corporate operational guidelines for implementation. An important task thereby is the creation of a corporate directive for agreements regarding the cooperation with suppliers and the propagation of business risks to suppliers in strategic supply networks. So far it was sufficient for strategic purchasing to check direct suppliers with regard to critical regions or political impact. Now all nodes of a strategic supply network have to be verified. Furthermore, it turned out that an involvement of strategic suppliers in product design and product development led to process improvements and increased efficiency for both the buyer and the supplier (Carr & Pearson, 1999, p. 513). Additionally, efficient agreements for environmental protection and recycling are needed. Environmental needs as well as the protection of fundamental living conditions obtain more and more importance. Hence, efficient agreements comply not only with legal requirements but avoid cost significantly. All nodes of a supply network need therefore to be involved in an environment-friendly purchasing strategy, including the usage of environmentally sound goods and transportation facilities as well as reusable packages and fillers. Criteria on environmental protection and recycling need therefore to be considered while selecting supply networks.

Another important task of the purchasing strategy is the *definition of a consumption or safety strategy.* Consequential use of a company's demand power on the purchasing market results in favorable prices and best conditions, whereas it is important to assure availability of purchasing goods (Jahns et al., 2001, p. 40). The decision whether a consumption or safety purchasing strategy is applied has an impact on the composition and development of supply networks. If the main focus is set on supply safety, then long-term and stable relationships with supply networks are desirable. In the case of a consumption strategy, it is important to identify comparable supply networks in order to select the one that fits best in the sense of prices and conditions in a concrete purchasing situation. Such a consumption strategy is used especially for standardized goods, allowing a good comparison of supply networks.

In order to *define a concrete sourcing strategy,* it is necessary to distinguish between different sourcing strategies (e.g., single sourcing vs. multiple sourcing, local sourcing vs. global sourcing or insourcing vs. outsourcing). Single sourcing defines the supply of a good without using a contest between different supply networks. It is possible for strategic purchasing to ensure good prices, for example, by establishing long-term contracts with entire supply networks as it is managing direct suppliers. Multiple sourcing is aimed at the competition of existing and potentially new supply networks. Depending on which decision criteria (e.g., price, availability, lead time and quality) are used while comparing supply networks, the process of selecting a supply network is much more complex than selecting a single direct supplier. Local sourcing restricts purchasing on markets in the company's home country—cost savings (e.g., because of a shorter route of transport) and higher reliability because of stronger control possibilities are the main advantages (Large, 1999)—whereas global sourcing describes international purchasing activities using worldwide resources. In the case of global sourcing, opportunity and risk profiles need to be elaborated. It is reasonable to use the strategic decision on local or global sourcing as a parameter while identifying and modeling supply networks. Decisions on make or buy (in- or outsourcing) need to be considered while sourcing entire modules or even systems (Large, 1999). Such a decision has significant influence on the company's vertical range of manufacture and permits drastic reduction of internal costs.

Choosing the right strategy for a purchasing good depends on the importance of the good for the corporate goods and services. With high quality, non-standardized goods the safety and single sourcing strategy is desirable. On standardized goods with low complexity a company may choose a consumption strategy and use a multiple sourcing strategy to achieve low purchasing prices. Another important task area of strategic purchasing is the reduction of complexity and variety of goods while at the same time transparency needs to be increased. This can be achieved by using standardized goods and a corporate classification system.

Calculate Strategic Demand

In order to consolidate demands, the purchasing goods need to be categorized into a corporate classification system. The *classification of purchasing goods* therefore needs to be performed for goods which are already in use as well as for all new goods. Fuhry et al. (2002) suggests to classify the purchasing goods into three groups: indirect material, basic direct material and strategic direct material. Indirect materials are goods and services which are not directly necessary for the production of an end product (e.g., office equipment). The focus of such goods lies, therefore, on the optimization and increase of efficiency of the order management and invoice processes (e.g., by using e-procurement systems). The share of this group is about ten percent of the total purchasing volume. Basic direct materials are directly used in the end product (e.g., raw materials and pre-fabricated parts). With this group of material, the competition can be increased by standardization and transparency in the market, which results in a direct decrease of cost. The use of IT-Systems like online auctioning or automated bidding systems can significantly increase the efficiency of the purchasing process. The share of this group of material is about 30% of the total purchasing volume. Strategic direct materials are complex components, pre-fabricated goods and systems or extensive services, which are used in the end product (e.g., motors and car seats). With this group of material, it is important to develop and maintain long-term and high quality relationships with the suppliers, and therefore with the related strategic supply networks. In addition, it is necessary to involve the suppliers that are participating in such strategic supply networks at an early stage into product planning and product development. The share of this group of material is about 60% of the total purchasing volume.

For the classification of goods it is possible to use classification standards (e.g., eClass and UN/SPSC). The value based share of the purchasing volume of a good can be calculated by using the ABC- or the portfolio analysis (Hirschsteiner, 2000, p. 11).

The extension of the view from a supplier-centric to a supply network approach has significant influence on the purchasing of strategic direct material. In most cases, these goods are purchased with a safety strategy and single sourcing. Selecting and qualifying of appropriate supply networks is hereby an important task. The transparency of a supply network is a prerequisite for the buyer to evaluate and develop a supply network.

Demand consolidation combines demands of several divisions and locations of a company in order to use the appearance on the purchasing market to strengthen the negotiating position. Prerequisites for a successful demand consolidation are the standardization and consistent classification of goods as well as the explicit identification of supply networks. Demand consolidation can improve the purchasing conditions.

Supply marketing has the responsibility to *analyze purchasing markets* and identify powerful supply networks on the supply markets (Schifferer, 2001, p. 68). The bases for it are the basic conditions defined within the supply policy, such as transfer of business risk to supply networks or the compliance with environmental regulations. Adequate supply networks can be found through Internet search engines, external service providers (e.g., international yellow and white pages) or other data sources, such as up-to-date company profiles and key performance indicators. Based on supplier self service information, a concise profile is generated in order to decide for a supply network. With the help of supply market research, a transparency is established and continuously improved in order to provide information and outlook on future market trends and their interference with the decision strategy. A further task of supply market research is the exposure of competitors and their demand potential for specific services of a supply network. Thus, significant changes in the purchasing price can arise. Further important influencing factors are so called quantity or tool monopoly. It is necessary to recognize whether only one supply network can deliver the amount of goods or whether only one node of a specific supply network can implement and operate a special tool (Strache, 1983, p. 19). Furthermore, it is important to identify the critical path in a supply network in order to take appropriate action for adjustment if a node on this critical path fails.

Define Operational Framework

Methods and procedures for risk management, controlling of purchasing and conflict management are provided by strategic supply network development in order to manage operational purchasing.

The perception of the purchasing market research needs to be applied in order to establish effective *risk management*. Risk management deals with early detection of market, service and financial risks. Based on the business objectives and the purchasing policy of the company, concrete risk strategies are defined (e.g., fundamental risk avoidance or risk degradation strategies). Subsequently, the actual purchasing situation is analyzed, considering risk types, risk areas and risk reasons. Thus, it is examined from which countries and which industries goods are to be purchased in order to identify high-risk regions. These can be countries having high political risk, high inflation rates, high currency risks or even companies with the risk of insolvency. Through the gathering of such information, it is possible to create and evaluate quantitative and qualitative predictions (Das & Teng, 1998, p. 22).

The *controlling of purchasing* accompanies the purchasing process throughout the entire purchasing organization. It consists of the definition of operating figures and their target values. The actual values are periodically measured and compared with the target values. Deviations are analyzed and appropriate action is taken. Controlling therefore ensures the ability of a company to adapt and react as well as to coordinate and innovate. The definition and monitoring of these values is supported by design and safety goals. Regarding design goals, the controlling defines target values in order to reduce the maximum number of supply networks or the purchasing quote related to framework agreements (Schifferer, 2001, p. 62). The target values are monitored by analyzing whether the goods needed in the corporate processes are supplied in the right quantity and the right quality at the right time and the right place. Sample measures are: resource consumption, cost of purchasing staff and cost of handling the purchasing tasks but also adherence to delivery dates, quantity stipulations and the price behavior of supply networks. Furthermore, it is monitored that buying is based on a purchase order. It is recommended to use balanced score cards to compile the operating figures. The method of the balanced score card allows, with a limited number of operating figures, implementation of a very efficient and flexible mechanism to manage a purchasing organization.

The *introduction of conflict management* processes is necessary in order to avoid conflicts in purchasing. Conflicts can occur while defining tasks and decision competency between the strategic and the operational parts of the purchasing organization. This may apply to selecting supply networks while conducting a single purchasing. A large conflict potential may also arise if operational purchasing does not adhere to strategic instructions, such as cost limitations, amounts or dates. Companies having more than one production facility or having decentralized purchasing divisions may have the same problems while purchasing identical goods. Conflicts may also arise if the purchasing staff does not stick to corporate framework contracts with supply networks due to individual connections to suppliers. An effective incentive system helps to implement the objectives of strategic purchasing. This can be established by using the extensive data gathered by controlling. It is measured how the supply objectives are achieved. The cost savings reached by the employees involved are the basis for a bonus system. Besides the cost savings, a strategic purchaser can be measured as well on the quote of newly negotiated framework contracts. An operational purchaser can be measured on the adherence to supply lead time or the securing of a specific quality level on purchased goods (Schifferer, 2001, p. 90).

Strategic Demand Planning: Business Process and Data Models

The elementary function *classify purchasing goods* (see Figure 2) is used to illustrate how the process organization is established and which information objects are used in the domain of strategic supply network development. The business processes for introducing material group codes and planned conversion of material strategies are modelled in Figure 3 and Figure 4, whereas the data model for purchasing goods can be found in Figure 5. For modeling the business domain, the ARIS (Scheer, 1999) method has been used.

The classification of purchasing goods in the company builds the basis for a material-specific purchasing strategy and is a prerequisite for effective purchasing marketing, for a consolidation of demands as well as an optimized supply network management. Initially, all purchasing goods are listed in order to decide whether a proprietary material code is being used or whether a standardized method like eClass or UN/SPSC needs to be introduced (Figure 3). It is important that all existing and new goods are grouped with a consistent material code. While working with supply networks, the material code needs to be based on a standard such that all nodes of the supply network adhere to the same method. If it is necessary to use a proprietary material code, this code has to be distributed to the entire supply network. It may be necessary to provide assistance to the nodes of the supply network in order to show how to implement and use the material code.

According to the strategic decision for a material group code, either a standardized method is adapted (preferred while working with supply networks) or a proprietary material group code is defined. This material group code is then implemented in the entire purchasing organization. The purchasing divisions are now asked to classify all purchasing goods with

Figure 3. Business process for the introduction of a material group code

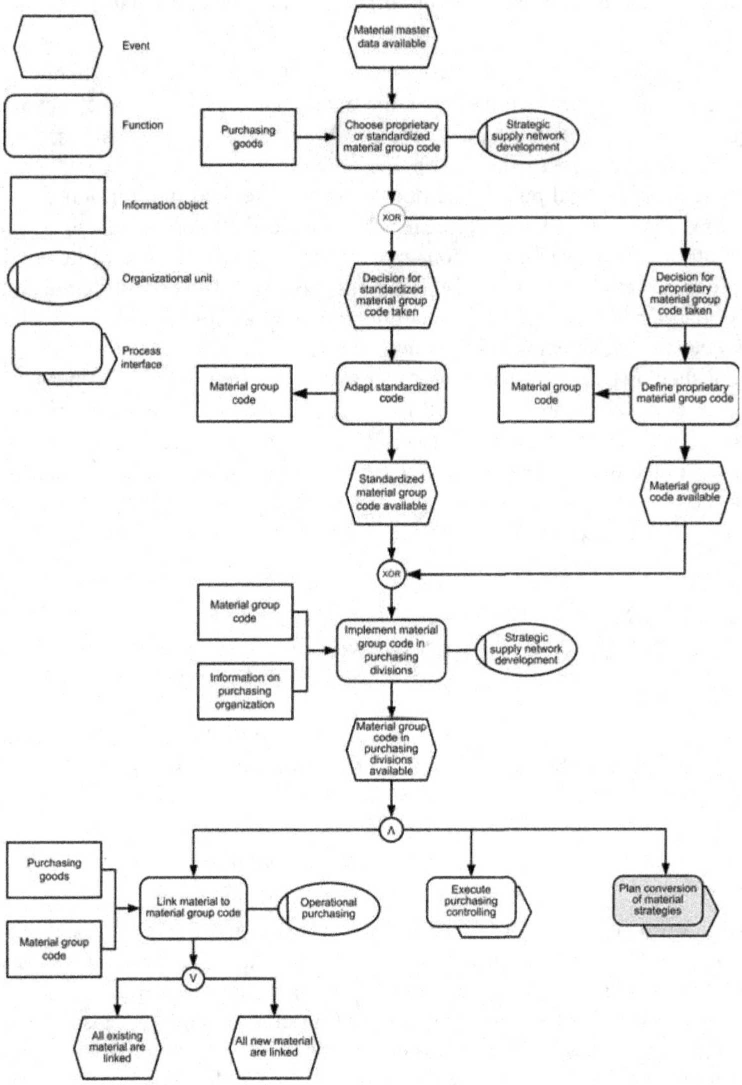

this material group code. In doing so, purchase controlling needs to observe the progress of this process (e.g., supported by a balanced scorecard). Besides the material group code, other criteria (e.g., the purchasing volume or the importance) are used to further group the purchasing goods. The process of structuring goods according to their share of the total purchasing volume and starting specific actions is illustrated in the process flow *plan conversion of material strategies* in Figure 4.

Figure 4. Business process for planning conversion of material strategies

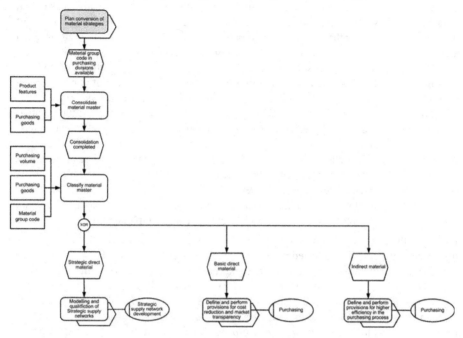

Figure 5. Semantic data model for purchasing goods

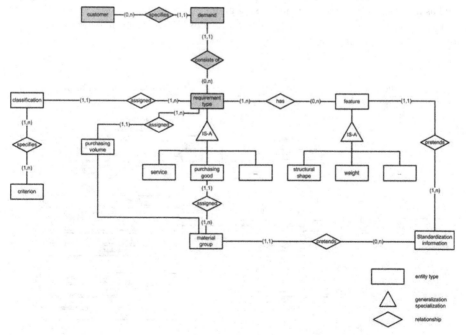

The consistent classification of purchasing goods allows for the standardization of products and recognition of product correlations. Such a consolidation of the material master can reduce the variety of goods, which are required in the company. Purchasing goods are of different importance for the success of a company. Therefore, purchasing goods are grouped according to their relevance and their purchasing volume in three groups: indirect material, basic direct material and strategic direct material. For each of the groups, individual activities are deduced. While purchasing indirect material, for example, it is important to design the purchasing process as efficiently as possible. This can be achieved by the use of e-procurement processes and systems. While purchasing basic direct material, a minimization of the purchasing costs can be achieved by arranging auctions or biddings. While purchasing strategic direct material, the main focus is set on the development and maintenance of long-term relationships with supply networks. Therefore, the modeling and qualification of supply networks is of great importance. In order to describe the information objects of the strategic supply network development, a semantic data model is created within the scope of this reference model. An extract, showing the information objects of the process flows illustrated above, is presented in Figure 5 in an entity relationship diagram.

Starting with the specification of the demand of a *customer* (e.g., the demand for strategic direct material), data are collected not only from the direct suppliers but also from all upstream suppliers in order to support the strategic supply network development. The specific *demand* (as shown in the upper center of the picture) consists either of *services, purchasing goods* or other requirement types which are subsumed to the term *requirement type*. Every requirement type has *features*, such as *structural shape, weight,* and so forth. A purchasing good belongs to exactly one *material group*, which is identified by a material group code. Features as well as material groups are provided by *standardization information*. A requirement type belongs to a *classification* (e.g., strategic direct material). A classification is defined by different *criteria*. The *purchasing volume* of a requirement category as well as the material groups or the purchasing goods can be criteria for the classification of requirement categories. The objects, which are shadowed, will later on be found again in the extension of the semantic data model.

Figure 6. Function decomposition diagram of the function model strategic supply networks

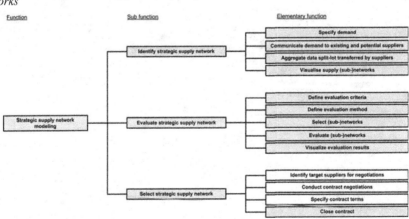

Figure 7. Example for result of identification process

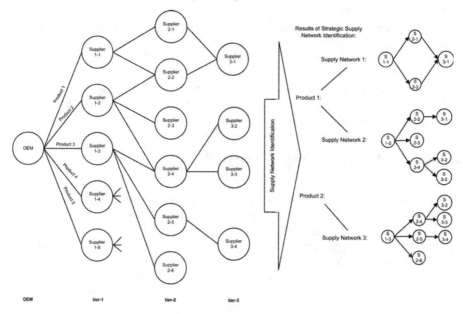

Strategic Supply Network Modeling

To model a supply network in a structured way, potential supply networks need to be *identified, evaluated* and then *selected*. Figure 6 shows the sub- and elementary-functions of *model strategic supply networks*, which are described in detail in the following sub sections.

Identify Strategic Supply Networks

For the identification of potential supply networks, a specific strategic demand for an offer to a product to be built is *specified* and *communicated* from the OEM *to existing and/or potential suppliers*. Figure 7 illustrates an example for an identification process and its results.

In the example, the OEM is connected to a potential network of suppliers as shown in the left part of Figure 7. It is assumed that the OEM needs to order two products externally, product 1 and product 2. During the identification process, the OEM sends out demands for these products to its strategic suppliers in tier-1. In the example, it is assumed that supplier 1-1 and supplier 1-2 get the demand for product 1 while supplier 1-3, supplier 1-4 and supplier 1-5 receive the demand for product 2. These suppliers check whether they can fulfill the demand internally and, if not, send out subsequent demands to their respective suppliers. Each node executes the same process as described until the demand has reached the last tier. The requested information is then *split-lot transferred* to the OEM, *aggregated* and finally *visualized* as a supply network, in which each participant of the supply network constitutes a network node.

This process may result in the identification of several possible supply networks as shown in the right part of Figure 7, where, for exmple, product 1 can be provided by two supply networks, supply network 1 (root node S1-1) and supply network 2 (root node S1-2), whereas product 2 can only be provided by supply network 3. It is now up to the OEM to decide which of the potential strategic supply networks (in the example above for product 1) will be selected to fulfill its original demand. The basic information needed for the selection results from the evaluation of potential networks.

Evaluate Strategic Supply Networks

Based on *defined evaluation criteria*, potential networks are evaluated. Evaluation criteria may span from simple facts to highly complex considerations. One of the simplest criterion is the minimum number of nodes in the supply network, which can be used to minimize overall complexity of supply networks. Criteria with more complex calculations, for example, are the shortest total delivery time, the minimum total cost or the regional only sourcing (indicating, that only those suppliers are selected which are located within a certain region). Complex criteria are maximization of product quality or delivery time liability, since these criteria implicate the evaluation of past experience. While considering critical areas in the supply network, it is also of main importance to know which nodes have absolute monopoly with their supply value or which are involved in more than one potential supply network (see S2-2 and S3-1 in the example in Figure 7).

After having specified the evaluation criteria, the next step is to *define the evaluation method.* In most cases, a method is represented by an algorithm which itself is related to the selected evaluation criterion. For example, the criterion minimum number of nodes involves a simple algorithm counting the nodes in potential tree graphs, comparing the results and selecting the tree (supply network) with the least number of nodes. Assuming that the identification process will provide several possible supply networks for different products, the function *select supply network(s)* will select the supply networks related to a specific product in order to *evaluate* them using the evaluation criteria and methods as just introduced above. The result of the evaluation process is a rated list of all supply networks related to a specific product. This list can therefore be *visualized* and used for the selection of strategic supply networks in order to produce the specific product.

Select Strategic Supply Networks

Based on the evaluation results of potential supply networks, *target suppliers* are *identified for negotiation.* In order to *close a contract* with those suppliers, *contract negotiations* are conducted first in order to *specify the contract terms* relevant for ordering the required goods. Those elementary functions highlighted in white in Figure 6 express that the steps cannot be automated and therefore need face-to-face communication in order to be executed.

Figure 8. Semantic data model for the function strategic supply network modeling

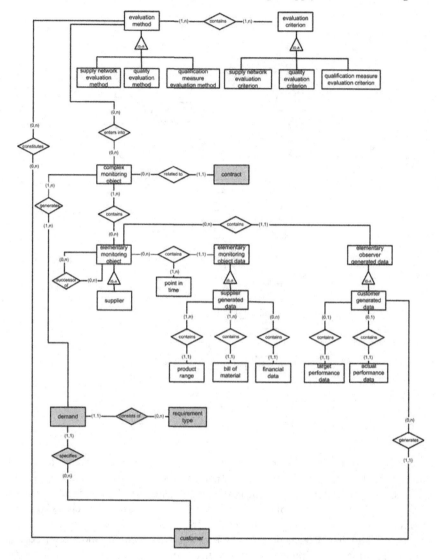

Strategic Supply Network Modeling:
Business Process and Data Models

The semantic data model, introduced in Figure 5 has been extended with data objects used for the identification of supply networks.

The extension of the model can be found in Figure 8. The objects, which are shadowed, connect the different semantic data models to each other (see Figure 5 and Figure 10). Starting from

Figure 9. Business process for the identification of strategic supply networks

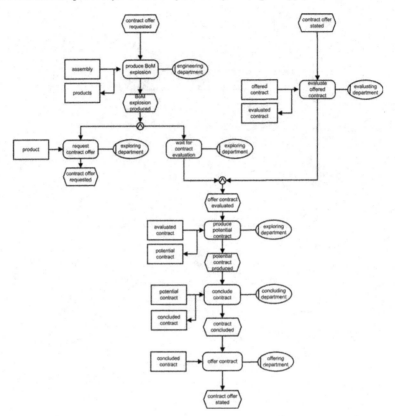

the demand of a *customer*, it is relevant to collect data not only from the suppliers in tier-1, but also from all suppliers in tier-n. A whole supply network specified by a demand is a network of suppliers, providing information to the customer, which is used for the development of the supply network. This network of suppliers is represented in the data model as a *complex monitoring object,* whereas a single supplier is represented as an *elementary monitoring object.* With the affiliation of elementary monitoring objects to a complex monitoring object, and with the identification of predecessors and successors of such elementary monitoring objects, the whole supply network is defined. Each complex monitoring object is related to a *contract* which has been offered to the customer for delivering a requested product. At a particular time, each elementary object provides information about the *product range, bill of material, financial data* or more. This information is known as *supplier generated data.* In addition, the customer generates their own data, called *customer generated data,* specifying the performance of the respective supplier of the elementary monitoring object. Examples for data generated by the customer are *target performance data* and *actual performance data.* Target performance data are guidelines for the supplier, and the actual performed data are the work performed by the customer. With the acquisition of supplier generated data and

Figure 10. Semantic data model for the identification of strategic supply networks

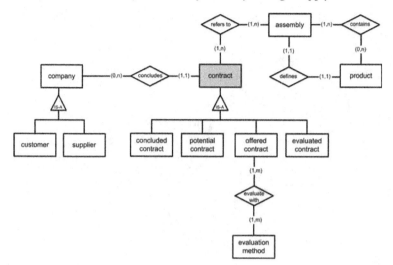

with the definition and the measurements of performance data, the customer holds all the needed to evaluate different complex monitoring objects of the supply network. Different *evaluation methods* are defined by different *evaluation criteria*.

The whole process of modeling the supply network for a specific demand sent by a customer is shown in Figure. 9. The process modelled holds for each company in the network. Requests from a customer may arrive (*contract offer requested*) for a specific product, or different contract offers from one or more suppliers (*contract offer stated*) may be sent to the company examined. If the company has received a request for a specific product, a *bill-of-material-explosion* is produced in order to identify the products, which need to be ordered from suppliers. Contract offers need therefore to be *requested* from the respective suppliers. A request for one and the same product may be sent to different suppliers. The company examined *waits* for the different contract offers of the suppliers in order to *evaluate* them and *conclude* their own contract, containing the contract aspects of all suppliers involved. The contract is then *offered* to the requesting customer. Since each node in the network performs the process just described, the contract offered to the customer includes all contract aspects of the supply network.

The semantic data model introduced in Figure 5 and Figure 8 has been extended with the contract information objects shown in Figure 10.

Each node in the network is a *company*. A company can either be a *customer* or a *supplier*. One and the same company can be a supplier for a specific product, and at the same time a customer ordering goods necessary for production of the requested product. A company concludes *contracts* with their customers and suppliers for a specific product. An *assembly* defines a *product*, which may contain additional products. A contract has different states. Each contract, which has been received from a supplier, is an *offered* contract. Such a contract is then evaluated with *evaluation methods*, reaching the state of an *evaluated contract*.

Figure 11. SSND supply network for an electronic motor

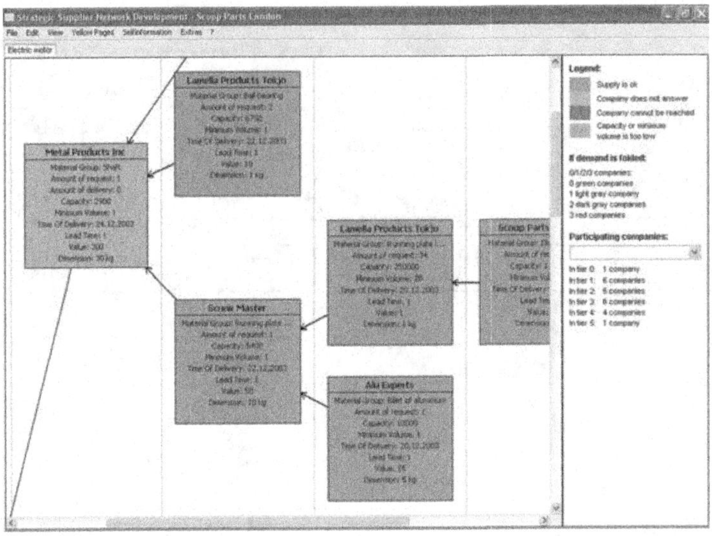

Evaluated contracts with good evaluation results may become *potential contracts,* which are then *concluded* and accumulated to a *concluded contract*, which again is offered to the requesting customer.

Prototype Implementation of SSND

For proof of concept, the prototype tool SSND has been implemented providing the functionality for the identification and dynamic modeling of strategic supply networks. A sample view of a supply network with detailed information about every supplier contributing to an example demand for the production of an electronic motor is shown in Figure 11. Only a selected area of the whole supply network is shown. The rectangles represent the different companies of the supply network visualized with important information about the node contributing to the supply network of the electronic motor. Relevant information for the requestor about the suppliers is, for example, name of the company, material group the supplier is producing, minimum volume necessary to be ordered and capacity per day. The companies are visualized in the SSND prototype in different colors, differentiating between (a) suppliers who are able to deliver the product and amount requested, (b) suppliers who are not answering to the demand sent, (c) suppliers who are not online or where a communication problem exists and therefore can not be reached and (d) suppliers who do not have enough capacity for producing the required product, or where the volume required by the client is too low.

The tool provides different modes of visualizing the network—adding more detailed information to the nodes, showing just parts of the network, and so forth—in order to support the client with all necessary information for developing the strategic supply networks.

Conclusion

Challenges in today's economy are more and more transforming formerly closely-linked value chains into flexible networks, thus significantly changing the buyer/producer-supplier relationship. As laid out in this chapter, this is especially true for the field of strategic purchasing, where an extension from a supplier-centric to a supply network perspective is required. In order to accomplish this extension, complexity issues connected with the modeling of supplier networks have to be overcome. Having identified the need for managing the complexity of supplier network modeling, a reference model for the domain of strategic supply network development has been developed. It contributes to the class of theoretical constructs of potential business challenges and describes functional, data and process aspects in strategic sourcing in order to optimize the purchasing function in a network perspective. In this chapter, an overview of the reference model has been given detailing the functions of demand planning and identification of supply networks. Additionally, a prototype of the model has been implemented in order to evaluate the described concepts.

Since the reference model is classified as a theoretical construct, and the prototype implementation has until now only been evaluated in small examples, additional work needs to be investigated in validating the concept in practice. Additionally, the prototype needs to be extended in order to allow additional product classifications next to eClass. Such an enhanced version of the existing prototype, based on a consistent and validated reference model, would constitute a basic component in an IT-infrastructure that enables companies to efficiently develop and maintain their strategic supply networks.

References

Albani, A., Bazijanec, B., Turowski, K., & Winnewisser, C. (2004a). *Component framework for strategic supply network development*. Paper presented at the 8th East-European Conference on Advances in Databases and Information Systems (ADBIS-04), Budapest, Hungary (LNCS 3255).

Albani, A., Keiblinger, A., Turowski, K., & Winnewisser, C. (2003a). *Domain based identification and modelling of business component applications*. Paper presented at the 7th East-European Conference on Advances in Databases and Information Systems (ADBIS-03), Dresden, Deutschland (LNCS 2798).

Albani, A., Keiblinger, A., Turowski, K., & Winnewisser, C. (2003b). *Dynamic modelling of strategic supply chains*. Paper presented at the E-Commerce and Web Technologies: 4th International Conference, EC-Web 2003 Prague, Czech Republic (LNCS 2738).

Albani, A., & Müssigmann, N. (2005). *Evaluation of supply networks*. Paper presented at the International Workshop on Modelling Inter-Organisational Systems (MIOS), in conjunction with the OTM 2005 Federated Conferences, Larnaca, Cyprus (LNCS).

Albani, A., Winnewisser, C., & Turowski, K. (2004b, 25.09. - 29.09.). *Dynamic modelling of demand driven value networks*. Paper presented at the On The Move to Meaningful Internet Systems and Ubiquitous Computing 2004: CoopIS, DOA and ODBASE, Larnaca, Cyprus (LNCS).

Ammer, D. (1968). *Materials management* (2nd ed.). Irwin, Homewood, IL.

Angeli, R. (2002). *Development and coordination of dynamic enterprise networks*. Paper presented at the Wissenschaftssymposium Logistik der BVL. [in German]

Burtler, P., Hall, T. W., Hanna, A. M., Mendonca, L., Auguste, B., Manyika, J., et al. (1997). A revolution in interaction. *The McKinsey Quarterly, 1/97*, 4-23.

Carr, A. S., & Pearson, J. N. (1999). Strategically managed buyer-supplier relationships and performance outcomes. *Journal of Operations Management, 17*, 497-519.

Carr, A. S., & Smeltzer, L. R. (1999). The relationship of strategic purchasing to supply chain management. *European Journal of Purchasing & Supply Management, 5*(1), 43-51.

Das, T. K., & Teng, B. S. (1998). Resource and risk management in the strategic alliance making process. *Journal of Management, 24*(1), S. 21-24.

Dodel, J. H. (2004). *Supply chain integration: Reduction of the logistic criticality in the automotive industry*. Unviersity of St. Gallen, Switzcrland. [in German]

Fettke, P., & Loos, P. (2004). Reference modeling research. *Wirtschaftsinformatik, 46*(5), 331-340. [in German]

Fuhry, G., Valdes, L., & Reinecke, N. (2002). *Digital sourcing-purchasing in the next generation*. Retrieved 5.7. 2004 from, www.digitaltransformation.de [in German]

Gulati, R. (1998). Alliances and networks. *Strategic Management Journal, 19*, 293-317.

Gulati, R., Nohria, N., & Zaheer, A. (2000). Strategic networks. *Strategic Management Journal, 21*, 203-215.

Hagel III, J. (1996). Spider versus spider. *The McKinsey Quarterly, 1*, pp. 5-18.

Herman, J. (2002, July/August). Global value webs. *Supply Chain Management Review*, pp. 30-37.

Hirschsteiner, G. (2000). Purchasing in the company. In S. Schötz (Ed.), *Einkauf, methoden, werkzeug und arbeitshilfen für den industriellen einkauf* (Chap. 3.2.1). Kissing: WEKA Praxis-Handbuch. [in German]

Houlihan, J. B. (1985). International supply chain management. *International Journal of Physical Distribution and Logistics Management, 15*(1), 22-38.

Jahns, C., Middendorff, A., & Schober, H. (2001). Repositioning of the purchasing function . In K. Kohlhammer (Ed.), *Beschaffung aktuell, materialwirtschaft, einkauf, logistik*

(Vol. 2/2001, pp. 38-43). Organ des Bundesverbandes Materialwirtschaft, Einkauf und Logistik e.V. [in German]

Jarillo, C. J. (1988). On strategic networks. *Strategic Management Journal, 9*, 31-41.

Jones, T., & Riley, D. (1985). Using inventory for competitive advantage through supply chain management. *International Journal of Physical Distribution and Logistics Management, 5*, 16-22.

Kaufmann, L. (2002). *Purchasing and supply management-a conceptual framework. In Handbuch industrielles beschaffungsmanagement* (2. Auflage ed., pp. 3-33). Wiesbaden: Hahn, D, Kaufmann, L. (Hrsg.).

Kopanaki, E., Smithson, S., Kanellis, P., & Martakos, D. (2000). *The impact of inter-organizational information systems on the flexibility of organizations*. Paper presented at the Proceedings of the Sixth Americas Conference on Information Systems (AMCIS), Long Beach, CA.

Lambert, D. M., & Cooper, M. C. (2000). Issues in supply chain management. *Industrial Marketing Management, 29*(1), 65-83.

Large, R. (1999). *Management of strategic purchasing*. Wiesbaden: Gabler. [in German]

Malone, T. W., & Lautbacher, R. J. (1998, September-October). The dawn of the e-lance economy. *Harvard Business Review*, 145-152.

Malone, T. W., Yares, J., & Benjamin, R. I. (1987). Electronic markets and electronic hierarchies. *Communications of the ACM, 30*(6), 484-497.

McIvor, R., Humphreys, P., & McAleer, E. (1997). The evolution of the purchasing function. *Journal of Strategic Change, 6*(3), 165-179.

Miles, R. E., & Snow, C. C. (1984). Fit, failure and the hall of frame. *California Management Review, 26*(3), 10-28.

Osterloh, M., & Frost, J. (2003). *Process management as core competence* (Vol. 4). Wiesbaden: Gabler Verlag. [in German]

Picot, A., Reichwald, R., & Wigand, R. T. (2003). *The boundless enterprise: Information, organization and management* (5th ed.). Wiesbaden: Gabler Verlag. [in German]

Pine, B. J., Victor, B., & Boynton, A. C. (1993). Making mass customization work. *Havard Business Review, 36*(5), 108-119.

Prahalad, C. K., & Gary, H. (1990). The core competence of the corporation. *Harvard Business Review, 68*(3), 79-91.

Scheer, A.-W. (1999). *Aris-business process modeling* (2nd ed.). Berlin: Springer.

Schifferer, S. (2001). *Process oriented management of the purchasing organisation*. Unpublished Dissertation, Technische Universität, München. [in German]

Strache, H. (1983). How to purchase in monopolistic environments? Accurate purchasing behaviour for purchasing agents. *Praxis für Materialwirtschaft und Einkauf, Volume 3, Nürnberg*. [in German]

Tapscott, D., Ticoll, D., & Lowy, A. (2000). *Digital capital: Harnessing the power of business webs*. Cambridge, MA: Harvard Business School Press.

Thorelli, H. B. (1986). Networks: Between markets and hierarchies. *Strategic Management Journal, 7*, 37-51.

vom Brocke, J. (2004). Reference modeling research . *Wirtschaftsinformatik, 46*(5), 390-404. [in German]

Chapter XII

E-Business Reference Models

Vojislav B. Mišić, University of Manitoba, Canada

J. Leon Zhao, University of Arizona, USA

Abstract

A number of reference models have been proposed to facilitate the development of e-business systems and applications. A comparative analysis of existing models and their pertinent characteristics should be the first step in selecting the right one to be used as the foundation for the system being developed. This chapter addresses that goal through an exposition of different reference models to be used for the development of e-business systems and applications, as well as of suitable quality evaluation frameworks to be used for their assessment.

Introduction

Electronic business (or e-business, for short) may be succinctly defined as the ability to perform exchanges of goods, services, content, assets and money, using electronic tools and techniques (Zwass, 1994). E-business transactions may be conducted by individual customers, businesses (including non-profit organizations) and various governmental agencies and departments. The main promises of e-business include cost reduction, new ways of accessing customers and the ability to overcome geographical distance and other physical obstacles. In order for all these benefits to be realized, and for the development of e-business systems to be ultimately successful, proper foundation is needed—part of which is the use of suitable *models*.

The concept of a model has at least two meanings in the study of e-business. Those meanings are distinct yet not altogether mutually exclusive, as will be seen from the following. From the business perspective, an e-business model is "a description of the roles and relationships among a firm's consumers, customers, allies, and suppliers that identifies the major flows of product, information, and money, and the major benefits to participants," according to Weill and Vitale (2001). This concept does not differ in essence from the more traditional view of a business model as "the organization (or 'architecture') of product, service, and information flows, and the sources of revenues and benefits for suppliers and customers" (Timmers, 1999). Thus defined, the business model provides the vision and the foundation upon which strategies to pursue their respective business goals are developed and implemented in practice.

From the definitions given above, it may seem that e-business is just another form of business, having the same goals as any other business and requiring the convergence of business capabilities in order to achieve those goals. However, the prefix "e-" is more than a simple designation for a convenient vehicle to be used in the pursuit of those goals—it is the indication that another kind of convergence is needed, the "convergence of multiple technologies into an integrated electronic infrastructure" which is a *sine qua non* for conducting e-business (Weill & Vitale, 2001). The synergy of business and technology is the single most important characteristic of e-business.

From the technology perspective of the IS and computer science, on the other hand, an e-business model can be understood and employed as a reference model for the development of e-business systems and applications. A reference model, as defined by the ISO 7498 standard (ISO, 1984), describes a standard decomposition of a known problem domain into a collection of interrelated parts, or components, that cooperatively solve the problem; furthermore, it describes the manner in which the components interact in order to provide the required functions. In this manner, a reference model provides a shared mental model that facilitates learning, improves understanding and leads to better communication among all the stakeholders (Osterwalder & Pigneur, 2004). A reference model can also be used to develop more specialized models that support specific requirements and scenarios, such as specialized markets or business applications. It also provides the foundation for the development of e-business systems and applications. Finally, a reference model provides the contextual framework to identify the need for, develop and coordinate related technology standards, without which flexible and interoperable e-business systems would be impossible to build (Mišić & Zhao, 2000). It is this latter meaning of the concept of an e-business reference model that we will focus on in this chapter.

We stress that the need for reference models exists regardless of the particular strategy and implementation path (or paths) chosen for the development of e-business applications. Ideally, such systems and applications should be developed in a structured, top-down and architecture-centric fashion (Bass, Clements, & Kazman, 2002). In practice, however, few businesses have the luxury of being able to develop their respective systems and applications in this manner, starting from zero (although some projects may be developed in that manner). Most of the others already utilize a multitude of existing systems and applications—often referred to using the qualifier "legacy"—that were developed over the years on heterogeneous hardware, software and application platforms. While sometimes inadequate and most often incompatible with one another, legacy systems cannot simply be discarded since they encapsulate crucial business logic and manage vast quantities of operational data; instead, they should be integrated with one another and with newly developed e-business systems. (Such development is often referred to as evolutionary.) In both cases, the availability of a suitable model to govern the development is a necessary precondition for success.

A number of reference models for the development of e-business applications have been proposed over the years. Developed by both individual companies and organizations and industrial consortia, they offer markedly different perspectives and different sets of features. Selecting the most appropriate one under a given set of requirements and constraints that hold in a given environment is a non-trivial undertaking. Therefore, the study of e-business reference models should help both researchers and practitioners to develop better and more advanced e-business application systems, and thus help implement the business vision and strategies defined by e-business models. To aid in that process, this chapter provides a compendium of e-business reference models, primarily from the technology perspective, with a twofold objective: first, to outline the available architectural options and choices in the design of e-business applications and systems, and second, to highlight the tradeoffs incurred in the selection process. Of course, an exhaustive enumeration of all models, architectures and frameworks relevant to e-business is not possible. Yet we have tried to include all the developments with theoretical and practical relevance, as well as some of the others that highlight certain important aspects of e-business reference models.

The remainder of the chapter is organized as follows. First, the chapter outlines the basic concepts relevant to the e-business reference models, using some of the models proposed in the literature to illustrate and clarify them. A brief historical overview of the development of e-business reference models is then given, followed by the discussion of a number of important models. Particular attention will be paid to the models that use Web services, which are quickly becoming the dominant paradigm for the development of flexible, interoperable e-business systems, not least on account of their ability to integrate heterogeneous systems and applications, including legacy ones (Booth et al., 2004; Fletcher & Waterhouse, 2002; Gottschalk, Graham, Kreger, & Snell, 2002). The next section addresses the ever important issue of quality of reference modeling and presents a brief overview of a quality framework suitable for evaluating that quality. Finally, the chapter summarizes the chapter's content and outlines some promising avenues for further research.

Characteristics of E-Business Reference Models

In this section, a number of pertinent characteristics of e-business reference models, as identified by Mišić and Zhao (2000), will be listed, discussed and illustrated using actual e-business models that feature them.

Orientation

E-business, as its very name implies, is built on the dual foundations of business and technology (Zwass, 1996). Successful development of e-business systems thus requires that both business- and technology-related issues are addressed in an interdependent way. This interdependence has been recognized since the beginnings of e-business in the early nineties, yet most of the research work reported so far can readily be classified as primarily business- or technology-oriented. While this dichotomy is not quite unexpected—after all, e-business systems are quite complex in terms of both the number of features and the diversity thereof, and researchers themselves are not always ready to step outside their narrow area of expertise—it does play a crucial role in determining the scope and focus of much of the research work reported. In doing so, the issues related to the other side (i.e., business issues, in case of technology-oriented models, and vice versa) may be implicitly assumed to be easy or already solved. While the latter may well be the case, the former is almost never true, and may incur serious risks in later development.

As an example of a definite orientation, consider the classification of Internet business models originally proposed by Timmers (1998), which is shown in Figure 1. Although, strictly speaking, it is not a reference model, it is nonetheless interesting on account of its clear business orientation and because it provides a useful, albeit somewhat limited, taxonomy of different e-business models. Similar taxonomies have been described by other authors, using different criteria for classification; among the better known ones are the eight atomic models described and analyzed in detail by Weill and Vitale (2001), and an exhaustive ontology of e-business models by Osterwalder and Pigneur (2004). A more detailed discussion of those

Figure 1. Classification of Internet business models (According to Timmers, 1998)

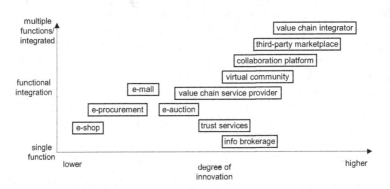

taxonomies is beyond the scope of this chapter, as our primary focus is the discussion of e-business reference models as vehicles to aid and facilitate the development of e-business systems and applications.

Perspective and Viewpoint Support

The existence of distinct, mostly independent and (sometimes) mutually orthogonal views was recognized in several areas, in particular in relationship with architectural modeling of software-intensive systems (Bass et al., 2002; Kruchten, 1995; Shaw & Garlan, 1996). A view (often referred to as a viewpoint or perspective) attempts to describe the system from the perspective of a related set of concerns, most often corresponding to the requirements put up by a specific group of stakeholders (IEEE, 2000). In fact, even the dichotomy between business and technology orientation mentioned above can be considered as an instance of multiple perspectives. This approach is adopted by the ISO Open EDI Standard, which describes "two perspectives of business transactions" through business aspects and information technology aspects (ISO/IEC, 1998). The modeling methodology of the recent ebXML standard also distinguishes between business and information technology aspects of business transactions, described through business operational view and functional service view, respectively (Eisenberg & Nickull, 2001).

However, many proposed models include more than two perspectives. According to Bussler and Jablonski (1994), descriptions of business systems commonly include functional, informational, behavioral and organizational perspectives. Technology-oriented models sometimes include even more: Witness the ISO/IEC reference model for open distributed processing which defines no less that five viewpoints: enterprise, information, computational, engineering and technology (ISO/IEC, 1992); the same number of views has been identified in the area of software architecture (Kruchten, 1995). Regarding e-business itself, Holsapple and Singh (2000) have defined a total of five such views: the trading view, the information exchange view, the activity view, the effects view and the value chain view.

Therefore, a reference model of e-business should (a) account for as many different perspectives as possible, and (b) specify the perspective or (preferably) perspectives it takes into

Figure 2. Reference model for electronic markets (After Schmid & Lindemann, 1998)

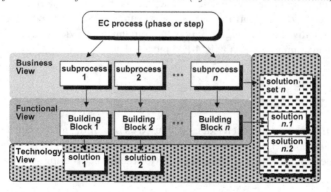

Figure 3. EBES/EWOS building blocks architecture

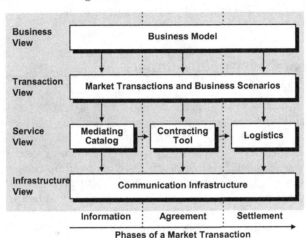

account. The former property may be considered as yet another facet of the completeness property.

The reference model for electronic markets (RM-EM) proposed by Schmid and Lindemann (1998) is shown in Figure 2. This is a business-oriented model that supports multiple views, arranged to support the decomposition of a business transaction into information, agreement and settlement phases. Similar phase decomposition, but with an additional support or communication phase *after* the settlement, was proposed by Selz and Schubert (1998).

A similar approach has been adopted by the project on Building Blocks for Electronic Commerce (EBES/EWOS, 1997), where the concepts of sequential and hierarchical decomposition are used as the main analytical tools. Business activities are sequentially decomposed into five steps or high-level commercial processes of marketing, contracting, logistics, settlement and interface with administrations. (Notice the similarity with the RM-EM model.) These processes are, in turn, decomposed into lower-level activities referred to as building blocks, such as "consult product catalogues," "request price quotation" and the like. The technology-dependent implementation of a building block is called a "solution," which is to be integrated into appropriate applications or services; a number of integrated products or services used to provide support for one or several subprocesses is called a "solution set." This is schematically shown in Figure 3; note the combination of views and layering which indicates another similarity with the RM-EM model.

Layering

Layering or stratification has been extensively used as one of the main vehicles to reduce the complexity of models. Probably the best known example of layering is the ISO OSI reference model (ISO, 1984), predominantly used to describe networking systems, which has

Table 1. Hierarchical framework of e-commerce (Adapted from Zwass, 1996)

meta-level	level	function
products and structures	7	electronic marketplaces and electronic hierarchies
	6	products and systems
services	5	enabling services
	4	secure messaging
infrastructure	3	hypermedia/multimedia object management
	2	public and private communication utilities
	1	wide-area telecommunication infrastructure

no less than seven different layers; although few actual systems use all the layers (and even the layers which are used cannot always be unambiguously defined), this model is considered as a significant milestone in the area of networking, and it is widely used in research, education and practice ever since. Note that structural properties, such as number of layers, partitioning of system functionality between them, the level of abstraction of each layer, the manner in which components interact (both within each layer and between different layers) and the like, can be used to compare and evaluate different layered models.

In the e-business area, layered models have been used from the very beginning. In fact, one of the first surveys of e-commerce research (Zwass, 1996) describes a three-layer, seven-sublayer framework for e-commerce. This framework, not unlike the original ISO/OSI reference model (ISO, 1984), is shown in Table 1. A similar framework, but with a different layering structure, has been proposed by Kalakota and Winston (1996).

Most other e-business models are also layered, with the number of layers ranging from three to seven. Moreover, several of those models possess more than one level of decomposition, resulting in an even wider range of layers. Of course, the optimum number of layers in a reference model cannot be prescribed in advance.

Technology (In)Dependence

An important characteristic of e-business models, tightly coupled to the business vs. technology dichotomy explained above, is their technology independence or lack thereof. E-business systems are ultimately implemented using available technology; but the models themselves should be as little dependent on any particular technology as possible. The reasons for this are nearly self-evident:

- As the number of decisions and choices to be made in actual system implementation is large, using a model tied to a particular technology restricts those choices and deprives us of possible benefits brought on by more advanced technology. On the contrary, the use of a technology-independent model provides the freedom to choose the implementation technology on the basis of other criteria, and thus minimize the cost-benefit ratio and maximize the return on investment.

- The use of a model tied to a particular technology may preclude reuse of tools and components already available, thus increasing the cost of developing the new system.

- The use of a technology-independent reference model ensures its longevity, thus protecting our initial investment, both monetary and intellectual, made in the development of that model.

- Finally, the use of a technology-independent model facilitates the interoperability with other e-business systems and thus allows for easy integration of both existing and newly developed applications into a coherent enterprise system.

Typically, models with dominant business orientation exhibit the least amount of technology independence. As for the models with definite technology orientation, some of them are tied to a particular technology while others are not; examples for both kinds of models will be provided. On the other hand, technology orientation does not automatically imply technology dependence: Some among the reference models with clear technology orientation are essentially technology-independent. This distinction essentially vindicates our approach to separately consider the dependence/independence and orientation properties.

Interoperability and Openness

One of the main tenets of e-business (and any other business, for that matter) is interaction between two or more business partners. In order to enable and facilitate the communication between their respective e-business systems, those systems should adhere to some protocols and standards. This decision has to be reached by consensus within the community, as there is no central authority to mandate the use of a particular protocol or standard—although such attempts often happen as vendors attempt to gain market share and force the use of proprietary standards onto the user community. Such attempts sometimes succeed, and indeed proprietary standards may sometimes offer certain advantages in terms of performance, reliability or otherwise. Yet the use of open standards is considered beneficial in the long term, if only because it avoids vendor lock-in and thus results in distinct economic advantages.

Another facet of this property is openness, defined as the ability of the system to interface to other systems and actors in the outside world (Mišić & Zhao, 2000). Openness is certainly facilitated through the use of established and widely accepted standards and protocols.

The Role of Standards

We note that protocols exist almost as long as humans have communicated (any natural language is, in essence, a general purpose protocol), and the importance of standards in industrialized society hardly needs mentioning. Yet the impetus for development, formal specification and verification of protocols is inextricably linked to the development of data communication through computer networks (Stallings, 2005). As a result, a number of standards for communication between independent business systems and applications have been proposed over the years. Some of those standards have enjoyed rather wide acceptance: SWIFT, a secure messaging standard developed and used throughout the financial industry (ISO, 2004), and eectronic document interchange, or EDI, a standard for electronic document interchange (FIPS, 1996), to name but two among the best known ones.

However, the advent of the Internet and e-business, together with the characteristics of Internet communications and the underlying TCP/IP family of protocols, have introduced the need for new and improved standards. A number of standards evolved from the existing ones, or have been developed from scratch. The list includes Open EDI (ISO/IEC, 1998), Open buying on the Internet (OBI, 1999), and open trading protocol (IOTP, 1998), among others. Unfortunately, those protocols did not succeed in achieving wider acceptance, mainly on account of the following factors:

- Most of those protocols cover only a fraction of possible e-business scenarios and activities. For example, the OBI protocol (OBI, 1999) deals with payment only, and payment is but one phase in any e-business transaction. Consequently, the benefits achievable through deploying such a protocol were perceived as insufficient to offset the high initial cost in infrastructure and manpower.

- As some of the new protocols were extensions of the existing ones (e.g., Open EDI has evolved from EDI), business that did not use the original protocols had little incentive to jump start the new ones.

- The sheer number of such protocols meant that there was no clear winner in sight. Therefore, a majority of businesses were rather reserved in deploying them, deferring the costly switching to the new technology until they could be assured of widest possible interoperability. In contrast, the World Wide Web has been readily embraced by most businesses—but a universally interoperable standard was available (HTML), and the costs incurred were seen as justified in view of the increased reach and presence.

Consequently, each developer of e-business systems was free to design its own interoperability standard without any concern regarding interoperability with the others. This was further aggravated by the relative immaturity of e-business, as the traditional business models and approaches were found inappropriate for the new business environment, and new modes of conducting business had to be devised, validated and perfected. Note that similar situations are quite common in many industries, in particular in information technology-related markets at an early stage—remember the number of *incompatible* PC-based operating systems, word processors and spreadsheets that were available in the early eighties, and compare it to the numbers available in the respective markets now. However, as the markets mature, the number of competitors tends to diminish. Quite often, a new standard (or a new set of standards) appears that replaces the existing ones, either as a synthesis of their best features or merely as their least common denominator—but at least only one standard remains upon which new, interoperable systems can be built.

The problems mentioned above could be addressed in different ways. In one approach, standards are built in a bottom-up manner, starting from the lowest common denominator that all interested parties can agree upon, and then gradually adding more functionality as needed. Such a "minimalist" approach was adopted by the proponents of Web services, a recent interoperability standard endorsed by all major players on the market: BEA, IBM, Microsoft, Sun and others (Erl, 2004; Fletcher & Waterhouse, 2002). While the Web services paradigm provides just the bare interoperability between applications (which means it is not too useful in practice), it also offers a common conceptual and technical foundation upon which models and systems catering to specific business requirements can be built.

Another approach gives preference to depth over breadth, as it attempts to leverage the advances in organizational knowledge. Namely, when new application domains arise, requirements are initially vague and first systems invariably suffer from the lack of focus and well defined scope. As a result, such systems, including reference models, are not very successful—as production-quality solutions, that is, but they do allow us to clarify and refine the requirements, and ultimately improve our knowledge. As the market matures, our knowledge of it improves—we know more about both problems and their solutions, and we can choose more promising routes to follow in solving those problems. The qualitative and quantitative improvement obtained in this manner is inversely proportional to the scope of the domain: The narrower the scope, the greater the improvement that can be achieved. This enables the development of standards and practices that distill and embody that knowledge, for the benefit of all parties involved. Such a "specialist" approach is perhaps best exemplified by the development of two recent families of standards known as ebXML (Eisenberg & Nickull, 2001) and RosettaNet (Kak & Sotero, 2002), both of which build upon existing standards at different levels, including Open-EDI and XML (among others), while focusing on their respective application areas in depth. A more detailed description of both standards is given in Section 4.

Extendibility

Extendibility refers to the ability of the model to evolve over time. Evolution includes accommodating new or changed requirements, which may (and ultimately will) emerge over time. Requirements may change because of new or changed business needs, technology changes due to new advances or phasing out of obsolete technologies or changes in the business environment. Yet regardless of their particular cause, changes must be absorbed and seamlessly integrated into the model, if it is to remain a coherent foundation for the development of e-business systems. Extendibility might also mean that existing standards are enriched or extended using certain new facilities: For example, the SWIFT messaging standard for financial industry has recently been enriched with appropriate UML models and XML message structure (ISO, 2004).

E-Business Models: Past and Present

This section will briefly present a number of e-business reference models, including some that have already been mentioned, in historic succession.

Figure 4. Main roles and interactions in IOTP architecture (After IOTP, 1998a)

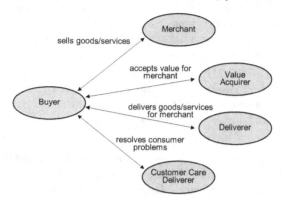

Early Attempts

A number of early attempts at creating a reference model for e-business are worth mentioning:

*   The DoD electronic commerce model, in fact an extension of the EDI standard (Jo, Pottmyer, & Fetzner, 1995).
*   A layered model described by Kalakota and Winston (1996), which is similar to the Zwass (1996) framework mentioned above.
*   The EBES/EWOS model mentioned above (EBES/EWOS, 1997) was sponsored by the European Commission through EBES (European Board for EDI/EC Standardisation) and EWOS (European Workshop for Open Systems); both bodies were later superseded by the European Committee for Standardisation (CEN).

Building on Existing Pre-Internet Models

Soon enough, as more experience in various aspects of e-business was obtained, a number of more mature models began to appear.

*   The Internet open trading protocol standard focused on the problems of business transactions—primarily business-to-consumer, but other forms were not precluded—conducted over a public (and rather open) network such as the Internet (IOTP, 1998a, 1998b). A number of roles, schematically depicted in Figure 4, were identified, and a number of protocols, essentially defined as workflows enacted by participants in designated roles, were developed.

A notable characteristic of the IOTP protocol is that the actual payment mechanism is deliberately left out of the standard. The intention was to make the IOTP-compliant systems extendible so that different payment protocols could be plugged in at will, but it was mostly seen as a deficiency rather than an advantage, since the necessary protocols for payment over the Internet were not available at the time.

Another characteristic of the IOTP is that it was one of the first reference models to propose the use of XML-compliant language for communication between participants in an e-business transaction. To that end, an elaborated message structure was devised and formulated as an XML DTD (XML schemas were not available at the time).

- Two rather interesting reference models were made public at about the same time. The first one was the eCo system architectural framework developed by the CommerceNet industry consortium (Tenenbaum, Martin, Chowdhry, & Hughes, 1996). While the overall structure of the eCo system framework is layered, as in other reference models, it is perhaps worth mentioning that it is, in fact, intended to serve as a meta-framework. (The term "framework" is used here to denote an almost complete application that can be customized or extended to address specific needs.) In this manner, it can accommodate models that cater to mutually orthogonal perspectives or viewpoints; each of the viewpoints can model a distinct business process or service for building Internet markets. Different frameworks can then be built on top of each other, and a shared services infrastructure is thus made available to all applications. Each of the eCo system "frameworks" specifies the core services that all application objects from that layer must provide, a set of messages for requesting the core services, known as the network services interface (NSI), the business objects on which the services operate and the application programming interface (API) for any software modules involved in delivering these services. The NSI messages, together with business objects and product taxonomies, constitute the common business language (CBL) intended to be an alternative to the *ad hoc* text strings currently used in EDI systems.

- The second was the secure electronic marketplace for Europe (SEMPER) is a project sponsored by the European Commission (Schunter & Waidner, 1997). The SEMPER model of electronic commerce assumes that any business scenario consists of a number of standard business processes, which may be further decomposed into a sequence of unidirectional and/or bidirectional exchanges of business items. (SEMPER documentation uses the terms "transfers" and "fair exchanges," respectively.) In that respect, the model appears to be a well thought out combination of business and technology orientation; it is shown in Figure 5.

The SEMPER model has another very interesting feature. Namely, it is based on the unified concept of "business items": payments, credentials and documents or statements. Each business scenario is, in fact, a sequence of *exchanges* of business items of different types: payments, credentials and/or documents, each of which is managed by a separate service in the exchange management layer. Thus (multiple) existing implementations can be integrated into a unified service framework. For example, the payment manager can provide generic services for handling account- and cash-style payments, together with the negotiation of the means of payment. In this way, different payment systems may be simultaneously installed

Figure 5. Architecture of the SEMPER model (Adapted from Schunter & Waidner, 1997)

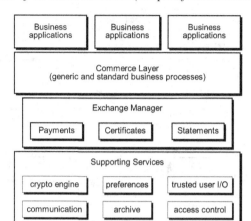

and any of them can be used in an actual transaction, while the appropriate negotiation may be entirely transparent to the user. It is interesting to note that XML message exchange in the Web services paradigm is rather reminiscent of the concept of business items and exchanges thereof, as defined in the SEMPER reference model.

•   Another industry consortium, the Object Management Group, has joined forces with CommerceNet and formed the OMG Electronic Commerce Domain Task Force (EC-DTF). The EC-DTF has developed a high-level object-oriented framework for specification of requirements for e-business systems (OMG/CommerceNet, 1997), which is fully compliant with OMG's Object Management Architecture (Soley, 1995) and its rather successful common object request broker (CORBA) framework (OMG,

Figure 6. Structure of OMG/CommerceNet open architecture for electronic commerce (Adapted from McConnell, Merz, Maesano, & Witthaut, 1997)

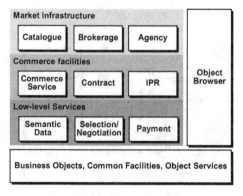

Figure 7. Main roles and interactions in the OBI architecture (Adapted from OBI, 1998)

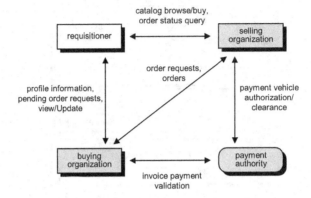

2002). This framework, shown in Figure 6, is known as OAEC, or an open architecture for electronic commerce (McConnell, Merz, Maesano, & Witthaut, 1997). This architecture has well defined functional blocks arranged (as usual) in a three-layer stratified structure. Since the model is based on object-oriented systems architecture, each facility is handled as a real object, offering interfaces to other objects. Detailed semantics for the facilities' interfaces are provided, including (in some cases) high-level protocols of their usage.

However, this model does exhibit heavy dependence on the CORBA architecture (OMG, 2002) which limits its usefulness. This is particularly pronounced in dynamic environments which are not well supported by CORBA components.

- Open buying on the Internet, or OBI (OBI, 1999), is another interesting reference model, albeit limited in scope—it is predominantly geared toward payment processing. The basic premise of OBI was that an open communication infrastructure such

Figure 8. Java electronic commerce framework architecture (Adapted from Sun Microsystems, 1998a)

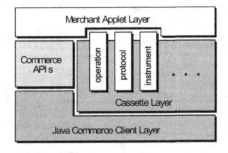

as the Internet poses new problems in terms of payment, and that e-business cannot grow unless those problems are addressed. The other focus of OBI is business-to-business transactions, the volume of which is known to be at least three to five times the volume of consumer-to-business transactions. The basic roles and interactions in the OBI architecture are shown in Figure 7.

It should be noted that most, if not all, of the models presented here are building upon the foundations developed in the pre-Internet era. While some of them do address specific problems brought on by the use of the Internet, their basic structure still carries distinct marks of their roots. (For example, OBI does bear more than a passing resemblance to the electronic payment protocol SET developed jointly by a consortium of financial industry led by Visa and Mastercard—which, incidentally, did not gain wider acceptance, mostly because it was perceived as being too difficult to implement.) Models specifically designed with Internet communications in mind had yet to appear.

Coming of Age

The use of the Internet and the development of models and tools to build Internet applications have grown hand in hand, and a number of models have appeared to support the development of e-business systems.

- The Java electronic commerce framework (JECF) is an extendible framework for conducting consumer-to-business transactions over the Internet or within corporate intranets (Sun Microsystems, 1998a). Its initial component was the Java Wallet, a client-side application to be distributed as a core component of the Java environment (Sun Microsystems, 1998b). The Java Wallet enables the users of any Java-enabled Web browser to conduct commerce transactions with JECF-compliant merchant pages anywhere on the Internet. A number of downloadable "cassettes" implement specific business functions; unlike Java applets, they remain on the client system after use. In this manner, a "customized" e-business layer may be gradually built for a specific consumer. The JECF architecture is depicted in Figure 8. Although JECF does allow developers to build actual e-business systems, it does not provide much help in terms of structuring them to address business needs—it has a definite technology orientation.

Figure 9. Web service roles and interaction model (After Champion et al., 2002)

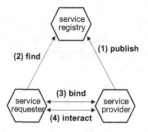

Figure 10. Microsoft Web services architecture stack (After Ballinger, 2003)

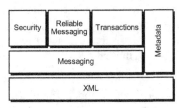

It is just a way of structuring applications using specific infrastructure, rather than a fully developed reference model for e-business.

- At the business side, the reference model for electronic markets (Schmid & Lindemann, 1998), described in section 2, appeared at about the same time. A number of other, both more general and business-specific, reference models have appeared, including updated versions of some of the models mentioned above. The real changes, however, have occurred only with the advances in the Web services paradigm.

Internet AND XML

The rapid growth of the Internet as the ubiquitous communication medium has led to the development of reference models that use the Internet as the primary communication medium, and XML as the dominant information packaging paradigm. Two distinct approaches can be identified: the horizontal integration advocated by Web services and the vertical integration models of ebXML and RosettaNet.

Web Services

Web services are a recent development paradigm that is part of a broader technological shift toward the so-called service-oriented software systems (Erl, 2004, 2005; Fletcher & Water-house, 2002). Web services are based on direct interaction of self-described, autonomous entities that can be published, discovered and invoked over the Internet or Internet-based networks (Booth et al., 2004; Gottschalk et al., 2002). The concept of Web services originally aimed for enabling asynchronous, stateless, communication of discoverable software services, and thus had no business perspective *per se*. However, its potential for seamless integration of business systems built on widely differing technological foundations over the years was quickly recognized. On account of this potential, it is expected that a large portion of existing systems, including a majority of e-business systems, will switch to Web services-based implementation in the near future (Gill, 2003), the more so because all major software vendors offer support for Web services.

In the Web service interaction paradigm, a service description is written using the Web service description language (WSDL). The service provider submits this description to a

Figure 11. IBM Web services conceptual architecture (Adapted from IBM, 2001)

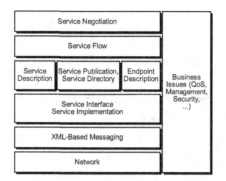

dedicated service registry using the universal description, discovery and integration protocol (UDDI). The client in need of a specific functionality queries the registry through UDDI in order to find out whether an appropriate service exists and, if so, how it can be invoked. Having found a suitable service, the client contacts the provider in order to initiate a binding, following which the client and the server may cooperate to achieve the desired goal. All the messages are exchanged using the simple object access protocol (SOAP), and all protocols are XML-compliant. The roles and the sequence of interactions are schematically shown in Figure 9, where numbers correspond to the temporal ordering of those interactions.

All major vendors, including BEA, IBM, Microsoft, Sun and Oracle, have developed architectures, infrastructure and support tools needed to develop Web services-based applications. However, their architectures differ—although the differences are not substantial, as will be seen from the following.

- The Microsoft Web services architecture, in its simplest form, is shown in Figure 10 (Ballinger, 2003). The most fundamental underpinning of this architecture is its reliance on XML messaging through a lightweight SOAP protocol, although other messaging protocols can be substituted if and when available. Network functionality is based on a proprietary .NET framework.

- The IBM Web services architecture (IBM, 2001) adds several enhancements to the basic model, as can be seen from Figure 11. The most important among those enhance-

Figure 12. Sun Web services reference model (After McGovern, Tyagi, & Mathew, 2003)

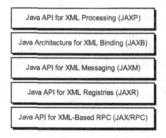

Figure 13. BEA WebLogic architecture stack (After BEA, 2001)

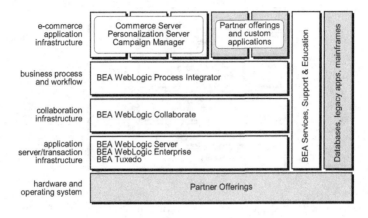

ments relate to areas like security and transaction processing support, where existing standards and solutions may not suffice and additional facilities have to be provided for applications that need them—which is the majority of real-life applications. Note that the criteria for decomposition into different layers are obviously based on different aspects of Web services, most of which are technology-oriented. At the same time, business-related issues are covered in a summary fashion, as a simple listing of issues that span all other layers but are specified in much less detail.

- While IBM and Microsoft have been working together on defining their Web services architecture specification, Sun has developed a Web services architecture of its own (McGovern et al., 2003), which is shown in Figure 12. As is the case with JECF, each of the layers is seen as an application programming interface (API) that lets the developers write Web service applications entirely in the Java programming language. All of the Java APIs for XML support industry standards, thus ensuring interoperability. They also define strict compatibility requirements to ensure that all implementations deliver the standard functionality, but they also give developers a great deal of freedom and flexibility to provide implementations tailored to specific uses. It should be noted that the Sun Web services reference model is heavily dependent on the use of Java language and associated frameworks and libraries. While the use of Java technology is indeed widespread in industry, it is nonetheless a dependence on a specific technology, which may be a disadvantage in certain situations.

- It may be informative to compare those architectures with other existing architectures which are not necessarily Web services-based. As an example, consider the architecture proposed by BEA (2001), shown in Figure 13. As can be seen, the architecture is again layered, but it is heavily geared toward using proprietary commercial products and, possibly, products offered by commercial partners. Also, incorporating Web services in this architecture would necessitate a major redesign of most, if not all, of the components in it—although the final architecture would probably not look very different from the current one.

ebXML and RosettaNet

Basic Web services standards such as WSDL, UDDI and SOAP, are lacking important functionality in the areas of quality of service, security, dynamic service selection, trust and reputation
among others. Some of these shortcomings are addressed—to a certain extent—by a recent
series of standards commonly referred to as second generation Web services technologies, or
WS-* (Erl, 2005). While a more detailed discussion of those issues is beyond the scope of
this chapter, suffice it to say that most, if not all, of the new standards follow the minimalist
philosophy of the original standards: they enable certain aspects of functionality at the lower
layers of the architecture but leave the upper layers open. Furthermore, both older and newer
standards are developed by technology providers, rather than business providers. As a result,
they strive for universal "horizontal" interoperability—they tend to cover certain aspects of
functionality regardless of the particular business area. A radically different approach has
been undertaken by two business consortia, resulting in sets of standards known as ebXML
(Eisenberg & Nickull, 2001) and RosettaNet (Kak & Sotero, 2002). Although both families of
standards are based on XML-compliant components, just like the Web services, their primary
objective is universal "vertical" interoperability: that is, the standardization and subsequent
automation of business processes within a specific supply chain or business model.

The ebXML architecture (Eisenberg & Nickull, 2001) builds upon the foundation provided
by the EDI standard and its successors through the use of XML-compliant data interchange
formats and associated business systems and applications. In this manner, businesses that have
embraced EDI can leverage their prior investments, while those that have not done so can
enjoy the full benefits of the interoperability and openness of the ebXML standard. Standard
mechanisms are provided for describing business processes and the associated information
models, including relevant constraints and procedures, registering and storing those models so
as to make them publicly accessible and discoverable over the Internet and creating negotiable
collaboration protocols, subject to the constraints associated with respective processes and
models. All of those capabilities are supported through both standardized and configurable messaging protocols, as well as through XML compliant information models. While this approach
closely parallels the one adopted in Web services, its support for business processes is much
more elaborated; in fact, the Web services paradigm provides no such support, even with the
WS-* family of specifications. Furthermore, the ebXML meta-model observes the distinction
between business and technology perspectives (referred to as the business operational view
and the functional service view).

The RosettaNet family of standards is an attempt to automate the interactions of different
participants in a supply chain (Kak & Sotero, 2002). Interoperability both within a supply
chain and between supply chains must be ensured, which requires both horizontal and vertical
XML-based components. To that end, a full complement of components, shown in Figure
14, is developed to provide a total e-business process. As can be seen, this architecture is
conceptually equivalent to those proposed for Web services, the main difference being their
original goals and the evolution path chosen by their developers.

It is worth noting that some of the shortcomings of Web services—most notably, security, quality of service, trust and reputation—are absent from both ebXML and RosettaNet standards.
Therefore, their main advantage over Web services seems to be the availability of ready-made
solution blueprints and business dictionaries or ontologies that can significantly shorten the
time to market.

Quality of Reference Models

A crucial ingredient for successful development and deployment of e-business reference models is the availability of methods and tools for evaluation or assessment of their quality. Despite its importance in practice, this problem has yet to receive the attention it deserves, in both research and industry communities, and only a handful of authors have addressed it. Two main directions are observed: Fettke and Loos (2003a) and Schütte (1999), among others, have adopted an ontological approach based on the work of Wand and Weber (1989), while Mišić and Zhao (2000) have based their work on the linguistics-based evaluation framework by Lindland, Sindre, and Sølvberg (1994).

In the former approach, the reference model is evaluated in a four-step process (Fettke & Loos, 2003a). First, the so-called representational and interpretational mappings are developed to map the constructs of the reference model under consideration onto the constructs of an equivalent ontological model. The two-step approach allows for detection of deficiencies such as incompleteness, redundancy, excess and overload. Those deficiencies are identified and, if possible, resolved, in order to facilitate the normalization of the ontological model. Finally, the normalized ontological model is assessed, taking into account the previously defined mappings and the deficiencies that were identified. This assessment can be used to evaluate the quality of the model under consideration in isolation, as well as to compare it with other models analyzed in the same manner.

In the latter framework, the properties are grouped into three major categories: syntactic, semantic, and pragmatic (Mišić & Zhao, 2000). Those categories roughly correspond to the relationships of the model itself with the three cornerstones of the modeling process: language, domain and target audience. Syntactic properties describe the model in terms of the modeling language constructs used to define it, without considering its meaning (Lindland et al., 1994). Syntactic quality, then, describes how well the model corresponds to the rules of the language used. Syntactic properties include layering or stratification, level of abstraction and level of detail. While those properties do not directly correspond to quality, they define a context within which the quality of the model may be assessed by examining other, semantic and pragmatic properties, and comparing it to other models (Mišić & Zhao, 2000).

Figure 14. RosettaNet component set (Adapted from Kak & Sotero, 2002)

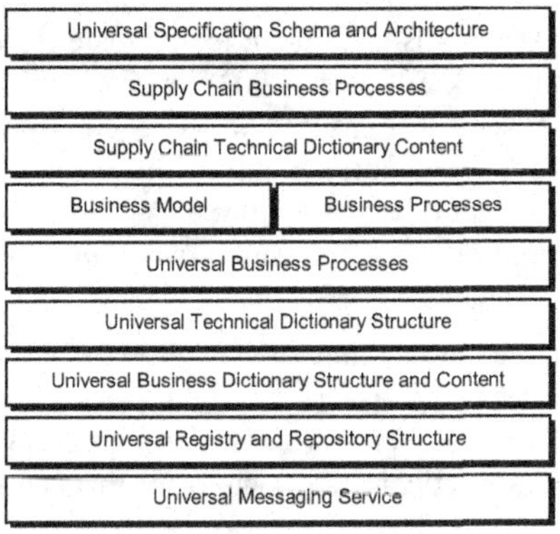

Semantic properties describe the model from the viewpoint of the domain being modeled, focusing on the meaning of the model. Semantic quality, then, depends on how well the model corresponds to its domain. General semantic properties include completeness, (internal) consistency and coherence. Semantic properties specifically relevant to e-business reference models include orientation, scope, perspective (viewpoint) support and support for different transaction types and phases.

Finally, pragmatic properties describe the relationship of the model with its intended audience, and pragmatic quality quantifies how well the model corresponds to the interpretation by its audience (Lindland et al., 1994). In case of reference models intended to be used as the foundation for system building, the audience includes modelers, architects and developers; pragmatic quality, then, primarily translates into ease of comprehension and use. Most important pragmatic properties are extendibility, openness, interoperability and technology dependence.

Note that the distinction between semantic and pragmatic properties is not always clear-cut, as some of the properties of the former category have significant implications in practice. Nonetheless, it seems to be a useful distinction to make in the context of quality evaluation of reference models, and it can often be resolved by distinguishing the property itself from its implications that belong to a different category. A further complication stems from the fact that the properties are often interrelated: For example, scope and completeness can be considered as two facets of a single property, or two different properties. This is a common problem arising in the assessment of high-level conceptual designs.

In general, the approach of Fettke and Loos (2003a) is slightly more theoretical and almost independent of any particular technology, while the approach of Mišić and Zhao (2000) aims for a comprehensive evaluation from different viewpoints, including technology-related ones. In practice, it would be beneficial to use several different approaches simultaneously—that is, to adopt a multi-perspective evaluation, since in this manner we can leverage their particular strengths (Fettke & Loos, 2003b). Obviously, more work is needed in this area, the more so because the choice of a reference model has a profound impact on subsequent system development (Bass et al., 2002).

Problems and Open Issues

Future research in the area of e-business reference models has at least two paths to explore in further detail. The first path is the development of new and improved reference models. Although our discussions clearly show a substantial level of agreement between different models, primarily in the areas of layering and perspective/viewpoint support, new models can (and most certainly will) be proposed. More benefits can be gained, however, by enriching the existing models with provisions for specific business requirements or specific types of business activities. This approach is likely to be more interesting in practice, especially for organizations that already have an e-business system in place and just need to adapt to new markets or cater to changed requirements.

A number of open issues related to e-business reference models can be identified. Three among them appear most urgent at the time of this writing. The first issue is the lack of specific security and quality of service provisions in most of the models, in particular, the recent standards that rely on the Internet and XML. Both security and quality of service have to be addressed in a generic and comprehensive manner, rather than as being put aside by simply referring to cryptographic provisions, as the case is now.

The second issue is the relationship between the Web services-based models and vertical integration models such as ebXML and RosettaNet. Both families are based on the similar paradigm and both use XML-compliant languages for information modeling and communication. As both of these families of models have attracted substantial support in industry, their convergence, or at the very least, interoperability, would be of great practical significance.

The last issue is related to the quality of e-business reference models and the availability of suitable quality evaluation frameworks, of which there are only a few at this time. Further developments in the area of e-business reference models cannot be made without more such frameworks, and without more detailed analysis and assessment methodologies.

References

Ballinger, K. (2003). *NET Web services: Architecture and implementation*. Menlo Park, CA: Addison Wesley.

Bass, L., Clements, P., & Kazman, R. (2002). *Software architecture in practice* (2nd ed.). The SEI Series in Software Engineering. Reading, MA: Addison-Wesley.

BEA (2001). *Future-proof your business with the BEA WebLogic e-business platform* (white paper). San Jose, CA: BEA Systemsc.

Bussler, C., & Jablonski, S. (1994). An approach to integrate workflow modeling and organization modeling in an enterprise. In *Proceedings of the 3rd IEEE Workshop on Enabling Technologies: Infrastructure for Collaborative Enterprises*, Morgantown, WV (pp. 81-95).

Booth, D., Haas, H., McCabe, F., Newcomer, E., Champion, M., Ferris, C., & Orchard, D. (2004). *Web services architecture* (W3C working draft). Retrieved from http://www.w3.org/TR/2004/NOTE-ws-arch-20040211/

Currie, W.L. (2004). Building out the Web services architecture: The challenge of software application integration. In W. L. Currie (Ed.), *Value creation from e-business models* (pp. 370-407). Amsterdam, The Netherlands: Elsevier Butterworth-Heinemann.

EBES/EWOS (1997). *Building blocks for electronic commerce*. Final report (version 5.1) deliverable to the European Commission DG III/B2, European Board for EDI/Electronic Commerce Standardization.

Eisenberg, B., & Nickull, D. (2001). *ebXML technical architecture specification v.1.0.4*, The organization for the advancement of structured information standards (OASIS).

Erl, T. (2004). *Service-oriented architecture: A field guide to integrating XML and web services*. Upper Saddle River, NJ: Prentice Hall.

Erl, T. (2005). *Service-oriented architecture: Concepts, technology, and design*. Upper Saddle River, NJ: Prentice Hall.

Fettke, P., & Loos, P. (2003a). Ontological evaluation of reference models using the Bunge-Wand-Weber model. In *Proceedings of the Ninth Americas Conference on Information Systems AMCIS 2003,* Tampa, FL (pp. 2944-2955). Atlanta, GA: Association for Information Systems.

Fettke, P., & Loos, P. (2003b). Multiperspective evaluation of reference models—towards a framework. In M.A. Jeusfeld & O. Pastor (Eds.), *Conceptual modeling for novel application domains* (pp. 80-91). Berlin, Germany: Springer-Verlag.

Fletcher, P., & Waterhouse, M. (Eds.). (2002). *Web services business strategies and architectures*. Chicago: Expert Press.

FIPS (1996). *Standard for electronic data interchange (EDI)*. Federal Information Processing Standards Publication 161-2. Gaithersburg, MD: U.S. Department of Commerce/National Institute of Standards.

Gill, L. (2003, February 28). How Web services will change e-business. *E-Commerce Times*. Retrieved August 20, 2006, from http://www.ecommercetimes.com/perl/story/20874.html

Gottschalk, K., Graham, S., Kreger, H., & Snell, J. (2002). Introduction to web services architecture. *IBM Systems Journal, 41*(2), 170-177.

Grühn, V. (1995). Business process modeling and workflow management. *International Journal of Cooperative Information Systems, 4*(2-3), 145-64.

Holsapple, C. W., & Singh, M. (2000). Electronic commerce: From a definitional taxonomy toward a knowledge-management view. *Journal of Organizational Computing and Electronic Commerce, 10*(3), 149-170.

IBM. (2001). *Web services conceptual architecture WSCA 1.0* (white paper). Armonk, NY: IBM Corp.

IEEE. (2000). *Recommended practice for architectural description for software-intensive systems*. IEEE Standard No. 1471-2000. Piscataway, NJ: IEEE.

IOTP. (1998). *Internet open trading protocol, part I: Business description; Part II: Specification*. IETF Internet Open Trading Protocol Working Group.

ISO. (1984). *ISO 7498, basic reference model for open systems interconnection*. Geneva, Switzerland: International Standard.

ISO. (2004). *Financial services: Universal financial industry message scheme*. Geneva, Switzerland: International Standards Organization.

ISO/IEC. (1992). *ISO/IEC 10746-1, basic reference model of open distributed processing, Part 1: Overview and guide to use*. Draft International Standard ISO/IEC JTC1/SC21 N 7053. Geneva, Switzerland: International Standards Organization.

ISO/IEC. (1998). *ISO/IEC CD 14662, information technology: Open EDI reference model*. Draft International Standard ISO/IEC JTC1/SC30. Geneva, Switzerland: International Standards Organization.

Jo, K. Y., Pottmyer, J. J., & Fetzner, E. A. (1995). DoD electronic commerce/electronic data interchange systems modeling and simulation. In *Proceedings of MILCOM 95* (Vol. 2, pp. 479-483). San Diego, CA.

Kak, R., & Sotero, D. (2002). *Implementing RosettaNet e-business standards for greater supply chain collaboration and efficiency* (white paper). Lawrenceville, NJ: RosettaNet. Retrieved February 6, 2006, from http://www.rosettanet.org

Kalakota, R., & Whinston, A. B. (1996). *Frontiers of electronic commerce*. Menlo Park, CA: Addison-Wesley.

Kruchten, P. B. (1995). The 4+1 view model of architecture. *IEEE Software, 12*(6), 42–50.

Lindland, O. I., Sindre, G., & Sølvberg, A. (1994). Understanding quality in conceptual modeling. *IEEE Software*, 11(2),42-49.

McConnell, S. editor (1997). *The OMG/CommerceNet joint electronic commerce white paper*. Needham, MA: The Object Management Group.

McGovern, J., Tyagi, S., & Mathew, S. (2003). *Java web services architecture*. San Francisco: Morgan Kaufmann.

McConnell, S., Merz, M., Maesano, L., & Witthaut, M. (1997). *An open architecture for electronic commerce*. OSM response to OMG Electronic Commerce Domain Task Force RFP-2, OSM.

Mišić, V. B., & Zhao, J. L. (2000). Evaluating the quality of reference models. In *Proceedings 19ᵗʰ International Conference on Conceptual Modeling ER2000* (pp. 484-498). Salt Lake City, UT.

OBI. (1998). *Open buying on the Internet* (white paper). Palo Alto, CA: The Open Buying on the Internet Consortium.

OMG. (2002). *Common object request broker architecture: Core services, revision 3.0* (OMG Document no. 91.12.1). Needham, MA: The Object Management Group.

OMG/CommerceNet. (1997). *The OMG/CommerceNet joint electronic commerce whitepaper* (technical report). Needham, MA: The Object Management Group.

Osterwalder, A., & Pigneur, Y. (2004). An ontology for e-business models. In W. L. Currie (Ed.), *Value creation from e-business models* (pp. 65-97). Amsterdam, The Netherlands: Elsevier Butterworth-Heinemann.

Schmid, B. F., & Lindemann, M. A. (1998). Elements of a reference model for electronic markets. *Proceedings of the 31ˢᵗ Annual Hawaii International Conference on System Sciences* (Vol. 4, pp. 193-201).

Schunter, M., & Waidner, M. (1997). Architecture and design of a secure electronic marketplace. In *Proceedings of the 8ᵗʰ Joint European Networking Conference (JENC8)*, Edinburgh, UK (pp. 712-1 to 712-5).

Schütte, R. (1999). Architectures for evaluating the quality of information models: A meta and object level comparison. In *Proceedings of the 18ᵗʰ International Conference on Conceptual Modeling ER99*, Paris (pp. 490-505).

Selz, D., & Schubert, P. (1998). Web assessment: A model for the evaluation and the assessment of successful electronic commerce applications. In *Proceedings of the 31ˢᵗ Annual Hawaii International Conference on System Sciences,* Kohala Coast (Vol. 4, pp. 222-231).

Shaw, M., & Garlan, D. (1996). *Software architecture: Perspectives on an emerging discipline*. Englewood Cliffs, NJ: Prentice Hall.

Shin, K., & Leem, C. S. (2002). A reference system for internet based inter-enterprise electronic commerce. *The Journal of Systems and Software, 60*, 195-209.

Soley, R. M. (Ed.). (1995). *Object management architecture guide* (3rd ed.). New York: John Wiley & Sons.

Stallings, W. (2005). *Business data communications* (5th ed.). Upper Saddle River, NJ: Prentice Hall.

Sun Microsystems (1998a). *The Java electronic commerce framework white paper*. Mountain View, CA: Sun Microsystems, Inc.

Sun Microsystems (1998b). *The Java wallet architecture white paper*. Mountain View, CA: Sun Microsystems, Inc.

Tenenbaum, J. M., Chowdhry, T. S., & Hughes, K. (1997). *eCo system: CommerceNet's srchitectural framework for Internet commerce* (White Paper & Prospectus, version 1.0). Cupertino, CA: CommerceNet, Inc.

Timmers, P. (1998). Business models for electronic markets. *International Journal of Electronic Markets, 8*(2), 3-8.

Timmers, P. (1999). *Business models for electronic commerce*. Chichester UK: John Wiley & Sons.

Wand, Y., & Weber, R. (1989). An ontological evaluation of systems analysis and design methods. In E.D. Falkenberg & P. Lindgreen (Eds.), *Information systems concepts: An in-depth analysis* (pp. 79-107). Amsterdam, The Netherlands: North-Holland.

Weill, P., & Vitale, M. R. (2001). *Place to space: Migrating to e-business models*. Boston: Harvard Business School Press.

Zwass, V. (1996). Electronic commerce: Structures and issues. *International Journal of Electronic Commerce, 1*(1), 3-23.

Chapter XIII

Evaluation of Selected Enterprise Reference Models

Jean-Paul Van Belle, University of Cape Town, South Africa

Abstract

This chapter describes a comprehensive evaluation of ten enterprise reference models, including the models underlying the two leading ERP systems (SAP and Baan) and a number of prominent data model libraries. The main purpose of the chapter is to explore how well various model evaluation criteria and the associated metrics can be applied to real-life enterprise models. The analysis is structured into syntactic, semantic and pragmatic criteria. Not all criteria can be measured using clear or unambiguous metrics and some novel, exploratory approaches are suggested. The chapter does not only provide an insight in how some of the better-known enterprise models compare against each other, but it also highlights the many practical problems and issues encountered with applying evaluation criteria to industrial-strength models.

Introduction

The importance of enterprise reference models is growing thanks to the increasing adoption of CASE tools as well as the demand for enterprise information architectures to support more integrated, agile systems and enterprise-wide data warehouses.

This trend is reflected in an ever-increasing number of modeling methodologies and tools. But, while there is a significant body of literature available on the evaluation of modeling tools and methodologies, far less has been published on actual evaluation of the *output* from these methodologies, namely how to actually evaluate specific reference models. While the importance of assessing the quality of a methodology is not questioned, it is abundantly clear from industry experience that employing a good modeling technique, tool or process does not necessarily guarantee the production of a quality reference model. Thus, when evaluating competing reference models, the practitioner is often left in limbo looking for an appropriate and suitable set of evaluation criteria.

This chapter, therefore, applies a comprehensive set of model quality metrics which have been proposed in the literature to a selection of ten published enterprise reference models in an attempt to explore the practical issues that arise if one uses the various model evaluation metrics which have been suggested in the literature for comparing real-world reference models. Not all evaluation criteria attempt to measure quality; model size, cost or the degree of overlap between models are important evaluation criteria but have little or no direct bearing to model quality.

The focus in this chapter is on *static* models. However, parallel but independent research has developed a similar framework to evaluate dynamic models (Taylor & Sedera, 2003). Also, this chapter concentrates on the evaluation of enterprise reference models, but much of the analysis should be equally applicable in *other modeling domains,* such as embedded systems or specific functional areas within the enterprise. Finally, note that this chapter uses the term "validity" fairly loosely. However, Van Belle (2003) gives a more detailed discussion of the different types of validity and how they apply to the metrics used in the framework.

Prior Work and Analysis Framework

Prior Work on Evaluation of Models

Research on the evaluation of models and similar conceptual structures can be found in a number of different reference disciplines, such as software engineering, ontology research, methodology engineering and enterprise reference architectures. Most researchers simply provide an unstructured sequential list or table of model evaluation criteria (e.g., Benyon, 1990; Claxton & McDougall, 2000; Halpin, 2001) without supplying sound arguments for the completeness of their lists.

Other researchers organise their evaluation criteria into comprehensive frameworks. Most of these frameworks are found in context of evaluating the *quality* of modeling approaches and methodologies (e.g., Khaddaj & Horgan, 2004; Brazier & Wijngaards, 1998). Perhaps best known by practitioners are the matrix presentations of "software" quality factors which originate from the software engineering community: McCall's quality factors, the very similar Böhm model and Gillies' hierarchical quality model (Böhm, 1976; Gillies, 1997). A comprehensive framework for analysing the quality of information models was suggested by Krogskie et al. (1995) and Lindland et al. (1994) and in subsequent work they were among the first to attempt to empirically validate their quality framework (Moody et al., 2003). However, previous research appears to have focussed on empirical validation of relatively small models and was generally restricted to *quality* criteria only. This chapter will focus on the empirical analysis of ten *large* real-world enterprise reference models and also includes non-quality related but useful criteria.

Analysis Framework

In order to structure the various criteria in a logical and systematic manner, a framework is required. Here a framework with a structuring principle grounded in semiotics is adopted. It classifies criteria in syntactic, semantic and pragmatic categories, as suggested in Stamper (1997) and Taylor and Sedera (2003). *Syntactic* analysis focuses on the (mainly numerical or statistical) reference model's structure: the model elements it contains, how they are grouped and the relationships between them. Here, any names or descriptions are treated as mere "alphanumeric labels." Syntactic metrics, typically proposed by computer scientists and software engineers, tend to be algorithmic in nature and can often be computed automatically.

The *semantic* analysis of models is concerned with the intrinsic *meaning* of the reference model, that is, the correspondence between the model (as an abstract or intellectual construct) and the underlying domain or reality that is being modelled. It is not easily automated and usually involves considerable human input.

Pragmatic model analysis considers information regarding the use, environment or context of the model. This information is not found within the reference model and concerns issues such as model popularity, availability, cost, flexibility, adaptability, currency, maturity and support. Pragmatic criteria usually involve a high degree of subjective interpretation and often reflect the intended use of the reference model.

The framework classifies only simple or atomic evaluation criteria. Criteria that do not fit into one semiotic category are likely to be of a composite nature. For instance, the rather fluid and context-dependent concepts of model usability and model quality are composites of a number of atomic criteria.

Table 1 lists suggested reference model evaluation criteria using the framework. These criteria have been distilled from a literature survey numbering well over 100 publications. Some of the more comprehensive sources include Benyon (1990), Claxton and McDougall (2000), Orli et al. (1996), Fox and Gruninger (1998), Böhm et al. (1976), and Gillies (1997). Since authors may use different definitions and meanings, criteria have been grouped into "clusters." The finer distinctions in meaning can then be accommodated when selecting specific metrics to quantify the evaluation criteria. The framework should be seen as open-ended and researchers should feel free to add their own criteria.

The empirical validation of the framework requires that each of the evaluation criteria can be measured by means of practical metrics. Where possible, metrics were adopted from the literature although a number of new ones were suggested where no valid metric could be found. Sample metrics are listed in Table 1, though not all are discussed in this chapter due to space considerations. For a full discussion of the validity of these and other metrics that were omitted, refer to Van Belle (2003).

Selection of Enterprise Reference Models

The main purpose of the chapter is to evaluate real-world, industrial-strength reference models. Hence the selection of appropriate and well-known models is crucial. *Ten* medium-sized to large enterprise reference data models were chosen for analysis[1]. To qualify for

Table 1. Summary of framework criteria and metrics

	Evaluation Criteria	Sample Metrics or Measures
SYNTACTIC	Size	CASE (concept) count and adjusted CASE count
	Correctness; consistency	Syntax error, consistency and standards level score
	Modularity	Number of groupers, group levels and diagrams
	Structure; hierarchy	Multiple inheritance; mean inheritance depth, reuse ratio\
	Complexity; density	Relative connectivity; average fan-out; harmonic mean of fan-out; fan-out distribution (chart)
	Architectural style	Layout aesthetics (various metrics)
SEMANTIC	Genericity	Percent mapping to domain
	Coverage	Domain coverage score; core concept coverage
	Completeness	[Ranking of] absolute lexicon coverage
	Efficiency; conciseness	Relative lexicon coverage
	Expressiveness	Weighted expressiveness score
	Similarity & overlap with other models	Plot of similarity coefficients; most similar neighbours; similarity dendrogram; most important concepts
	Perspicuity; comprehensibility; under-standability; readability	Normalised rank-adjusted weighted perspicuity count based on user lexica
	Documentation	Completeness, extensiveness and readability (e.g., Flesh Reading Ease score)
PRAGMATIC	Popularity; validity; authority; user acceptance	Academic author citations, Google Page Rank and sales
	Flexibility; expandability; adaptability	Composite flexibility score
	Currency; maturity	Descriptive table
	Purpose; goal; relevance; appropriateness	Descriptive table
	Availability	Medium and status
	Cost	Purchase cost
	Support	Tool and vendor support, user base

inclusion, models had to have at least 100, preferably more than 200, entities/object classes and needed to be publicly available. The following gives a brief overview of the generic enterprise models which were selected.

Two enterprise models underlying the world's leading integrated enterprise resource planning (ERP) applications were captured: the original *SAP* R/3 reference model (Sheer, 1998) and the relational data model underlying the *BAAN* IV system. Instead of using the real system tables, the latter was "re-engineered" from the public description given in Perreault and Vlasic (1998) in order to respect IP rights. Both ERP systems have a tremendous impact on organisations worldwide and the underlying models are thus of particular significance. However, it should be noted that the models described in both books are only a partial reflection of the actual models underlying the latest ERP system implementations. In addition, four generic data model libraries were captured from their respective publications: Hay (1996), Silverston et al. (2001), Marshall's BOMA (2000) and the analysis patterns of Fowler's model (1997). These models are specifically geared toward the enterprise modeller and are generally well-regarded in the practitioners' community. The first two models are published in EERD notation, the other two use UML notation. In addition, two somewhat dated and relatively small academic enterprise reference models were included: Purdue's reference model for CIM in DFD notation and the ARRI's small integrated manufacturing enterprise model in IDEF0 notation (Williams, 1991). Finally, two enterprise ontologies were selected to complete the library of enterprise reference models, namely the enterprise ontology developed by the AIAI in Edinburgh (Uschold et al., 1998) and TOVE from EIL in Toronto.

Syntactic Analysis

Model Size

Arguably the most important syntactic measure to be considered within any discipline is *size*. However, an unambiguous and acceptable size measure for objects of a relatively heterogeneous and complex nature, such as reference models, is quite difficult to find. This is partly due to the close relation between size and complexity: "Size metrics are usually used in conjunction with complexity metrics and the distinction between them is sometimes unclear" (Brito, 1994, p. 6).

Thus, many different size metrics have been proposed for models (Shepperd, 1995). The CASE (or concept) count looks at the number of unique instances of the various modeling elements—such as would typically be stored in the CASE repository or modeling tool database. Since the CASE count can be inflated artificially by high numbers of modeling elements which require little or no modeling effort, an *adjusted CASE count* can be used which only includes the more important types of modeling elements or applies a relative weighting factor to various types to reflect the notional degree of modeling effort required.

Only three *size* measures are listed in Table 2: the entity or class count, the (adjusted) CASE size or concept count (entities + relationships + grouper elements) and the full CASE size (concept count), which includes additional meta-modeling elements such as attributes.

Table 2. Syntactic model analysis

Model	Size			Correctness				Complexity					
	Nr of Entities	Adjusted CASE Size	Full CASE Size	Accuracy	Consistency	Standards	Combined Score	Cyclomatic Complexity	Relative Connectivity	Average Fan-Out	De Marco's Data Bang	Average Data Bang	(Harmonic) Mean Fan-out
AIAI	94	270	510	2	3	2	7	30	1.82	3.32	220	4.99	1.81
ARRI	128	430	790	2	2	1	5	79	2.09	3.31	592	4.97	1.81
BAAN	328	1086	1927	2	2	2	6	377	2.29	5.24	2018	8.7	2.23
BOMA	183	552	770	3	2	2	7	65	1.68	3.00	557	4.35	1.81
Fowler	120	375	579	2	2	2	6	37	1.67	2.76	372	3.92	1.71
Hay	291	1292	3465	2	3	2	7	491	3.13	6.17	2470	10.5	2.42
Purdue	106	343	866	0	0	1	1	136	2.11	5.03	711	7.99	3.82
SAP	396	1218	1917	3	3	2	8	285	1.97	3.73	1851	5.64	2.30
Silverston	267	1269	2235	2	3	2	7	114	1.51	3.08	950	4.55	1.76
TOVE	564	1937	2042	2	1	2	5	678	2.28	4.51	3876	7.19	2.33

Although the values are highly correlated, it is suggested that the adjusted or full CASE size metric be used because it favours the more fully specified models above the shallower models. Although it may come as a surprise that the SAP and BAAN models rank behind the data models published by Hay and Silverston, it must again be stressed that the former are only a partial model of the underlying ERP systems.

Model Correctness

One of the most important model quality attributes is model correctness and, not surprisingly, it features prominently amongst the evaluation criteria from most authors. "By model correctness, we understand the correctness of the model against the modeling language. Model correctness is certainly a very important aspect unfortunately ignored by many specialists in the modeling domain. How else could we possibly explain a series of errors found in different UML models?" (Chiorean, 2002,p. 71).[2]

A number of different aspects of correctness can be measured. *Intrinsic correctness* looks at anomalies such as the existence of orphan entities (without relationships), circular inheritance relationships or the uniqueness of model element names. *Consistency* concerns consistent ways of defining model elements, listing attributes or possible conflicts between different diagrams. Finally, *standards* enforce the use of naming conventions of elements (e.g., concatenation, capitalization and use of plurals) and the strict adherence to a modeling notation or subset. Correctness problems with reference models should be viewed in a harsh light since most modeling tools are able to eliminate these in the first place. If a reference model contains syntactic correctness problems, it is likely to have many other quality problems as well and it should be viewed very critically.

Unlike the size metrics, correctness is usually evaluated using a categorical scale. Here, a composite "correctness score" was used. Errors and consistency were rated 3 for (almost) no problems or errors, 2 for minor ones, 1 for medium and 0 for major problems. In addition, a score between 0 up to 2 was allocated for adhering to stringent standards for naming, diagramming, etc. This score was awarded based primarily on problems encountered during the capture of the models. Thus, the combined and admittedly somewhat subjective "correctness score" ranges from 0 to 8, with a higher score indicating a more correct model. Not surprisingly, the well-validated SAP model achieves the highest score with most of the other well-known practitioner models following immediately after. Reflecting somewhat badly on the academic community, the lesser-known research models obtained a low score: Purdue has serious correctness problems, and both TOVE and ARRI also score a relatively poor 5.

Complexity and Density

A multitude of systems *design* and a smaller number of system *analysis* metrics have been proposed. Especially high-level analysis metrics are of relevance to reference models. The most commonly calculated model complexity metrics are cyclomatic complexity, relative connectivity, fan-out and data bang. An averaged complexity measure, such as relative connectivity or average fan-out, can also be said to measure model *density*.

The *cyclomatic complexity* is the classic complexity metric proposed by McGabe (1976) to measure program complexity. Edmonds (1999) rated cyclomatic complexity the most efficient and applicable out of a list of 48 syntactic complexity measures. *Connectivity* (the number of inter-connections or relationships) was also found to be a good measure of model complexity, although relative connectivity should be calculated in order to adjust for model size. The connectivity metric can include or exclude the structural (inheritance and grouper) relationships. *Fan-out* is another complexity metric. The original measure referred to subordinate (program) modules but recognized an orthogonal version based on (directed) relationships. Here, an *entity's fan-out* refers to the number of relationships in which it participates. Finally, De Marco suggested two *"bang"* metrics, with *Data Bang* being the one relevant to data models. It is the sum of all entities' "COBI" (corrected OBject increments)—a number indicating the connectedness of an entity based on an empirically derived table.

Table 2 shows only McGabe's cyclomatic complexity, the relative connectivity (including the inheritance structure), average fan-out and De Marco's data bang. It appears that the overall model size still exerts a very strong influence on the complexity measures. None of these appear to convey the subjective feeling of model network density well and the measures do not yield to easy or intuitive interpretation.

A more promising approach, at least for static models, involved comparing the frequency distributions of the entity/class fan-outs. These were found to yield a distinctive and characteristic size-independent signature of the underlying model complexity (Van Belle, 2002). The *(harmonic) mean of the fan-out distribution* was found to be the single most descriptive statistic for the average "density" of the model network, but since a compact model can easily achieve a relatively high complexity (e.g., Purdue), the harmonic mean fan-out is best compared among similarly sized models. Interestingly, SAP and Baan exhibit similar complexity as do the fairly comparable BOMA, Fowler and Silverston.

Other syntactic measures relating to groupers and inheritance structure as well as architectural metrics relating to diagram layout and aesthetics were computed for the reference models, but exhibited low validity. Interested researchers can find full details in Van Belle (2003).

Semantic Analysis

Semantic analysis investigates what the entities or relationships actually represent, that is, their correspondence to the underlying enterprise domain. Thus, it is concerned with the degree of correspondence between a model (as an abstract or intellectual construct) and its underlying domain (reality). Semantic analysis does not lend itself easily to objective or automated analysis. Because it is a relatively under-researched sub-discipline in modeling, this section is more exploratory in nature with an emphasis on possible "lines of attack," rather than strict prescriptions about which thesaurus or wordlist to use. The key reference disciplines for semantic analysis are linguistics, ontology research and lexicography, with much of the analysis concentrating on readability, similarity, correspondence and cluster analysis.

Genericity, Domain Coverage and Completeness

In the context of *enterprise reference models*, genericity refers to how well a model can be applied across different types of organizations. A possible, but subjective, approach to measure model genericity is to analyse a number of very different (types of) organisations and assess the applicability of the reference model to each. Organisation theory suggests a number of classification dimensions: organisation structure (e.g., matrix or hierarchical), industry type (i.e., product or service produced), process type, size (both absolute and geographic distribution), etc. Alternatively, a suitable general framework (such as the Zachman framework) could be used to check how well the reference models comply with all the dimensions of the framework. However, the high-level nature of most frameworks is likely to prevent detailed conclusions.

Table 3 shows an *illustrative* application of these criteria whereby the applicability of the model to five different types of organisations was rated subjectively by the researcher. In practice, a panel of domain experts using an iterative process such as the Delphi-technique is suggested. Thus, the table should be seen as illustrative rather than definitive. The ratings shown ranged from 1 (very low applicability) to 5 (excellent applicability).

A first suggested measure of genericity (G1) takes the average score for each model to serve as a quantitative expression of how well all model elements can be applied to different types of organisations. When ranking the scores, the most generic model is AIAI's fairly abstract and high-level enterprise ontology, followed by Fowler's high-level patterns. This is an encouraging validation since both are specifically designed to be as generic as possible. By

Table 3. Model genericity

Model	Manufacturer	Service Org	Virtual Org	Micro-business	NGO	Average (G1)	Ranking (G1)	St.Dev. (G2)	Ranking (G2)
AIAI	5	5	5	5	4	4.8	1	0.45	1
ARRI	5	4	4	5	3	4.2	3	0.84	3
BAAN	5	3	3	2	1	2.8	9	1.48	7
BOMA	5	5	4	4	3	4.2	3	0.84	3
Fowler	5	5	5	4	4	4.6	2	0.55	2
Hay	5	5	4	2	1	3.4	6	1.82	10
Purdue	5	4	4	2	1	3.2	8	1.64	9
SAP	5	3	3	2	1	2.8	9	1.48	7
Silverston	5	4	4	2	2	3.4	6	1.34	6
TOVE	5	4	4	3	3	3.8	5	0.84	3

contrast, the larger ERP models, Baan and SAP, score relatively badly but may be unduly handicapped because many of their constructs are not applicable in many situations.

This suggests a possible alternative genericity measure (G2) that looks at how the scores *change* when the domain (the type of organisation) is changed. This is a conceptually different but equally plausible interpretation of the concept of genericity. If a model's rating of coverage stays constant, regardless of which domain is being modelled, and the number of redundant concepts also stays fairly constant, then it can be argued that the model has many generic constructs across the different domains. Thus, one can operationalise G2 as the standard deviation of the genericity scores. These are given in the second to last column and ranked in the last column.

For most models, G1 and G2 correlate quite closely, but there are a few very significant shifts. The ERP models SAP and Baan, as well as Purdue (a CIM model) all score low. This is perhaps somewhat unfair: their authors probably never intended them to be applied to a small business or NGO, but rather across different manufacturing industries, possibly those with continuous or mass production processes. In this context, organisations from different industries instead of different sectors could be used. The method remains the same, but the interpretation of the "range" of genericity is different. Nevertheless, the genericity measures remain perhaps the most problematic metrics suggested in this chapter, and they were included expressly for their particular relevance to reference models.

Domain coverage is the complement of genericity: How well does the reference model cover a given domain. In a sense, if genericity measures the (horizontal domain) width, coverage measures the (vertical) depth to which the domain has been modelled. The higher the domain coverage of a reference model, the less customization or additional modeling effort will be required to apply the model to a given organisation. Consequently, a methodology similar to measuring domain coverage can be used as for measuring genericity.

Select one (or several) prototypical organisations and rate the domain coverage for each of the reference models under consideration, possibly again through a subjective assessment by experts such as consultants who have used the reference model in a number of real life situations. Alternatively, a detailed domain analysis by, for example, a team of business analysts who are very familiar with the domain, can be conducted. However, these efforts effectively duplicate the initial analysis that was conducted by the model authors and, thus, do not represent a realistic approach.

An alternative approach to model coverage (or completeness) is to measure directly how much of the domain has been covered by looking at an ideal description of the domain. Since this accepted and complete description of the model domain is unlikely to be available, in practice an approximation will have to be found. For static models of the enterprise, a possible candidate is a comprehensive business lexicon. Here the same business lexicons as for the perspicuity analysis were used and it was calculated how many distinct concepts within the lexicon are covered, that is, the more words or concepts that are covered, the better. The analysis was enhanced by an intermediary mapping process which uses synonyms (found in WordNet) to enable the matching of meanings instead of word tokens (see Table 4). Not surprisingly, using this measure, the larger models tend to be more complete although it is interesting that there is no strict linear relationship. The ERP models cover most of the business domain. The smaller CIM models (ARRI and Purdue) and AIAI, the smallest ontology, rank lowest. Although this validates the measure, the actual usefulness of the metric is debatable.

Where a relatively large number of reference models is available, an alternative approach can be followed. In this case, model elements which appear across a majority of reference models can be tallied and extracted to create a set of core constructs or a consensus domain model. The coverage of each of the reference models can then be measured against this core set. However, this analysis did not yield any additional insights (Van Belle, 2003).

Model Expressiveness

A much more straightforward semantic criterion is the *expressiveness* of a model, which investigates the richness of the modeling language used in the model. For example, by its nature, a relationship has to contain a reference for the "To-Entity" and the "From-Entity," but models may also include a relationship definition, a name, cardinalities and role names for bi-directional relationships. A model may even distinguish between different types of relationships and/or specify relationship constraints.

The expressiveness of a model is intrinsically bound by the modeling language used. UML class diagram notation is potentially richer than ERD, since the former allows for various types of relationships including generalization, aggregation and composition as well as constraints over relationships, but UML is not as rich as KIF, which allows formal definitions of relationships, including default values or domain ranges. However, not all models expressed in a particular language necessarily make use of the power of the language: Merely re-drawing an ERD as a UML class-diagram does not make the model richer or more expressive. Hence, the expressiveness metric looks at the extent to which a model actually used the various features of its modeling language.

Table 4. Semantic model analysis

Model	Expressiveness		Perspicuity		Completeness	
	Unweighted Expressiveness	Weighted Expressiveness	GPC	NRAWPC	Completeness1	Completeness2
AIAI	10.5	13.0	85%	68%	80	272
ARRI	7.3	8.5	86%	77%	121	346
Baan	6.3	8.0	95%	81%	235	636
BOMA	9.7	12.0	91%	77%	156	452
Fowler	6.8	8.5	88%	68%	100	336
Hay	9.3	12.0	93%	76%	201	574
Purdue	6.5	7.5	93%	79%	116	383
SAP	8.8	10.5	94%	82%	236	632
Silverston	8.8	11.5	95%	81%	141	461
TOVE	9.5	12.5	77%	60%	226	571

A straightforward approach to measuring the expressiveness of modeling notations was suggested by McLeod (1998). In attempting to quantify the "complexity" of a methodology, he used a composite weighting index, analogous to the function point metric, to rate how much of the semantics of a modeling notation was used in a given methodology. In general, the expressiveness of the enterprise model must be measured against a meta-model. Here, the following expressiveness attributes were used (unless specified otherwise, a weight of 1 was applied): degree of formality (weight of 3), use of diagrams, directed graphs, generalisation, multiple inheritance; entity definitions, entity examples, entity attributes, relationship names, relationship role names (x2), relationship cardinalities, relationship types, definitions for relationships/groupers, minimal depth of inheritance tree and number of grouper levels (x2) and the use of additional constructs such as constraints.

The results are also listed in Table 4. It comes as no surprise that the ontologies in the sample (TOVE and AIAI), which use semantically very rich languages, scored very high. So did the object-oriented model (BOMA) whose developer was, incidentally, also involved with the specification of the UML standard. The exact final composition of any expressiveness metric should obviously be modified to suit the ultimate requirements of the model analysis. The weighting does not appear to affect the ranking of the models very much.

Perspicuity and Readability

Model *perspicuity* and *readability* refer to the extent to which a model can be understood or comprehended by the intended users or readers of the model. It also measures how self-describing or self-explanatory the model is. This is not an absolute measure, because it depends on the language used by the model users. A complicating issue is the fact that models often have different groups of model users, each using their own jargon (e.g., a model may serve both IT professionals and business managers). Since reference models are often created by computer scientists or IT professionals, the perspicuity of the model is especially important from the perspective of people working within the business domain. The term "model perspicuity" is used here in preference to model comprehensibility or understandability because the latter terms often imply a dependence on structural, syntactic model characteristics, such as model complexity, and the choice of modeling notation.

A simplistic approach to perspicuity analysis is to calculate the readability scores or indices for model descriptions or documentation. However, it was found that measures such as the Flesh Reading Ease or Flesch-Kincaid Grade Level score had extremely low validity (Van Belle, 2004). Attempting to retain the benefit of a metric that can be computed fairly automatically, an alternative approach was adopted by matching or comparing model element names and their descriptions against common domain vocabulary lists. For example, in the case of enterprise reference models intended to be used and understood by a business audience, an appropriate business lexicon could be used. However, although several business lexicons exist, they may not properly reflect the actual vocabulary of the intended business audience. Hence, the use of a well-validated corpus-based business language list annotated with word frequency statistics was found to yield slightly better results, especially if wordlist preparation and synonomy-based matching algorithms are used. Possible wordlist preparation measures include normalisation of word tokens to extract word stems by removing suffixes and plurals, standardizing capitalization and hyphenation. More sophisticated matching algorithms compensate for word frequencies (indicating a user's familiarity with words) and relative lexicon/model size.

Several business lexicons were tested. Using Someya's (1999) well-validated corpus-based business language list annotated with word frequency statistics yielded the best results, especially when slightly more sophisticated wordlist preparation and matching algorithms are used. The GPC ("gross perspicuity count") measures what percentages of model element labels exist in the business word list, whereas the NRAWPC Normalizes for the size of the model, is Rank-Adjusted for word use frequency and applies a Weighting to concatenated or multiple word labels.

It is encouraging to find the measure validated by the high ranking of the well-known ERP models and the published data models. The low scores for AIAI and TOVE demonstrate that the "ontologies" tend to use a more obscure or even obtuse language.

Similarity and Cluster Analysis

A very interesting analysis is measuring how closely related reference models are to each other (i.e., how much overlap exists between models). Because this entails looking at the model meaning, it falls under the category of semantic analysis.

One approach suggested by Chen-Burger et al. (2000) is based on a "heuristic similarity assessment function" to "quantify the quality of a match" between entities in their generic model advisor. This function matches models on the basis of structural relationships but, although their tool offers some assistance, it still requires significant user interaction to identify matches.

A more sophisticated approach for determining similarity using meaning instead of structural similarity was suggested by Honk (1998) to measure document similarity. The principle for measuring this type of model correspondence or overlap is simple: Attempt to map each model construct to a semantically equivalent construct in other model(s). Corresponding model constructs increase the similarity between the models, whereas model elements for which no corresponding element can be found in another model increase the semantic distance between the models concerned.

The overall methodology can be broken down into three distinct steps, each posing unique challenges. First, the model elements from each reference model must be mapped to the corresponding elements in other models. This involves semantic processing and results in large lists with cross-linked concepts. Because very few models in the sample included relationship names, relationships had to be excluded from the correspondence analysis. This lack of incorporating relationship, or structural information, in the model comparison represents a serious weakness which future research will hopefully remedy. To get around the problem of dealing automatically with synonomy and hypernomy, a linguistic resource (here: WordNet) was used. Alternatively, more expensive methods such as topic signatures or human experts could be used. Based on the mappings, the similarity (or distance) between each possible pair of reference models can then be calculated. This requires a particular choice of similarity measure but common candidates are dice, cosine and Jaccard coefficients. The final challenge is to analyse and interpret the similarity indices. The distance table (Table 5) represents a multi-dimensional space and is difficult to interpret at first sight. However, a three-dimensional surface plot eases interpretation (Figure 1). Cluster analysis techniques can also be employed; for instance a dendogram summarizes the relatedness between reference models very neatly (Van Belle, 2003).

Table 5. Semantic overlap between models (dice similarity coefficients)

	AR	PU	FO	BO	HA	SI	BA	SA	AI
TO	16%	12%	17%	21%	23%	18%	24%	23%	17%
AI	24%	17%	30%	27%	30%	25%	26%	27%	
SA	33%	36%	33%	45%	47%	43%	48%		
BA	29%	32%	37%	43%	45%	43%			
SI	24%	31%	38%	44%	47%				
HA	29%	36%	39%	45%					
BO	29%	30%	34%						
FO	22%	25%							
PU	31%								

Figure 1. Surface plot of dice similarity coefficients between models

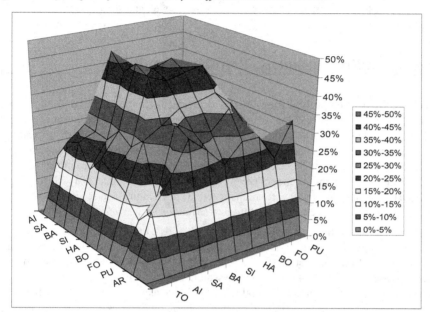

The dice similarities show that the highest degree of similarity exists between the two ERP models with an overlap of almost half of the concepts in the SAP and Baan models. Also very similar are the pure data model libraries of Silverston, Hay and BOMA—between them as well as with the ERP models. The only exception is the more conceptual set of data patterns presented by Fowler, which are much more abstract in nature. This analysis also shows that the ontologies appear to use very much an own, unique terminology when modeling the domain with relative overlap between the ontologies themselves as well as the other models.

Pragmatic Analysis

Pragmatic model analysis is concerned with metrics and criteria which cannot be assessed purely on the basis of the information contained within the model, but which require the consideration of information regarding its use, environment or context. Most analysis relies on the searching, ranking or categorizing of certain specific information details. The criteria usually involve subjective interpretation. By definition, many criteria depend on the actual purpose for which the evaluation is carried out. The discussion is therefore limited to two pragmatic measures, mainly for purposes of illustration. In practice, other criteria such as cost or tool support are likely to be important as well and should be included on an as-needed basis.

Model Validity, Authority, Popularity, and Use

Model validity is a complex measure. The most succinct definition of validity, "how well the model matches reality" (Williams, 2002), is best represented by the concept of *content validity* and, in the absence of statistical and experimental measures, by means of *face validity* (i.e., the acceptance of the model by practitioners in the field). However, model acceptance in the market place is often influenced by the authority of the developers of the model (i.e., the source of the model). In the absence of contrary information, the product of a well-respected academic research group or software company will be rated higher and accepted better than that of lesser known sources. This is referred to as *authoritative validity.*

Measuring the *face* validity of a set of enterprise models can be done through a panel of expert analysts, requesting them to evaluate the various enterprise models using a Delphi approach. Apart from the cost factor, the selection of the panel introduces another methodological problem. Bergholtz and Johannesson (2000) have used such an approach for model fragments using automated natural language-based explanation generation, but their approach is not feasible for large models even though a more rigorous and elaborate process was used by Moody et al. (2003).

Model *authority* or *popularity* refers to the acceptance of the model by practitioners in the field. Depending on the publishing medium of the model, metrics that are relatively easy to collect are the sales figures for book-based models (Table 6 gives historical book sales ranking from Amazon.com, though these vary substantially over time) and the popularity of a Web page by counting the number of external hyperlinks to the page for Web-based models (e.g., using the Google PageRank™ system). The latter is problematic for the models which are not available on the Web. A surrogate but pragmatic proxy is *authoritative validity* (i.e., the reputation of the authoring person, team, or organisation). As an illustrative example, an academic references metric was calculated by counting the number of unique academic references to the lead author using the NEC Research Index online citations database (http:// citeseer.nj.nec.com/cs). In situations where *all* reference models under consideration have a unique name, the references should be taken to the model name. The numbers seem to be representative, indeed, of the academic standing of the lead authors of the models: Mark Fox, A-W. Scheer, Theodore Williams and Mike Uschold are respected academics, while Martin Fowler is a well-known practitioner. Unfortunately, the achievements of practitioners such as Chris Marshall and Len Silverston go unrecognized when measuring citations. Comparing A-W. Scheer with Jan Baan does confirm, however, the sounder academic and theoretical grounding of SAP vs. the Baan ERP.

A practitioner's alternative is the Google PageRank metric for the home page of the *author* (organisation). Interestingly, and despite the huge methodological problems, these two very different measures exhibit a fair degree of correlation (correlation coefficient = 0.47). The highest authority was accorded to large commercial organisations, such as for the ERP systems, as well as the better known research organisations which devised the ontologies (Table 6).

Flexibility and Adaptability

Flexibility refers to the extent to which models can be adapted to different situations. This consists of a number of aspects. The first aspect looks at whether the model is available in digital format and in which technical format. Note that this could also be considered to be a separate criterion namely (ease of) model availability.

The second aspect is how easily the model can be customised, extended and/or reused. *Customisability* refers to the ability to change existing constructs to suit differing circumstances. *Extendibility* refers to how easy it is to add *new* (usually more specialized) constructs and requires, for example, that the hierarchical structure is clear and well-designed. *Reusability* refers to how easy it is to use the same model for different purposes and requires, *inter alia*, proper documentation as well as genericity of application. Although the distinction is important for programming code, the difference is much more subtle in the context of models. It is important to realize that reference enterprise models are almost by definition customisable since the overall purpose of these models is to apply them to specific situations.

Table 6. Pragmatic model analysis

Model	Authority & Popularity				Availability		Flexibility		
	# of Lead Author Citations	PageRank™ for organisation URL	Google PageRank™ for model	Book Sales (Amazon Ranking)	Physical Size (pages/ file size)	Digitally available?	Customizable/ reus- able	Implementation independence	Overall flexibility score
AIAI	20	7	7	NA	85 KB	Yes	Some	Low	1.50
ARRI	19	5	3	NA	132 KB	No	No	Med.	0.50
Baan	0	7	0	16012	576 pp.	Yes	Some	Med.	2.25
BOMA	0	4	0	31295	30.2 MB	Yes	Some	High	2.25
Fowler	25	7	0	36515	356 pp.	No	Yes	High	2.00
Hay	3	5	5	34589	268 pp.	No	Yes	High	2.00
Purdue	17	6	4	NA	10.7 MB	No	Limited	Med.	0.75
SAP	30	8	0	819742	770 pp.	Yes	Some	Med.	2.25
Silverston	0	5	0	13019*	355 pp.	Yes	Yes	High	3.00
TOVE	47	6	4	NA	7.83 MB	Yes	Some	Med.	2.00

Finally, a third flexibility measure, the *implementation independence*, refers to how dependent the model (in its source format) is on the availability of a particular platform, in particular whether proprietary application software is required.

The above factors were rated subjectively and combined into a composite flexibility score. The top score was obtained by Silverston's reference models, which were in fact designed specifically as a set of templates for model development. The ERP and other data models also scored high, whereas the more obscure academic models (ARRI and Purdue) scored very low. Surprisingly, the AIAI ontology which is supposedly aimed at re-use also scored relatively low.

Other Pragmatic Criteria

Many other pragmatic criteria can be considered by the reference model adopter. The *cost* of reference models is often non-trivial, for example, the "visible universal model" retails for $100,000 and the public petroleum data model is available to members only, with corporate annual membership rates well above $20,000. However, all of the models used here are publicly available. *Intellectual property rights* as embodied in the licensing terms which may restrict the duplication of the model within an organisation, or the incorporation of the model into another intellectual product, such as an information system or concrete information architecture. *Model currency and maturity* refer to how often the model is updated, what the update policy (including version control) is and when the last update or change occurred. *Model support* includes the following dimensions: tool support, vendor support and user base. Support is probably often closely correlated to the model currency and maturity. Another pragmatic but subjective consideration concerns the *alignment* of the model with the context in which it is to be used. This requires an investigation of the *theoretical foundation* of the model, its effect on business or ease of integration, its reference discipline and the model's *purpose* or *goal*. As illustrated, for all pragmatic criteria, the choice of metric and actual rating of models is likely to remain subjective and the collection of data subject to considerable methodological problems.

The Meaning of a Composite Model Evaluation Score?

It is natural to question whether an overall score can be calculated to capture, perhaps, the essence of overall model value or quality. A superficial problem is the fact that metrics use different scales. Although this can be addressed—Van Belle (2004) gives an approach based on model rankings—the overall validity of a single composite evaluation must be questioned for more fundamental reasons. "[C]alculating and understanding the value of a single overall metric for (…) quality may be more trouble than it is worth. The major problem is that many of the individual characteristics of quality are in conflict; added efficiency is often purchased at the price of portability, accuracy, understandability, and maintainability" (Böhm, 1978, p. ix). Comparing reference models is best done by analysing the scores for the individual criteria and weighing these up subjectively rather than attempting to integrate these into one single, relatively meaningless number.

However, comparing the relative positions of models *within the same reference discipline* sometimes yields discernable trends or patterns. For example, between the two ERP models, SAP consistently beats or matches Baan across most criteria. However, the "Baan model" here is not the original conceptual model, which is not publicly available, but has been re-engineered from a description of its relational implementation. This implies a quality handicap so the results should not be read as reflecting on the actual ERP packages. Nevertheless, there is support for the contention that the SAP model has a better theoretical foundation as well as represents significantly more analysis effort: Historically the SAP model was developed through a decade-long concerted research effort and it is grounded in a previous CIM model, whereas the Baan system developed more organically by bundling a number of different applications together.

Comparing the data models, it must be admitted that any quality differences between Silverston and Hay are marginal. However, among the more "pattern-like" models, the lagging position of Fowler stands out clearly and this can be explained because of its highly conceptual nature.

The comparative scores for the ontology-based models correspond very well with the amount of ontology engineering and analysis effort invested in each. TOVE represents significantly more engineering effort than AIAI. However, although it is smaller, AIAI is a more homogenous model and at a conceptually higher level, which is perhaps not fully reflected in the score. Regarding the CIM models, it must be recognized that although ARRI is a much cleaner, more correct and rounded model than Purdue, the latter is a better representation of the enterprise domain and represents significantly more modeling effort than ARRI.

Conclusion

The overall research objective was to empirically evaluate a number of real-world reference models. A structuring framework was used which easily accommodated the large number of evaluation criteria which have been suggested in the literature. The structuring principle of the framework is based on the explicit separation of syntactic, semantic and pragmatic criteria or factors. Each of these tends to have metrics with a very distinct tone, reflecting a certain paradigmatic approach. Syntactic analysis has a strong pure science and engineering flavour, drawing heavily from computer science metrics, systems engineering graph-theory and even architectural concepts. Semantic analysis relies mainly on lexicography and computational linguistics, as well as more conceptual information sciences such as meta-analysis or information frameworks. Finally, pragmatic analysis focuses on practical business or commerce issues such as support, pricing, purpose, organizational impact, etc. The framework thus brings the basic constituent reference disciplines of information systems together quite neatly.

Ten non-trivial real-world enterprise reference models were evaluated. It was found that the models underlying two large, widely implemented ERP systems—SAP and Baan—scored consistently high and strongly across all criteria, with the SAP model generally ranking at the top. Scoring almost equally well were most of the data model libraries which are well-known by enterprise modeling practitioners. The reference models from academic origin, ontologies as well as CIM reference models, often scored lower on a wide range of criteria.

Generally, it was found that a large number of metrics can be calculated but, unsurprisingly, not all metrics are equally valid or relevant to high-level reference model analysis. In general, the semantic and pragmatic criteria and metrics are open to a large degree of subjectivity and the results reported here should be seen as exploratory. More valid interpretations could, no doubt, be made by adopting more rigorous but expensive processes such as the Delphi technique. It would also be interesting to repeat the research for reference models in other domains and compare whether the metrics return comparable results. Finally, a more theoretically valid approach to combining individual criteria into composite metrics, such as model quality or usability, remains an open research question, although this may well prove to be an illusive goal.

References

Avison, D.E., & Fitzgerald, G. (1995) *Information systems development: Methodologies, techniques and tools*. London: McGraw Hill.

Benyon, D. (1990) *Information and data modelling*. Oxford, UK: Blackwell.

Bergholtz, M., & Johannesson, P. (2000). Validating conceptual models utilising analysis patterns as an instrument for explanation generation. In *Fifth International Conference on Applications of Natural Language to Information Systems* (pp. 325-339). Berlin: Springer Verlag

Böhm, B., et al. (1978). *Characteristics of software quality*. New York: Elsevier North-Holland.

Brazier, F. M. T., & Wijngaards, N. J. E. (1998). A purpose driven method for the comparison of modelling frameworks. In *Proceedings of the 11th Workshop on Knowledge Acquisition, Modeling and Management*, Banff, Canada (p. 18). London: Chapman & Hall.

Courtot, T. (2000). What to look for in packaged data models/databases. In *Proceedings of the Meta Data Conference*, Arlington, VA.

Chen-Burger, Y.H., Robertson, D., & Stader, J. (2000). Formal support for an informal business modelling method. *International Journal of Software Engineering and Knowledge Engineering, 10*(1), 49-68.

Chiorean, D., Carcu, A., Pasca, M., et al. (2002). UML model checking. *INFORMATICA, XLVII* (1), 71-88.

Claxton, J. C., & McDougall, P. A. (2000). Measuring the quality of models. The *Data Administration Newsletter*, (14). Retrieved May 27, 2004, from http://www.tdan.com/i014ht03.htm

Edmonds, B. (1999) *Syntactic measures of complexity.* Doctoral thesis, University of Manchester, UK.

Fowler, M. (1997) *Analysis patterns.* Reading, MA: Addison-Wesley.

Fox, M. S., & Gruninger, M. (1998, Fall). Enterprise modelling. *The AI Magazine,* 109-121.

Gillies, A. (1997). *Software quality: Theory and management.* London: Thomson.

Halpin, T., & Bloesch, A. (1999). Data modeling in UML and ORM: A comparison. *The Journal of Database Management, 10*(4), 4-13.

Hay, D. C. (1996) *Data model patterns.* New York: Dorset House.

Khaddaj, S., & Horgan, G. (2004). The evaluation of software quality factors in very large information systems. *Electronic Journal of Information Systems Evaluation, 7*(2), 43-48.

Krogstie, O. I., Lindland, & Sindre, G.(1995). Towards a deeper understanding of quality in requirements engineering. In *Proceedings of the 7th International CAiSE Conference,* (LNCS 932, pp. 82-95).

Lindland, O.I., Sindre, G., & Sølvberg, A. (1994). Understanding quality in conceptual modeling. *IEEE Software, 11*(2), 42-49.

Marshall, C. (2000). *Enterprise modelling with UML. Designing successful software through business analysis.* Reading, MA: Addison-Wesley.

McGabe, T.J. (1976). A software complexity measure. *IEEE Trans. Software Engineering, 2,* 308-320.

McLeod, G. (1998). Method points: Towards a metric for method complexity. *Australasian Journal of Information Systems, 6*(1), 48-58.

Moody, D.L, Sindre, G., Brasethvik, T., & Sølvberg, A. (2003). Evaluating the quality of information models: Empirical testing of a conceptual model quality framework. *Proceedings of the 25th International Conference on Software Engineering,* Portland, OR (pp. 295-305).

Ngo, D., Chek L., Teo, L., et al. (2000). *A mathematical theory of interface aesthetics.* Unpublished working paper. Retrieved May 27, 2004, from http://www.mi.sanu.ac.yu/vismath.ngo

Noy, N.F., & Musen, M. A. (2000). PROMPT: Algorithm and tool for automated ontology merging and alignment. In *Proceedings of the 17th National Conference on Artificial Intelligence (AAAI-2000),* Austin, TX (pp. 450-455).

Orli, R., Blake, L., Santos, F., & Ippilito, A. (1996). *Address data quality and geocoding standards.* Unpublished report. Retrieved May 27, 2004, from http://www.kismeta.com/Address.html

Perreault, Y., & Vlasic, T. (1998) *Implementing Baan IV.* Indianapolis, IN: Que.

Scheer, A.-W. (1998). *Business process engineering. Reference models for industrial enterprises* (2nd ed.). Berlin: Springer-Verlag.

Shepperd, M. (1995). *Foundations of software measurement.* London: Prentice-Hall.

Silverston, L., Inmon W.H., & Graziano, K. (2001).*The data model resource book. A library of universal data models for all enterprises* (2nd ed.). New York: Wiley.

Someya, Y. (1999). *A corpus-based study of lexical and grammatical features of written business English.* Masters Dissertation, Dept of Language and Information Sciences, University of Tokyo.

Stamper, R. (1997).Semantics. Critical issues in *Information Systems Research.* In R.J. Boland & R.A. Hirschheim (Eds.) (pp. 43-78). Chichester, UK.

Taylor, C., & Sedera, W. (2003).Defining the quality of business process reference models. In *Proceedings of the 14th Australasian Conference on Information Systems (ACIS)*, Perth [electronic].

Uschold, M., King, M., Moralee, S., & Zorgios, Y. (1998).The enterprise ontology. *The Knowledge Engineering Review (Special Issue on Putting Ontologies to Use), 13*(1), 31-89.

Van Belle, J.P. (2002).Towards a syntactic signature for domain models: Proposed descriptive metrics for visualizing the entity fan-out frequency distribution. In *Proceedings of the SAICSIT Conference,* Port-Elizabeth, South Africa (pp. 19-29).

Van Belle, J.P. (2003).*A framework for the analysis and evaluation of enterprise models.* PhD Thesis, Department of Information Systems, University of Cape Town.

Van Belle, J.P. (2004).A framework to evaluate the quality of information system models. *Ingénierie des Systèmes d'Information, Special Issue on IS Quality, 9*(5).

Williams, T. (Ed.). (1991).*A reference model for computer integrated manufacturing (CIM). A description from the viewpoint of industrial automation.* CIM Reference Model Committee, International Purdue Workshop on Industrial Computer Systems, the Instrument Society of America: Research Triangle Park, North Carolina.

Williams, T. (2002). *Modelling complex projects.* Chichester, UK: Wiley.

Endnotes

[1]   For the initial validation of the metrics, more than 20 enterprise models were captured and analysed but many cannot be considered reference models. The comprehensive database with the models (in XML format) is available on request from the author. The model capture, at well over 500 person-hours, proved to be rather laborious. A comprehensive meta-model was used to standardize the data capture (Van Belle, 2004).

[2]   The above description is a syntactic interpretation of model correctness—a stance generally adopted in computer science. However, many business analysts perceive correctness to also include a semantic component, namely how correctly the model portrays the domain. Here, the purely syntactic definition will be adopted and the term "model validity" will be used to measure how well a model corresponds (semantically) with its domain.

Section IV

Reference
Modeling Context

Chapter XIV

Reference Model Management

Oliver Thomas, Institute for Information Systems (IWi) at the German Research
Center for Artificial Intelligence (DFKI), Saarbrücken, Germany

Abstract

*Reference modeling is located in a field of conflict between research and practice. Despite
the array of theoretical concepts, there is still a deficit in knowledge about the use and
problems inherent in the implementation of reference models. Accordingly, in the past years
the supply-sided development of reference models predominant in the science world has
distanced itself from their demand-sided use in business and administration. This contribution will analyze the causes of these problems and present a solution in the form of an
integrative approach to computer-supported management of reference models. The task to
be carried out with this solution approach will be concretized using data structures and a
system architecture and then prototypically implemented in the form of a reference model
management system.*

Introduction

Business Process Modeling and Reference Modeling

The central idea in reference modeling is the reutilization of the business knowledge contained in reference models for the construction of specific information models (Hars, 1994; Scheer, 1994b; Schütte, 1998; vom Brocke, 2003; Becker & Schütte, 2004; Fettke & Loos, 2004; Thomas, 2006a). Reference models provide companies with an initial solution for the design of organization and application systems. The possibility of orienting oneself with the specialized content in a reference model can, on the one hand, decisively save time and costs for the model user and, on the other, can increase a model's quality because reference models present general recommendations for the subject area under analysis.

Towards the end of the 1990s, a certain "reference modeling euphoria" could be detected which could be attributed to the strong influence of process-oriented paradigms, such as business process reengineering (Hammer & Champy, 1993) or continuous process improvement (Robson, 1991). However, while process consulting and, especially, software tools for business process modeling established themselves as a separate market segment (Gartner Inc., 1996), a development in the opposite direction can be observed for reference modeling—despite the often mentioned close connection to business process modeling.

Today, the systematic development of reference models is seldom seen in practice. Reference models are rarely oriented towards customer segments or enterprise processes. The potential for improvements which result from the enterprise-specific adaptation of reference models is usually not consequently integrated into them. Modeling tool providers are discontinuing modeling projects due to restrictions in time, personnel and finances. Few reference models exist on the basis of a modeling method which offers comprehensive support for model adaptation—the few exceptions here are the reference models from some providers of ERP systems.

Reference modeling as a field of research in the information systems discipline finds itself conflicted between theory and practice. This field of conflict is characterized by the fact that the theoretic foundation of reference modeling propagated by researchers is rarely consistent with the pragmatic simplicity of reference models and the manageability of their enterprise-specific adaptation called for in business practice. This discrepancy can, for the most part, be ascribed to the problems discussed below.

Problems in Reference Modeling

Research Diversity

The number of scientific contributions on the topic of reference modeling has multiplied in the last few years. From the contextual perspective, works come to the fore which support the development of reference models for branches of trade not considered up to now, such as public administration, health care systems or credit and insurance business (Fettke & Loos, 2003). Today's literature also provides a multitude of different suggestions from the methodological perspective for the construction and usage of reference models. The number of modeling methods and techniques applied with the corresponding approaches is so diverse, that even their classification has become a subject of reference modeling research (Fettke & Loos, 2002b). Up to now, few recommendations for the case-specific selection of classes of methods or individual techniques of reutilization have been made. The question also remains open, as to whether the technologies examined can be integrated into construction processes. The fact that most of the examined technologies are geared to a certain modeling language (Fettke, et al., 2002b, pp. 18 ff.) should at least make an integrated usage difficult. Reference model developers and users are therefore hardly in the position of deciding which of the methods, techniques and languages suggested in literature are adequate for their use cases. In this connection, it becomes clear why so few "unique" languages in reference modeling (e.g., Lang, 1997; vom Brocke, 2003) or reference modeling-specific extensions of established languages in information modeling (e.g., Remme, 1997; Schütte, 1998; Schwegmann, 1999; Becker, Delfmann, Knackstedt, & Kuropka, 2002) have so far not found great acceptance in practice.

Findings Deficit

There is a considerable degree of unanimity in literature regarding the application possibilities of reference models. Nevertheless, few empirical studies on the topic of "reference modeling" are documented. The only German-language empirical study on the creation and usage of reference models was carried out in the spring of 1997 at the University of Muenster (Schütte, 1998, pp. 75 ff.). A survey of 390 reference model users in business practice was planned for the questionnaire campaign (planned random sample). The actual sample size (final sample size) however, with only 22 questionnaires filled out (rate of return approx. 5.6%) (Schütte, 1998, p. 371), was so low that no statistically significant statements could be made. Thus, a deficit still exists regarding the benefits and problems inherent in the use of reference models.

Implementation Deficit

The deficit in findings in reference modeling mentioned above is also reflected in the lack of IT implementations. Despite the diversity of the theoretical solutions for sub-problems in reference modeling, only a few of these concepts were implemented technically or tested in practice. Thus, in connection with his approach for using reference process building blocks, Lang (1997, p. 8) explicitly points out the fact that modeling tools are circumstantial, because one can fall back on existing tools. He does not, however, explain how this is to be done. Schwegmann (1999, p. 2) completely differentiates his approach to object-oriented reference modeling from implementation-technical problems, although he sees the information systems represented by reference models in a more or less technical light through the use of the object-oriented paradigm.

One reason for the lack of IT implementations is the low "degree of formalization" in the respective approaches—usually, it is a consequent transfer of the requirements definition to a data-processing concept that is lacking. This would, for example, allow the integration into a professional modeling tool and, in doing so, allow many users to be reached and practical experiences made.

Reference Model Management

Objective and Subject Area

In light of the problems shown in reference modeling, the author is of the opinion that the current significance of reference modeling in research does not so much result from the necessity of methodically analyzing it, but is rather much more the realization in operational practice that, in times of dynamic markets, knowledge about application system and organization design has become a critical factor for business success.

The current occupation with reference models focuses on a central question in business information systems: "How can application systems and organizations be designed so that they meet the demands of their environment as best possible?" The analysis of this problem pertains to many interdisciplinary fields of work, such as organizational theory, systems theory, enterprise modeling, business process management, knowledge management, innovation management and software engineering. However, respective theoretical concepts often neglect the competition-relevant role of knowledge about the design of application systems and organizations. Therefore, based upon the theoretical concepts, the following modified question should also be asked regarding the problem discussed above: "How is the knowledge concerning the design of application systems and organizations planned and controlled?" Moreover, if one understands reference models as memories for explicit domain knowledge, then one must interpret reference modeling as an instrument, which aims at the transfer of business and IT knowledge (Scheer, Habermann, Thomas, & Seel, 2002, pp. 209 ff.; Fettke et al., 2003, pp. 35 ff.), and if one summarizes the terms planning and control in the term "management," then the resulting question can be none other than: "How can reference models be managed?" The author will do his part in answering this question, as expressed in the title of this contribution, in the following.

As touched upon in the previous paragraph, this article understands *reference model management* (RMM) as the planning and control of the development and usage of reference models. The terms "management of reference models" and "reference model management" will be used here as synonyms.

Core Functions

The management of reference models can be conceived as a process. This process is characterized by creativity and is highly complex due to its multifariousness and dependency on human judgment. Procedure models have established themselves in reference modeling—in analogy to software engineering—as being useful in making this complexity controllable. These procedure models which are presented by, among others, Schütte (1998, pp. 184 ff.), Schwegmann (1999, pp. 165 ff.), Schlagheck (2000, pp. 77-91), Fettke and Loos (2002a, pp. 9 ff.) and vom Brocke (2003, pp. 320-344), emphasize the developmental phase of a reference model on the one hand and, on the other, the phase of creation of enterprise-specific models based on a reference model (i.e., the usage of a reference model). In both cases, a process of construction must be gone through and this process can be supported by operationalizable approaches to the creation of models. The processes of development and usage of a reference model are, however, usually chronologically, as well as contextually and organizationally separated from one another (Thomas & Scheer, 2006):

- **Chronological separation:** The chronological separation of the construction process results directly from the definition of a reference model. A model can be referred to as a reference model when used to support the construction of other information models. Thus, the construction of a reference model always precedes the construction of specific models.

- **Contextual separation:** Usually, the reference model constructor does not know the demands regarding the content of future reference model adaptations. He must therefore try to foresee them. This problem occurs especially when construction techniques, such as the configuration (e.g., Rosemann & van der Aalst, 2003) are used, whereas in dependence of specific conditions, construction results from the reference model are selectively adopted.

- **Organizational separation:** The model provider and customer, respectively constructor and user, are usually different people, departments or companies. An enterprise is, for example, either the provider of the knowledge in the reference model or—through the enterprise-wide introduction of a modeling tool—a customer for the reference model. This organizational separation can lead to the fact that, on the one hand, the customer-requirements on the reference model are not adequately fulfilled by the supplier and on the other, that the customer's experiences using the reference model are not used continuously for the improvement of the model.

This separation of the processes "reference model development" and "reference model usage" as regards time, context and organization is seen here as a problem of integration. In general language use, integration is understood as the recreation of a whole. From the system theoretic perspective, integration means the linking of elements and components to form a complete system. This integration can take place by merging or connecting elements and components which logically belong together. One can refer to integration as either the process of recreating a whole or the result of such a process. For the field of information systems, integration means connecting man, task and technology—the components of an information system—to form a whole.

If we transfer this understanding of the term to the topic dealt with here, then we can identify the development, usage and integration of reference models as the core functions of reference model management (cf. Figure 1):

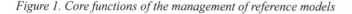

Figure 1. Core functions of the management of reference models

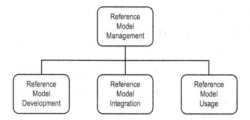

- **Reference model development:** The planning and realization of reference model construction. The development of reference models encompasses the acquisition of and search for relevant information sources and content, as well as the explication and documentation of an employee's application system knowledge and organizational knowledge. The development of reference models refers to the development of new reference models, as well as the modification and continual improvement of existing ones.

- **Reference model usage:** The planning and realization of the construction of information models using reference models. The usage of reference models comprises the search and navigation of the reference models relevant for the use-case, their selection and distribution to the persons concerned, the presentation of knowledge content, as well as the support of the reference model adaptation. It also comprises the retroactive evaluation of the reference models used and associated information.

- **Reference model integration:** The fusion of the separated processes in the development of reference models and the use of reference models for the construction of enterprise-specific models in the sense of the (re) creation of a whole.

IT-Support

The usage of reference models for the construction of enterprise-specific information models is a fundamental idea resulting from paperless, tool-supported data-processing consulting (Scheer, 1994a). Thus, this contribution will not deal with the question as to *whether it* makes sense to economically develop a computer-aided information system for the management of reference models from the research perspective, as well as from the practice perspective. This question has long been "answered" by the economic success of modeling and analysis-tool providers (Sinur, 2004). On the contrary, we must investigate the question of *how* an information system should be designed so that it can support reference model management adequately.

Because it is the design-objective of information systems in the sense of the planning, construction and modification of operational reality and supportive information systems that is emphasized in this contribution, the goal to be achieved cannot be found in design alone but rather, also in the creation of an information system which can support the management of reference models. This information system will be referred to as a *reference model management system* (RMMS).

Concretion of the Challenge

The framework shown in Figure 2 will be used as a guideline for the challenge to be carried out. Due to its system-theory character, it illustrates the most important components of an RMMS, as well as their functional interaction.

The graphic is oriented on the contextual and technical interface-concepts for modeling tools which allow die retention of various IT-platforms (Scheer, 1994a). This allows the consideration of the underlying networking of conceptual research results, prototypes and professional software developments. The RMMS-framework is also oriented on studies concerning instruments and processes for the access to and usage of information models which, among other things, lead to the conception of a model library (Mili, Mili, & Mittermeir, 1998). In addition, results from the prototypical development of an integrated information system for the documentation, networking and design of operational measures for business process improvement have been used for its construction (Scheer et al., 2002).

The framework consists of seven components, which are arranged in five layers. The components are represented by rectangles, the relations existing between them by shaded grey connecting lines and the system limits by a rectangle with rounded corners (cf. Figure 2).

In addition to the support in the development and usage of reference models, a third main function was identified for the management of reference models: reference model integration. These functions also form the core functionalities of the information system for the support of reference model management on the *tool layer*. The link between the elements "reference model development" and "reference model usage" is created by the element "reference model integration." This "bracket" is illustrated by the arrangement of the components, as well as

Figure 2. Framework for a reference model management system

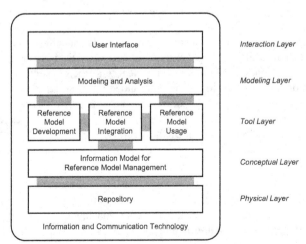

by the connections representing the relations between the components in Figure 2.

The information model for reference model management, derived from the *conceptual layer*, can be seen as the core component for the organizational framework. It identifies and links the most important information objects of the reference model management as well as associated information objects and, at the same time, forms a basis for its physical management. It is a semantic data-model, which—against the background of the research diversity discussed in the first section—is used to clarify relevant terms, as well as to define a uniform terminology.

The RMM-information model forms the technical basis for the functionality "reference model integration" of the RMMS on the tool layer. It is, however, also the basis for the logical database structure of the RMMS on the *physical layer*. It is also referred to as a repository. Both relationships are illustrated in Figure 2 by way of the connections plotted between the components.

Because established products exist in the field of information, and especially business process modeling, the complete new development of an RMMS is not necessary, but rather only the extension of existing systems. Thus, on the *modeling layer* especially, professional tools were used for the design of the component "modeling and analysis." The functionalities necessary for the development and usage of reference models which, for example, require a model modification, have already been implemented in corresponding systems. Functionalities which, however, serve the documentation of a construction process or a certain procedure in the usage of reference models may require a new implementation. Moreover, the deficit in findings discussed above is met through the implementation of the RMMS as an integrated part of a professional tool for business process modeling.

The user-interface of the RMMS is designed on the *interaction layer*. In addition to human judgment, the user interface of the RMMS represents a large bottleneck in the implementation of computer-aided information systems. Great importance must therefore be attributed to its design.

In the following, the design target defined by the RMMS-framework, that is, the description of the individual components of the framework, as well as their interactions, will be pursued. In doing so, the conceptual aspects of the RMM-information model, as well as the technical aspects in the form of an RMMS-system architecture, will be discussed.

Reference Model Management System

Information Model

The RMM-information model pursues two goals. First, the model, as the core component of the RMMS-framework on the conceptual level, builds the foundation for the design of the RMMS-functionality "reference model integration" on the tool level. This was identified as the "link" between the RMMS-functionalities for the development and usage of reference models before. Thus, the RMM-information model must identify and connect the most important information objects for the development and usage of reference models. In addition to the technical analysis of the field of application, the RMM-information model also pursues another goal. It serves as a starting point for the technical implementation of the information system and forms the foundation for the database-structure of the RMMS on a physical layer (RMMS-repository). The modeling language in which the RMM-information model is explained must therefore allow the representation of the relevant business content and be so formalized that a subsequent transfer of this content to information technology can be accomplished. The class diagram from the unified modeling language (UML) (http://www.uml.org/) was selected as a modeling language.

With the help of an object-oriented model, many classes and associations are constructed in the description of the application field "management of reference models." Due to the resulting complexity of the total model, a structuring approach is required which abstracts from details while at the same time illustrating them, clarifying the underlying "superordinate" structure. The differentiation of information models according to the attribute "degree of aggregation" in macro- and micro-information models is such a structuring approach. While macro-information models represent aggregated and contextually similar objects (of another information model) and can be broken down into finer elements, micro-models contain no aggregated information and cannot be broken down into finer elements. The package diagram performs this task in the UML. It will be used in the following to show the fundamental dependencies between the components of the reference model management on a highly aggregated level (macro-modeling). In the next step, these components will be analyzed more closely and their "inner" structure will be constructed (micro-modeling). The UML-package diagram model presented in Figure 3 identifies the most important components for the management of reference models, as well as their interactions.

Reference models created within the framework of a construction or enterprise-specific information models designed during the adaptation of a reference model by persons, departments or enterprises can generally be interpreted as output. The usefulness of this output can be acknowledged by its recipients (for example, customer or a certain company-internal department). This interrelationship is represented in Figure 3 by the two packages *Organizational Unit* and *Reference Modeling Output*, as well as by their relationship to one another.

Figure 3. Macro-model of the reference model management

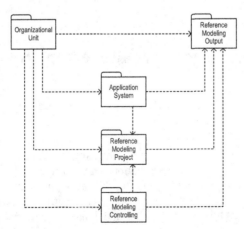

During the structuring of the macro-model, the idea was pursued that certain processes must be run through for the development and usage of reference models. These processes generally possess project-character due to their chronological and contextual restrictions. The respective reference modeling projects are therefore realized using concrete measures initiated and carried out by organizational units. The reference modeling projects, in turn, aim at creating reference modeling output. Thus, the package *Reference Modeling Project* is also introduced and is the center of the macro-model in Figure 3. The connection described is illustrated by the relationships between the packages *Organizational Unit*, *Reference Modeling Project* and *Reference Modeling Output*.

Reference models are recorded in electronic form or conventionally on paper. The models stored electronically can be assigned to application systems, such as modeling, and analysis tools as supporting media. The package *Application System* addresses this point.

Reference Model Controlling also carried out by organizational units, plans and controls the costs resulting from the activities in connection with reference modeling output and in addition, evaluates the reference modeling measures carried out according to their economic aspects.

The application field "Reference Model Management" is characterized in a survey-like manner with the UML-package diagram model. We will concentrate in the following on the classes assigned to the individual packages in this macro-model and the associations existing between them. Due to reasons of space, the description is limited only to the central package Reference Modeling Project (cf. Figure 4).

Figure 4. Micro-model of the reference model management (section)

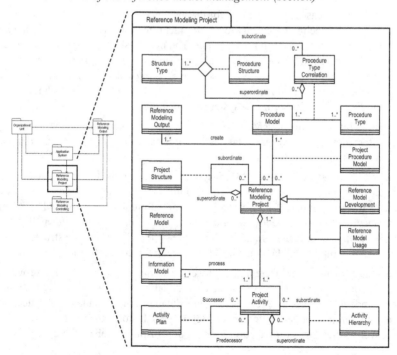

Reference modeling projects are instantiated from the homonymous class *Reference Modeling Project* which refers to the interface of the corresponding package in the macro-model. A reference modeling project is comprised of the concrete project activities with which a target reference modeling output is to be created. A "network" is constructed here as a general procedure structure for project activities. The association class *Activity Plan* states that an activity can, but must not, have several successors and predecessors. The association class *Activity Hierarchy* suggests the possibility that an activity can consist of several sub-activities and is an element of a superordinate activity. The data structure for describing procedure models is also illustrated in Figure 4. Procedure models describe standard procedures for certain project types and can be used for the specification of concrete project procedures. Procedure types, instantiated as objects from the class *Procedure Type*, can be assigned to the class *Procedure Model* over the association class *Procedure Type Correlation*. This allows the reutilization and redundancy-free storage of procedure types. The various possibilities for the structural connection of procedure types are expressed by the class *Structure Type*. The contextual relation between the classes *Reference Modeling Project* and *Procedure Model* is created by the association class *Project Procedure Model*. Depending on the complexity of the project, several procedure models can be assigned to a reference modeling project. They are then processed within the framework of the total project as more or less independent sub-projects.

Information System Architecture

The primary technical aspects of the tool for the management of reference models refer to the definition of the technological platform, the identification of the IT-components and the description of their DP-logical relationships. The main task below consists in selecting individual technologies and integrated technology systems, and arranging these in a network so that the user is supported as best as possible in carrying out his or her tasks within the framework of the reference modeling project. The selected information technologies are illustrated in Figure 5 in the form of a system architecture.

The system architecture of the RMMS is that of a client/server. Due to the multitude of RMMS-system elements, these are "classically" structured in three layers—the data management, application and presentation.

The *data management-layer* of the RMMS-system architecture is divided up into database and file management. While the structured data (human resource and customer data, as well as as-is and reference models) is managed in relational databases, the weakly-structured data (text documents, spreadsheets, presentation graphics, images, video and audio files, as well as links to further documents), is stored in a file system. The database structure is built upon the logically integrated data models developed on the conceptual level.

The data management-layer differentiates between four databases—an enterprise-wide human resource database, an enterprise-wide customer database, an as-is-model database and a reference model database. The reference model database, in particular, is a systematized collection of reference models (reference model library). It stores the reference model constructs, as well as their structural relationships, model attributes such as name, identification

Figure 5. RMMS-system architecture

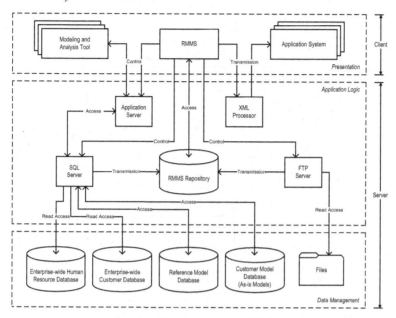

number, type of model (for example, EPC or ERM), description, time of creation, originator and last modification or last processor. The customer model database is also a model database, as is the case with the reference model database. It contains documented as-is-models, that is, sections of the customer's enterprise-structure interpreted by the creator of the model at the time of modeling.

The external databases in Figure 5 manage the data needed by the RMMS. Together they form the "minimum configuration" of the external RMMS-database. The individual data-bases in Figure 5 are represented as logical entities for purposes of simplicity, which, as a rule, consist physically of several distributed databases. For example, the reference model database could consist of several external databases. This is the case, for example, when in modeling projects reference models from different modeling tools are used to manage the models in their own databases.

The *application layer* comprises the server-services and data (RMMS-repository) which are used to carry out the technical tasks. The programs in this layer receive the user's (client's) instructions and carry them out on the relevant data. By using a client/server-architecture, several applications and users can access the same database at the same time and process it.

The RMMS-repository, in the center of the application layer, is completely defined by the data model designed above (cf. Figure 6). It structures the information objects necessary for the development and usage of reference models and can be searched. As already mentioned, textual project documents (for example, offers, commissions, specification sheets and bills) and presentation graphics or multimedia files (for example, audio and video recordings)

Figure 6. RMMS-repository and databases

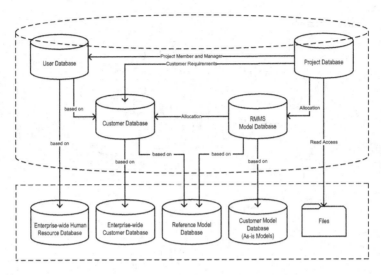

are not stored in the RMMS-repository. They are managed in the file system of the data management layer and processed with external programs. Nevertheless, the search for and in these files is controlled with the help of links to the repository. It is especially the connection of structured and weakly structured documents via the database and file-server that is of importance here. The repository-data is stored in an XML-structure for internal processing. Through this, the integrated application of the structured data (database), as well as the weakly-structured data (files) are guaranteed, because they can be managed independently of their format. Thus, for the user, the database and file system appear to be one.

The project database is at the center of the RMMS-repository. It manages internal and external reference modeling project commissions between organizational units by storing data such as project name, type, objective, time period and status or progress. The data-structure of the project database corresponds to the UML-class-diagram model in Figure 4. Project documents, such as project commissions, structure plans, schedules, minutes and status reports or specification sheets, are not directly stored in the RMMS-repository. These documents are created by the users locally and managed in an external file directory. The project database also supports project management by managing the number, type and logical order of all activities with which a reference modeling project is to be realized, as well as by storing model histories. With the help of relations to the user database, each reference modeling project is assigned a project leader and a group of project members. Associations to the customer database take reference modeling-specific customer requirements into consideration. The project-related new development, configuration or reengineering of reference models, as well as the documentation of changes in the knowledge basis, require access to the reference model database.

While read-access to the weakly-structured data is controlled via the FTP-server, the SQL-server controls the read and write-access to the external databases and the data transfer to the repository (cf. Figure 5). The application server gives the RMMS-users access to the modeling and analysis tools. The application-server allows the flexible modification and extension of the RMMS-system architecture. When, for example, a new modeling and analysis tool is added, all that must be done is to adjust the respective software on the application-server.

The components of the RMMS with which the user has contact are assigned to the presentation layer (cf. Figure 5). They make the input and output user-friendlier and are represented by a graphic interface. The operational concept of the RMMS and its graphic user interface should be adapted to the interface design of established modeling and analysis tools. This way, the separate systems appear to be a logical entity for the user—from the technological point of view. This also makes access to the RMMS easier for users familiar with modeling tools.

The central element of the presentation layer is the RMMS-client. This term refers to the graphic user interface for the reference model management system in Figure 5. The access to the repository data, as well as the control of the SQL and FTP-servers, takes place over the interface of the RMMS. In addition, the requirements to the modeling and analysis tool are routed to the application-server and, when necessary, data are transferred to the XML-processor.

While the RMMS-components are used for processing information which is important for the development and usage of reference models, the creation, processing and deletion of information models remains the task of the modeling and analysis tools. Several different modeling and analysis tools may be used here. This is illustrated by the rectangles arranged one after another in Figure 5. In order to not focus on the integration capability of modeling tools (Mendling & Nüttgens, 2004) the use of only *one* modeling and analysis tool will be assumed. Not the interactions between several modeling tools, but rather the general exposure to reference models and associated information objects are the subject here. It is important, thereby, to secure the compatibility of the database of the modeling tool with the model databases in the data management-layer.

A decisive difference exists between the components "modeling and analysis tool" and "application system" (cf. Figure 5) on the technical side. While the modifications of the modeling and analysis tools flow back into the database of the RMMS, the information from the RMMS is only transferred to the application systems. This means that the knowledge won from these systems does not flow back into the RMMS-repository.

The repository-data is stored as XML-documents. Due to the independence of these documents from logical and physical structures, the integration of other application programs which use these documents is facilitated in the RMMS-system architecture. Applied RMMS-interfaces are conceivable in the software categories of office information (for example, word processing, spreadsheets and presentation graphics), computer-aided software engineering, computer-supported cooperative work, document management, enterprise resource planning, knowledge management, organizational memory and project management or workflow management. A simple implementation would be, for example, the integration of components which help to generate and output HTML-descriptions of process models. This can be especially useful in international reference modeling projects, where separate project groups operate. It allows the discussion of modeling results via Internet and Intranet. Some manufacturers of modeling tools already offer such components.

Prototype

The graphic user interface of the RMMS is illustrated in Figure 7. The prototype, implemented in the platform independent programming language Java (http://java.sun.com/), differentiates between a project and a model view of the tasks associated with the development and usage of reference models.

The project view has been selected in the screenshot in Figure 7. The RMMS workspace is divided up into an explorer and a viewer. These are connected logically with each other—a project selected in the explorer is displayed in detail in the viewer and can be manipulated there. The project active in Figure 7 is called "Reference Model for Event Management" and is used for the development of a reference model for the application domain "event management."

The title, the project's customer segment and information concerning the project period, progress and type were selected by the project manager while setting up the project with the help of the assistant (project wizard). This information can, in addition, be modified using the buttons "Project" and "Subject." A detailed representation of the customer assigned to the activated reference modeling project (i.e., his or her address, branch of business, turnover, number of employees, range of products, etc., can be reached using the button "Customer"). This functionality also allows the user to call up information such as customer description,

Figure 7. Graphic user interface of the RMMS

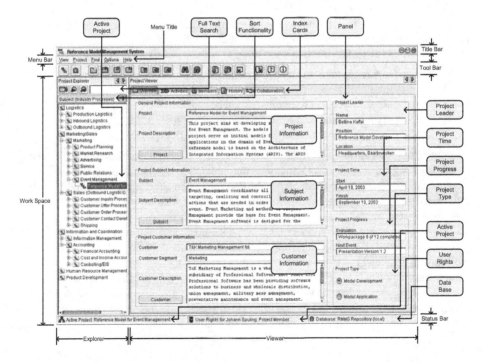

goals or requirements. While this assignment in the use of reference models pertains more to individual customers, projects in reference model development are usually assigned an entire customer segment, as reference models are constructed for a whole class of use cases.

The Viewer is divided up into index cards, which can be selected using their respective tabs. The index card "Overview" (cf. Figure 7) basically characterizes the modeling projects. The elements in this card form important criteria according to which the projects stored can be sorted or searched.

The index card "Activities" contains the tasks or activities necessary for the realization of the targeted reference modeling project. Furthermore, descriptions of the above, activity plans and hierarchies are also stored here. These tasks are individually assigned to project members (via a link to the index card "Members"), as well as to project documents, such as meeting minutes or the presentation of results (linked to the index card "History").

The creation of the team, which will work together in realizing the reference modeling project, takes place using the index card "Members." This card also contains the name, position, location, organizational unit and contact information for each member of the team, as well as the respective tasks assigned to them.

In addition to the project activities and employees involved in business engineering projects, one should also document information about the progress of the tasks and the problems met, as well as possible and ultimately selected measures for solving these problems. The history

Figure 8. Interaction-design between the RMMS and the ARIS-Toolset

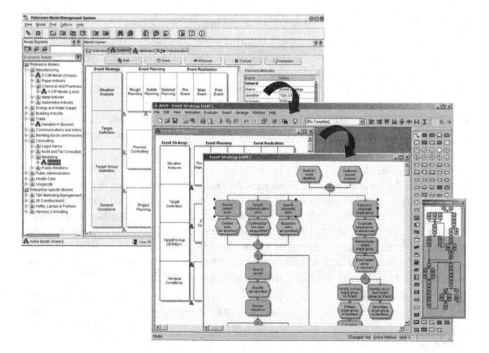

of the reference modeling project is therefore documented in a project history ("History"). This can be used by the project members as a source of information regarding the project history and can support the user in planning future projects.

The collaboration between employees in different departments and at different locations is also customary in the development and usage of reference models (vom Brocke, 2003). The RMMS thus has functionalities which support collaboration during reference modeling projects. To this purpose, an asynchronous communication medium (discussion) is offered on the "Collaboration"-card. One is also given the possibility of reviewing project documents.

The workspace in the RMMS-model view is also divided up into an explorer and a Viewer (cf. Figure 8, screenshot in the background). In the model explorer, all of the information models managed by the RMMS are displayed. This pertains to reference models constructed in development projects, as well as enterprise-specific models created in application projects.

The index card system in the "Model Viewer" is used to manage the most important model-related information for the management of reference models.

The information models managed by the RMMS are characterized on the index card "Overview" of the model view. This is similar to the corresponding card in the project view. The elements of the card "Overview" provide criteria similar to the corresponding information in the project view, according to which the information models stored can be sorted or searched. Potential sorting criteria, which can be selected in the corresponding pulldown menu in the upper part of the "Model Explorer" are: branch-of-trade, model name, application domain, model developer, period of development, modeling progress and modeling language. In the screenshot in Figure 8, the criteria "Economic Activity" is selected, which differentiates between branches of trade at the top level. The reference model selected, which due to its form is referred to as "Event-E," is assigned to the branch "Marketing."

A graphic representation of the model to be constructed in the modeling project is made possible with the card "Graphic." Figure 8 illustrates the connected requirements clearly, as well as the resulting interactive-design between the RMMS and the modeling tool ARIS-Toolset (IDS Scheer AG, 2003). The example illustrates that the user can make modifications on a version of the reference model organizational framework for event management. To do so, he or she must open the ARIS-Toolset by clicking the "Edit" button. In addition to reading, editing or deleting models and model elements, the user is given further functionalities of the modeling tool.

The subject of the dialogue which can be reached using the "Versions" button on the "Graphic"-card (cf. Figure 8) is the management of the models and model element versions (model history) created in the course of the reference modeling project. In addition to the most important model data, such as name, type or creation and modification dates, other data such as time, responsibility (link to the card "Members"), description, reason, priority and status of the model modifications, as well as the corresponding project activities (link to the card "Activities"), are recorded. The structure of this dialogue is based upon the findings on the version management of reference models (Thomas, 2006b).

The display of characteristic information, with which certain information models can be recognized, can be viewed on the index card "Attributes." Similarities and differences between the models are emphasized and used for other activities (for example, similarity analyses and searches).

The RMMS gives you diverse functionalities for the support of distributed reference modeling. In the Project View, these referred to the support of administrative project tasks, complemented by the asynchronous communication medium of the discussion forum. These functionalities have been extended by way of a synchronous communication medium on the index card "Collaboration," a shared whiteboard for the interactive viewing and annotation of graphic data.

Related Work

"Reference model management" is a term rarely used in science and in practice for the description of the management tasks associated with the development and usage of reference models. Therefore, a few examples for the use of this term will be discussed below.

Within the framework of his approach to the computer-aided use of reference data models HARS (1994, p. 11) sees the purpose of meta-models in creating a more favorable structure for the storage and *management of models*. What he means by this term, however, is not explained.

In a paper within the framework of the research project, "Business Process Design with Integrated Process and Product Models" (GiPP) Klabunde and Wittmann (1998), see the reference character of information models anchored in a "broad" basis of knowledge. This could be guaranteed when instruments and procedures for the access and efficient and flexible use of reference models were developed and would make it possible to fall back on existing models, discuss their content, compare them with other models and continue models development. They see the *DP-supported management of reference models* in libraries as one of the central challenges here (Klabunde & Wittmann, 1998, p. 16).

Gerber and Müller-Luschnat (1999) describe a method for business process-modeling projects for the "Sparkassenorganisation" (SKO), consisting of three components which serve the "coordination of diverse modeling projects, … the use of synergies in modeling and … the prevention of multiple developments" (Gerber & Müller-Luschnat, 1999, p. 27). In addition to the procedure model, which describes the individual project phases and the reference process model which serves the reutilization of process templates, they define *process model management* as a third component. This model "describes the processes necessary for the permanent care and further development of a reference model" (Gerber et al., 1999, p. 28). They declare the consistency of the reference process model during the usage of models from different BPR-projects to be the main task in process model management.

The goal of the project "Transformation of Reference Models for Standard Business Software" (TREBES) is the development of a theory for procedure model transformations with special regard to the requirements of business process engineering and reference model-based customizing (Oberweis, 2003). Petri-nets are used as a modeling language. According to existing procedure description methods, business objects are integrated and described using the extensible markup language (XML). The simultaneous transformation of several models during customizing (delta analysis) and the *computer-based management of reference models* are seen as problematic areas.

In addition, the term "model management" is often discussed by consulting firms in connection with the integration of enterprise applications. Model management then refers to the integration and contextual adjustment of models (for example, organization models, process models, data models and object-oriented models) within the same task and is seen as an important medium for increasing quality in software development (Resco GmbH, 2002). While model management deals primarily with instance models with respect to the degree of abstraction from the original, enterprise model management aims at type and cluster models. *Enterprise model management* (EMM) integrates and consolidates models on the project-level and tries to generalize their facts, so that the models can be applied on the department, division or enterprise level. The resulting models are, in turn, adjusted to each other and by adding other areas, further generalized.

Critical Discussion of the Results and Further Research

The instrument "reference modeling" has not yet established itself extensively in business practice. This is due to the particular field of conflict between research and practice in which reference modeling is at home. Thus, there is still a deficit in knowledge about the use and problems inherent in the implementation of reference models despite the array of theoretical concepts. Accordingly, in the past the supply-sided development of reference models predominant in the science world has distanced itself from their demand-sided use in business and administration. This contribution has been devoted to this problem.

The rationale for the "reference model management" approach selected here is based on an analysis of the state of the art in reference modeling, whereby potentials were seen in two respects. First, we have shown that the contributions at hand comprehensively address the design of construction results but, however, disregard the corresponding construction processes which make the retraceability and, thus the reuse of the results, difficult. On the other hand, results pertaining to the design of the construction processes are available; they concentrate, however, either on the development or the use of the reference models or they do not sufficiently reduce the chronological, contextual and organizational separation between both processes. Reference model management was therefore formulated explicitly with the purpose of recreating the connection between the separated processes in reference model development and usage. Thus, within the framework of a process-oriented interpretation, the integration of both processes has been identified as a third function in reference model management next to the development and usage of reference models. The design and realization of an information system for the management of reference models were concretized as objectives here because, due to the magnitude of the models in modeling projects, the economic construction and use of models is only possible with the help of IT-tools. The development of this information system referred to as a reference model management system was structured by a framework.

The knowledge won in this analysis can be used as a starting point for more detailed research work. Thus, for example, empirical studies could be made to investigate whether the insights won more or less deductively coincide with the reality of business practice. One could also investigate how the use of the RMMS affects efficiency in modeling projects.

The investigation of the effects of this prototype in operational business reality is seen as a future challenge for the author in his research activities.

The reasons for further research in the field of reference modeling lie in the fact that up to now no uniform reference modeling language has been established in theory or practice. Even the reference modeling-specific extensions of established languages in information modeling created primarily for research are rarely used in practice. Reference modeling research must carefully weigh formal precision against pragmatic manageability when developing such a modeling language: If modeling languages have formal semantics then they are suited to machine processing, but the interpretation of real-world connections can become more difficult. In this case, studies should be carried out to resolve this conflict. Thus, one of the central tasks in the future of reference modeling researchers should be to not only present the consequences of their results for science, but also for modeling practice.

Obviously, more fundamental research is required in order to understand the effects connected with the creation and usage of reference models in science and practice. However, this topic is dealt with in the future in reference modeling research, the compilation of improved knowledge about application system and organization design remains a central task in the field of information systems. With the cognition won within the framework of this study, a concept and a prototypical implementation for the management of this knowledge, which is represented by reference models, are to be available.

Acknowledgments

The system presented in this article was developed at the Institute for Information Systems (IWi) at the German Research Center for Artificial Intelligence (DFKI) in Saarbruecken. The development of the system was funded by the "Deutsche Forschungsgemeinschaft" (German Research Foundation) within the research project "Reference Model-Based (Reverse-) Customizing of Service Information Systems" as part of the initiative BRID. The author is also grateful to Johann Spuling for supporting the implementation of the presented prototype.

References

Becker, J., Delfmann, P., Knackstedt, R., & Kuropka, D. (2002). Configurative reference modeling. In J. Becker & R. Knackstedt (Eds.), *Wissensmanagement mit Referenzmodellen. Konzepte für die Anwendungssystem- und Organisationsgestaltung* (pp. 25-144). Berlin: Springer. [in German]

Becker, J., & Schütte, R. (2004). *Retail information systems* (2nd ed.) Landsberg/Lech: Moderne Industrie. [in German]

Fettke, P., & Loos, P. (2002a). The reference modeling catalogue as an instrument for knowledge management—methodology and application. In J. Becker & R. Knackstedt (Eds.),

Wissensmanagement mit Referenzmodellen : Konzepte für die Anwendungssystem- und Organisationsgestaltung (pp. 3-24). Heidelberg: Physica. [in German]

Fettke, P., & Loos, P. (2002b). Methods for reusing reference models: Overview and taxonomy. In J. Becker & R. Knackstedt (Eds.), *Referenzmodellierung 2002: Methoden—Modelle—Erfahrungen* (pp. 9-33). Münster: Westfälische Wilhelms-Universität. [in German]

Fettke, P., & Loos, P. (2003). Classification of reference models: A methodology and its application. *Information Systems and e-Business Management, 1*(1), 35-53.

Fettke, P., & Loos, P. (2004b). Reference models for retail enterprises. *HMD - Praxis der Wirtschaftsinformatik, 235*, 15-25. [in German]

Gartner Inc. (Ed.). (1996, June 20). *BPR-Tool Market* (Gartner's Application Development & Maintenance Research Note M–600–144). Stamford, CT: Gartner Research.

Gerber, S., & Müller-Luschnat, G. (1999). Are reference process models useful in practice? In J. Desel, K. Pohl, & A. Schürr (Eds.), *Modellierung ,99: Workshop der gesellschaft für informatik e. V. (GI), März 1999 in Karlsruhe* (pp. 27-42). Stuttgart: Teubner. [in German]

Hammer, M., & Champy, J. (1993). *Reengineering the corporation: A manifesto for business revolution* (1st ed.). London: Brealey.

Hars, A. (1994). *Reference data models: Foundations for efficient data modeling.* Wiesbaden: Gabler. [in German]

IDS Scheer AG. (Ed.). (2003). *ARIS Toolset, ARIS Version 6.2.1.31203* [Computer software]. Saarbrücken: IDS Scheer AG.

Klabunde, S., & Wittmann, M. (1998). *Reference models and model libraries.* Saarbrücken: Institut für Wirtschaftsinformatik [in German].

Lang, K. (1997). *Business process management with reference model components.* Wiesbaden: DUV. [in German]

Mendling, J., & Nüttgens, M. (2004). XML-based reference modelling: Foundations of an EPC markup language. In J. Becker & P. Delfmann (Eds.), *Referenzmodellierung : Grundlagen, techniken und domänenbezogene Anwendung* (pp. 51-71). Heidelberg: Physica.

Mili, A., Mili, R., & Mittermeir, R. T. (1998). A survey of software reuse libraries. *Annals of Software Engineering, 5*(0), 349-414.

Oberweis, A. (Ed.). (2003). *TREBES: Transformation von Referenzmodellen für betriebswirtschaftliche Standardsoftware.* [in German] [On-line]. Retrieved August 17, 2003, from http://lwi2.wiwi.uni-frankfurt.de/projekte/trebes/

Remme, M. (1997). *Designing business processes.* Wiesbaden: Gabler. [in German]

Resco GmbH (Ed.). (2002). *EMM : Enterprise model management.* Hamburg: Resco.

Robson, G. D. (1991). *Continuous process improvement: Simplifying work flow systems.* New York: Free Press.

Rosemann, M., & van der Aalst, W. M. P. (2003). *A configurable reference modelling language* (Rep. No. FIT-TR-2003-05). Brisbane: Queensland University of Technology.

Scheer, A.-W. (1994a). A software product is born. *Information Systems, 19*(8), 607-624.

Scheer, A.-W. (1994b). *Business process engineering: Reference models for industrial enterprises* (2ⁿᵈ ed.). Berlin: Springer.

Scheer, A.-W., Habermann, F., Thomas, O., & Seel, C. (2002). Cooperative organizational memories for IT-based process knowledge management. In M. Blay-Fornarino, A. M. Pinna-Dery, K. Schmidt, & P. Zaraté (Eds.), *Cooperative systems design: A challenge of the mobility age. Proceedings of the 6ᵗʰ International Conference on the Design of Cooperative Systems (COOP2002)* (pp. 209-225). Amsterdam, The Netherlands: IOS Press.

Schlagheck, B. (2000). *Object-oriented reference models for controlling processes and projects*. Wiesbaden: DUV. [in German]

Schütte, R. (1998). *Guidelines for reference modeling*. Wiesbaden: Gabler. [in German]

Schwegmann, A. (1999). *Object-oriented reference modeling*. Wiesbaden: DUV. [in German]

Sinur, J. (2004). *Magic quadrant for business process analysis, 2004*. Stamford, CT: Gartner Research. Gartner's Application Development & Maintenance Research Note M-22-0651, March 4, 2004.

Thomas, O. (2006a). Understanding the term reference model in information systems research: History, literature analysis and explanation. In C. Bussler & A. Haller (Eds.), *Business process management workshops, BPM 2005 International Workshops, BPI, BPD, ENEI, BPRM, WSCOBPM, BPS,* Nancy, France, September 5, 2005, *Revised Selected Papers* (pp. 484-496). Berlin: Springer.

Thomas, O. (2006b). Version management for reference models: Design and implementation. In *Multikonferenz Wirtschaftsinformatik 2006 (MKWI'06). Universität Passau*. Accepted for presentation and publication in the track "reference modeling."

Thomas, O., & Scheer, A.-W. (2006, January 4-7). Tool support for the collaborative design of reference models—a business engineering perspective. In R. H. Sprague (Ed.), *Proceedings of the 39ᵗʰ Annual Hawaii International Conference on System Sciences,* Kauai, HI. Abstracts and CD-ROM of Full Papers. Los Alamitos, CA: IEEE Computer Society Press.

vom Brocke, J. (2003). *Reference modelling: Towards collaborative arrangements of design processes*. Berlin: Logos. [in German]

Chapter XV

Configuration Management for Reference Models

Robert Braun, Technische Universität Dresden, Germany

Werner Esswein, Technische Universität Dresden, Germany

Andreas Gehlert, Technische Universität Dresden, Germany

Jens Weller, Technische Universität Dresden, Germany

Abstract

In this chapter we analyse how a configuration management system can support reference modelling activities. We argue that a configuration management system can not only record the changes made to a single model but also administer different relations between models. To show how such a system can be useful for reference modelling, we analyse the different relations between models from a reference modelling perspective and formulate our findings as requirements for an ideal system. In the next step, we show how configuration management operations map to these requirements. Finally, we demonstrate that the usage of a configuration management system can significantly increase the productivity of the reference modelling activities.

Introduction

Since their first appearance, models have become increasingly important in the economy. Together with modelling languages and methods, models have significantly influenced the way software systems are developed today. At the beginning of the 1990s, accompanied by new findings in management science, the generally positive experiences with modelling were transferred from software systems engineering to organisational issues (Fettke & Loos, 2003). Established modelling techniques are broadly applied for describing business processes and corporate structures in an organization (Scheer, 2000). The significance of the modelling discipline is embodied by the proposal to define it as the core of the information systems discipline (Weber, 2003).

Understanding models as outcomes of processes and means for knowledge management within an enterprise, all active models are constantly changing. These changes are induced by the flow of the environment of that enterprise. As a consequence, a permanent evolutionary cycle of each model results after the model was initially constructed (see Figure 1).

In order to plan and execute a modelling project, it is essential to record all changes made to all models. This documentation can be used, first, to go back to a model version in the case of a faulty development, and second, to learn from the modifications for future modelling projects (see also method use rationale in Rossi, Ramesh, Lyytinen, & Tolvanen, 2004).

Documenting the modifications of an artefact in general has a long tradition within the software development and production industry. This tradition was manifested in the ISO 9001:2000 norm. According to this norm, a certification of a company requires a *configuration management system* (ISO, 2000), which enables a systematic recording of all changes made to artefacts within this company. Additionally, such a configuration management system is a prerequisite to reach CMM level two (SEI, 2002).

Contrary to the software industry, where the artefacts are mainly the application's source code, we focus here on models only. Consequently, the need for a model configuration management system arises (Esswein, Kluge, & Greiffenberg, 2002). By definition, a *model configuration management system* includes methods to record, control and manage all

Figure 1. The general evolution cycle of a model

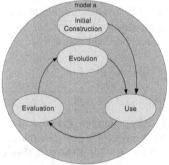

Evolution Cycle

changes made to a model through its entire lifetime (Esswein, Kluge, & Greiffenberg, 2002; Greiffenberg, 2003).

A *model* is generally understood as "… the result of a construction done by a modeller, who examines the elements of a system for a specific purpose such as redesign of an organization or the development of an information system at a given point of time with a specific language" (Schütte & Rotthowe, 1998, p. 243). The model is the result of modellers' abilities to structure a universe of discourse (Dresbach, 1996; Molière, 1984; Schütte & Rotthowe, 1998).

Reference models are an important model type. A *reference model* is a model, which structures and guides the creation of an *enterprise model* (Fettke & Loos, 2003). The main idea of a reference model is to reduce the costs of the construction of an enterprise model by re-using knowledge already specified in the reference model (Rosemann & Aalst, in press). The reference character, however, is not an intrinsic property but a role of one model in relation to another. This *referencing relation* is characterised by the knowledge of the reference model incorporated into the enterprise model (vom Brocke, 2003). Furthermore, as reference models are models, they are constantly changing as well. Thus, the need to document these changes arises as well.

We provide an in-depth analysis of the relationships between reference and enterprise model and show in which ways a model configuration management system can support the reference modelling process from the creation of the reference model till the creation of the enterprise model.

The chapter is organised as follows: We introduce the notion of reference modelling as well as software and model configuration management in section 2. Requirements for an ideal system for supporting reference model construction and use are raised in section 3. In section 4, we show how these requirements can be supported by a configuration management system. In section 5, we discuss questions, which are subject to further research, and conclude the chapter in section 6.

Background

This section is divided into three subsections. In subsection one (reference models) we discuss the state of the art of reference modelling and use. The main result of this discussion is to specify the different roles of and relations between models. In subsection two (configuration management) we give an overview of the software configuration management discipline and describe the main configuration management operations. Last, we apply this knowledge to model configuration management (subsection three).

Reference Models

As the reference modelling discipline matured, different techniques were put forward to structure the adaptation of reference models (Becker, Delfmann, Dreiling, Knackstedt, & Kuropka, 2004; Becker, Delfmann, & Knackstedt, 2004; vom Brocke, 2003; Recker, Rosemann,

Aalst, & Mendling, 2005; Rosemann & Aalst, in press; Turowski, 2002). Becker, Delfmann, and Knackstedt (2004) provided the following classification of these techniques:

1. **Rule-based techniques**[1]: This set of techniques is based on specific constructs in the reference model's grammar. These constructs provide formal means for adapting the reference model. This set includes model type selection, element type selection, element selection as well as a notational and representational variation. All these techniques are tailored to hide or exchange special parts of the reference model during the adaptation process (see Table 1 for details).

2. **Formative techniques:** Formative techniques are based on creative activities of the person who adapts the reference model. These techniques include analogous construction, specialisation, instantiation and aggregation. In contrast to rule-based techniques, formative techniques do not only remove content from the reference model but also add additional knowledge (see vom Brocke, 2003, and Becker, Delfmann, & Knackstedt, 2004, for details).

Table 1. Overview of rule-based techniques (Source: Becker, Delfmann, & Knackstedt, 2004)

Operation	Description	Usage
ModelTypeSelection	Selects parts of the reference model, which are instances of a specific meta model (modelled in a specific grammar)	Delete all data modelling content from the copy of a reference model
ElementTypeSelection	Enables or disables all elements which are an instance of a specific type	All elements that are an instance of the concept entity-type might be deleted from the copy of a reference model
ElementSelection	Reference model elements are enabled or disabled according to specific criteria these model elements employ	Delete all fully automatable processes from the copy of a reference model
NotationalVariation	Replaces the model element notations	A model element "invoice" may be called "bill"
RepresentationalVariation	Replaces the model element symbols	Changing the representation of model elements belonging to the model element type "function" by using a desktop-symbol instead of the ordinarily used symbol of a rectangle or new arrangement of the model elements from top/down to left/right

The distinction of the two different adaptation techniques above has an important consequence for the quality of the referencing relation between the reference and the enterprise model:

- **Strict referencing:** The relation between one model (reference model) and another model (enterprise model) is said to be strict if and only if the reference model was created with a reference modelling grammar containing constructs which implement rule-based techniques (Rosemann & Aalst, in press) and the enterprise model was created solely by using these rule-based techniques.

- **Loose referencing:** The relation between one model (reference model) and another model (enterprise model) is said to be loose if the enterprise model was not derived by configuration mechanisms provided by the reference model.

Both referencing relations can be distinguished by their degree of formality. While in a strict referencing relation the enterprise model is derived by using formal notions within the reference model, in a loose referencing relation the enterprise model is derived by using creative techniques. In the first case the relation between both models is formally defined while in the second case the relation exists only informally.

To illustrate these referencing relations, we use the research framework shown in Figure 2. Model II represents a model which is supposed to serve as a reference model. We assume that this model is created in a modelling grammar containing the constructs needed to establish a strict referencing relation to another model. The sets of models I and III have no special features. From this setting we can distinguish three relations between the model(s) I, II and III as shown in the figure.

Figure 2. Theoretical foundation: A role-based framework for referencing

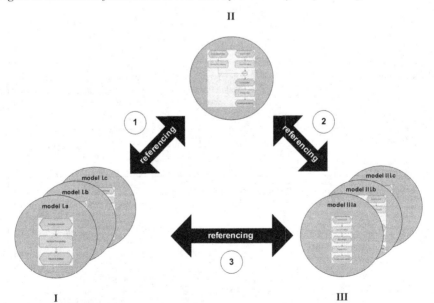

We explain the research framework in line with the process of construction and using reference models (configuration and build time) proposed by Rosemann and van der Aalst (in press):

1. The first step represents the creation of a model, which should be used as a reference model later on (referencing Relation 1, reading direction: upward from I to II). This can be done by either constructing the model from scratch based on theoretical foundations or by incorporating best practices (Scheer, 1994). Within the latter approach, two or more models (I.a…I.c) can be compared in order to find commonalities and differences. The consolidation forms model II (Rosemann & Aalst, in press). Additionally, the differences of the models in I are attached to this common core of model II using the rule-based mechanisms described above. In this setting the models in I are reference models of model II. The relation between these models is a loose referencing relation since model II is not derived using rule-based mechanisms. The same mechanism cannot only be used to construct model II but also to evolve it.

2. If the model II is created, it can be used to derive enterprise models by applying the rule-based mechanisms (referencing Relation 2, reading direction: downward from II to III). The result of the operation is one or more enterprise model(s) (III). Since the rule-based mechanisms have been applied, there is a strict referencing relation between model II and the set of models III. The mechanisms can also be applied to evolve an existing model in set III.

3. Since all models undergo constant change, there might be the need to incorporate new knowledge of the models in III back into the model II (referencing Relation 2, reading direction: upward from III to II). In this situation, the models in III become reference models for model II. Since in our setting the set of models III does not have any rule-based constructs, the relation between III and II is a loose referencing relation.

4. The same can be said about the relation between model II and the set of models I. If model II is modified, these modifications might be reflected in one of the models in set I (referencing Relation 1, reading direction: downward from II to I). The referencing relation is loose and the formative techniques are applied.

Additionally, loose referencing relations can also be identified between the sets of models I and III. If a model in I is constructed by applying formative techniques to a model in set III, the latter model becomes a reference model of the former and vice versa.

Configuration Management

Configuration management (CM) has been intensely discussed in the software engineering literature (Conradi & Westfechtel, 1998; Estublier, 2000; Feiler, 1991; Thompson, 1997; Zeller, 1997). In this context, CM serves two different purposes. First, as a management support discipline, CM is basically used for controlling the evolution of software. Second, CM can be seen as a means for supporting software development. In this sense, CM is used to control the modification of software artifacts (code) and to support cooperative work in software development teams. Software configuration management "… is the discipline that enables us to keep the evolving software products under control, and thus contributes to satisfying quality and delay constraints" (Estublier, 2000, p. 1).

Recently, configuration management was discussed as a general means and thus independently from software artifacts. Today CM does not primarily focus on software artifacts but is used to control changes of products in general. The term configuration management is therefore more generally defined as an "…activity that applies technical and administrative direction over the life cycle of a product, its configuration items, and related product configuration information" (ISO, 2003, p. 4). While the focus changed, the superordinated aim of configuration management did not. Even in respect to a more general view, CM is used to increase process and product quality (ISO, 2000).

The basic element of a configuration management system is the *configuration item*. A configuration item is an element (product, source code, model, etc.) which is controlled by the system. A *version* represents a state of a configuration item (Conradi & Westfechtel, 1998; Zeller, 1997). Generally, each time a change in the item is made, a new version of it is created. Particularly, the type of changes, which results in a new version of the item, is prescribed at the beginning of all configuration management activities. This prescription is necessary because of the different complexity of the configuration items.

1.   Changes made to the configuration item for the purpose of the development or maintenance are called historical versions or *revisions* (Thompson, 1997; Zeller, 1997). Revisions are important for tracking changes of such a configuration item made over time. These revisions are ordered chronologically so that each revision usually has exactly one predecessor (see Figure 3, revisions-axis). There is only one exception to this rule: If two versions are merged (see below), the resulting version has multiple predecessors (Conradi & Westfechtel, 1998).

2.   In contrast to revisions, we speak of logical *variants* if more than one version of a configuration item exists concurrently at a given time (Conradi & Westfechtel, 1998; Zeller, 1997). The main rational for creating variants is an adaptation of one and the same configuration item for different purposes (e.g., producing the same product for different customers with only minor differences; see Figure 3, variants-axis).

Figure 3. Version graph of a version family (Source: Zeller, 1997, p. 11)

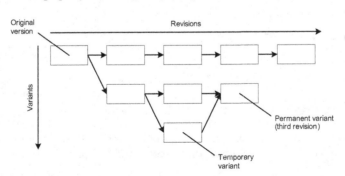

3. Special kinds of variants are *temporary variants*. Like variants, temporary variants will be created in parallel to existing versions. However, these variants are only created for the purpose of simultaneously working on one and the same configuration item. The main difference between variants and temporal variants is that temporal variants are considered to be merged to one version after a short period of time (Feiler, 1991; see also Figure 3, temporary variant).

A *configuration* represents "… the functional and physical characteristics of a product…" (ISO, 2003, p. 4). The configuration concept is necessary because in the CM system, the versions of different configuration items are independent from each other (Estublier, 2000). However, each configuration item is only one part of the product. A configuration is, therefore, a bundle of versions of configuration items. It is itself a configuration item and comprises a version. As a consequence, if one item belonging to a configuration is modified, a new configuration with a new version is created. This new configuration succeeds the previously existing one.

A *version family* is a collection of all versions of exactly one configuration item. In general, a version family is illustrated by the use of version graphs (Conradi & Westfechtel, 1998; Zeller, 1997; see also Figure 3).

A *configuration management system (CMS)* is a socio-technical system that implements configuration management. However, we only focus on the automatable parts of a CMS and use

Table 2. Configuration management operations

Operation	Description	Usage	Specialization
CheckOut	Transferring a version from one workspace to a *sub*ordinated workspace	Cooperative working	Export
CheckIn	Transferring a version from one workspace to a *super*ordinated workspace	Consolidation of temporary variants	Import Merge
Branch	Creating a new development path for a configuration item	Parallel versions of one product because of slightly different requirements	—
Merge	Integration of two versions of configuration items of the same version family	Consolidation of temporary variants modified by different users at the same time	—
Lend	Transferring configuration items into other configurations	Copying parts of a product into another product	—

the term configuration management and configuration management system synonymously. Software implementations of the automatable parts of the CMS store all configuration items, including all modifications made to such an item in a central repository. The repository is the top-level workspace, which has one ore more subordinated workspaces. A *workspace* is "… the individual area of a developer, isolating him from changes made by others, and isolating others from his changes" (Zeller, 1997, p. 43). Modifications are not applied to the repository itself but only to the subordinated workspaces. This raises the need to transfer configuration items between workspaces.

The operation CheckOut (CheckIn) transfers configuration items from the repository (user's workspace) to a user's workspace (repository). Additionally, CheckIn leads to a new revision of a configuration item. While the CheckIn operation creates new revisions, the Branch operation leads to a new variant within the repository. The number of variants within the repository is theoretically unlimited. The integration of several variants is done by the Merge operation. In this case, a revision of a development path DP_1 is firstly transferred into a local workspace (CheckOut operation) and secondly transferred back into the repository by defining the target development path DP_2 (Merge operation).

Because we intensively discuss the usability of merging configuration items later in this chapter, we shortly present the principles of this operation below. Although different strategies for realising the Merge operation can be found in CM literature, we concentrate on the *three-way-merge* presented by Conradi and Westfechtel (1998) because it reduces the number of decisions to be performed by the user and is therefore used in most of today's CM tools. Using the three-way-merge, the variants V_1 and V_2 to be merged must have a common predecessor V_0 (if there is no common predecessor, V_1 and V_2 represent different configuration items). Firstly, a so-called delta analysis is performed, which compares V_1 and V_2 to V_0. The results of this analysis is *delta* (V_0, V_1) and *delta* (V_0, V_2). Secondly, both deltas are compared to each other. The result of this comparison is depicted in Table 3. Lastly, the creation of V_R is afterwards performed on the basis of the decisions made in the second step.

All CM operations affect configuration items. In practice, however, it is common to use the presented operations on configurations too, because it is interesting for a user to know how changes of a configuration item affect the whole product represented by the configuration. In this case, the CM operations are simply accomplished on all items of the chosen configuration (e.g., transferring all items of a configuration into a user's workspace using the CheckOut operation).

Model Configuration Management

As we discussed in the introduction, models change during their entire lifetime. Thereby, configuration management can support the creation and maintenance of these models. In the literature, however, this problem achieved only little attention. Esswein, Kluge, and Greiffenberg (2002) presented a model configuration management system. The authors argue that CM can increase the quality of the modelling process as well as the quality of the resulting models. The feasibility of this theoretical building block has been proved by implementing the model configuration management system into a generic modelling tool (Cubetto Toolset, 2005).

Table 3. Resulting versions of the Merge *operation*

	Delta (V_0, V_1)	Delta (V_0, V_2)	Resulting action (content of V_R)
(1)	$V_0 = V_1$	$V_0 = V_2$	$V_R = V_1$ or $V_R = V_2$ (same result because $V_1 = V_2$)
(2)	$V_0 \neq V_1$	$V_0 = V_2$	$V_R = V_1$ (only V_1 changed)
(3)	$V_0 = V_1$	$V_0 \neq V_2$	$V_R = V_2$ (only V_2 changed)
(4)	$V_0 \neq V_1$	$V_0 \neq V_2$	Result strongly depends on the kind of configuration items stored in CMS. In software engineering, source code files are compared and will be merged line by line in general (Zeller, 1997). Regarding more complex configuration items, a merge of properties or a decision from the user is necessary.

The configuration management of models is based on the experiences made in the software engineering. Thus, the structure and terms are identical to the ones introduced above. The model CM fully implements the before-mentioned CM operations. Model elements are represented as configuration items in the configuration management system. A complete model represents a configuration.

Because of the principles of the CM to store all changes as revisions, it is always possible to go back and forth in the revision graph, for instance, to restore an older version of a model. The need to document the modifications of the models as demanded in the introduction of this chapter is furthermore supported by version documents linked to each model element version. Version documents contain a general description of the model element (configuration item) as well as the name of the users who created, modified or deleted that element (Greiffenberg, 2003).

Additionally, model CM supports cooperative development of conceptual models. "In this case, multiple developers work in parallel on different versions" (Conradi & Westfechtel, 1998, p. 240). Therefore, all modifications of a model are made in workspaces (Esswein, Kluge, & Greiffenberg, 2002). Via the operation CheckOut, users can copy a model from the repository into their local workspaces (see Figure 4, number 3). Because local workspaces are independent from each other, modifying the model in a local workspace has no influence on the local copy of the model inside a different workspace. As we mentioned in subsection two (configuration management), the checkout operation leads to temporary variants (models "$M_{B3.1}$" and "$M_{B3.2}$" in Figure 4). For an adequate support of teamwork, these temporary variants have to be integrated after all users have finished their work (Greiffenberg, 2003). In the model CM, the process of integration is realized by the Merge operation (see Figure 4, number 4).

We have identified two types of relations between models so far. The first type has its origin in the configuration management discipline and describes temporal relations between two models (predecessor/successor). The second type is motivated by the findings in the reference modelling discipline and describes a referencing relation between two models. We can map both relations to the configuration management concepts as follows:

- **Temporal relation between models:** Temporal versions are needed to trace changes made to models over time, to record the decisions associated with these changes (construction rationale) as well as to recover a previous version in the case of erroneous updates (Conradi & Westfechtel, 1998; Zeller, 1997). As argued in subsection two (configuration management), this type of relation between two models is directly supported by a configuration management system with the concept of a revision.

Figure 4. Relationship kinds between models

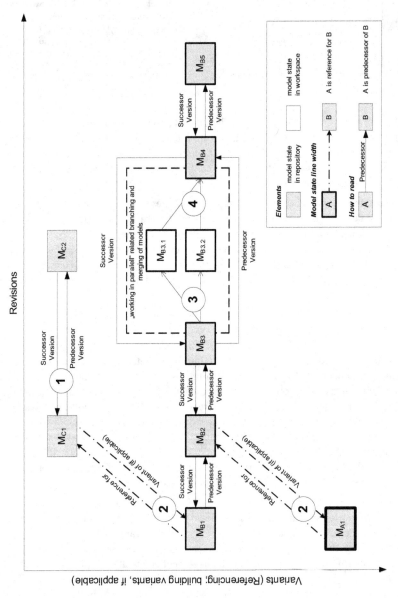

- **Referencing relation between models:** When applying a reference model to derive or evolve an enterprise model or to use the enterprise model for an evolution of a reference model, we talk about *referencing*. When the enterprise model is derived using the rule-based mechanisms of the reference model (strict referencing), the enterprise model can be seen as a variant of the reference model. Consequently, a model configuration management system supports this operation. When the enterprise model is derived using creative, formative techniques (loose referencing), the resulting enterprise model is neither a revision nor a variant of the reference model. Thus, loose referencing is not supported by a configuration management system.

The results of this analysis are depicted in Figure 4. Two important consequences can be drawn. First, while revisions produce temporal models of the same family (Figure 4, number 1), referencing splits (merges) the development path of one (many) model(s) into at least two (exactly one) distinct paths (path) (Figure 4, number 2, 3 and 4).

Requirements for Supporting Reference Model Construction and Use

As pointed out in the introduction, the aim of the chapter is to combine the formal means of a configuration management system with the requirements for a tool support which arise from the reference modelling discipline. In this section we use the understanding of reference models introduced in section 2 and derive requirements for a system which supports reference modelling activities.

According to Figure 2, a complete specification of all requirements can be achieved by investigating all referencing relations. In this chapter, however, we focus only on the relations depicted in Figure 5. The requirements of this subset of relations are derived in the following subsections.

Support for Reference Model Construction

Since the word *reference* signifies a role (reference), model creation undergoes the same process as the construction of any model. As previously described, building a model which is useful for deriving other models can be done in two distinct ways: First, the model can be created by the experience and theoretical knowledge of the modellers only. Second, it can be constructed by a comparison-based consolidation of different models (Rosemann & Aalst, in press; see also Figure 5, number i).

- **Re1:** The system should be able to extract the core of two or more models by comparing them.

Figure 5. Use cases within the reference model framework

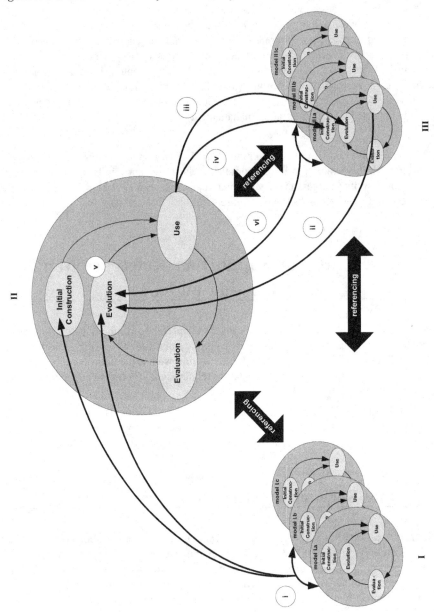

Furthermore, the reference model might evolve in the same (comparison-based) way (see Figure 5, number i (again) and number vi). Additionally, it might desirable to compare the reference model with an enterprise model derived from this reference model in order to extract, analyse and include the changes made to the enterprise model over time back into the reference model (see Figure 5, number ii).

- **Re2:** The system should support the unification of a reference model with its enterprise models to detect and analyse the changes made to the enterprise model.

The contrary might be desirable as well in the following use case. An enterprise model was derived from a reference model. If the reference model undergoes changes over time, it might be necessary to incorporate these changes into the enterprise model (see Figure 5, number iii).

- **Re3:** The system should support the unification of an enterprise model with its reference model for the purpose of reflecting the changes made to the reference model within the enterprise model.

Requirements Re2 and Re3 represent a specialisation of Re1. Consequently, the evolution of a reference model as well as an enterprise model can also be implemented by comparing the respective models. However, as we examine later in this chapter, supporting Re1 is generally difficult while supporting Re2 and Re3 is not. For this reason we treat these three requirements separately.

While Re2 and Re3 focus on the evolution of (reference) models, both are based on existing models that were created out of a reference model. In the reference modelling field it is therefore essential to support the creation of enterprise models out of reference models using the techniques leading to strict referencing.

- **Re4:** The system should support the creation of enterprise models out of reference models (Figure 5, number iv).

Lastly, it might also be desirable to store different versions of one and the same model to be able to roll back to a past version in case of an erroneous update (see section 2 and Figure 5, number v, as an example).

- **Re5:** The system should support the recovery of a past version of a model.

Support for Reference Model Use

Since the paper aims to combine the formal means of a configuration management system and the operations for the adoption of a reference model, we will focus on the rule-based techniques presented in section 2 only.

Figure 6. General procedure of a Configuration *(Adapted from Brocke, 2003)*

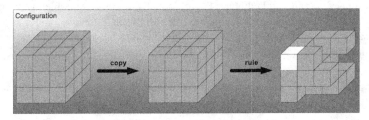

For the subsequent description, we consider the following use-case when adapting a reference model (see Figure 6). First, the reference model is fully duplicated. Second, the reference model is modified using the rule-based techniques. From this use-case we can derive the first requirement:

- **Re6:** The system must be able to duplicate the reference model.

As described above, a model might comprise divergent views on the problem domain using different modelling grammars to express their content. On the highest granularity level, the ModelTypeSelection operation operates on the meta-model level. It selects parts of the reference model, which are instances of a specific meta-model (modelled in a specific grammar). In our use-case, the model type selection operation is used to delete certain grammars, such as all data modelling content, from the copy of the reference model (Becker, Delfmann, & Knackstedt, 2004).

The ElementTypeSelection operation operates on the meta-level too, but employs a finer granularity. This operation deletes all elements which are an instance of a specific type from the copy of the model. For example, all elements that are an instance of the concept entity-type might be deleted from the specific model in our use-case by applying this operation (Becker, Delfmann, & Knackstedt, 2004).

To achieve a finer granularity, ElementSelection was introduced. This operation is employed on the instance level. These model elements employ model elements deleted according to specific criteria. This operation might delete all fully automatable processes from the reference model (Becker, Delfmann, & Knackstedt, 2004).

We can derive three requirements from the model: type selection, element type selection and element selection operations:

- **Re7:** The system must be able to delete model elements according to their attribute's values.
- **Re8:** The system must be able to define a named collection of model elements.
- **Re9:** The system must be able to define a named collection of meta-model elements.

Figure 7. Relations between requirements

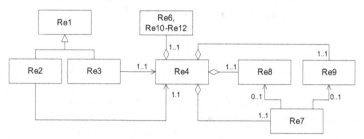

Requirement Re7 provides direct support for element selection. Since model type selection deletes all model elements of a certain type, it can be traced back to model element selection under the condition that the instance-of relation between model elements and model types is available (Re8). The same can be said about the relation between model element types and model types. If a named collection of model element types is defined, the model type selection technique can be reduced to element type selection (Re9).

Notational variation applies to the model as a whole. The idea is to be able to replace all domain language expression within the model by appropriate synonyms ("bill" for "invoice"). Thus, we derive the following requirement:

- **Re10:** Domain language expressions are handled independently from the model elements. The system supports the definition of synonymous expressions.

Representational variation takes the symbolic nature of the modelling language symbols into account. As the notational variation, it operates on the model as a whole as well and replaces the model element symbols. Additionally, a new arrangement of the model elements (top down vs. left-right) might also be supported. This leads to requirements:

- **Re11:** The graphical symbols must be separated from the model elements. The definition of alternative symbols must be supported.
- **Re12:** The system applies graphical layout algorithms to change the arrangement of the symbols according to the requirements of the user.

Relations Between Requirements

Having analysed the requirements, we can now derive the dependencies between them (see Figure 7). As described above, requirement Re2 and Re3 are specialisations from requirement Re1. Furthermore, Re2 and Re3 depend on requirement Re4 because these requirements are based on the existence of at least one reference model. Requirement Re4 calls for the creation of enterprise models by adapting a reference model. This creation includes the requirements Re6-Re12. Additionally, to implement the model type selection and the element type selection, requirement Re7 can be used (associations from Re7 to Re8 and Re9).

Configuration Management Support
for Reference Modeling

This section will present an overview of the state of the art in configuration management support for reference modelling. We use the requirements derived in the previous section and explain how these requirements can be fulfilled by configuration management operations presented in section 2. This overview is structured according to section 3. First, we show how configuration management can support the construction of reference models (Re1-Re5). Second, we analyse if, and in the positive case, how, configuration management supports the adaptation of reference models (Re6-Re12).

Figure 8. Update of a reference model by the incorporation of knowledge from (a new revision) an enterprise model

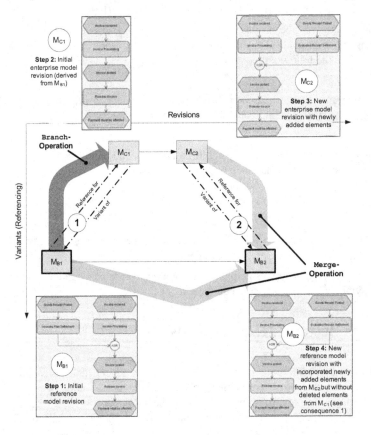

Configuration Management Support for Reference Model Construction

Configuration management operations provide a technology for the construction and evolution of reference models (see again Figure 5, numbers i, ii and vi). This subsection deals with the advantages and disadvantages as well as the limitations of using configuration management operations for this purpose (Re1-Re5).

Initial Reference Model Construction

Configuration management enables the merging two completely different models via the Lend operation. Since all configuration mechanisms build upon the sucessor/predecessor relations of different versions of the configuration items, a merge of different models with the Lend operations results in copying one model into another. It is, therefore, impossible to support a comparison-based consolidation of two or more models by extraction of a common core. Instead, mechanisms are needed to compare models on a semantic level (see section 5 for a short further discussion):

* **Conclusion 1:** Requirement Re1 cannot be supported with configuration management.

Reference Model Evolution

To incorporate the knowledge acquired in the enterprise model back into the reference model (Re2), the Merge-Operation can be applied. The enterprise model "M_{C1}" was initially derived from the reference model "M_{B1}" (see Figure 8, number 1).[2] Because of the modification made to the enterprise model, a new revision of this model was created, "M_{C2}." Merging "M_{C2}" with "M_{B1}" results in a new revision of the reference model ("M_{B2}," Figure 8, number 2).

It seems that there is an alternative way to the merge operation. It includes branching the enterprise model "M_{C2}" to derive the reference model "M_{B2}." Besides the fact the "M_{B2}" looses the relation to its predecessor "M_{B1}," all rule-based techniques of a reference model will not be included in "M_{B2}" since they are not present in the enterprise model (Rosemann & Aalst, in press) and cannot be added during the branching process. Therefore, this alternative should be generally avoided.

Carrying out the merging operation has the following consequences:

1. All model elements of "M_{B1}" that are deleted while adapting the reference model revision "M_{B1}" when deriving the enterprise model revision "M_{C1}" do not occur in "M_{B2}" (strongly undesired use case; this is depicted as an example within Figure 8).

2. All model elements of "M_{B1}" that are copied into the enterprise model revision "M_{C1}" do occur again in "M_{B2}." All modifications made to such a model element in "M_{C2}" will be reflected in the new revision of the reference model "M_{B2}" (desired use case).

Figure 9. Update of an enterprise model by the incorporation of knowledge from (a new revision) a reference model

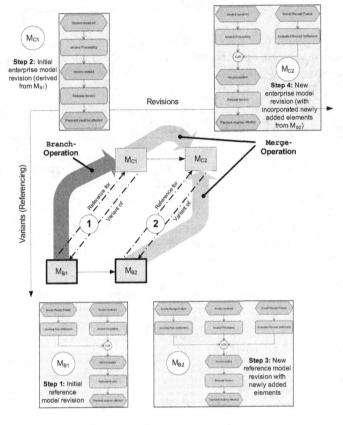

3.   All model elements added to "M_{C2}" appear in "M_{B2}" after the merge (desired use case).

4.   If both models, the reference model "M_{B1}" and the enterprise model "M_{C1}," were modified concurrently, the merge operation might include a conflict resolution (desired use case).

•   **Conclusion 2:** Requirement Re2 can be well supported with a configuration management system. Section 5, "Future Trends," discusses possibilities to enhance the applicability of the system.

Model Evolution

To update an enterprise model by the incorporation of knowledge from (a new revision of) a reference model (Re3), the Merge-operation can be applied as well. This use case is analogous to the one described in the previous subsection. Figure 9 depicts the following: "M_{C1}," the initial revision of the enterprise model "M_C" was created by the adaptation of the reference model "M_{B1}" using the branch operator (Figure 9, number 1). While using the enterprise model, a new revision of the reference model might evolve ("M_{B2}"). To incorporate this new knowledge into the enterprise model, the model "M_{C1}" must be merged with the new revision of the reference model "M_{B2}" (Figure 9, number 2).

Since the mechanism described here is very similar to the one described in the previous subsection, the question arises if it is feasible to use the adaptation of the reference model "M_{B2}" in the same way as "M_{C1}" was initially derived. This method, however, has the disadvantage of loosing the relationship between "M_{C1}" and "M_{C2}" within the configuration management system. This means that any modification made to "M_{C1}"will not be reflected in "M_{C2}." Consequently, this possibility is not desirable.

With respect to the underlying logic of the versioning of configuration items (see again section 2, Table 3), merging "M_{C1}" and "M_{B2}" has the following implications for the resulting model "M_{C2}":

1.   All model elements of "M_{B1}" that remain unchanged in the revision "M_{B2}" and that were deleted while adapting the reference model when deriving the enterprise model (version "M_{C1}"), still remain deleted in the enterprise model revision "M_{C2}" (desired use case).

2.   All model elements of "M_{B1}" that remain unchanged in the revision "M_{B2}" and that were *not* deleted while adapting the reference model when deriving the enterprise model (version "M_{C1}"), still remain in the enterprise model revision "M_{C2}" (desired use case).

3.   All model elements of "M_{B1}" that were modified between the reference model revisions "M_{B1}" and "M_{B2}" and that were actually deleted while adapting the reference model when deriving the enterprise model revision "M_{C1}." appear again in the enterprise model after the merge (undesired use case).

4.   All model elements of "M_{B1}" that were modified between the reference model revisions "M_{B1}" and "M_{B2}" and that were *not* actually deleted while adapting the reference model when deriving the enterprise model revision "M_{C1}," will appear modified in the enterprise model revision "M_{C2}" (desired use case).

5.   All model elements newly added to "M_{B2}" will appear in "M_{C2}" (might be desired use case; is depicted as example within Figure 9).

6.   Again, if the reference model and the enterprise mode were changed concurrently, a conflict resolution activity might apply (desired use case).

As in the previous subsection we can conclude:

•   **Conclusion 3:** Requirement Re3 can be well supported with a configuration management system. "Future Trends" discusses possibilities to enhance the applicability of the system.

Reference Model Adaptation and Recovery

To handle the creation of enterprise models out of a reference model and to administer the relationships between them (Re4), both should be stored in the configuration management system. Thereby, the reference model as well as the enterprise model are under versioning control and all CM operations can be used upon them. As described above, deriving an enterprise model requires copying the reference model and applying the rule-based techniques to it afterwards (see again Figure 6). This operation requires four different steps. First, to tell the configuration management system that the new enterprise model differs from the reference model, a branch must be created. Second, to duplicate the reference model it must be checked out into the local workspace. Third, the rule-based mechanisms can be applied to the local copy. Last, the resulting enterprise model can be checked back in the repository (see also Figure 11).

- **Conclusion 4:** Configuration management largely supports requirement Re4.

Because changes on configuration items within a configuration management system do not override older versions but lead to the creation of new revisions, the recovery of past (reference) models is always possible, which leads to:

- **Conclusion 5:** Configuration management directly supports requirement Re5.

Figure 10. Duplication of a reference model via branching

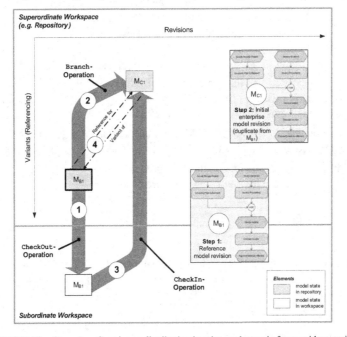

Configuration Management Support for Reference Model Use

In this subsection we describe how a configuration management system can support the requirements needed to adapt a reference model (Re6-Re12).

Requirement Re6 is directly supported by a configuration management system. The following operations can be used (see Figure 10):

1. CheckOut: Allows the transfer of a reference model revision to a subordinated workspace (Figure 10, number 1).
2. Branch: Allows the creation of a new development path (variant) for the reference model (in the repository, Figure 10, number 2).
3. CheckIn: Allows assignment of the reference model revision to the new development path (Figure 10, number3).

The referencing-relationship between "M_{B1}" and "M_{C1}" (see Figure 10, number 4) is the result of the execution of the three above-mentioned configuration management operations. We, therefore, conclude:

*   **Conclusion 6:** Configuration management directly supports requirement Re6.

Figure 11. Incorporation of configuration management operation and adaptation rules

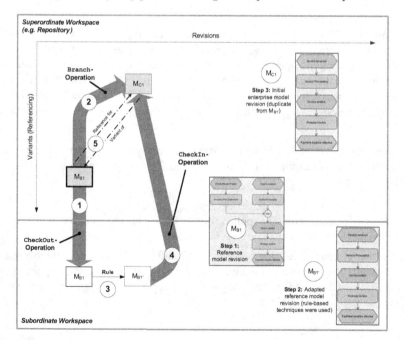

Table 4. Overview of the requirements of reference modelling supported by a configuration management

Requirement	Current support by CMS	Feasible support by future CMS
Re1: The system should be able to extract the core of two or more enterprise models.	No	By generalising of the Merge operator.
Re2: The system should support the unification of a reference model with an enterprise model derived from the reference model to detect and analyse the changes made to the enterprise model.	Partial support	Feasible by recording the reasons of model changes as well as the relations between models.
Re3: The system should support the unification of an enterprise model with a reference model for the purpose of reflecting the changes made to the reference model within the enterprise model.	See Re2	See Re2
Re4: The system should support the creation of enterprise models out of reference models.	Fully supported	-
Re5: The system should support the recovery of a past (reference) model version.	Fully supported	-
Re6: The system must be able to duplicate the reference model.	Fully supported	-
Configurational mechanisms (Re7-Re12)	Not supported	Not feasible.

Requirements Re7 to Re12 cannot be supported by a configuration management system, because these operations manipulate the model itself. In contrast to manipulating a model, a model configuration management system only documents the changes made to the model (see section 2). Furthermore, as pointed out above, adapting the reference model using the rule-based techniques requires a specific modelling grammar. Since the model CM operates on any model regardless of its grammar, it cannot support any grammar-specific operations.

•   **Conclusion 7:** A model configuration management system does generally not capture any adaptation mechanism of reference models. Thus, requirements Re7-Re12 cannot be supported.

The rule-based techniques must be applied after the CheckOut operation and before performing the CheckIn operation (see Figure 11, number 3).

However, the referencing relation between "M_{B1}" and "M_{C1}" (Figure 11, number 4) has a different quality than the one in Figure 10 (number 4) as it includes not only the copying operation but also the modifications made to the reference model (Figure 11, number 3) by applying the rule-based techniques.

Future Trends

As we have discussed in the previous section, a model configuration management system can support many reference modelling activities. However, the following open issues remained:

1. Configuration management operations provide a technology for models in general and for the life cycle of reference and enterprise models in particular. Problems remained when merging the reference model and the respective enterprise model to either an updated enterprise model or an updated reference model (see section 4).

2. Furthermore, formative techniques for reference model adaptation, such as analogous construction, specialising, instantiation and aggregation have been excluded from this chapter. As we found that the configuration management cannot support the rule-based adaptation techniques of reference models, this might indicate that the above-mentioned formative techniques might not be supported. However, further research is required in this field.

3. Last, the support for extracting a common core of two or more enterprise model(s) to construct or enhance a reference model was not evaluated in detail in this chapter, because configuration management does not support this activity. More work needs to be done on this issue also.

These issues are discussed in detail in the following subsections.

Proposal for Solving the Critical Merge Implications

The undesired use cases derived when merging an enterprise model with a reference model can be reduced to one underlying problem class. Changes made to a reference model when adapting cannot be distinguished from the changes made to a model during its life cycle. The solution can be sketched out as follows: Figure 11 visualises that the difference between "M_{B1}" and "M_{C1}" is the result of an adaptation of the reference model and the operations made to this model in the subordinated workspace. These operations are enclosed between a CheckOut and a CheckIn operation of the associated configuration management system. Obviously, the intentions of both operations are completely different. The adaptation of the reference model is used to derive the enterprise model (change of purpose). The modifications made to the model to enhance that model and to tailor it for the situation at hand must be carefully separated from the adaptation process. Consequently, the reasons of these changes must be recorded structurally within a configuration management system. If this information has been recorded, it can be used in the subsequent Merge operation. Therefore, the undesired use-cases can be avoided.

Furthermore, the result of a Merge operation differs if two models are merged which evolved during a normal model life cycle, if the reference model is merged with the enterprise model and if the enterprise model is merged with the reference model. Consequently, the merge operation must take the relations between these models into account. The configuration management system needs additional information when carrying out the branch operator.

Finally, it must be clear, that the resulting model of a merge operation can only guide the modeller to construct a new (reference) model. Usually it is necessary to revise the resulting model according to the modellers intent.

Comparison-Based Construction and Evolution of Reference Models

As analysed in Section 4, building a reference model from two or more (enterprise) models requires a semantic merge operation to find commonalities and differences between these models. Further research has to develop a method for performing such a comparison and to incorporate it into the configuration management. According to Pfeiffer and Gehlert (2005), most techniques to compare conceptual models focus on the formal comparison of both models. However, to achieve sound results of this operation, a semantic comparison of both models is necessary. Research is underway to describe such a method.

Conclusion

Although configuration management is a well established discipline in the software industry, the topic has gained surprisingly little importance in the modelling field (Esswein, Kluge, & Greiffenberg, 2002; Greiffenberg, 2003). To the best of our knowledge, only one partial implementation exists today (Cubetto Toolset, 2005). However, as we showed in this Chapter, configuration management is an important means to support not only modelling activities but also the creation and use of reference models. We concluded that configuration management can support important parts of this process (see Table 4).

Further research is underway to analyse, design and implement future features of a configuration management system.

References

Becker, J., Delfmann, P., Dreiling, A., Knackstedt, R., & Kuropka, D. (2004). *Configurative process modeling—Outlining an approach to increased business process model usability.* Paper presented at the Innovations Through Information Technology: Proceedings of the 15th Information Resources Management Association International Conference (IRMA 2004), New Orleans, LA.

Becker, J., Delfmann, P., & Knackstedt, R. (2004). Construction of a reference modelling language: A framework to specify adapatation techniques for information models. *WIRTSCHAFTSINFORMATIK, 46*(4), 251-264. [in German]

Conradi, R., & Westfechtel, B. (1998). Version models for software configuration management. *ACM Computing Surveys (CSUR), 30*(2), 233-282.

Cubetto Toolset. (2005). Retrieved August 17, 2005 from, http://wise.wiwi.tu-dresden.de

Dresbach, S. (1996, January 3-6). *Modeling by construction: A new methodology for constructing models for decision support.* Paper presented at the 29th Hawaii International Conference on System Sciences (HICSS), Wailea.

Esswein, W., Kluge, C., & Greiffenberg, S. (2002). *Model configuration management.* Paper presented September 10 at the MobIS 2002, Nürnberg, Germany. [in German].

Estublier, J. (2000). *Software configuration management: A roadmap*: Dassault Systèmes / LSR, Grenoble University.

Feiler, P. H. (1991). *Configuration management models in commercial environments* (Technical Report). Pittsburgh: Software Engineering Institute (SEI), Carnegie Mellon University.

Fettke, P., & Loos, P. (2003). Classification of reference models: A methodology and its application. *Information Systems and e-Business Management, 1*(1), 35-53.

Greiffenberg, S. (2003). *Method engineering in economy and public administration.* Hamburg: Dr. Kovač [in German].

ISO. (2000). *Quality management systems—requirements (ISO 9001:2000).* International Organization for Standardization (ISO).

ISO. (2003). *Quality management systems—guidelines for configuration management (ISO 10007:2003).* International Organization for Standardization (ISO).

Molière, F. d. (1984). *Principles of model design: A model theory-based and construction-oriented view.* Technische Hochschule Darmstadt. [in German]

Pfeiffer, D., & Gehlert, A. (2005, October 24-25). *A framework for comparing conceptual models.* Paper presented at the Enterprise Modelling and Information Systems Architectures (EMISA 2005), Klagenfurt, Austria.

Recker, J., Rosemann, M., Aalst, W. v. d., & Mendling, J. (2005, September). *On the syntax of reference model configuration—transforming the C-EPC into lawful EPC models,* accepted for Workshop on Business Process Reference Models (BPRM 2005) at the 3rd International Conference on Business Process Management (BPM 2005), Nancy, France.

Rosemann, M., & Aalst, W. M. P. v. d. (in press). A configurable reference modelling language. *Information Systems.*

Rossi, M., Ramesh, B., Lyytinen, K., & Tolvanen, J.-P. (2004). Managing evolutionary method engineering by method rationale. *Journal of the Association for Information Systems, 5*(9), 356-391.

Scheer, A.-W. (1994). *Business process engineering—reference models for industrial companies* (2nd ed.). Berlin: Springer.

Scheer, A.-W. (2000). *ARIS—business process modeling* (3rd ed.). Berlin: Springer.

Schütte, R., & Rotthowe, T. (1998). *The* guidelines of modeling: An approach to enhance the quality in information models. In *Proceedings of the 17ᵗʰ International Conference on Conceptual Modeling* (LNCS 1507, pp. 240-254).

SEI. (2002). *Capability maturity model integration for systems engineering, software engineering, integrated product and process development, and supplier sourcing (CMMI-SE/SW/IPPD/SS, V1.1).* Pittsburgh, PA: Software Engineering Institute (SEI), Carnegie Mellon University.

Thompson, S. M. (1997). Configuration management: Keeping it all together. *BT Technology Journal, 15*(3), 48-60.

Turowski, K. (Ed.). (2002). *Standardized specification of business components: Memorandum of the working group 5.10.3 component oriented business application system,* February 2002. University of Augsburg, Augsburg.

vom Brocke, J. (2003). *Reference modeling: Design and distribution of construction processes.* Berlin: Logos. [in German]

Weber, R. (2003). Editor's comments: Still desperately seeking the IT-artifact. *MIS Quarterly, 27*(2), iii-xi.

Zeller, A. (1997). *Configuration management with version sets: A unified software versioning model and its applications.* Braunschweig.

Endnotes

[1]   vom Brocke (2003) actually uses the term "configurative techniques." Because of the different usage of the word *configuration* in this chapter, we use the term "rule-based" instead.

[2]   Please note that all examples in this chapter are in the event-driven-process chain notation (EPC) and were taken from Rosemann and van der Aalst (in press).

Chapter XVI

Interchange Formats for Reference Models

Jan Mendling,
Vienna University of Economics and Business Administration, Austria

Gustaf Neumann,
Vienna University of Economics and Business Administration, Austria

Markus Nüttgens, University of Hamburg, Germany

Abstract

This chapter presents interchange formats as an enabler for reference model reuse on a technical level. We use a framework to describe the interplay of modeling tools and interchange formats. Based on an extended framework, we discuss the potential of interchange formats for the reuse aspect of reference models. Furthermore, we distinguish four cases of different technical sophistication that are needed to make interchange work. As it is unrealistic that everybody will use the same tool, the standardization of open interchange formats is the second best solution to leverage reference model reuse across different tools. After briefly sketching XMI, BPEL, XPDL and PNML, we focus on event-driven process chains (EPCs) since they are frequently used as a language for process reference models. The introduction to EPC markup language serves as an example to illustrate the design of an open interchange format for a reference modeling language.

Introduction

Since the advent of XML as a standard for the definition of structured data, considerable effort has been put into the specification and standardization of domain-specific XML schemas. Such an XML schema defines the set of allowed XML elements and attributes and the structure in which they may appear for a certain application domain. An individual XML file is said to be valid if and only if its elements and attributes comply with the structure rules of a related XML schema. By this means, the XML schema specifies the set of XML instances which are valid against it. The names of XML elements and attributes are usually taken from the application domain of the schema. Precise data semantics have to be clarified in additional human-readable documents. The overall goal of specifying a domain-specific XML schema is to facilitate the interchange of structured data between different parties related to that domain, for example, business partners exchanging XML-based business documents over the Internet.

The success of XML soon had an impact on how modeling languages were defined and used in practice. One prominent example from the area of workflow modeling is the business process execution language for Web services (BPEL4WS or BPEL) (see Andrews et al., 2003). This language has been defined as an XML schema accompanied by a specification document. XML instance files that are valid against the BPEL schema represent BPEL process models. The advantage is that BPEL models can be processed by and interchanged between different modeling tools and execution engines. Beyond that, interchange formats have also been defined for existing modeling languages. There are various examples such as the PNML schema for Petri nets, the EPML schema for event-driven process chains, and the XMI interchange concept for the unified modeling language (UML).

Throughout this chapter, we discuss that this recent trend has the potential to leverage the application of reference models in practice. In the following, we define reference models as generic conceptual models that formalize recommendations for a certain application domain in order to be reused as best practice recommendation (see Fettke & Loos, 2003). Interchange formats are of particular importance as an enabler for reference model reuse on a technical level (see Brocke & Buddendick, 2004) because they facilitate model exchange between different tools and applications. In Section 2 we present a framework for discussing the interplay of modeling and interchange formats. This framework includes model user, modeling tool, model and metamodel repository, import/export interfaces, model file and interchange formats and it explains how they are related to each other. In section 3 we extend this framework in such a way that the reuse aspect of reference modelling is depicted appropriately. Based on this extended framework, we distinguish four cases based on the level of technical sophistication that is needed to make interchange work. In this context, we discuss the advantages of open specifications of interchange formats from a reference modeling perspective. Section 4 presents current interchange format support for reference modeling languages. While XMI offers a rather mature interchange mechanism for UML-based reference models, considerable work is needed on interchange formats for business process modeling. As event-driven process chains (EPCs) are frequently used as a language for process reference modeling, we present the design of the EPC markup language. It serves as an example to illustrate the design of an open interchange format for a reference modeling language. Section 5 concludes the chapter and gives an outlook on future research directions.

Interchange Formats and Modeling

In this section we define a framework for discussing the relationship interchange formats and modeling. This framework includes model user, modeling tool, model and meta model repository, import and export interfaces, model file and interchange format schema (see Figure 1). The modeling tool is the central element of the framework because the complexity of real-life modeling projects is hard to manage without such a modeling tool. The model user interacts with a modeling tool via a graphical user interface. A model user can be a modeler who creates or changes models or a model reader who looks up information in models, as for example to find out in which order certain activities of a business process have to be executed. Models are stored in a model repository which is often based on a relational database system. The tool must also be aware of the meta-model of a model in order to process and visualize it correctly. A meta model is a model that defines the modeling language for a certain domain (see Karagiannis & Kühn, 2002). Flexible modeling tools allow the user to define meta-models and to store them in a meta model repository; in some tools meta models are hard-coded. Various modeling techniques have been be used for the definition of meta models, including entity-relationship-diagrams (see Chen, 1976), UML class diagrams (see OMG, 2004), graphs (see Winter, 2002), or XML Schema (see Beech, Lawrence, Moloney, Mendelsohn, & Thompson, 2001).

Most modeling tools offer import and export interfaces that read from and write to one or multiple models to a model file. The purpose of such interfaces is to provide a simple integra-

Figure 1. Framework illustrating the interplay of interchange formats and modeling

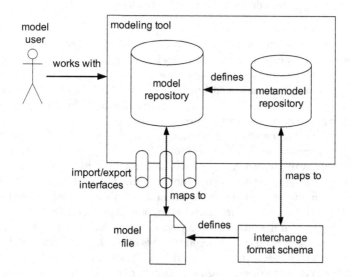

tion based on the same interchange format (see Hohpe & Woolf, 2004). The structure and elements of a model file have to be specified in an interchange format schema. From a formal point of view, the interchange format schema defines a serial representation that corresponds to a related meta-model. Accordingly, models of different meta-models are serialized to model files and have to be validated against different interchange format schemas. The problem is, though, that there is not only one definite mapping from a meta-model to an interchange format schema. Therefore, there are often different import and export interfaces included in a modeling tool. The interchange format must include all elements and relationships of the meta model in order to avoid loss of information while importing and exporting (see St-Denis et al., 2000). Basically, there are three different approaches for aligning meta models and interchange format schemas: interchange-format-only specification, mappings-only specification and joint specification (see Mendling, Neumann, & Nüttgens, 2005a).

- **Interchange format only:** Interchange formats like BPEL are specified only as an XML Schema. This schema can be regarded as the serialization of an implicit meta-model. Accordingly, no explicit mappings need to be defined between meta-model and interchange format.

- **Mappings only:** This approach is the foundation of XMI (see OMG, 2003). The XMI specification defines production rules (mappings) from the meta-object facility (MOF) (see OMG, 2002) to XML and XML schema. As MOF is the meta^{2}model of UML, these production rules can be used to derive a respective interchange format. This means XMI does not specify the interchange format for UML models, but the production rules that generate an interchangeable representation of those models.

- **Joint specification:** The joint specification of a meta-model and a respective interchange format is another option. The Petri net markup language (PNML) (see Billington et al., 2003) follows this approach. A UML class diagram defines its meta-model and a schema specifies the corresponding XML interchange format.

From the perspective of the modeling tool vendor and the model user, two kinds of interchange formats can be distinguished: proprietary interchange formats and open interchange formats. The purpose of the first is to store models as files and to exchange model files between installations of the same modeling tool. The structure of a proprietary interchange format does not necessarily need to be transparent or documented by the tool vendor. Some vendors prefer proprietary interchange formats because they offer a certain vendor lock-in effect since model data cannot be read by other tools. By contrast, open interchange formats seem to be more appealing to modeling tool users. The documentation of an open interchange format is publicly available, so that every tool vendor can implement compatible interfaces. This especially holds true for interchange format specifications of standardization bodies. Accordingly, such standardization is an important step towards the interoperability of tools (see Koegel, 1992). In general, open interchange formats provide interoperability without making assumptions on the internal representation of models in the tools. In Mendling, Neumann, and Nüttgens (2005a) this circumstance is called the pragmatic effect of an open interchange format. The advantage is that there is no discontinuity of media and re-entering if a model file can be loaded via an open interface. Furthermore, open interchange formats can serve as an intermediary for transformations between tools that support different interchange formats. This reduces the number of transformation programs (see Wüstner, Hotzel, & Buxmann, 2002).

Beyond that, open interchange formats have an economic effect and an effect of conceptual consolidation. The economic effect is related to competition between tool vendors. The specification of an open interchange format can leverage competition due to interchangeability of model files and to reduced vendor lock-in. The shift to another tool causes less effort and complementary tools can be integrated more easily (see Crawford, 1984). The development of new specialized tools becomes more attractive as models from existing model repositories can be imported via the interchange format. Moreover, the specification of open interchange formats can even create a new market as the case of multimedia applications shows (see Koegel, 1992).

The effect of conceptual consolidation stems from the specification process of open interchange formats. In order to be successful, the interchange format has to reflect at least the commonly used concepts of a certain domain without redundancies. Therefore, the principles of schema integration can help to define a common interchange format based on the criteria of completeness, minimality and understandability (see Batini, Lenzerini, & Navathe, 1986). As such, the specification of an interchange format explicates the concepts and provides a consolidation of terminology of a given domain (see Ohno-Machado et al., 1998). Beyond that, extensibility is a specific criterion for interchange formats (see Crawford, 1984; Koegel, 1992; St-Denis et al., 2000). It reflects the fact that interchange formats are subject to change and evolution; as such future developments and new requirements have to be taken into account from the very beginning. Extensibility enables the inclusion of additional information in a predefined way. This provides a smooth integration of new aspects.

Interchange formats are helpful when data has to be moved between different tools. The following section relates this aspect to the reuse focus of reference modeling. As such, interchange formats can be an important enabler for reference modeling on the technical level.

Interchange Formats and Reference Modeling

While we explained the relationships of the framework in the previous section, we abstracted from the fact that a single model user or a single organization running a centralized model repository do not have much benefit from interchange formats. As we have outlined before, we consider the intended reuse of reference models to be a constituent feature. This implies that there are two actors involved in reference modeling: a reference modeler and a reference model user. Figure 2 extends the framework to reflect this separation of model design and model usage. The reference modeler as well as the reference model user utilize modeling tools of their own. As a consequence, the modeling tool, the interchange format and the meta-model may be different. Such differences represent obstacles to reference model reuse on a technical level. According to Brocke and Buddendick (2004), such characteristics of technology may have an impact on transaction costs of reusing reference models and therefore also on the appropriateness of certain coordination mechanisms.

Figure 2 shows the two actors involved in the reuse of reference models, the reference modeler and the reference model user as well as their modeling tool infrastructure. The reuse of reference models implies that a model file supplied by the reference modeler needs to be imported into the modeling tool of the reference model user. Based on how easy the two modeling tools can be integrated, the following four cases can be distinguished:

1. **Same tool:** In the simplest case, both reference modeler and reference model user use the same modeling tool. As the modeling tool is the same, the same interchange formats are supported. The reference model can either be exported to a model file of a proprietary or an open interchange format. It is recommended to use the proprietary format in this case, because proprietary interchange formats usually provide a lossless export and import of models and, furthermore, the import and export of model files in proprietary interchange format is often more efficient since the format is especially tailored to match the meta model of the tool.

2. **Same interchange format:** In this case, reference modeler and reference model user have different modeling tools. Still, at least one open interchange format is supported by both tools via import and export filters. The common format can be used to move the reference model from the first tool to the second. There may be a completeness problem when the modeling tool of the reference modeler offers details in the meta-model that cannot be mapped to an element of the open interchange format. Such details of a model might be omitted in the export process. A suitable interchange format should therefore include those meta-model features that are found in modeling tools in order to minimize potential loss of information.

3. **Same meta-model:** Even if the reference modeler and the reference model user work with different modeling tools that do not use the same open interchange formats, the

Figure 2. Framework illustrating the relationship between interchange formats and reference modeling

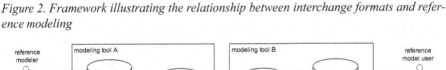
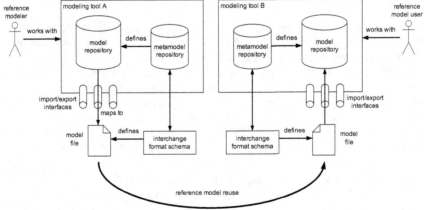

reuse of reference models can be facilitated by implementing a transformation from the interchange format of the first tool to the interchange format of the second tool. As the meta-models are equivalent, no semantic mapping is needed but rather a syntactic transformation between the formats. If both interchange formats are based on XML, the transformation can be easily implemented with XML processing techniques, such as SAX, DOM, XSLT, or XQuery.

4. **Different meta-models:** This case requires the most effort to move the reference model from the first tool to the second. A semantic mapping needs to be defined from the first to the second meta-model. The discussion on mappings from EPCs to Petri nets shows that such semantic mappings are often far from trivial. Beyond that, a respective transformation program must be implemented similar to the case of same meta-models.

From the perspective of reference modeling as an activity of model reuse, the first case is the most appealing. Yet, it is not realistic that everybody uses the same modeling tool. A study provided by Delphi Group (2003) reveals that heterogeneity of BPM modeling languages and tools is a fact. There have been more than 35 different tools in 2003 and the current popularity of BPM tends to a further increase as BPM-related tools are enhanced with BPM functionality. The definition of open interchange formats and their standardization is the second best solution in this context. Interchange formats can serve as an enabler for reference model markets as the user base of an interchange format defines the market for a reference model stored in that format. The model file then becomes an information product that can be marketed independent of the tool. Reference model catalogues as described by Fettke and Loos (2003) are a suitable means for retrieval in such a market. Accordingly, open interchange formats help to establish a market for reference models as envisioned in Leymann (2003) and elaborated by Brocke and Buddendick (2004). The following section discusses the current status of interchange formats related to reference modeling languages with a focus on EPCs.

Towards Open Interchange Formats for Reference Modeling

Open interchange formats for reference modeling have to be discussed separately for the modeling of static aspects and the modeling of behavior aspects. The unified modeling language (UML)—especially its class diagram—can be considered as the de facto standard for modeling static aspects. The meta-model of UML is defined as an instance of the meta-object facility (MOF) as its meta²model. Based on MOF, the Object Management Group (OMG) has specified the XML metadata interchange (XMI). XMI defines production rules to derive XML Schemas for MOF-compliant meta-models and to derive XML instance files for MOF-based models. Concerning UML, this implies that XMI maps the UML meta-model to an XML Schema. Furthermore, each concrete UML model defined by the modeler can be exchanged by serializing it according to the XMI production rules to a respective XML model file. XMI not only supports the interchange of model files and the derivation of XML Schemas, but also the exchange of model differences by the help of global identification mechanisms for model elements. XMI offers three different and complementary identifier attributes: id, label and uuid. The id attribute defines an identifier that must be unique within a single XMI document. The label attribute can be used to store a string label in which the user can put in any value. This means that uniqueness is not enforced. Furthermore, the uuid offers a globally unique identification of an element. All these identifiers can be referenced. XMI supports XLink and XPointer for this purpose. The XLink href attribute is used to reference other XMI documents or, via XPointer, parts of it. References within a document are specified via idref attributes. In order to express model differences, XMI defines Add, Delete, and Replace as primitives. The respective XML elements include references to the identifiers of the changed elements. This mechanism can also be used to trace back changes of a new version of a model.

For the modeling of behavioral aspects, especially process modeling, there are several open interchange formats available including BPEL, XPDL, PNML and EPML. The problem is that none of them is accepted as a de facto standard for business process modeling in general. We give a brief overview of the first three before turning to the details of EPML.

BPEL is an executable language for the definition of processes composed of a set of Web Services. It addresses the technical level of workflow execution. Its second version is currently standardized by OASIS. The main concepts of BPEL are basic and structured activities, variables, partner links, and handlers. In a simple case, a BPEL process includes partner links, variables, and activities. Partner links represent message exchange relationships between two parties. Via a reference to a partner link type the partner link defines the mutually required port types of a message exchange: The myRole and a partnerRole attributes defines who is playing which role. Partner links are referenced by basic activities that involve Web Service requests. Variables are used to store workflow data as well as input and output messages that are exchanged via Web services. Furthermore, the assign activity can write to variables. Scopes are specific structured activities that can define local variables and handlers within their scope. Handlers specify responses to unexpected behavior like time or message events, faults, compensation, or termination. The nesting of structured activities specifies the control flow in BPEL. There are specific structured activities for loops (while), sequential execution (sequence), conditional branching based on data (switch) or events (pick) and concurrent branches (flow). Additional synchronization constraints in a flow can be defined by links. So-called basic activities specify the actual operations of a BPEL process. There are three activities for Web services interaction: invoke for Web service calls, receive to wait for the receipt of a Web service message, and reply for responding to a remote request. All these activities reference a partner link and specify input and/or output variables for messages.

XPDL was originally defined as an XML-based interchange format for Interface 1 of the workflow reference model. In its new version 2.0 (WfMC, 2005), XPDL has been extended to additionally serve as an interchange format for BPMN (White, 2004). This realignment has been motivated by merger talks between the Workflow Management Coalition and the Business Process Management Initiative. As a consequence, the new XPDL version includes new concepts adapted from BPMN like Pools, Gateways or Events. The XPDL Package serves as a container for all information associated with a process definition including Pools, Processes, Participants, Applications, Type Declarations, and Data Fields. A Process (or

Workflow Process) defines Activities and their execution order as Transition arcs. Transition conditions serve as guards for Transitions. The operations of an Activity can relate to Participants, Applications and Data Fields. XPDL distinguishes several types of Activities. The Task/Tool activity describes an activity that is executed automatically without humans being involved. The Route activity specifies join and split conditions either based on data or events. The Block Activity defines an embedded sub-process that executes an Activity Set. In contrast to that, the Subflow represents a call to a sub-process of the Package. Different types of Events are adapted from BPMN as special types of Activities. In contrast to BPEL, XPDL can store statistical information for Activities via the deadline, limit and priority attributes. Furthermore, BPEL does not offer sub-processes, but XPDL does.

PNML was designed in order to facilitate the interchange of Petri net models between heterogeneous Petri net analysis tools (see Billington et al., 2003). PNML includes the standard Petri net elements (i.e., places, transitions and arcs between them). Furthermore, all these elements can have so-called labels. A label captures the specifics of a certain Petri net type. So-called Petri net type definitions specify the set of allowed labels to define a particular type of Petri net. This extensibility mechanism offers the flexibility to exchange arbitrary Petri net types with PNML. For further details on PNML refer to Billington et al. (2003). Further interchange formats for BPM are presented and compared in Mendling, Neumann, and Nüttgens (2005a). In the following section, we discuss the development of an open interchange format for event-driven process chains called EPML.

EPC Reference Model Interchange with EPML

EPC markup language (EPML) builds on the original definition of event-driven process chains (EPC) by Keller, Nüttgens, and Scheer (1992) and extends it with concepts for hierarchy as defined in Nüttgens and Rump (2002), concepts for so-called extended EPCs (see Scheer, 2000), yEPCs, as defined in Mendling, Neumann, and Nüttgens (2005b), and configurable EPC (C-EPC), as defined in Rosemann and Aalst (2005). Furthermore, EPML has elements for the graphical representation of EPC models in tools. In the following subsections, we will introduce each of these EPC-related concepts and illustrate their representation in EPML by examples. For a comprehensive introduction to EPML refer to Mendling and Nüttgens (2005).

Original EPC and Its Representation in EPML

Event-driven process chains (EPC) have been introduced as a modeling language for the representation of temporal and logical dependencies of activities in a business process (Keller et al. 1992). The standard EPC includes function, event, connector and arc element types. Functions are used to model activities of a business process. Such functions depend upon certain preconditions that have to be true before a function can be executed. The completion of functions triggers respective postconditions to become true. These pre- and postconditions are modeled as so-called events. The fact that certain postconditions are preconditions of other functions establishes an alternation of functions and events. In general, events and functions have one incoming and one outgoing arc that define the control flow. Exceptions to this rule are start and end events: The first have no incoming arc and the latter have no outgoing arc. EPCs' connectors define branching and merging of control flow. They can be differentiated in three ways. First, connectors have either one incoming and multiple outgoing arcs or multiple incoming and one outgoing arc. The former are called split connectors, the latter are called join connectors. Second, there are three types of connectors—AND, XOR and OR—that define split or join logic. Third, connectors between functions and events are called function-event-connectors, those between events and functions are called event-function-connectors. The AND split activates all subsequent branches in concurrency while the XOR split defines a choice to activate one of multiple branches. The OR split triggers one, two or up to all of multiple branches based on conditions. In both cases of the XOR and OR split, the activation conditions are given in events subsequent to the connector. Accordingly, event-function-splits are forbidden with XOR and OR as the activation conditions and do not become clear in the model. The AND join waits for all incoming branches to complete, then it propagates control to the subsequent EPC element. The semantics of the OR join have been debated for its non-local semantics—for an overview, see, for example, Kindler (2004). Non-locality means that the OR join synchronizes all incoming branches that are active. In order to do so, it must be aware of which branches are still active and which will never be active. In acyclic process models such synchronization can be achieved via dead-path-elimination, which was also proposed for EPCs (see Langner, Schneider, & Wehler, 1998). Yet, cycles cannot be handled with this approach. Kindler (2004) proposes an approach to resolve this problem. The XOR split has also non-local semantics: If there is only one branch active (which is the expected case) it activates the subsequent EPC element. Yet, if there are multiple branches active, it synchronizes them and blocks (see Nüttgens & Rump, 2002).

Figure 3 shows a simple EPC business process model and parts of its EPML representation. Note that although there is only one start event and one end event, EPCs may have both multiple start and end events. In an EPML file, the EPC is represented as an epc element identified by a unique epcId attribute and a name. Each EPC element is encoded as an element whose tag name is derived from its EPC element-type having a unique id and a name attribute. This means that, for example, the start event in Figure 3 is represented as an event element with the name "START." Functions are stored as function elements and connectors as and, or or xor elements. Control flow arcs are represented as arc elements. The direction is specified by the flow sub-element: The arc points from the element whose id is given in the source attribute to that referenced in the target attribute.

Hierarchical EPCs and Their Representation in EPML

Based on practical experiences with large models, process interfaces and hierarchical functions have been introduced as new EPC element types (see Nüttgens & Rump, 2002). Both these elements point to another EPC business process model. Process interfaces can be used to point from the end of a process to a subsequent EPC. In a technical sense, process interfaces can be regarded as an asynchronous call to a sub-process. Syntactically, they have some similarity to end events as they also have one incoming but no outgoing arc. In contrast to that, hierarchical functions point from a function to a refining sub-process. This is similar to a synchronous call to a sub-process that returns control to the hierarchical

Figure 3. Example of an EPC and its EPML representation

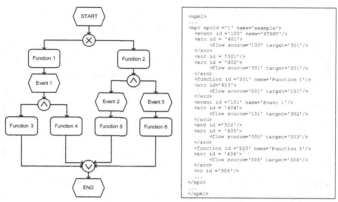

function after completion. Syntactically, the hierarchical function follows the same rules as usual function elements.

Figure 4 shows two related EPCs: The left EPC contains a function called "Function 3," that is decomposed to another EPC given in the middle of the figure. In EPML, both EPC models are stored in one file. One EPML file can contain an arbitrary number of EPCs. Furthermore, such a hierarchy is represented via the toProcess element. This element can be used as a child element in function elements and in process interface elements. Its linkToEpcId attribute references the epcId of another EPC. If it is a hierarchical function, navigation continues after that function when the sub-process has completed. If it is a process interface, the respective branch completes after triggering the sub-process.

Figure 4. Example of a hierarchical EPC and its EPML representation

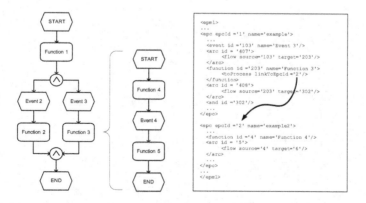

Extended EPCs and Their Representation in EPML

EPCs are an integral part of the architecture of integrated information systems (ARIS) (see Scheer, 2000). ARIS is a framework for enterprise modeling in which EPCs are used to integrate different perspectives. ARIS defines five perspectives. The *organization perspective* is modeled by defining relationships between organizational units, roles, positions, staff and sites. This results in an organization chart of the enterprise. The *data perspective* specifies the information entities and their relationships which are of importance to the enterprise. Entity-relationship-diagrams are adopted for this perspective. The *function perspective* defines the functional goals an enterprise wants to achieve. These are decomposed in a top-down way. The *output perspective* captures the products and services of an enterprise. Finally, the *process perspective* is used to integrate the four other perspectives. EPCs are used for this purpose, extended with the elements of the other perspectives. Accordingly, an eEPC is an EPC annotated with references to elements of other ARIS perspectives. The additional eEPC elements can be used to define responsibilities of organizational roles for the completion of certain functions; or to specify data input and output relationships between functions and data elements.

EPML offers dataField, application, participant and relation elements to represent eEPCs. The former three are identified by a unique id attribute and a name. The relation element defines a directed arc from the element whose id is referenced in the from attribute to that mentioned in the to attribute (see Figure 5). Each relation has a defRef attribute that links it to one of the relation definitions given in the EPML header. This mechanism grants that similar relationship types can be interpreted in a similar way.

yEPCs and Their Representation in EPML

The 20 workflow patterns gathered by Aalst, Hofstede, Kiepuszewski, and Barros (2003) have gained much attention as a benchmark for business process modeling languages. Al-

Figure 5. Example of an extended EPC and its EPML representation

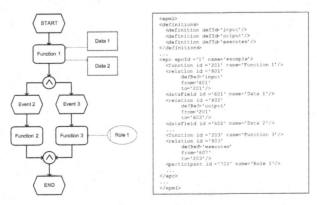

though EPCs already support a lot of these patterns, they fail to express multiple instantiation, cancellation and state-based patterns (Mendling, Neumann, & Nüttgens, 2005). The yEPC extension to EPCs introduces new element types to overcome this shortcoming. These include the empty connector for defining multiple incoming or multiple outgoing arcs for an event; multiple instantiation parameters and a cancellation concept. Both of the latter are adopted from YAWL, the workflow language that was defined to capture all workflow patterns (see Aalst & Hofstede, 2005).

Figure 6 illustrates the notation of yEPCs and their EPML representations. The circle after Event 1 is an empty split connector. It represents a deferred choice. This means that the first to start of Function 2 and Function 3 is executed and the other not. The second empty connector is a join representing a simple merge of the branches. Furthermore, there is a lariat attached to Function 2 that surrounds Function 1 and Event 1. This means that the elements within the latriat are cancelled after Function 2 has completed. In EPML each element to be cancelled is referenced in a cancel child element. Finally, multiple instantiation is specified via minimum, maximum, required and creation elements. The first three give the minimum and maximum cardinality of instances that can be created as well as the number of instances that must be finished in order to complete. The fourth parameter specifies whether instances can be created dynamically or only statically when the multiple instantiation function is started.

C-EPCs and Their Representation in EPML

The modeling of configuration aspects is especially interesting for reference modeling (see Soffer, Golany, & Dori, 2003). Such configuration aspects are included in configurable EPCs (C-EPCs). C-EPCs extend EPCs with five new concepts (see Rosemann & Aalst, 2005). First, *configurable functions* are special kinds of functions that can be configured to be included (on), to be excluded (off) or to be optionally included (opt) in a business process.

Figure 6. Example of a yEPC and its EPML representation

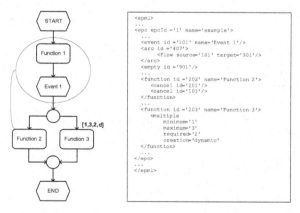

Second, *configurable connectors* can be set according to a partial order that defines which configurable connector type can be configured to which connector type (see Rosemann & Aalst, 2005). As an example, a configurable OR connector can be configured to OR, XOR, AND or Sequence. The latter specifies that one path must always be taken from the alternatives defined by the configurable OR. Furthermore, C-EPCs include a recommended *order of configuration*. *Configuration requirements* represent logical expressions over the values of the configurable nodes that must yield true. *Configuration guidelines* also give logical expressions that should evaluate to true. A configuration is then a mapping that assigns a set of configuration values to configurable elements. As such, a configurable process model is instantiated to a process model in a similar way as a process model is instantiated to a case (also called process instance).

Figure 7 gives the example of a C-EPC including a requirement, a configurable OR and a configurable function as well as its EPML representation as defined in Recker, Rosemann, Aalst, and Mendling (2005). In the C-EPC model, the configurable elements are highlighted by bold lines. In the EPML code, there is a configuration requirement over the elements referenced in the idRefs attribute. These are the configurable connector and the configurable function. The if sub-element defines the condition of the requirement as an XPath statement. If this condition evaluates to true, the implication given in the then element must also be true. In the example, it is required that if the configurable OR is set to seq, then the configurable function must be set to off. The following OR connector is identified as a configurable connector by a respective sub-element. The actual configuration is set in the configuration element. As its value is set to seq (i.e., the connector is replaced by a sequence continuing with the element mentioned in the goto attribute, the condition of the requirement is true). The function is also identified as a configurable function by a respective sub-element. Its configuration is set to the value off. Accordingly, the implication of the requirement is also true (i.e., the requirement is met).

Figure 7. Example of a C-EPC and EPML representation of a configuration

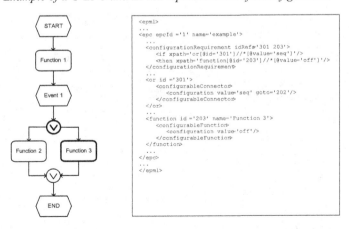

Graphical Information in EPML

Beyond the former XML elements which are derived from the meta-model of EPCs and its extensions, EPML includes further elements that are important for the graphical layout of the EPC model in business process modeling tools. In EPML, EPC elements and EPC arcs are graphically described by graphics child elements. These include information about position, fill, line and font. Furthermore, the coordinates element in the header of an EPML document can be used to define whether the x-axis runs from left to right or right to left as well as whether the y-axis runs from top to bottom or from bottom to top. General layout options for the entire EPML document can be defined via the graphicsDefault element.

Figure 8 illustrates that the four attributes of the position element refer to the smallest rectangle around the graphical element parallel to the axes. The x and y attributes define the offset, the width and height attributes specify the length of the edges of the container rectangle. Arcs should have at least two position elements to describe the two anchor points. Each additional position in-between is a bending point. The fill element describes the rendering of the interior of an object. It is not applicable for arcs. The color attribute must contain a RGB value or a predefined color of Cascading Stylesheets 2 (see Bos, Lie, Lilley, & Jacobs, 1998). The line element specifies the outline of an object. The shape attribute refers to how arcs are displayed: The value line represents a linear connection of anchor points to form a polygon; the value curve describes a quadratic Bezier curve. For the arc in Figure 8, the style is defined as solid. The font element holds family, style, weight, size and decoration attributes in conformance with Cascading Stylesheets 2.

Figure 8. EPML representation of graphical information

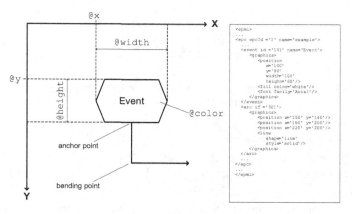

Conclusion

This chapter presented interchange formats as an important enabler for reference model reuse on a technical level. We presented a framework for discussing the interplay of modeling tools and interchange formats. Based on an extended framework, we distinguished four cases of different technical sophistication that are needed to make interchange work. As it is unrealistic that everybody will use the same tool, the definition and standardization of open interchange formats is the second best solution to leverage model reuse across different tools. While XMI offers a rather mature interchange mechanism for UML-based reference models, considerable work is still needed on interchange formats for business process modeling. There are several languages and related interchange formats that address specific aspects of process modeling. BPEL and XPDL are useful for the definition of executable workflow processes; PNML can be used to exchange Petri net models between analysis tools. EPCs and, accordingly, also EPML are mainly dedicated to documentation of business processes in visual models. We have used EPML in this chapter as an example to illustrate which kind of model information needs to be represented in an XML-based interchange format for a reference modelling language.

Currently, it is not clear which interchange format will become the de facto standard. BPEL is gaining increasing support from the industry to the disadvantage of XPDL. Yet both are not appropriate for conceptual modelling of business processes. At the time of writing, PNML is still in the process of standardization and the release of the standard is not yet scheduled. Meanwhile EPML is supported by EPC Tools, SemTalk and interfaces are implemented for the ProM framework. There is also a transformation between ARIS and EPC Markup Languages (see Mendling & Nüttgens, 2004). Regarding the existing heterogeneity of process modelling languages, it is likely that several interchange formats will coexist and that bilateral transformations will be implemented.

References

Aalst, W. M. P. v. d., & Hofstede, A. H. M. t. (2005). YAWL: Yet another workflow language. *Information Systems, 30*, 245-275.

Aalst, W. M. P. v. d., Hofstede, A. H. M. t., Kiepuszewski, B., & Barros, A. P. (2003). Workflow patterns. *Distributed and Parallel Databases, 14*, 5-51.

Andrews, T., Curbera, F., Dholakia, H., Goland, Y., Klein, J., Leymann, F., et al. (2003). *Business process execution language for web services, Version 1.1*. BEA Systems, IBM Corp., Microsoft Corp., SAP AG, Siebel Systems.

Batini, C., Lenzerini, M., & Navathe, S. B. (1986). A comparative analysis of methodologies for database schema integration. *ACM Computing Surveys, 18*, 323-364.

Beech, D., Lawrence, S., Moloney, M., Mendelsohn, N., & Thompson, H. S. (2001, May 2). *XML schema part 1: Structures* (W3C Recommendation)

Billington, J., Christensen, S., Hee, K. E. v., Kindler, E., Kummer, O., Petrucci, L., et al. (2003, June 23-27). The Petri net markup language: Concepts, technology, and tools. In W. M. P. v. d. Aalst & E. Best (Eds.), *Applications and theory of Petri nets 2003, Proceedings of the 24th International Conference, ICATPN 2003,* Eindhoven, The Netherlands (LNCS 2679, pp. 483-505). Springer-Verlag.

Bos, B., Lie, H. W., Lilley, C., & Jacobs, I. (1998, May 12). *Cascading style sheets, level 2* (W3C Recommendation).

Brocke, J. v., & Buddendick, C. (2004). Organisationsformen in der referenzmodellierung: Forschungsbedarf und Gestaltungsempfehlungen auf Basis der Transaktionskosten-theorie. *Wirtschaftsinformatik, 46,* 341-352.

Chen, P. (1976). The entity-relationship model: Towards a unified view of data. *ACM Transactions on Database Systems (TODS),* 9-36.

Crawford, J. D. (1984, June 25-27). An electronic design interchange format. In *Proceedings of the 21st Conference on Design Automation,* Albuquerque, NM (pp. 683-685).

Delphi Group. (2003). BPM 2003—Market Milestone Report.

Fettke, P., & Loos, P. (2003). Classification of reference models: A methodology and its application. *Information Systems and E-Business Management (ISeB), 1*(1), 35-53.

Hohpe, G., & Woolf, B. (2004). *Enterprise integration patterns.* Addison Wesley.

Karagiannis, D., & Kühn, H. (2002). Metamodelling platforms. Invited paper. In K. Bauknecht, A. M. Tjoa, & G. Quirchmayer (Eds.), *Proceedings of the 3rd International Conference EC-Web 2002—Dexa 2002,* Aix-en-Provence, France (LNCS 2455, pp. 182-196).

Keller, G., Nüttgens, M., & Scheer, A. W. (1992). *Semantische Prozessmodellierung auf der grundlage ``Ereignisgesteuerter Prozessketten (EPK).* Saarbrücken, Germany.

Kindler, E. (2004). On the semantics of EPCs: Resolving the vicious circle. In J. Desel, B. Pernici & M. Weske (Eds.), *Business Process Management: Second International Conference (BPM 2004),* Potsdam, Germany (Vol. 3080, pp. 82-97): Springer Verlag.

Koegel, J. F. (1992, November 12-13). *On the design of multimedia interchange formats.* Paper presented at the Network and Operating System Support for Digital Audio and Video, Proceedings of the Third International Workshop, La Jolla, CA.

Langner, P., Schneider, C., & Wehler, J. (1998). Petri net based certification of event-driven process chains. In J. Desel & M. Silva (Eds.), *Application and Theory of Petri Nets 1998, 19th International Conference (ICATPN '98),* Lisbon, Portugal (Vol. 1420, pp. 286-305). Lisbon: Springer.

Leymann, F. (2003). Web services: Distributed applications without limits. In H. S. Gerhard Weikum, Erhard Rahm (Ed.), *BTW 2003, Datenbanksysteme für Business, Technologie und Web, Tagungsband der 10. BTW-Konferenz* (LNI 26, pp. 2-23).

Mendling, J., Neumann, G., & Nüttgens, M. (2005a). A comparison of XML interchange formats for business process modelling. In L. Fischer (Ed.), *Workflow handbook* (pp. 185-198). FL: Lighthouse Point.

Mendling, J., Neumann, G., & Nüttgens, M. (2005). *Towards workflow pattern support of event-driven process chains (EPC).* In M. Nüttgens, J. Mendling (Eds.), *Proceed-*

ings of the 2nd Workshop XML4BPM 2005. CEUR Workshop Proceedings (Vol. 145, pp. 23-38).

Mendling, J., Neumann, G., & Nüttgens, M. (2005b). *Yet another event-driven process chain.* Paper presented at the Proceedings of the 3rd International Conference on Business Process Management (BPM 2005), Nancy, France.

Mendling, J., & Nüttgens, M. (2004). Transformation of ARIS markup language to EPML. In F. R. Markus Nüttgens (Ed.), *Proceedings of the 3rd Workshop on Event-Driven Process Chains (EPK 2004)* (pp. 27-38).

Mendling, J., & Nüttgens, M. (2005). *EPC markup language (EPML): An XML-based interchange format for event-driven process chains (EPC).* Vienna University of Economics and Business Administration.

Nüttgens, M., & Rump, F. J. (2002). Syntax und semantik ereignisgesteuerter prozessketten (EPK). In J. Desel & M. Weske (Eds.) (Vol. 21, pp. 64-77).

Ohno-Machado, L., Gennari, J. H., Murphy, S. N., Jain, N. L., Tu, S. W., Oliver, D. E., et al. (1998). The GuideLine interchange format. *Journal of the American Informatics Association, 5*, 357-372.

OMG. (2002). *Meta object facility version 1.4*: Object Management Group.

OMG. (2003). *XML metadata interchange (XMI) version 2.0*: Object Management Group.

OMG. (2004). *Unified modeling language version 2.0*: Object Management Group.

Recker, J., Rosemann, M., Aalst, W. v. d., & Mendling, J. (2005). On the syntax of reference model configuration. Transforming the C-EPC into Lawful EPC Models. In E. Kindler & M. Nüttgens (Eds.), *Proceedings of the Workshop on Business Process Reference Models (BPRM 2005)*. Nancy: Springer.

Rosemann, M., & Aalst, W. v. d. (2005). A configurable reference modelling language. *Information Systems,* to appear.

Scheer, A.-W. (2000). *ARIS: Business process modeling.* Berlin: Springer.

Soffer, P., Golany, B., & Dori, D. (2003). ERP modeling: A comprehensive approach. *Information Systems, 28*, 673-690.

St-Denis, G., Schauer, R., & Keller, R. K. (2000, January 4-7). Selecting a model interchange format: The spool case study. In *Proceedings of the 33rd Annual Hawaii International Conference on System Sciences (HICSS-33),* Maui.

WfMC. (2005). *Workflow process definition interface: XML process definition language.* Version 2.0.

White, S. (2004). *Business process modeling notation (BPMN).*

Winter, A. (2002). GXL—Overview and current status. In *Proceedings of the International Workshop on Graph-Based Tools (GraBaTs),* Barcelona, Spain.

Wüstner, E., Hotzel, T., & Buxmann, P. (2002). Converting business documents: A classification of problems and solutions using XML/XSLT. In *Proceedings of the 4th International Workshop WECWIS.*

Chapter XVII

Lessons Learned in Reference Modeling

Wolfgang Höhnel, PPI Consulting Group GmbH, Germany

Daniela Krahl, PPI Consulting Group GmbH, Germany

Dirk Schreiber, University of Applied Sciences Bonn-Rhein-Sieg, Germany

Abstract

A reference model is always developed in order to support a specific purpose. The development environment is setting the broader context. Limitations are not only set by size and experience of the modeler team or by budget and time constraints. The intended usage scenario also defines the fundamental contour of a reference model. During the practical work with reference models, a range of key issues has come up to increase the suitability of reference models for daily use. As the result of many projects, the authors have summarized the key issues and formulated critical success factors for reference modeling projects.

Introduction

In the '80s, the overall target of discussions on reference models was aimed at "how to construct." Today, the focal point was shifted to "how to use." Since many reference models for various purposes are available now, the discussion on concrete usage aspects of the models is more important to the practitioners. In the same way, the types of usage scenarios for reference models have increased. Reference models do not only provide a basis for application development as an aid for navigation and structuring (Schuette, 1998). They are also used to model the business in terms of operational and organizational structures. In fact, the same reference model supports a "make or buy" decision for a business application as well as a definition of a migration path between two applications. Additionally, it provides the starting point for an individual application development or organization development project. Furthermore, the reference model can be used as a template for organizational decisions during evaluation and the customization process of a standard application (Becker & Knackstedt, 2003; Keller, Lietschulte, & Curran, 1999; Kruse, 1996). Steve Hitchman defines reference models also as a "framework of strategic thinking" (Hitchman, 2005). This framework is applicable to all operations of an enterprise and assists in designing the business processes.

We share the common criticism on usability of reference models (Patel, Sim, & Weber, 1998). Nevertheless, in our opinion an enterprise will have its advantages if models are being used in well-defined environments (Schuette, 1998). Some investment is necessary in order to benefit from the use of reference models as anticipated. There is a danger to underestimate the effort of preparing the modelers' training and of adopting the reference model to the changing requirements over time. In the following sections, we outline our lessons learned.

A long-time relationship with the organization-wide data model of the German Savings Bank Organization, also known as the SKO Data Model, has been the bases of our experience. The SKO Data Model covers efficiently all business areas of savings banks (Krahl & Kittlaus, 1998). It is a reference model that has been deducted and further developed from the IBM Financial Services Data Model (IBM FSDM) (Financial Services Data Model, 1993).

Typical processes to construct, to apply and to maintain reference models are described in section "The Process of Managing a Reference Model." In the section, "Critical Success Factors," we formulate a set of critical success factors to determine the success for conducting the processes described in the previous section. The section "Exemplary Scenarios for Using a Reference Model" illustrates the implementation of these identified factors by presenting three usage scenarios of the SKO data model. "Summary and Outlook: Perspectives on Reference Modeling" summarizes the lessons learned and points out some perspectives for reference modeling.

The Process of Managing a Reference Model

The activities in reference modeling can be grouped into three main processes: construction, customization and maintenance of the model.

Figure 1. The process of reference modeling

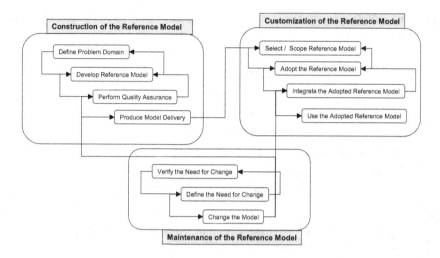

A model owner mainly drives the *construction* of the reference model. Considering the model as a product, the product "reference model" is under the control of a product management. The product management controls particularly the:

- **Management of the requirements:** Definition of scope, actual and future features of the model;
- **Management of the marketing activities:** Definition of the marketing mix, target groups and communication channels;
- **Management of the budget:** Definition of budget, construction process controlling and target pricing.

Customization of the reference model includes all activities that are necessary to adopt the reference model to the specific usage environment. These actions are necessary to find an adequate representation for the reference model in the selected business context.

While focusing on the change and impact management, the *maintenance* activities are following a mini construction cycle. In addition to the structure proposed by Fettke and Loos (2005), the *maintenance* activities are clustered in a separate process, since they are essential to the usability of a model.

Process: Construction of the Reference Model

The construction of a reference model consists of four major activity blocks.

Define the Problem Domain of the Reference Model

The answers to following questions are setting the frame of the reference model and its development:

*   Who should use the reference model?
*   What should be the context for the usage of the model?
*   What is the expected benefit for the user of the reference model?
*   Which set of problems should be addressed?
*   What is the marketable price for the model?
*   Which budget is available in developing the model?
*   Are comparable offers available?

After having identified all these parameters, the initial version of the development plan can be established and the required resources can be assigned.

Develop the Reference Model for the Problem Domain

The practical construction starts with defining the model architecture and outlining the meta-model, which is key to ensuring a defined level of quality and consistency. On top of that, the modeling methods and procedures as well as the training material for the developers should be at hand. The methods and procedures assist the modelers in harmonizing their individual modeling styles and in achieving compatible results.

Usually the entire set of modeling activities are performed incrementally.

Perform Quality Assurance for the Reference Model

The model has to be checked against the predefined quality criteria. There are two group groups of such quality criteria: criteria related to the format, such as meeting the required standards of documentation, and criteria related to the content of the model, such as asking whether the model describes the business context adequately. The formal criteria can be examined with specific tools, which are derived by applying the meta-model. These tool-checks are performed either *a priori* or *a posteriori*. The former might restrict the freedom of the developer, whereas the latter might require additional cycles of modeling, and, thus, consume more time.

Problem domain experts using walkthroughs, interviews, workshops and other techniques might verify the content.

Produce the Delivery Package of the Reference Model

A delivery of the reference model includes all necessary documents, models and teaching material. Various product packages might be necessary, since the reference model approaches different target groups. Therefore, specific language versions, specific distribution media as well as specific teaching material for different skill levels may be required.

Process: Customization of the Reference Model

Since a third party supplies the reference model, the individual customization of the model is a step of utmost importance. Even though a reference model may fulfill all predefined requirements—it might be useless unless its proper familiarization is carried out.

Select/Scope the Reference Model

It is essential to identify the model components that contribute most to the solution of a specific business problem. The basis for selection is a clear definition of functional and non-functional requirements. The number of satisfied requirements limits the choice of reference models that are available on the internal or external market. In most cases, the individual (project) model is cut out of the reference model.

Adopt the Reference Model

The major areas of adoption are:

*   **Adopt the model language:** Either the content of the reference model or the diagramming technique used has to be translated.
*   **Adopt the available specific model architecture.**
*   **Adopt the specific business context:** which means reduction, enlargement or enrichment of the model.

Alternatively, a full customization or a business-need-driven customization of the reference model is possible. The latter is the most efficient.

Integrate the Adopted Reference Model

It is mandatory to integrate the adopted and scoped reference model into the prefabricated model architecture and model landscape. Identifying, documenting and managing the overlaps and gaps among the various models and submodels is pivotal.

Use the Adopted Reference Model

Now, the refined and scoped model is ready for use. Before the first use of the adopted model, each modeler has to familiarize himself with the modeling standards, techniques and quality procedures. Similarly, the environment of the model management has to be prepared in advance.

Process: Maintenance of the Reference Model

The constant change of business is driving the need for change of models. In this section, we treat equally reference model and adopted model.

Verify the Need of Change

Numerous factors cause the need to modify a model. Alterations of the business requirements due to a change in legislation, reduction or enlargement of the project scope, changes in the architecture of the model or identified errors are such factors. All resulting modifications might affect the stability and coherence of the existing model. Therefore, the collateral affect of any modification has to be carefully examined. The formal change request is documenting each of the identified needs for need.

Define the Need of Change

In order to evaluate the impact of the envisaged change the request is being tested against the existing model. A documentation of the pre-and post change scenarios and a possible simulation of the change allow estimating the cost of implementation.

Change of the Reference Model

The verified change requests should be carried out in accordance with the existing model architecture, guidelines and quality criteria. Usually, many changes are bundled into a package that is implemented as a whole. After the completion of the change, the model is available for repackaging and delivery. The model documentation now also includes the change requests and the documented impact.

Critical Success Factors

This section describes critical success factors that we have identified in practical work in over 40 reference-modeling projects. In the section *Exemplary Reference Model Usage*

Scenarios, we describe some of the performed projects.

We learned that all the required steps described before are necessary but not sufficient to grant success. Failures are caused by a lack of user acceptance or by abundant complexity of the models. On the other hand, the richness in details may have the effect of lowering the threshold of getting acquainted to the model. Depending on the expectation of the user, the predefined content and structure of a reference model generates either relief or resistance.

We group the recognized success factors into five classes:

1.   Open communication
2.   Open construction principles and quality criteria
3.   Tool support
4.   Business justification
5.   Use what you bought

Open Communication (1)

(1.1) An open communication between the model designer and the potential user must be guaranteed.

An active communication between the expertise modeler and the potential model user supports the modeling process. Making the usually implicit assumptions explicit is the primary

Figure 2. The reference modeling experience base

	IBM Information Framework Models	IBM Insurance Models	SKO Data Model
Development of a reference model	Data Model (2) Process Model (1) Activity Model (1) Object Model (1) Data Warehouse Model (1)		Data Model (1) Process Model (1) Nomenclature (1) Object Model (1)
Customization on enterprise level	Data Model (7) Process Model (2) Object Model (1) Data Warehouse Model (2)	Data Model (1) Data Warehouse Model (1)	
Customization on Application or Business Domain Level	Data Model (4) Data Warehouse Model (2)	Data Warehouse Model (2)	Data Model (8)
Product Evaluation	Data Model (1)		Data Model (1)

aim of such communication. Even the best documentation cannot replace the one-to-one exchange of ideas.

Proven techniques are designer/user workshops in the problem domain or customer councils dealing with product management issues.

(1.2) Teaching material is a mandatory supplement of the reference model.

The teaching material should support the usage scenarios and reflect the distinct needs for induction. Such material can be delivered as self-teaching material, workshop material, train-the-trainer workshops or just handbooks. Additionally, worked examples from the practice are providing good insight into the reference model and its underlying principles.

Open Construction Principles and Quality Criteria (2)

(2.1) The principles of model design must be revealed.

The acceptance of the reference model stands and falls with the decisions taken with regard to the model design. Therefore, it is essential to disclose the modeling method applied. This is especially true of recurring structural design patterns. It is therefore indispensable to document these design principles, which emerge as creative assumptions and decisions during the construction phase. For a day-to-day use of the model, the internalization of the design principles by the user is necessary.

(2.2) The quality criteria have to be redefined on a regular base.

The quality criteria that were constituent for the construction should also be applied throughout the entire life cycle of the reference model, including the customized and extended versions of the model. The quality check should cover the model itself as well as its documentation. When individual elements are extracted from the entirety of the model, the avoidance of all inter- and intra-model conflicts has to be ensured.

(2.3) The meta model should be dealt with in total transparency.

The meta-model of a reference model is the foundation for formal quality criteria and a prerequisite for any tool support. Tool support is important to manage the model change, maintenance and documentation.

(2.4) The problem domain must be described as detailed as possible.

It is decisive to outline carefully the business context and the business assumptions. In particular, when submodels are derived from larger ones, the business and the model context should be documented thoroughly.

(2.5) All changes between model versions must be documented.

The documented trace between two model versions is essential for understanding the underlying rationale. If changes are to be reproduced in an already customized version, the change documentation is vital.

(2.6) Interaction must be managed between various models or model versions.

If more than one reference model is used, an integrative model architecture and model management is essential. Since it is unlikely that two reference models stick to the same design principles, the models must be made comparable and compatible. Rather than integrating the different meta-models, the management of the model architecture has to take care of hedging the problems arising from the coexistence of those models.

Tool Support (3)

(3.1) Adequate tools should support the management of a reference model.

Reference models may consist of thousands of elements (Fettke & Loos, 2004). It is, therefore, hard to assure the consistency of the model. Manual management or maintenance of a model of that size is difficult. Advanced toolsets provide assistance for decompositions of the model like model views, layers or sub systems. The integrated meta-model sets the framework for diverse perspectives and for associations between multiple model types. Additionally, the tool provides help for establishing traces between objects of different model layers (level trace) or model versions (history trace).

Business Justification (4)

(4.1) No use of a reference model without a business justification!

A business justification is setting the limitations for the use of a reference model. The justification sets a ceiling to the efforts, and determines the organizational boundaries of the project. A decision either to build one's own model or to use a reference model is also based on the initial justification. Furthermore, permanent project control based on the defined business cases and business scopes is an essential help for avoiding a mistaken investment.

Figure 3. Relationship between critical success factors and processes

	Process		
	Construction	**Customization**	**Maintenance**
Open Communication	Model Producer	Model User (generic)/ Model User (specific)	Producer/ Model User
Open Construction principles and Quality Criteria	Model Producer	Model User	Producer/ Model User
Tool support	Model Producer	Model User	Model Producer/ Model User
Business Justification	Model Producer	Model User	Model Producer/ Model User
Use what you bought		Model User	

(4.2) Before deciding to use a model, check the quality, the documentation and the integrity of the reference model package.

The value of the reference model depends on the accompanying verbal documentation. A formal representation of the model is incomplete without some explanatory words. Therefore, each model object needs a textual description. The description should enable less formally educated users to understand the rationale behind each model object. Tools may translate the graphical representation into continuous text or they may produce parts of the documentation.

Use What You Bought (5)

(5.1) Predefined design principles must be accepted and applied.

If the user of a reference model does not accept its design principles, his decision for a specific reference model should be put into question again. The phenomenon of resistance against models imposed from outside should not be underestimated. In the same way, the reluctant use of a model and the hesitant acceptance of its principles would clearly suggest departure from the reference model.

(5.2) If the model is overly restrictive, refrain from using it.

A reference model is always the representation of the reality seen from the perspective of the model designer. If the user does not share major elements of the designer's perception, than resistance can be anticipated.

Critical Success Factors and Process Relationship

Obviously, the reference model producer benefits most if he or she meets the criteria for success during the model construction process, whereas the reference model user is mostly supported by the success factors during the customization process. Because both groups are involved in model maintenance process, they can share the profit from fulfilling the critical success factors.

The applicable critical success factors are equally weighted; the absence of one factor does have a great impact on the reference-modeling project. The financial effect varies between "additional time needed" and "total loss," if the reference model isn't accepted by the community.

Exemplary Scenarios for Using a Reference Model

The activity "use the adopted reference model" is the most important, since at this point; the desired benefit is to be accomplished. The following examples are based on the SKO data model, which is described in detail in Eisenreich (2002) and Krahl and Kittlaus (1998).

From a data view, the following three usage scenarios illustrate how to apply the identified success factors:

Scenario I: "Green Field"

- **Step I.1. Evaluate the logical data requirements:** The establishing of the data household for a new application begins with analyzing the documentation of functional requirements. Accompanied with interviews, workshops and text analysis, the necessary business terms are identified. Recognized business terms are first categorized by main data concepts and then further decomposed into term hierarchies. New business terms are defined and adequately allocated. Existing terms are marked and the corresponding definitions are checked. Verified terms (new ones and already existing ones) are earmarked and discussed in a quality assurance workshop with the business users. For an easy understanding of the business terms, a graphical representation has turned out to be useful. The hierarchy structures help to identify open questions.

- **Step I.2. Build a project-specific conceptual data model:** The identified terms are translated into entity relationship structures. This can be supported by a trace between the aforementioned hierarchies and the organization-wide ER diagram. New Business Terms will be translated into entities, attributes, domains and domain values or relationships for enrichment of the reference ER-Model. Moreover, already existing model elements are verified again.

- **Step I.3. Specialize the conceptual model to the project environment:** The ER model representing the project scope mentioned in Step 2 has to be reduced according to the non-functional requirements. It is necessary to determine what data should be held in

Figure 4. Scenario I: "Green Field"

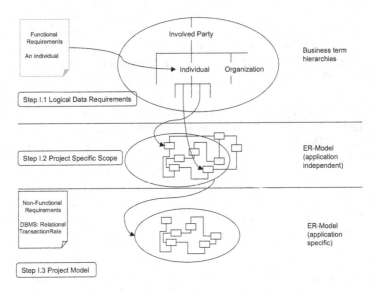

a new database and what data are already available through interfaces. Furthermore, logical super-subtype structures are simplified and adjusted to the available database technology.

This scenario describes the necessary activities to structure the data requirements for a new application, based on a given reference model, which is used like a warehouse catalogue.

The previous three steps transport the logical business data requirements into a format that can be used by a database designer and support the chosen technical architecture.

Since pre-defined business terms and data model structures are re-used, the reference model has accelerated the modeling process and improved the quality of the specification process. As a result, there is an involvement of the business user because they can easily recognize and verify their terminology without any bias of sophisticated modeling techniques (especially in Step I.1). Therefore, gaps and overlaps in the data requirements are revealed in an early project stage. Existing structures are re-used in a resulting application-specific ER model, which is modeled consistently, reflecting the functional and non-functional requirements of the application. The documented project model (including its links to the reference model) is also a valid base for future maintenance and functional enhancement projects.

Scenario II: "Migration" (From an Existing Application to a New One)

Migration from an application in use to a new application has many facets. The logical transition of the actual data elements into a new application is an essential task. Besides the difficulty with homonyms and synonyms, the handling of domain values is an additional challenge. Domain

Figure 5. Scenario II: "Migration"

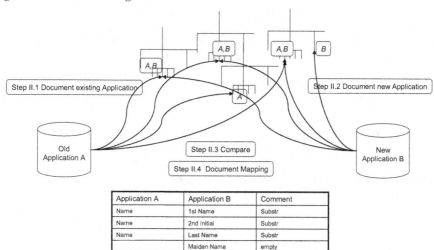

Application A	Application B	Comment
Name	1st Name	Substr
Name	2nd Initial	Substr
Name	Last Name	Substr
	Maiden Name	empty

values are mostly hidden in compound attributes, are coded or only accessible via functions. Nevertheless, these domain values are essential for a mapping between the new and the old applications.

- **Step II.1. Document existing application as reference model scope:** Existing data elements of the still active application are mapped against the business terms hierarchies of the reference model. This is necessary to analyze the semantic that is hidden in the data structures of the old application and to add more transparency to the existing application.

- **Step II.2. Document new application as reference model scope:** The new application is mapped as described in Step II.1.

- **Step II.3. Compare both scopes:** The (visual) comparison of the two business term scopes is supported by color-coding of the terms. Identical data elements have the same domain values pool. If data elements are identified only in the old application, it must be decided whether they are needed in future, or whether they have to be aggregated or decomposed. For non-pairing elements of the new application, an assessment has to be made whether the field has to be filled with a default value or populated from another source.

- **Step II.4. Document the data element mapping:** The functional specification for the data migration is derived from the detailed documentation between mapped data elements. Then, the technological details (technical field characteristics) are added and migration activities like data cleansing can be started.

The reference model is a neutral and single point of reference where both applications can be mapped. It offers a vast and ordered collection of business terms, which is independent of any specific application. Instead of a direct map between the two applications, the indirect map via the reference model ensures neutrality and transparency. It is a positive side effect of the mapping, that weak points of the existing data structure become obvious. The open questions can be clarified before the technical migration starts. Maintaining all these application specific data within a repository allows a machine-assisted comparison.

Scenario III: "Product Evaluation"

"Product evaluation" assumes that there are different alternatives available on the market that meet the specific requirements of the enterprise. It is expected that the requirements can be met at least after some intensive customization activities. The setting combines several steps of the previous scenarios. Thus, so the afore-mentioned arguments are also valid in this scenario.

- **Step III.1. Evaluate the logical data requirements:** Similar to scenario "Green field" Step I.1.

- **Step III.2.** Build a conceptual data model as target model by scoping the reference model: Similar to scenario "Green field" Step I.2.

- **Step III.3. Document conceptual data models of the products as reference model scope:** Similar to scenario "Migration" Step II.2.

- **Step III.4. Compare each alternative scope with the target model:** Similar to scenario "Migration" Step II.3.

- **Step III.5. Choose the product with the scope that fits most with the target model:** It is in general easier to compare products conceptually without regarding technical details. If the granularity of a product scope is nearly equal to the granularity of the target model, the product is suitable for the requirements of the evaluating enterprise.

Figure 6. Scenario III: "Product evaluation"

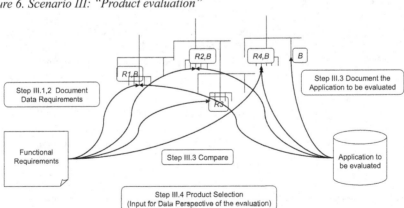

Figure 7. Relationship between critical success factors and exemplary scenarios

	Scenario		
	I. Green Field	**II. Migration**	**III. Product Evaluation**
Open Communication	Understand the problem domain and the reflection into the reference model. Communicate strength and weaknesses of the model proactively.		
Open Construction Principles and Quality Criteria	Understand the application of the implemented concepts as a tool to support the problem domain. Adopt the inherited quality criteria.		
Tool support	Use a consistent tool to document the decisions and to maintain the links between requirements, existing objects, new objects and assumptions.		
Business Justification	Since a reference model always takes time and does require a budget, the business justification should be evaluated first.		
Use What You Bought	If there was a decision to use the model, do not use the model as excuse.		

- **Step III.6. (Optional):** Specialize the conceptual model of the chosen alternative to prepare the customization of the acquired product environment.

- **Step III.7. (Optional):** Map the specialized conceptual model to the reference model.

Steps III.6 and III.7 are optional because the evaluation process in a narrow sense is already finished. In spite of this, it is useful to describe these steps in this scenario, because this connection of the customized product with the reference model is the base for further work.

In general, two types of usage scenarios can be identified. Reference models are used either as template, pattern and artifact or as "reference" point where different realities can be mapped. In the first class of scenarios (Scenario I), the model improves speed and quality of the specification process, whereas in the second group of scenarios (Scenario II and III) the model helps to make things comparable, even if they are using different "terminologies."

In summary, all the identified critical success factors can also be applied to the depicted scenarios.

Summary and Outlook: Perspectives on Reference Modeling

Certain success factors are necessary for an effective and efficient development and application of a reference model. In practice, methodological discussions about structure and content can be neglected. We have learned that methodological discussions are time consuming and sometimes artificial. Instead, questions concerning the manageability and practical usability are coming to the foreground. An adequate tool support is the main pre-requisite for manageability. Since model management is dealing with thousands of objects, a meta-model-based repository implementation, including model management tools, is a fundamental requirement.

The second fundamental requirement is the usability, which is defined as a low threshold of grasping the essence of the model and of applying it on the job.

A reference model is inevitably doomed to fail if these two requirements are not met. On the other hand, meeting the two requirements does not automatically suffice to grant success.

There is currently a remarkable renaissance in using reference models. Compliance and governance aspects are the main drivers for this. A reference model can be described as documented best practice and as a given pattern.

References

Becker, J., & Knackstedt, R. (2003). Construction and application of reference models for data warehousing. In W. Uhr, W. Esswein, & E. Schoop (Eds.), *Wirtschaftsinformatik 2003/Band II - Medien - Märkte – Mobilität* (pp. 415-433). Heidelberg: Physica. [in German]

Eisenreich, A. (2002). The SKO-data model: A reference model for savings banks. In J. Becker & R. Knackstedt (Eds.), *Referenzmodellierung 2002 - Methoden - Modelle - Erfahrungen. Tagungsband zur 6. Fachtagung Referenzmodellierung 2002 im Rahmen der MKWI 2002 in Nürnberg* (pp. 121–132). Münster. [in German]

Fettke, P., & Loos, P. (2004). Reference modeling research. Extension of an Article. *Arbeitsbericht des Instituts für Informationssysteme und Management Nr. 16*. Mainz. [in German]

Fettke, P., & Loos, P. (2005). Using reference modeling for business engineering. *HMD Forum der Wirtschaftsinformatik, 241, 18-26*. [in German]

Financial services data model reference, Volume 1: Model architecture release 1.01. (1993). Manassas: IBM.

Hitchman, S. (2005). Strategic conceptual modeling: An example from practice. *Journal of Conceptual Modeling, (31)*. Retrieved August 1, 2005, from www.inconcept.com/jcm

Keller, G., Lietschulte, A., & Curran, T. (1999). Business engineering with R/3 reference models. In A. Scheer & M. Nüttgens (Eds.), *Electronic business engineering: 4. Internationale Tagung Wirtschaftsinformatik* (pp. 397-423). Heidelberg. [in German]

Krahl, D., & Kittlaus, H.-B. (1998). The SIZ banking data model. In P. Bernus, K. Mertins, & G. Schmidt (Series Eds.), *International handbook on information systems* (pp. 667-687). Heidelberg.

Kruse, C. (1996). *Business process management.* Wiesbaden. [in German]

Patel, A., Sim, M., & Weber, R. (1998). Stakeholder experiences with conceptual modeling: An empirical investigation. In *Proceedings of the international conference on Information Systems*, Helsinki (pp. 370-375).

Schütte, R. (1998). *Guidelines for reference modeling.* Wiesbaden: Gabler. [in German]

About the Authors

Peter Fettke earned a master's degree in information systems (Diplom-Wirtschaftsinformatiker) from the University of Münster, Germany. Since April 2006 he has been a senior researcher in information systems, Institute for Information Systems (IWi) at the German Research Center for Artificial Intelligence (DFKI), Saarbrücken. Fettke has previously taught and researched at the Technical University of Chemnitz and the Johannes Gutenberg-University Mainz, both Germany. His research interests include information systems analysis and design, especially the use of conceptual modeling and component-based system paradigms. He has published numerous articles on reference modeling, conceptual modeling and component-based engineering in both national and international journals and conference proceedings. Furthermore, he is a member of the editorial board of the *Journal of Cases on Information Technology (JCIT)* as well as the *Journal of System and the Management Sciences (JSMS)* and serves as a regular reviewer for the *Information Resources Management Journal (IRMJ)*, *Data & Knowledge Engineering (DKE)* and *International Journal of Interoperability in Business Information Systems (IBIS)*. He recently finished his PhD thesis on structuralist foundations for the ontological evaluation of reference models.

Peter Loos (1960) is director of the Institute for Information Systems (IWi) at the German Research Institute for Artificial Intelligence (DFKI) and head of the Chair of Business Administration and Information Systems at Saarland University. His research activities include business process management, information modeling, enterprise systems, software development and implementation of information systems. Dr. Loos studied business administration and information systems at the University of Saarland and completed his degree

(Dipl.-Kfm.) in 1984. He wrote his PhD thesis on the issue of data modeling in manufacturing systems—awarded with the Dr.-Eduard-Martin-Preis—in 1991 as a research assistant at the Institute for Information Systems (directed by Professor Dr. Dr. h.c. mult. August-Wilhelm Scheer). In 1997, Dr. Loos received the venia legendi in business administration. During his earlier career, he had been chair of information systems & management at the University of Mainz (2002-2005), chair of information systems & management at Chemnitz University of Technology (1998-2002), deputy chair at University of Münster as well as a lecturer (Privatdozent) at Saarland University. Furthermore, he worked for six years as manager of the Department of Software Development at the software and consulting company IDS Scheer AG. Dr. Loos has written several books, contributed to 30 books and published more than 100 papers in journals and proceedings.

*   *   *

Frederik Ahlemann studied computer science until 2000 at the University of Münster, Germany, and worked as a consultant for project management for two years. Following this period, he joined the Faculty of Economics and Business Administration at the University of Osnabrück with the aim of obtaining his doctorate. Ahlemann is currently doing research in the area of information systems for enterprise-wide project management.

Antonia Albani studied computer science at the Swiss Federal Institute of Technology (ETH) in Zurich where she received her master's degree in 1995 and her PhD in 2000. After one year in IT consulting with focus on business process modeling, she was CEO and co-founder of an Internet start-up in the area of business process outsourcing. In January 2003 she started her habilitation at the Systems Engineering Group of the University of Augsburg, Germany, with specific focus on the research area of component-based, inter-organizational systems. Since February 2005 she has been a part-time assistant professor position at the Delft University of Technology, The Netherlands, in the Software Engineering Group.

Jörg Becker is a full professor for information systems and information management and head of the Department of Information Systems at the University of Münster, Germany, as well as managing director of the European Research Center for Information Systems (ERCIS). His research areas include information management, management information systems, information modeling, data management, logistics and industry information systems, workflow management and retail information systems. He has published seven monographs and numerous papers and articles in his research field. Dr. Becker holds a master's degree and a PhD in business administration from the University of Saarland, Germany. He also studied business administration and economics at the University of Michigan, Ann Arbor. Furthermore, he serves on the editorial boards of *Information Systems and e-Business Management*, *Wirtschaftsinformatik* and *Information & Management*.

Robert Braun studied business administration and engineering at Dresden University of Technology, Germany. Since 2002 he has been working as a research assistant at the Chair of Information Systems, especially systems development, at the same university.

Alexander Dreiling (PhD, 1975) is a researcher at SAP Research in Brisbane, Australia. Prior to joining SAP he worked as a research assistant at the European Research Center for Information Systems (ERCIS) in Münster, Germany and at the Centre for Information Technology Innovation in Brisbane. His research interests comprise conceptual data warehouse modeling, conceptual process modeling and process configuration. His research so far has led to approximately 25 refereed journal and conference publications.

Francisco J. Duarte is responsible for the Information Systems Group at the Department of Informatics at Blaupunkt Auto-Rádio Portugal (Braga, Portugal). He is also a teaching assistant in the Department of Information Systems, Universidade do Minho. He received a Lic. degree in informatics and systems engineering in 1993, and an MSc in informatics in 2002, both from Universidade do Minho. His MSc thesis, "Process-Oriented Software Engineering", addresses the usage of object-oriented concepts and processes, namely UML and RUP, to model process-oriented organizations and to develop software systems for those organizations. His research interests focus on software engineering, business process management, business modeling and requirements analysis.

Werner Esswein completed his PhD thesis at the University of Regensburg and worked as a research assistant at the Chair of Information Systems, especially systems and database development, at the Otto-Friedrich-University in Bamberg. Since 1994 he has been a professor of information systems, specializing in systems development, at Dresden University of Technology, Germany. Esswein founded the semture private limited company.

João M. Fernandes is an assistant professor at the Department of Informatics, Universidade do Minho, Braga, Portugal. He received a DEng in informatics and systems engineering in 1991, an MSc in computer science in 1994 and a PhD in computer engineering in 2000, all from U. Minho. From September 2002 until February 2003, he was a post-doctoral researcher at the TUCS Embedded Systems Laboratory, Turku, Finland. He is a (co-)author of several scientific publications with peer revision on international conferences, journals and chapters of books. He has already served as a scientific reviewer for an Addison-Wesley book, for several international conferences and for IEEE, Elsevier and Springer international journals. He has also served as a member of the Programme or Organizing Committees of international workshops and conferences, namely DIPES, TeaConc, ETFA, ICESS, DSOA, CPN, MOMPES, and ACSD. His research interests focus on software engineering, embedded software, software modelling, software process and management, methodologies for system development and history of computing. For more information, consult his Web site at http://www.di.uminho.pt/~jmf.

Ulrich Frank is a professor of information systems and enterprise modelling at the University of Duisburg-Essen, Germany. Prior to this position he headed the research group "Enterprise Modelling" at the University of Koblenz. His research interests include the design and evaluation of modelling languages and reference models, as well as software engineering and workflow management.

Heike Gastl studied business administration for the teaching profession with a major in computer science at the University of Mainz. In 2002 she joined the Business Technology Office of McKinsey & Company as a consultant. Currently she is working on her PhD, being a postgraduate student in the Department of Economics and Business Administration at the University of Osnabrück, Germany. In her thesis she focuses on building a reference model for enterprise-wide e-learning in major companies.

Andreas Gehlert studied information systems at the Dresden University of Technology, Germany. Since 2001 he has been working as a research assistant at the Chair of Information Systems, specializing in systems development at the same university.

Öner Güngöz has been a researcher at the Institute for Information System (IWi), Saarland University, since June 2001. Before working at IWi, Güngöz completed a bank traineeship followed by a business management degree course at the University of Saarland—part of this took place at the University of Technology, Sydney, Australia. During his time at IWi, Güngöz was responsible for several national and international projects; wrote a number of articles that were published in magazines, journals and books; and was also a lecturer at the University of Saarland. He is currently working as a guest lecturer on the topic of BPM at the Aoyama Gakuin University, Tokyo, Japan, and Cleveland State University, USA.

Wolfgang Höhnel studied business administration at the University of Cooperative Education Stuttgart and received a diploma degree. He worked for IBM as development team member of the IBM Information Framework and has conducted many reference model customization projects and modelling efforts during the last 15 years. He currently works for the PPI Consulting Group GmbH, Germany. Since 2000 he has held a lectureship at the University of Applied Science Bonn-Rhein-Sieg

Monique Jansen-Vullers (PhD, 1969) is an assistant professor at the Department of Technology Management at Eindhoven University of Technology (TUE), The Netherlands, and member of the BETA research group. Currently she is working on: (1) configurable reference models, (2) process mining in enterprise resource planning environments and (3) business process redesign. She is the author of several academic publications in the mentioned research fields.

Wolfram Jost has been a member of the management board at IDS Scheer AG in Saarbrücken, Germany, since October 2000, and is responsible for ARIS product development, product sales, product consulting, IDS Scheer technologies, business process management and marketing. After completing a degree in business economics at the University of the Saarland, he worked at the Institute of Economic Information Science at the University of the Saarland. After completing his doctoral thesis at the Law and Economics Faculty at the University of the Saarland he joined IDS Prof. Scheer GmbH, Saarbrücken (which became IDS Scheer AG in May 1999), initially as the head of ARIS product development and later as the head of ARIS Product Strategy. In 1994 he was promoted to senior management level, a post he held until he was appointed to the management board. Dr. Jost has written numerous articles for books and magazines and has also (co-)authored several specialist books. He is also a lecturer at the University of the Saarland.

Daniela Krahl, a computer scientist (diploma acquired at the Technical University of Berlin), worked as a lecturer for applied computer science. Since 1990 she held various positions within the German Savings Banks Organisation (SKO). First, she was the project manager for the organisation-wide reference model (SKO data model). Later on she developed architectural concepts for data mining and data warehouse projects. In 2005 she joined the PPI Consulting Group GmbH.

Ricardo J. Machado is a professor of software engineering and coordinator of the Software Engineering and Management Research Group (SEMAG) at the Department of Information Systems, Universidade do Minho (Guimarães, Portugal). He holds a PhD and an MSc in informatics and computer engineering (both from U. Minho), and a DEng in electronics and computer engineering (from FEUP). He is the president of the Portuguese technical committee (CT128) responsible for analyzing the documents produced by JTC1/SC7 from ISO/IEC and by TC311 from CEN/CENELEC in the software and system engineering domain. He is the president of the Portuguese representation in the IFIP Technical Committee in Computer Systems Technology (TC10), and he is member of the Portuguese Information Technologies and Telecommunications Quality Commission (CS03) of the National Council for Quality (CNQ). Professor Machado is one of the founding members of the IFIP WG10.3 special interest group on embedded systems (SIG-ES) and the IEEE-IES Technical Committee on Education in Engineering and Industrial Technologies (TCEDU). He is a regular scientific reviewer of IEEE Transactions on CAD and IEEE Transactions on Software Engineering. He acted as general chair of ACSD'03 conference, as co-organizer of MOMPES series of workshops, and he is presently acting as organizing chair of DIPES'06 conference. His current research interests include software engineering, embedded software and pervasive information systems. For more information, consult his Web site at http://www.dsi.uminho.pt/~rmac

Annett Mäuser works for IBM Business Consulting Services in Germany. Between 1994 and 1997 she studied at the Berufsakademie Stuttgart. She holds a degree in business administration (information systems). Since joining IBM in 1997, she has been working in several banking and insurance projects as a consultant. Mäuser supported the savings bank organization in various projects for more than seven years.

Jan Mendling is a research assistant at the Department of Information Systems and New Media at the Vienna University of Economics and Business Administration, Austria. Together with Markus Nüttgens, he is the author of the EPC markup language (EPML). Mendling has studied at University of Trier, Germany; UFSIA Antwerpen, Belgium; and University of Munich, Germany. He received a diploma degree in business computer science (Dipl.-Wirt.-Inf) and a diploma degree in business administration (Dipl.-Kfm.). Currently, he is working on his PhD thesis.

Vojislav B. Mišić is an associate professor of computer science at the University of Manitoba in Winnipeg, Canada. His research interests include software architecture and software engineering in general, architecture and design of service-oriented systems and modeling and performance evaluation of wireless and sensor networks. He has authored or co-authored four books, several book chapters, more than forty papers in archival journals and over 60 papers at various international conferences. He has received his PhD in computer science in 1993 from University of Belgrade, Serbia, Yugoslavia.

Nikolaus Müssigmann, after his studies of electrical engineering with focus on technical informatics at the University of Stuttgart, has worked several years in the high tech industry gaining practical experience mainly in business informatics aspects and projects. In different development and management positions he was responsible for e-business, logistics and purchasing strategies and applications. In November 2003 he started his own PhD project at the Systems Engineering Group of the University of Augsburg, Germany, concentrating on inter-organizational aspects in the domain of strategic supply networks.

Gustaf Neumann is chair of information systems and new media at the University of Economics and Business Administration (WU) in Vienna, Austria, since October 1999. Before joining WU he was a full professor at the University of Essen, Germany (1995-1999) and a visiting scientist at IBM's T.J. Watson Research Center in Yorktown Heights, NY (1985-1986, 1993-1995). In 1987 he was awarded the Heinz-Zemanek award of the Austrian Association of Computer Science (OCG) for best dissertation. Professor Neumann has published books and papers in the areas of program transformation, data modeling and information systems technology with a focus on e-learning applications. He is a founding member of the Virtual Global University, head of the EC IST project UNIVERSAL, the IST Project Elena, member of the steering board of the Network of Excellence ProLearn and technical director of the learn@wu project, which is one of the most intensively used e-learning platforms worldwide. Neumann is the author of several widely used open source software packages, such as the TeX-dvi converter, dvi2xx, diac; the graphical frontend package, Wafe; the Web-browser, Cineast and the object oriented scripting language, XOTcl.

Ovidiu Noran received his PhD in enterprise architecture from Griffith University, Australia, studying a meta-methodology for the creation and operation of collaborative networked organisations. He holds an engineering degree in building services and automation and also a master's degree in information and communication technology. Dr. Noran has been active as an engineer and business architecture/management consultant in companies based in Europe and Australia and is currently lecturing enterprise architecture, e-commerce and software engineering at Griffith University. He is a member of several professional bodies (e.g., Engineers Australia and Australian Institute of Management) and standardization committees, such as ISO/IEC SC7/WG7 (Software Engineering/Life cycle management) and ISO TC184 SC5/WG1 (Industrial Automation). His seminars, publications and regular involvement in conferences and journals highlight research interests in artificial intelligence, software engineering and enterprise architecture and a preference for the action research strategy.

Markus Nüttgens is a full professor of information systems at University of Hamburg, Germany. Prior to joining University Hamburg, Nüttgens was a teaching assistant at the CIM-Technology Transfer Center (CIM-TTZ), assistant professor at the Department of Law and Business Administration and deputy director of Institute of Information Systems, University of Saarland, Germany. He has conducted various research projects with a focus on information systems architecture and business process management in the industrial, service and public sectors. His research interests include methods and tools for business process modelling, analysis and optimization. He was initially involved in the development of the modelling technique, "event-driven process chain (EPC)," and is the head of the BPM-Laboratory at University Hamburg. He is a member of the steering committee of the German special interest group on information systems (German Society of Informatics e.V.). Nüttgens holds a PhD and a master's degree in business administration from the University of Saarland, Germany.

Jan Recker (1979) is a PhD student at the business process management research group at the Faculty of Information Technology at Queensland University of Technology, Brisbane, Australia. His research interests include business process modeling, conceptual model evaluation, process configuration and reference modeling for enterprise systems. He is also a part-time teacher of business process management-related units at the School of Information Systems at Queensland University of Technology.

Michael Rosemann (PhD, 1967) is a full professor of IS and co-leader of the Business Process Management Research Group at the Faculty of Information Technology, Queensland University of Technology, Australia. He is also a member of the Australian Research Council College of Experts. His research interests include business process management, information systems, process models, workflow management systems, enterprise systems and ontologies. He is the author and editor of five books and has published more than 120 refereed journal papers, book chapters and conference papers on these topics.

August-Wilhelm Scheer was the director of the Institute for Information Systems (IWi), at the German Research Center for Artificial Intelligence (DFKI) until 2005. In his current role he is a strategic consultant at IWi. Moreover he is also a consulting professor at Tongji-University, Shanghai and the Chinese Academy of Science. In 1996, Professor Scheer was awarded the "Medal of National Education" in Warsaw and received the "TMBE'96 Award for Achievement and Contribution to the Industry" in Washington. The following year, he was awarded an honorary doctorate from the University of Pilsen (Czech Republic) for his academic achievements. In 1999, he received the "IT-Precursor Award" from the computer magazine *IT Services* and also became a member of the founding committee of the Hasso-Plattner-Foundation (HPI). Professor Scheer was also a member of the Federal Council for Research, Technology and Innovation, founded by the German Federal Government, and of the Expert Board for Research and Technology in the Saarland. Since November 1999, he has represented the Prime Minister of Saarland in matters of innovation, technology and research. In 2001 he was awarded The Distinguished Service Medal of the Saarland and he also was awarded an honorary doctorate by the University of Hohenheim. Professor Scheer was a member of the supervisory board of SAP AG from 1988 to 1998 and returned to this role in 2002. In 2002, he was appointed honorary senator of the University of Music and Drama, Saarland. In January 2003, he received the Philip Morris Research Award. In May of the same year, he was appointed member of the board of trustees at the Chemnitz University of Technology. In 2003, he was honoured by Ernst & Young for outstanding entrepreneurial achievements in the category "Information Technology." In December 2005 he was awarded with the Federal Cross of Merit for his achievements as an "Internationally Successful Entrepreneur" by the Federal President. Professor Scheer is the founder and chairman of the supervisory board of IDS Scheer AG and of imc AG, both based in Saarbrücken. Professor Scheer has edited a number of books and journals. He has written over 300 essays and more than 10 books, many of which have been translated and published worldwide.

Dirk Schreiber has served as a professor in IS at the Faculty of Economics of the Applied University of Bonn Rhein Sieg, Germany (Sankt Augustin) since 2000. Having received his Diploma degree (Dipl.-Kfm.) and his PhD (Dr. rer pol.) both from the University of Siegen/Germany, he worked several years as analyst, project manager and CIO in mid-sized steel industry companies and in the banking sector. His research interest focuses primarily on business modelling, modelling techniques and applying information systems, especially for small and medium-sized enterprises.

Reinhard Schütte was born 1967 in Bremen. He received a master's degree in business administration at the University of Münster, Germany (master's thesis: Expert Systems in Production Planning and Control). Since 1992 he worked as a research assistant at the Institute for Information systems at the University of Münster. Later he worked at the Institute for Production and Industrial Information Management at the University of Duisburg-Essen. He is the author of more than 50 articles in journals and has published three monographs. Beside his academic career he worked as a business consultant and in 2001 joined the management board of Bremke & Hoerster Group, Arnsberg, as head of the division's of information technology, controlling, finance, accounting, audit, human resource as well as environmental. In 2003 he joined the Siegburg-based Dohle Group, which generated a turnover of controlling, IT, human resource, accounting and law. His present tasks have been the migration of all Hit stores to a new technical basis and the implementation of SAP, including XI, PDM and BW as Net Weaver components.

Oliver Thomas studied business administration at the Saarland University from 1995 to 1999. His major fields of study were mathematical economic theory, operations research, information systems, statistics and econometrics. He was a research assistant at the Institute for Information Systems (IWi) at the Saarland University from 1999 to 2002. In 2002, the institute was integrated into the German Research Center for Artificial Intelligence (Deutsches Forschungszentrum für Künstliche Intelligenz—DFKI GmbH) as a department. Mr. Thomas has been the deputy head of the Research Department and a senior researcher in this department since 2003. His fields of research are information modeling (in particular reference modeling), business process management, soft computing (in particular fuzzy-set-theory) and e-government. He also lectures at the Saarland University and holds the courses "Information Modeling—Languages, Techniques, Methods and IT-Support" and "Reference Modeling" for the Diplomstudiengang business administration, major Information Systems. In addition,

Mr. Thomas holds university teaching positions in information systems at the Verwaltungs- und Wirtschafts-Akademie Saarland (Academy for Administration and Economics), in MBA management and information systems at the Albstadt-Sigmaringen University for Business Process Management and at the Aoyama Gakuin University, in Tokyo (Japan) in the field of business process management.

Jean-Paul Van Belle is an associate professor in the Information Systems Department at the University of Cape Town, South Africa. Before joining UCT, he set up the Information Systems Department at the University of the Western Cape. He obtained his doctorate in the field of enterprise modelling. Currently, he is also researching various aspects of e- and m-commerce as well as the adoption of ICTs in a South African context. He supervises a number of post-graduate students in this area. He is a family man with 3 children and, despite his 44 years of age, still a keen and moderately competitive endurance athlete.

Wil van der Aalst (PhD, 1966) is a full professor of information systems and head of the information systems sub-department of the Department of Technology Management at Technische Universiteit Eindhoven, The Netherlands. He is also an adjunct professor at the Faculty of Information Technology of Queensland University of Technology, Australia. Wil van der Aalst directs the Eindhoven Digital Laboratory for Business Processes (EDL-BP) and is a fellow and management team member of the research institute BETA. His research interests include business process management, information systems, simulation, Petri nets, process models, workflow management systems, process mining, verification techniques, enterprise resource planning systems, computer supported cooperative work and interorganizational business processes. He has published more than 200 books, journal papers, book chapters, conference papers and reports on these topics.

Jan vom Brocke is an assistant professor at the Department for Information Systems at the University of Münster in Germany and a member of the European Research Center for Information Systems (ERCIS). He graduated with a Master of Information Systems (1998) and obtained his PhD at the Faculty of Business Administration and Economics of Münster (2002). Apart from Münster, he recently held research and teaching positions at the University of Saarbrücken in Germany and the Michael Smurfit Graduate School of Business at the University College Dublin in Ireland. At present, vom Brocke is supervising two Competence Centres at ERCIS and running research projects funded by industry, the German Federal Ministry of Education and Research as well as the European Commission.

Jens Weller studied information systems at the Dresden University of Technology, Germany. He worked as a software engineer after his studies. In 2004 he returned to Dresden University and is working as a research assistant at the chair of information systems, specializing in systems development.

Johannes Maria Zaha studied business informatics with emphasis on formal languages, distributed systems and industrial application systems at the Otto-Friedrich-University, Bamberg, Germany. From 2002 to 2005 he worked as research and teaching assistant at the chair of business informatics and systems engineering at the University of Augsburg, Germany. In July 2005 he received his PhD for his work titled "Automated Compatibility Tests for Software Components in Business Domains." Since September 2005 he has worked as postdoctoral research fellow in the Business Process Management Research Group at the Queensland University of Technology in Brisbane, Australia.

J. Leon Zhao is a professor and Honeywell fellow in MIS, University of Arizona, USA, and has taught previously at the Hong Kong University of Science and Technology and the College of William and Mary. He holds a PhD and an MS from the University of California, Berkeley, an MS from the University of California, Davis and a BS from Beijing Institute of Agricultural Mechanization. His current research focuses on business process automation and Web services and their business applications. Zhao is an associate editor of *Information Systems Research, Decision Support Systems, Electronic Commerce Research and Applications, International Journal of Business Process Integration and Management, International Journal of Web and Grid Services,* and *International Journal of Web Services Research.* He is also on the editorial board of *Journal of Database Management.* He has edited seven special issues in various journals. He has served as chairs of the Workshop on E-Business (2003), the 15th Workshop on Information Technology and Systems (2005) and the IEEE Conference on Services Computing (2006).

Index

P

paradigm 15
parameterization 102
partial enterprise model (PEM) 142
pattern-based 53
perspective 245
perspicuity 276
physical database scheme 212
physical layer 295
physical manifestation 148
planning 83, 91, 222, 228
policy deployment (PD) 103
pooled payment business 200, 201
potential configurable reference model 32
potential reference model 26
pragmatic model analysis 260, 268,
    279, 281
pre-Internet model 251
preliminary work 52
premium wage 108, 111, 113
principle of construction 52
problem definition 79, 83
problem domain 358
procedure model 292
process-aware information system 23
process-centered software engineering
    environment (PSEE) 101
process-orientation 23, 98, 99, 101, 102
process 39, 100, 179, 187
process mining 38, 39
process model 77, 81, 82, 84,
product and process model 169
production specifications 176
production system 170
product range 234
project management data (PMD) 82
Project Management Institute (PMI) 84
project planning 85
promotion business 202
protection of investment 130
prototype 236, 302
prototype implementation of SSND 236
purchasing policy and strategy 223
Purdue Enterprise Reference Architecture
    (PERA) 147
purpose or goal 148, 282

Q

quality 110, 120, 260
quality assurance 358
quality criteria 362
quality metrics 267

R

ranked list 159
rational unified process (RUP) 10
readability 276
reduced retail-H model 198
reference enterprise model 142
reference model 1, 3, 4, 6, 11, 23,
    39, 52, 67, 88, 118, 124, 145,
    182, 206, 217, 220, 243, 245,
    289, 291, 293, 322, 330, 355,
    357
reference model construction
    88, 321, 327
reference model for electronic markets
    (RM-EM) 246
reference model for organisational change
    and human resources 158
reference model for savings banks 206
reference model framework 7, 322
reference modeling language 6
reference model in enterprise architecture
    141
reference model integration 293, 295
reference model lifecycle 28
reference model management (RMM)
    288, 291, 294, 296, 297
reference model management system
    (RMMS) 294, 299, 303
referencing relation between models 321
relationship hierarchy 208
relationship model 120
relationship type 42
repository 299
repository-data 301
requirement 145, 325
research and development (R&D) 168,
    176
research diversity 289
retail-H 182, 191, 195, 200, 201
retail-H model 195